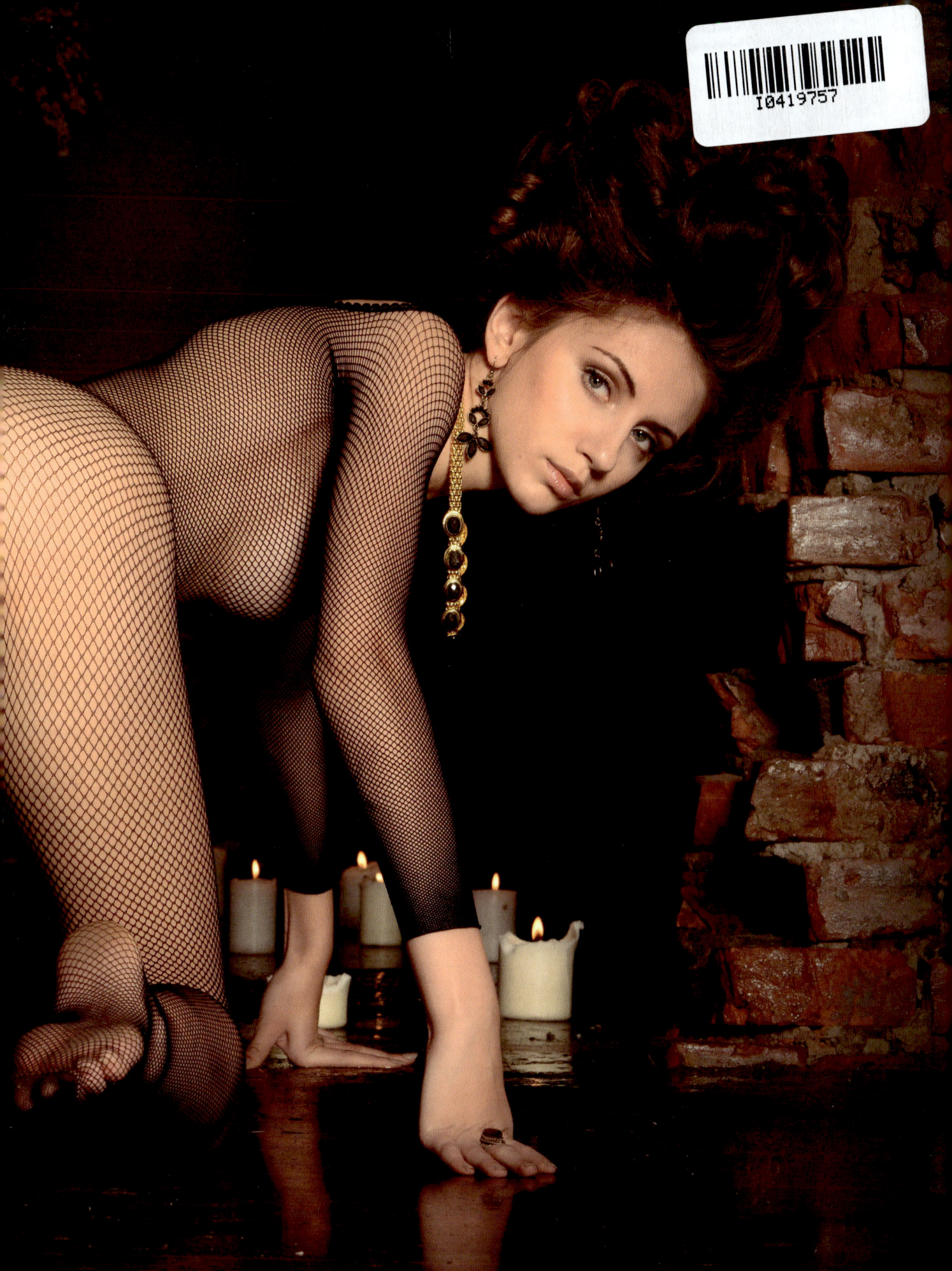

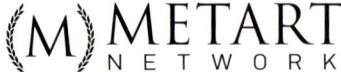

All photos © Copyright 1998–2024
by Metart TM HLP General Partners Inc.,
Hydentra HLP Int. Limited
9 Karpenisiou Street,
Nicosia 2021, Cyprus
www.metart.com

First edition 2024
Copyright © 2024 by Edition Skylight

EDITION SKYLIGHT
Rosengartenstr. 13B
CH-8608 Bubikon/Zürich
Switzerland
info@edition-skylight.com
www.edition-skylight.com

ISBN 978-3-03766-697-5

Bibliographic information published by Die Deutsche Bibliothek
Die Deutsche Bibliothek lists this publication in the
Deutsche Nationalbibliografie; detailed bibliographic data
are available in the Internet at http://dnb.ddb.de.

Printed in Czech Republik

Vanilla sex can be perfectly sweet, but if you crave something a little more adventurous, The Life Erotic is the place to come.

Established in 2009, The Life Erotic is renowned for pushing boundaries with beautifully daring film and photography. Gorgeous girls take a walk on the wild side, exploring the darker side of sensual pleasure as they indulge in kinky lesbian games and solo masturbation.

Role-playing, domination and submission, restraint, discipline, and other stimulating aspects of BDSM are experienced in delicious detail. Into ball gags and nipple clamps, Shibari (the art of Japanese rope bondage), and chains? Anything goes here, whether our star is a sweet 18-year-old eager to try handcuffs for the first time or a voracious thrill-seeker turned on by taking control.

If fetish outfits float your boat, you'll find plenty of like-minded experimenters here: not just leather, latex, and fishnet, but all manner of nylon lovers, panty stuffers, and lingerie addicts dressing up – and undressing, of course. Our unconventional beauties often express their sizzling sexuality through tattoos and piercings, as well as through their intriguing choice of clothing. Their imagination roams far beyond the naughty nurse or sassy college girl to some truly original and sometimes challenging styles of physical self-expression. Fully nude fun has its place here, too, naturally!

This is just the tip of the iceberg when it comes to the edgy themes uncovered by our ground-breaking team of artists. All manner of tantalizing fetish flavors are tried and tested – wax play, wet fun, exhibitionism, voyeurism, frottage, human puppy play, foot fetishism and high heels, hairy girls, shaving, massage, spanking, nipple clamps, improvised sex toys – you name it, there's a whole wide world of sensuality to explore. After all, what could be more invigorating and inspiring than subtly kinky, stylish creativity that fires up the imagination as well as the libido?

We pride ourselves on featuring a variety of attractive girls with a wide diversity of different looks and body types. They could be cute blondes, fiery redheads or statuesque Black goddesses, slender sweeties or voluptuous knockouts, but one thing unites them: the compelling desire to broaden their sexual horizons, and an eagerness to capture the experience on camera for your viewing pleasure.

You may wonder, what drives a strong, independent, modern woman to try kinky bondage games, to submit to a dominant partner and allow herself to be treated like a plaything? Well, many feminist writers believe that BDSM is an expression of sexual freedom, and therefore an empowering act.

After a day spent being strong and making decisions, perhaps it is a liberating feeling – and a major aphrodisiac – to surrender control to someone else. It's a pure jolt of sexual adrenaline that doesn't translate to any other area of life. Our girls may love being told what to do in the bedroom but don't try it in the boardroom – unless you're bending her over the desk, that would be hot!

BDSM is all about desire. It's about somebody clearly knowing what they want and how far they are prepared to test their boundaries. It's about the fierce pleasure that lies in giving pleasure. It's about trust, risk, and being brave enough to relinquish control to open oneself up to whatever comes next.

In fact, it has been argued that in BDSM play, the submissive person is the one with the power, as they actually control what happens – for example, by using a 'safe' word. Power games take place in a safe psychological space, where authentic desires are acknowledged, rules are observed, and external pressures to behave in a certain way can be escaped.

Do we have to reconcile our sexual self to the self we present in other areas of our life – or can we allow ourselves the freedom to experiment, to experience pleasure without limits and shame? Here at The Life Erotic, the expression of authentic sexuality in all its wild variety is an empowering act of self-love.

The Life Erotic is part of the Metart Network, the world leader in high-class adult entertainment, presenting stunning girls who are confident, sexy, and desirable – modern women for a modern world. From cute new models posing naked for the first time to captivating lesbian lovers expressing their mutual passion in tastefully explicit action, our award-winning sites are often imitated but never equaled.

High-resolution photos put you right in the middle of the action, so you'll enjoy every gasp of pleasure as these uninhibited beauties live out their forbidden secret fantasies in the most explicit and arousing ways imaginable. Their bold sexual games are the ultimate orgasmic thrill. We only feature girls who are genuinely eager to try something that will open up a whole new world of sexual experimentation to them. Check it out – you can be sure it will be a wild ride!

— *Rose Eden*

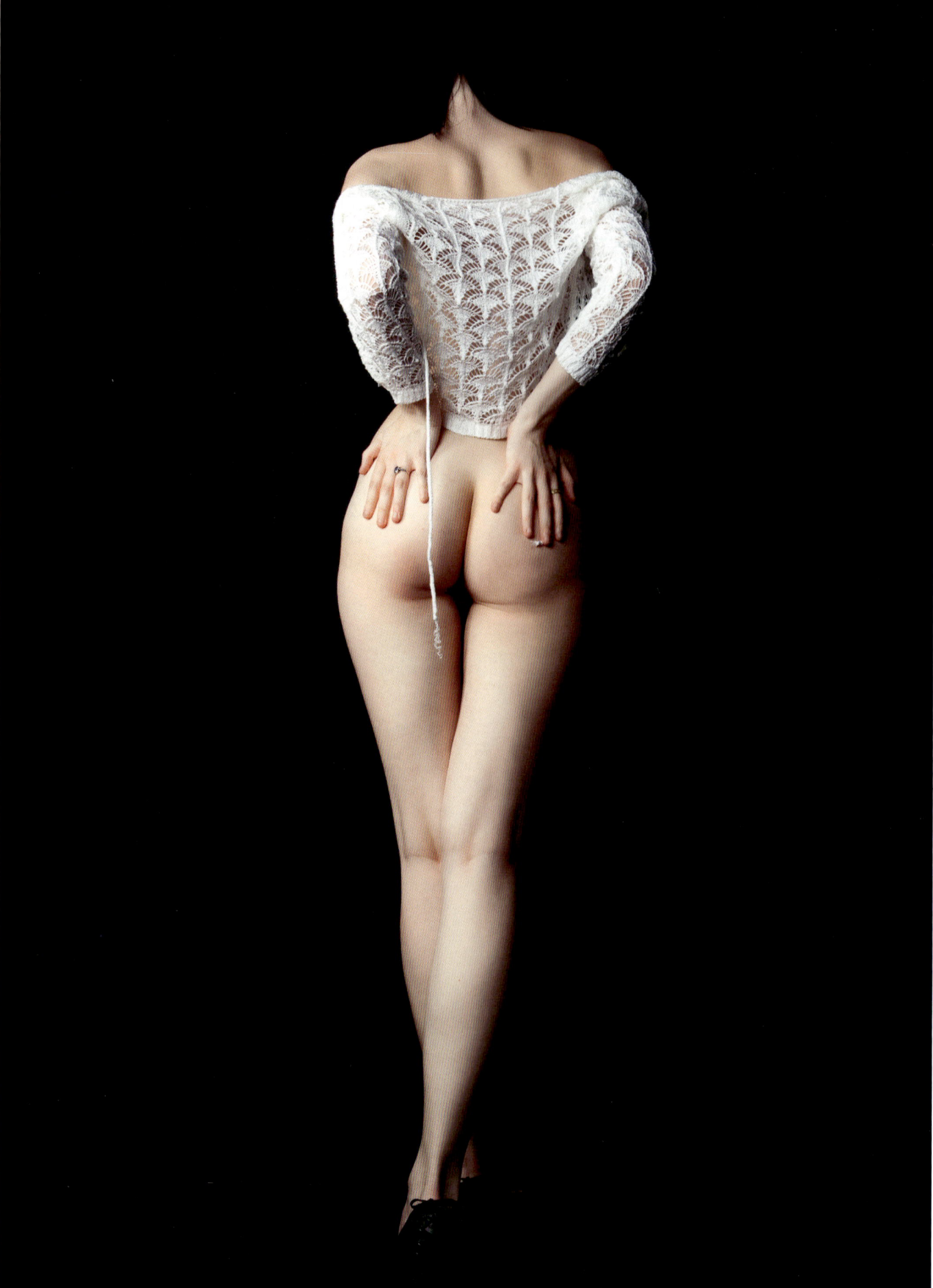

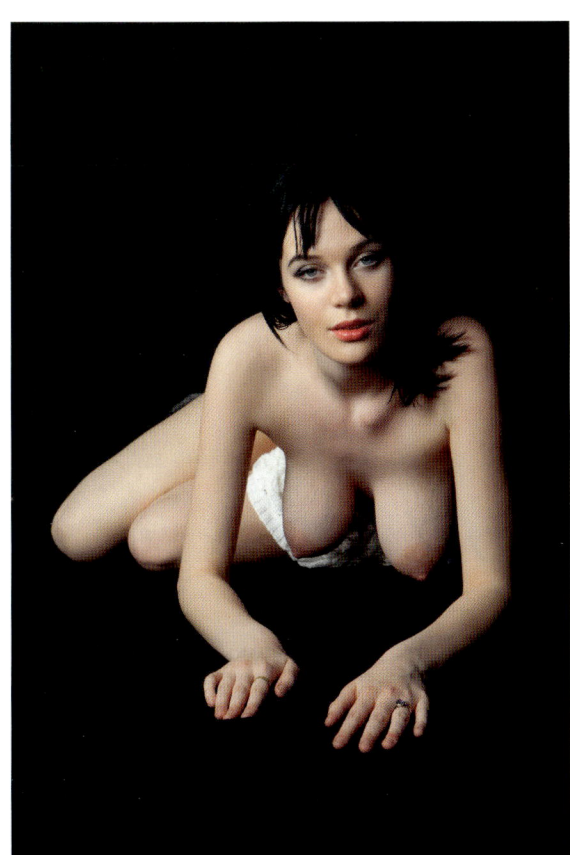

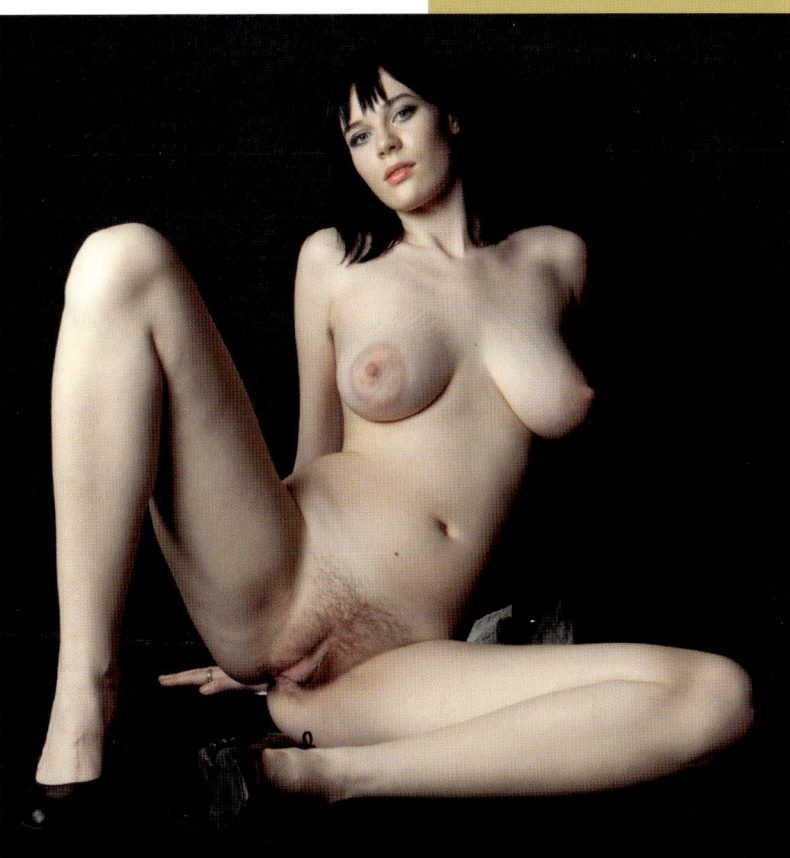

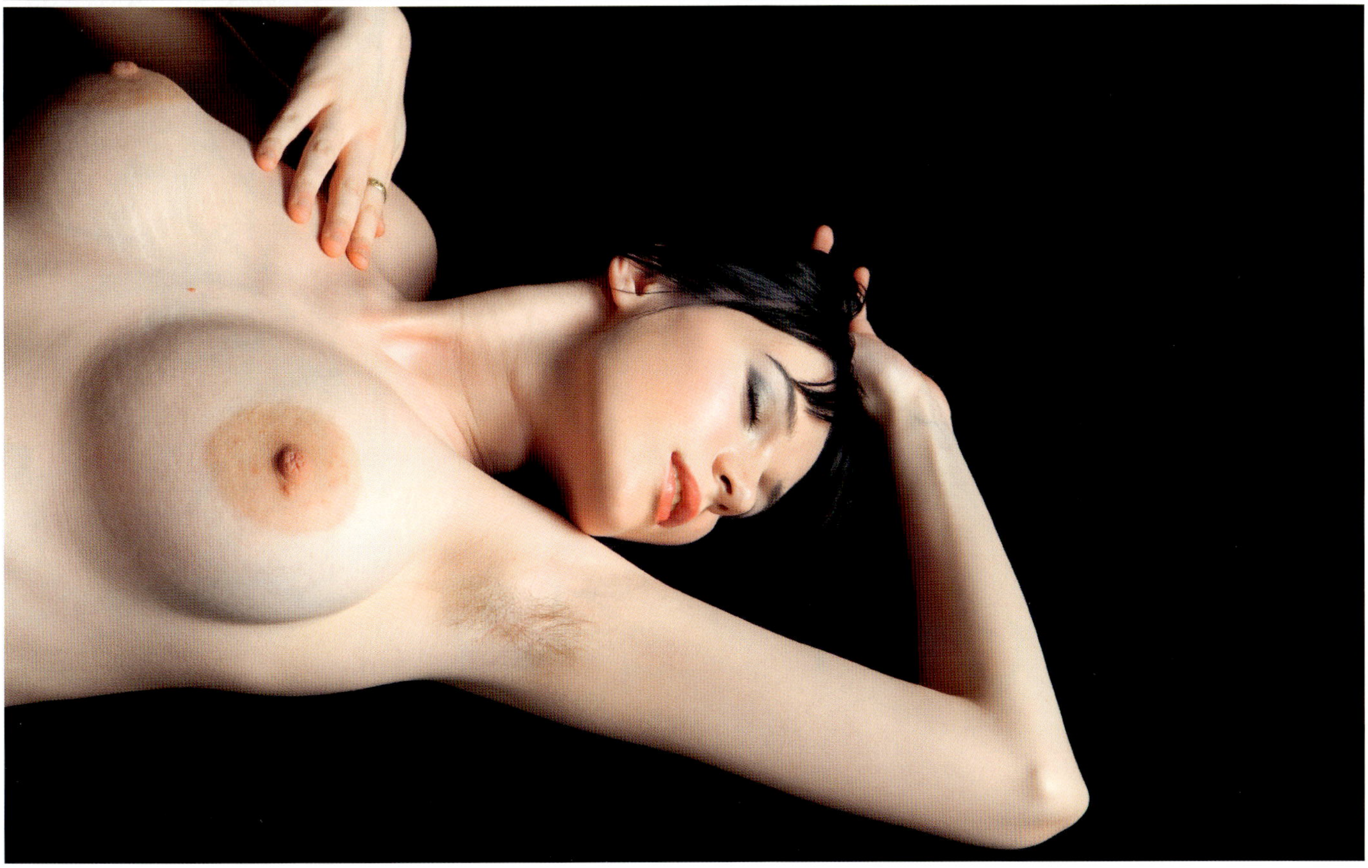

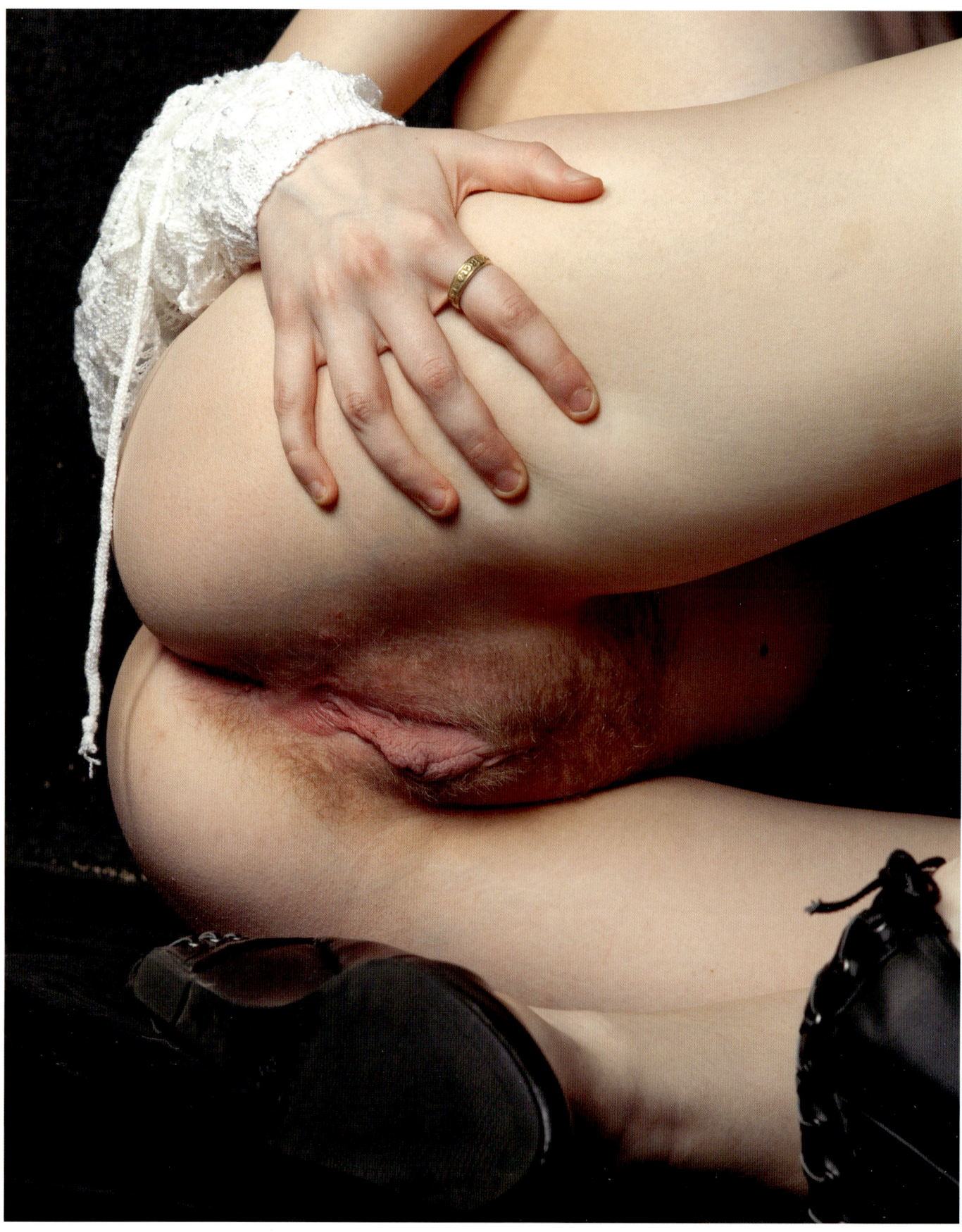

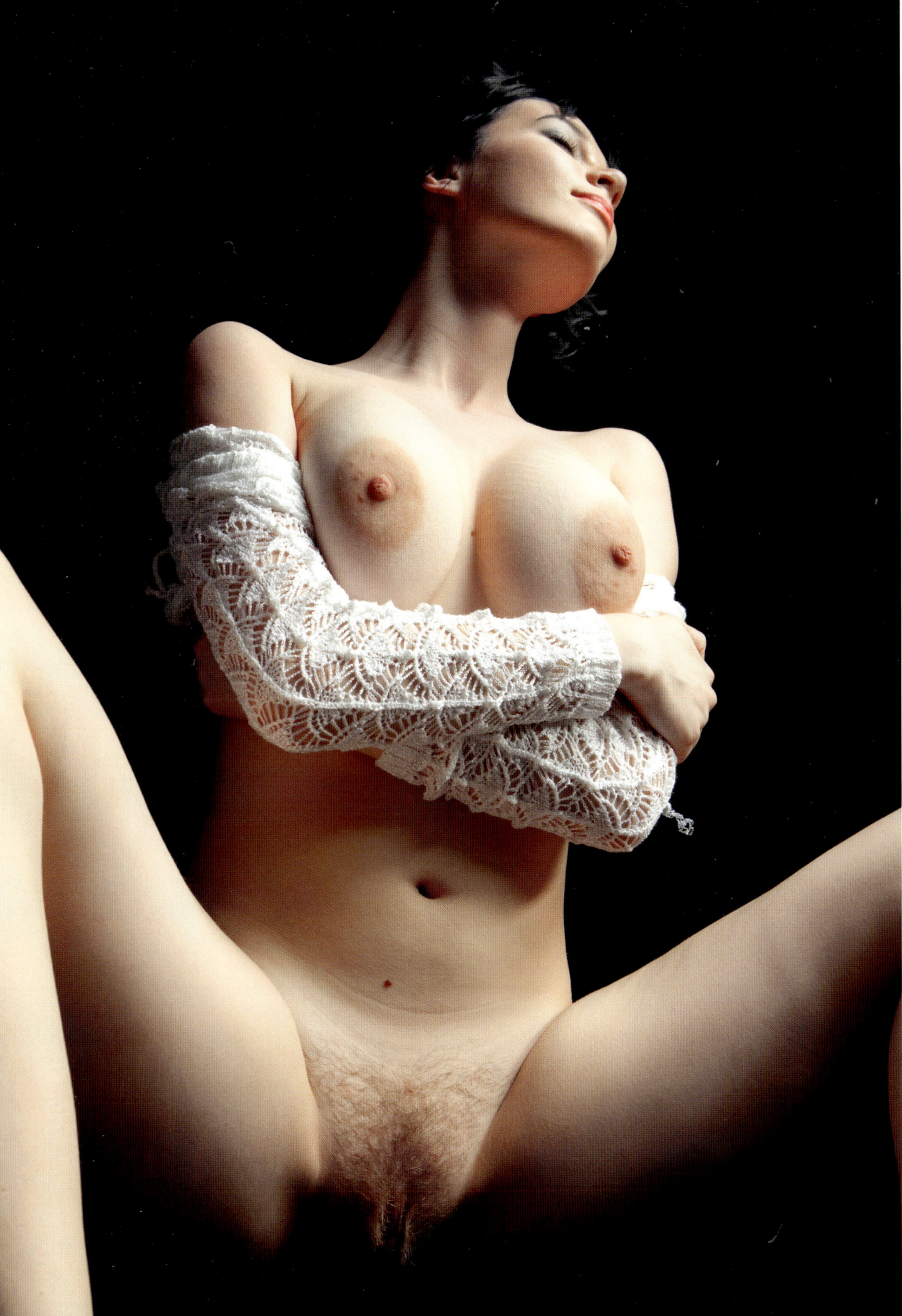

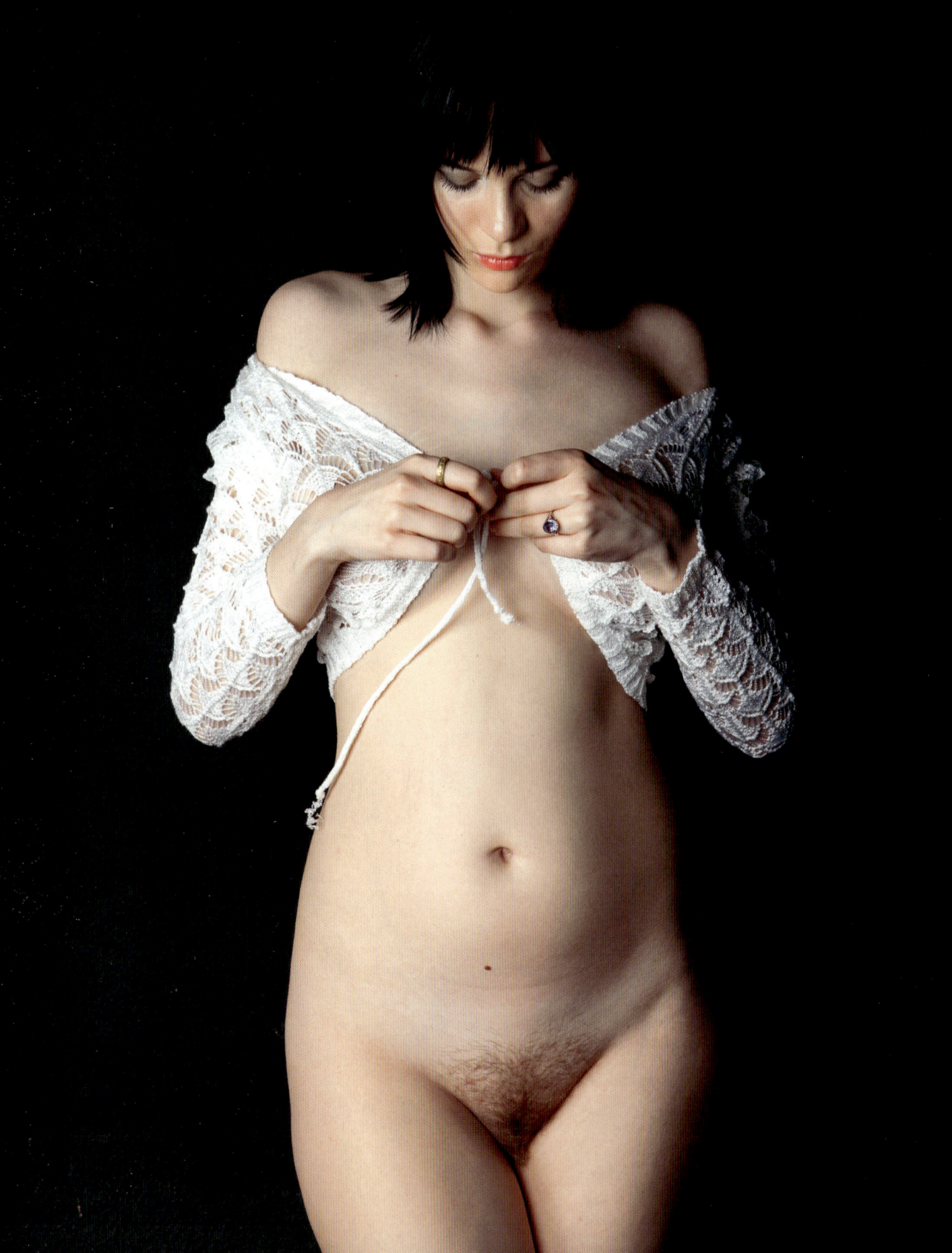

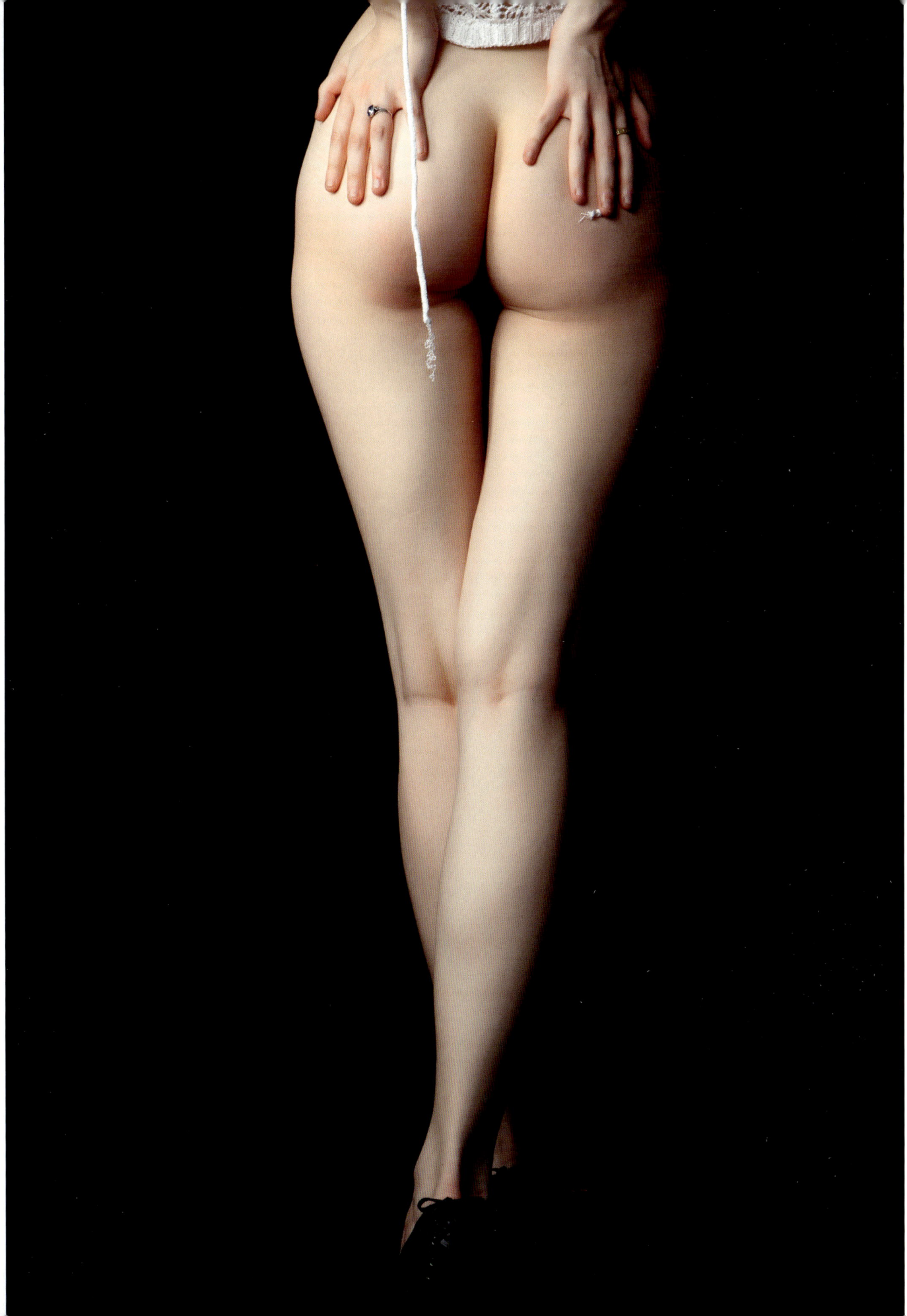

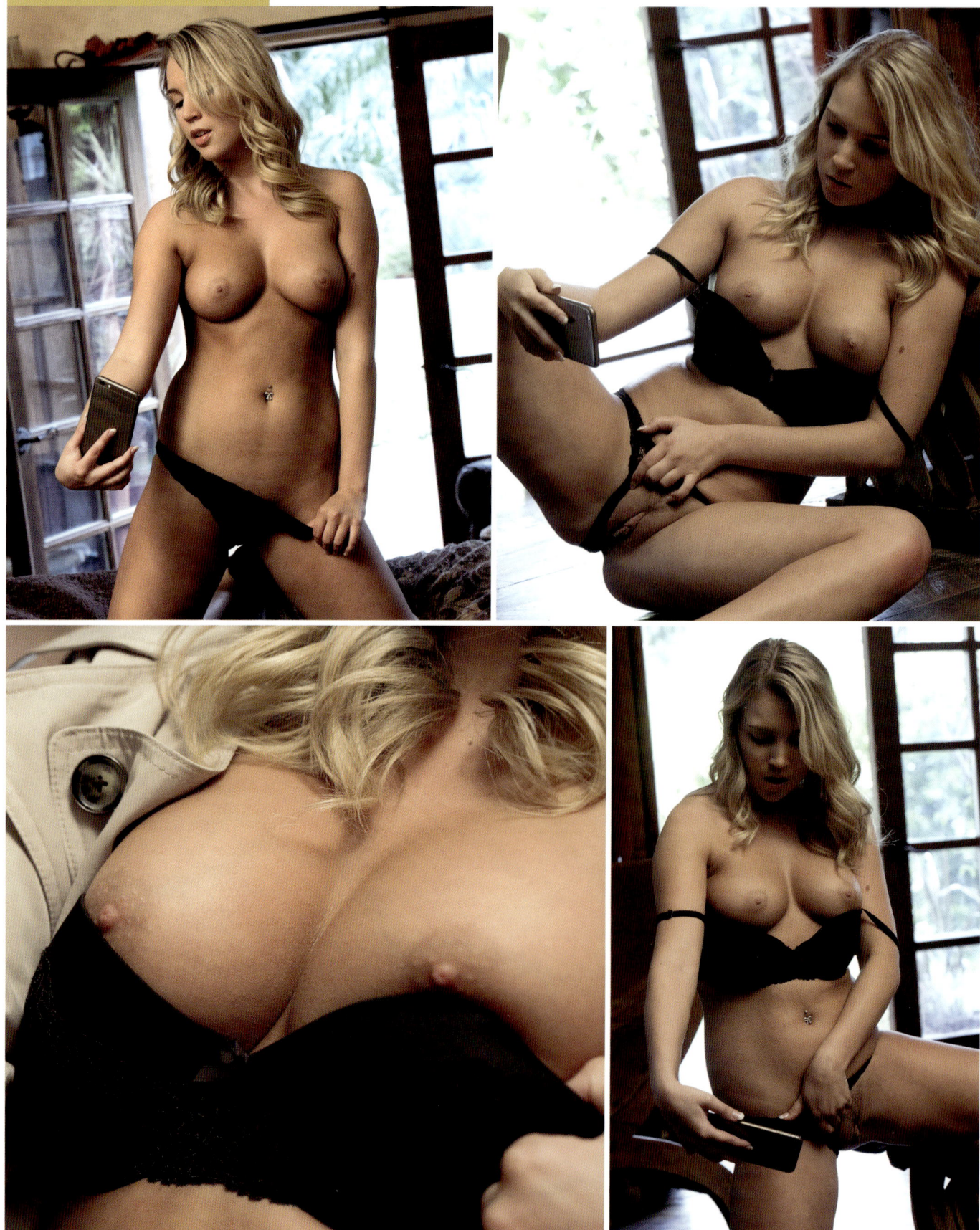

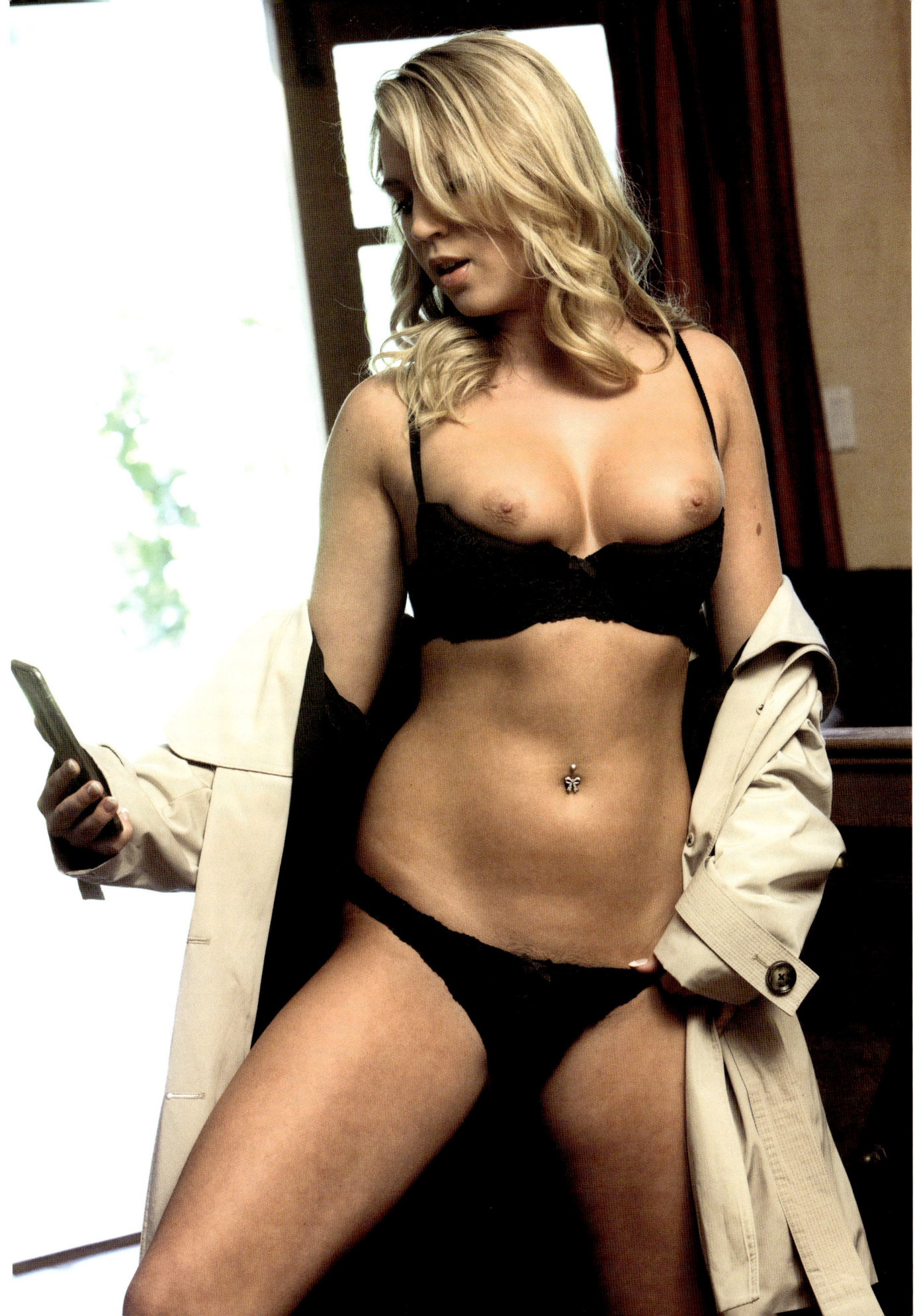

Yassa

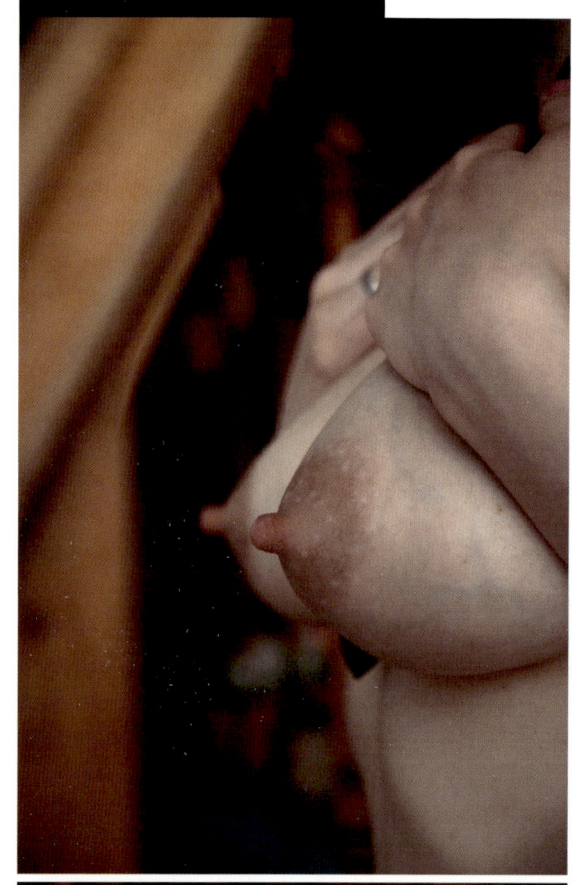

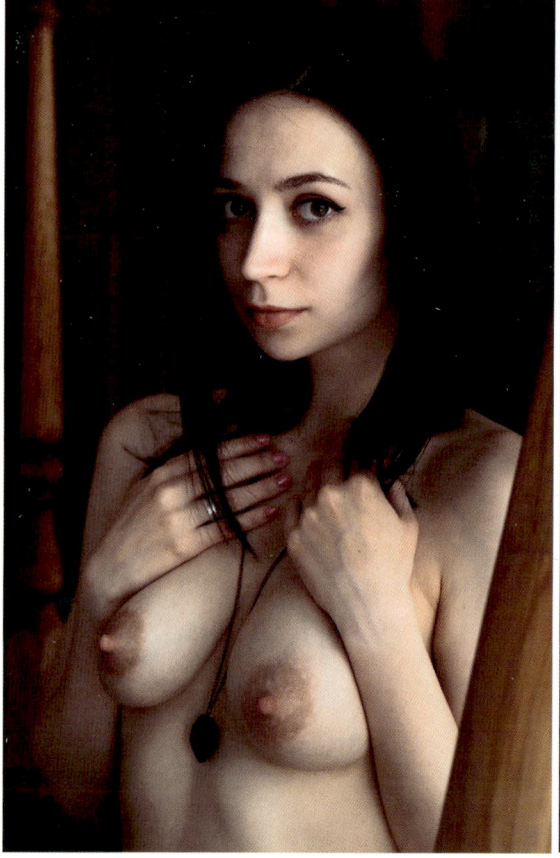

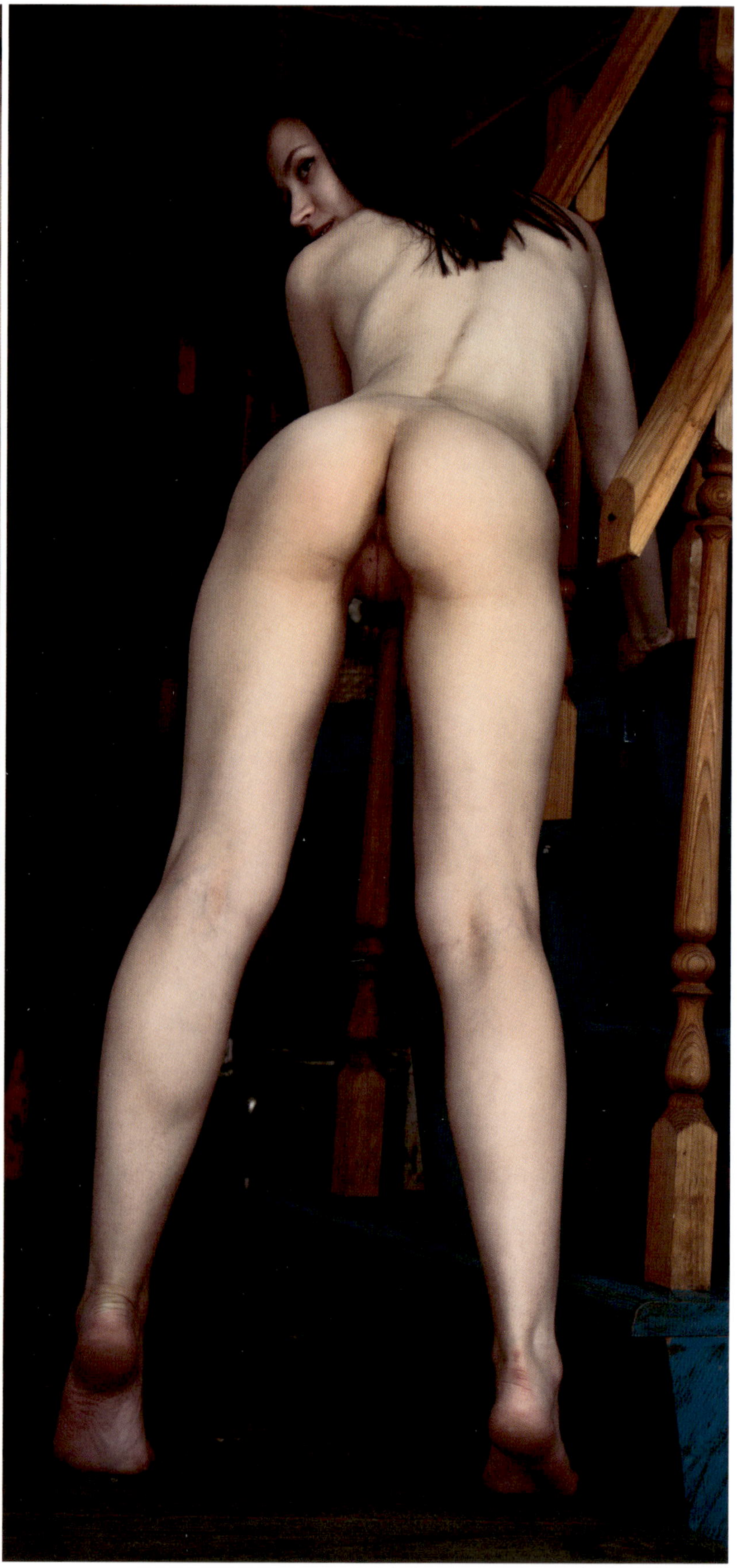

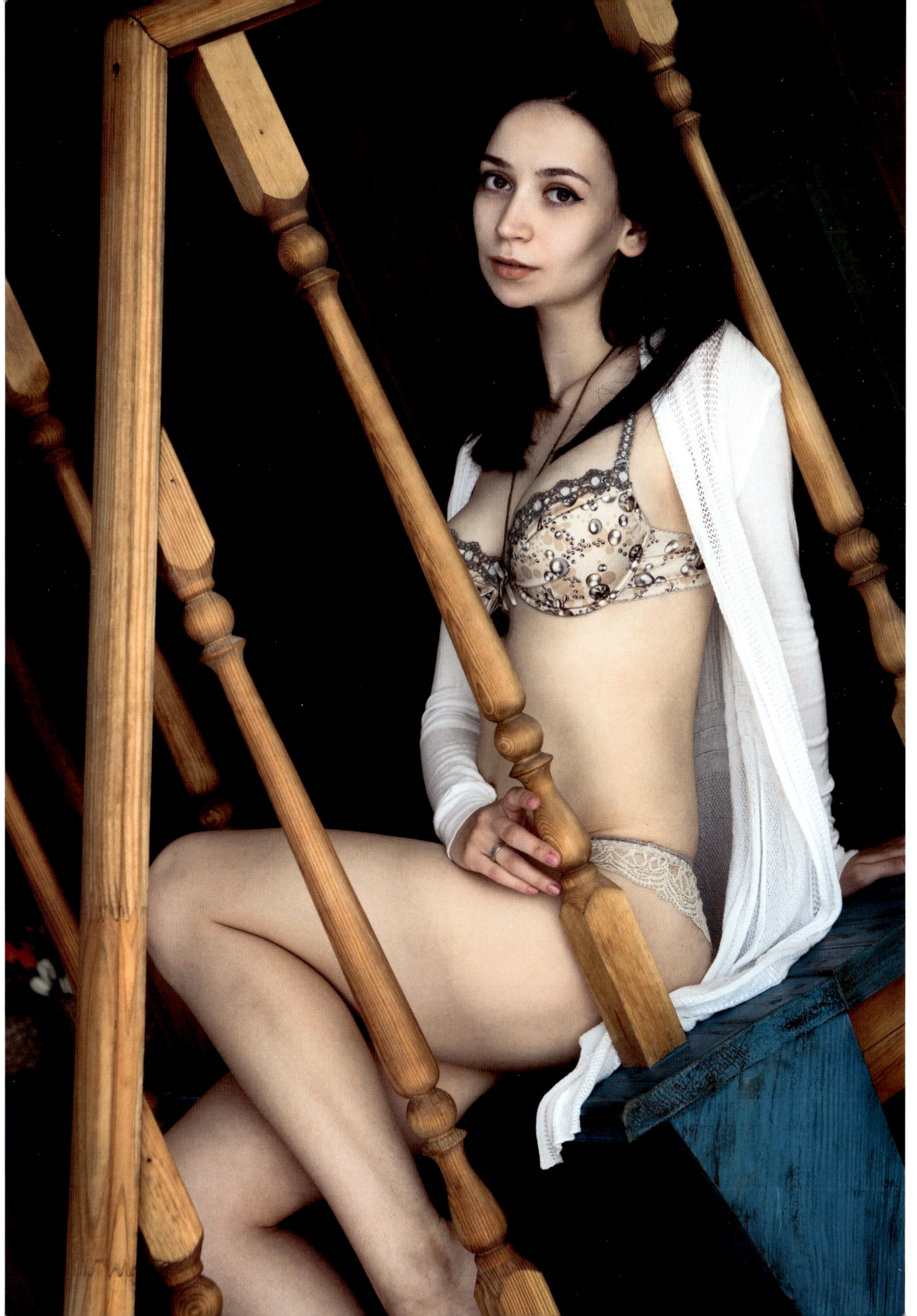

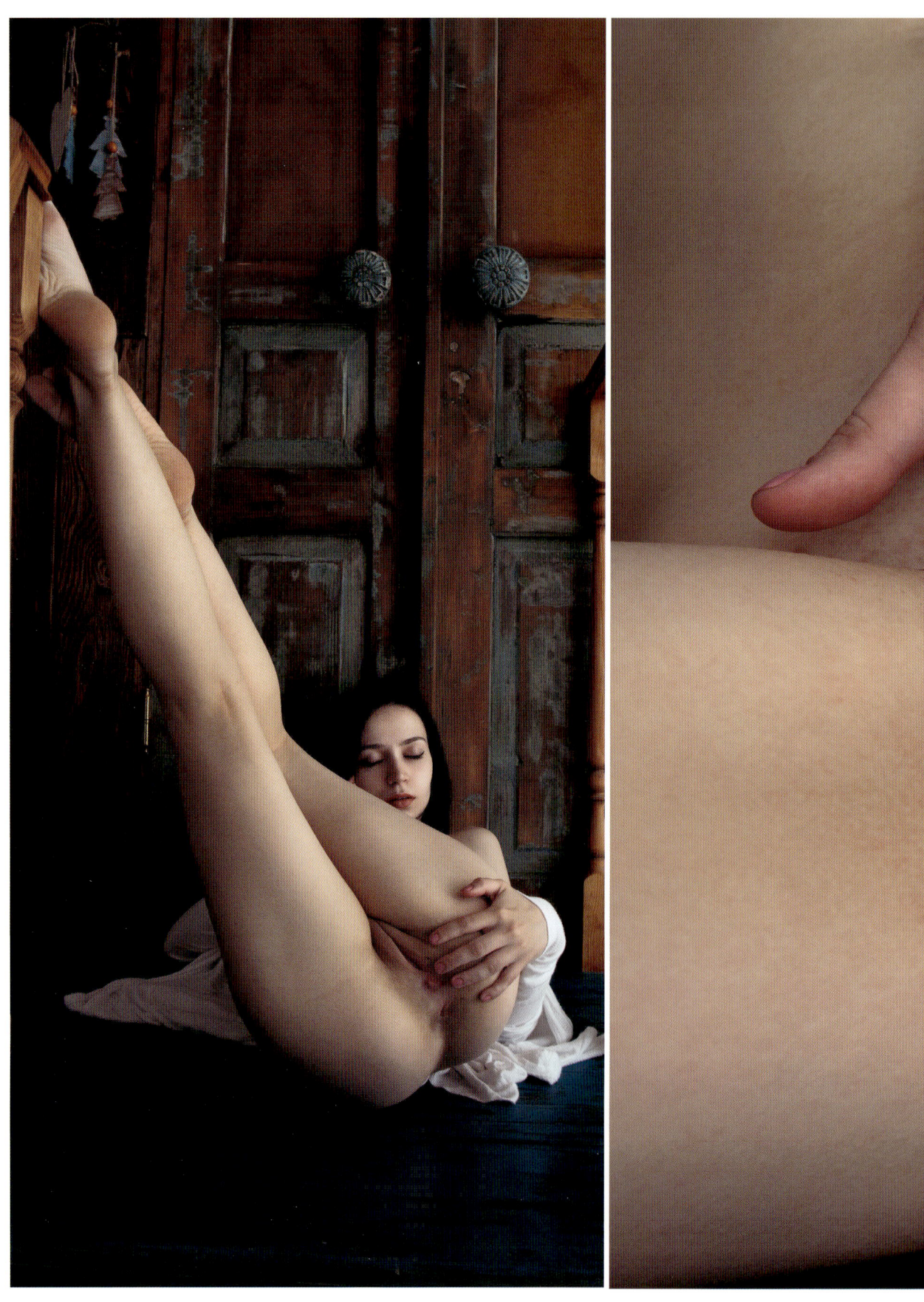

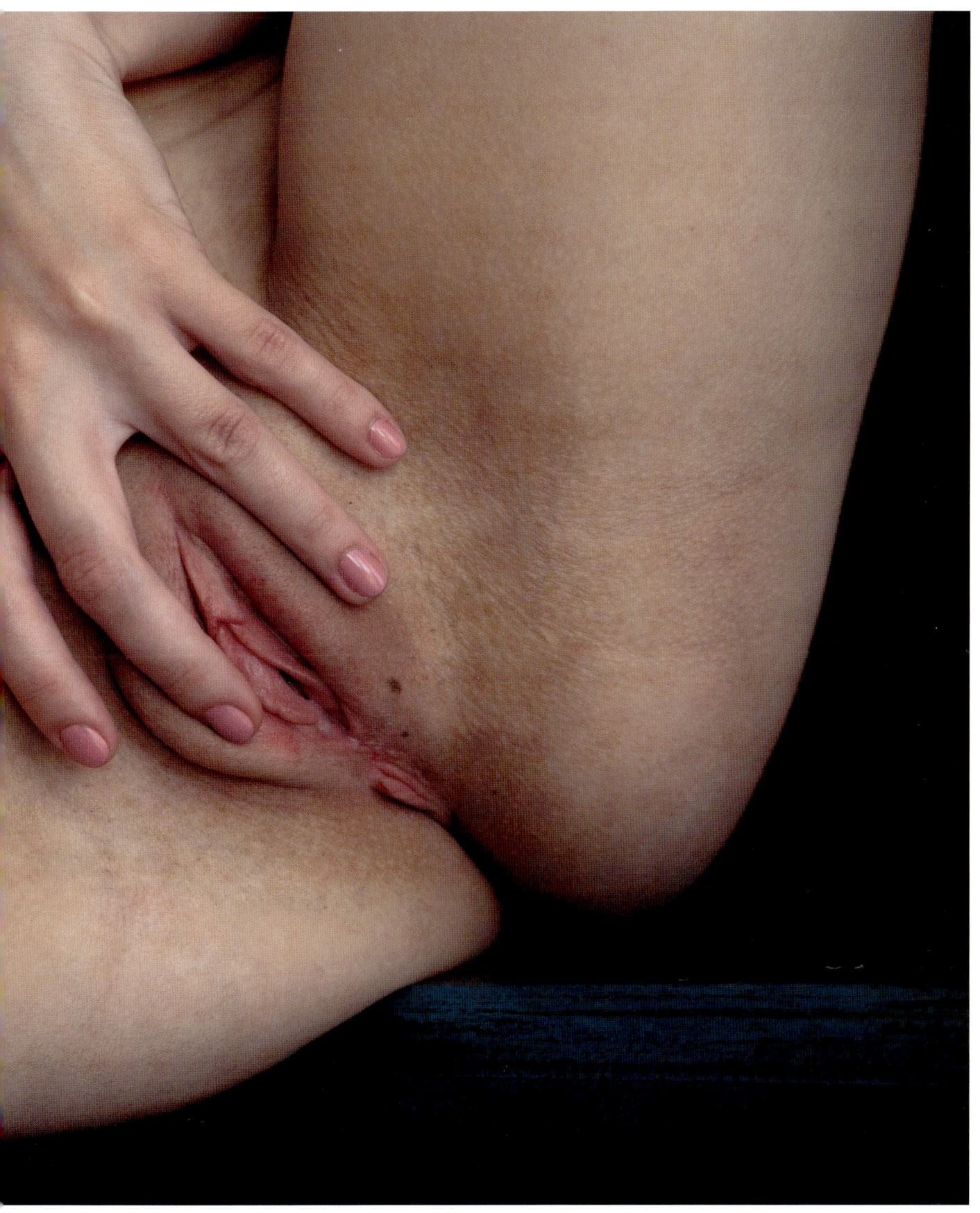

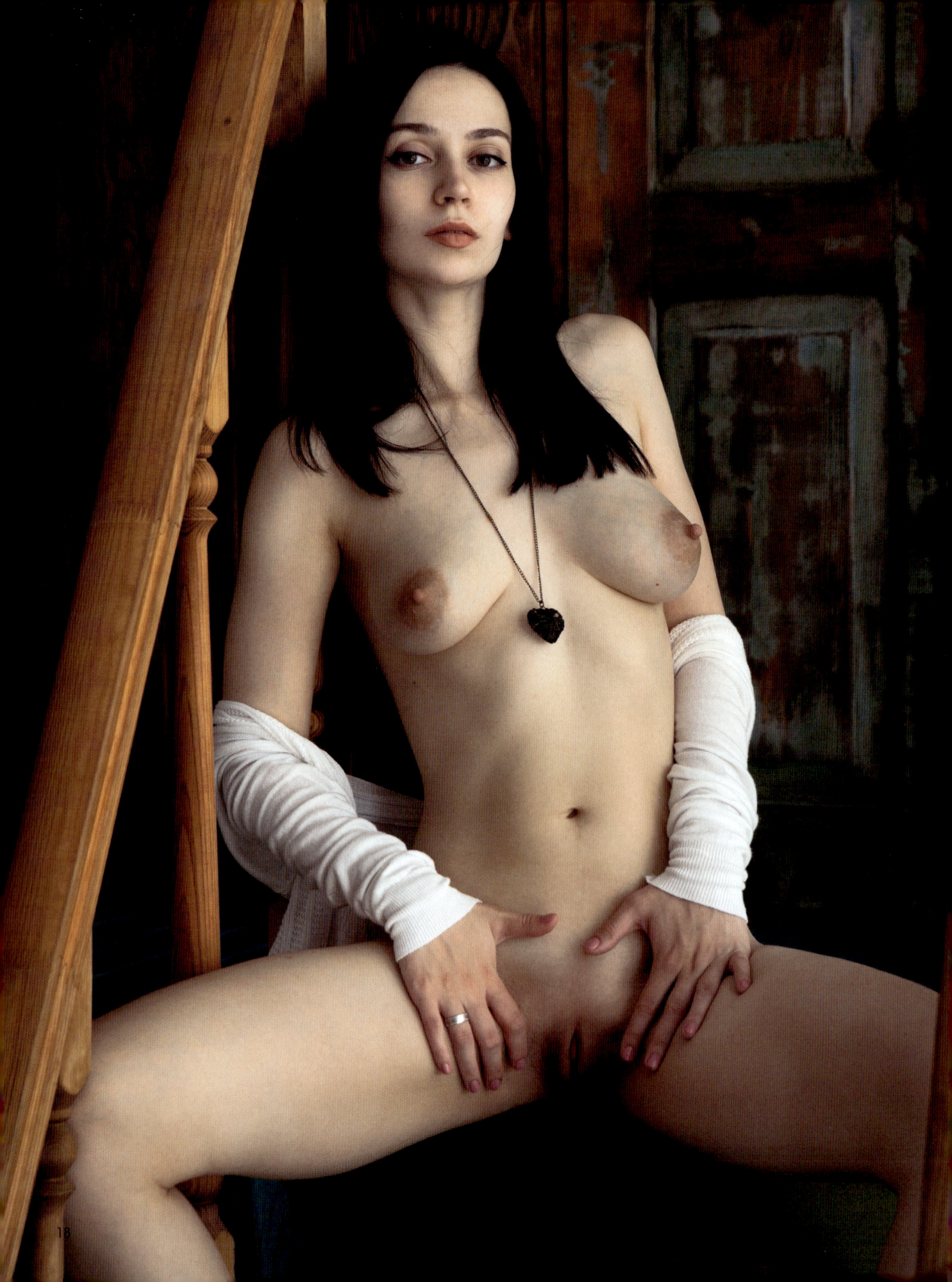

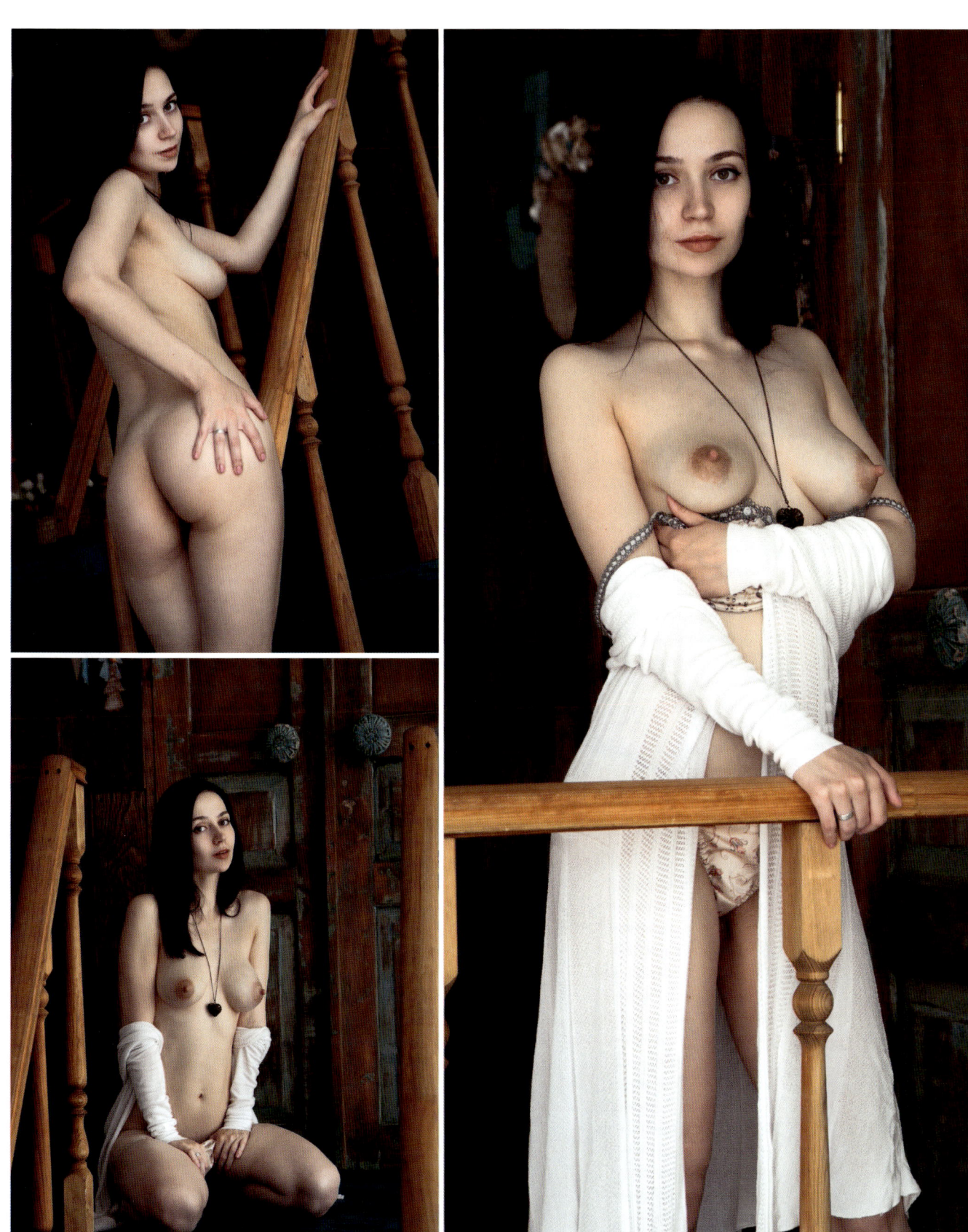

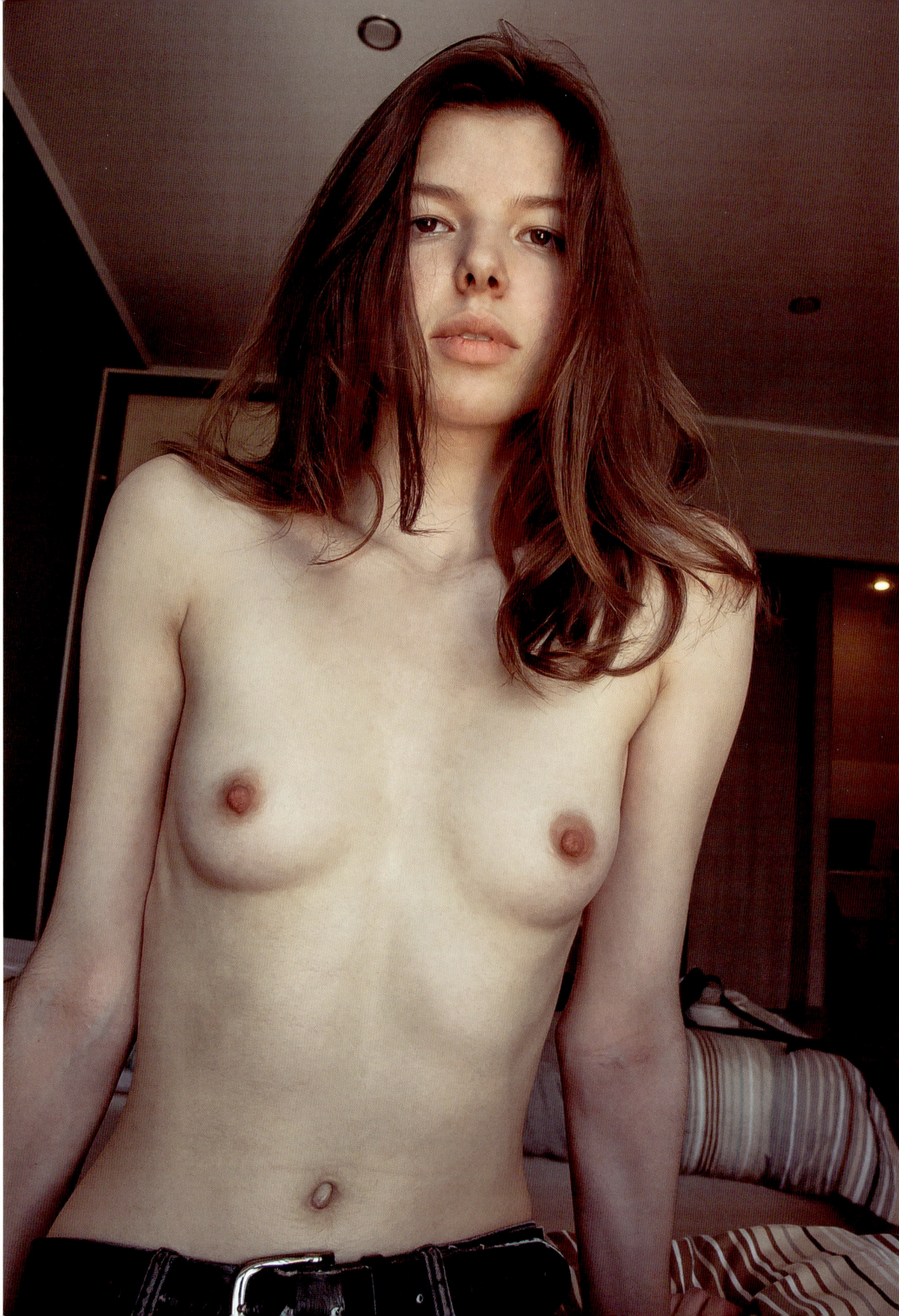

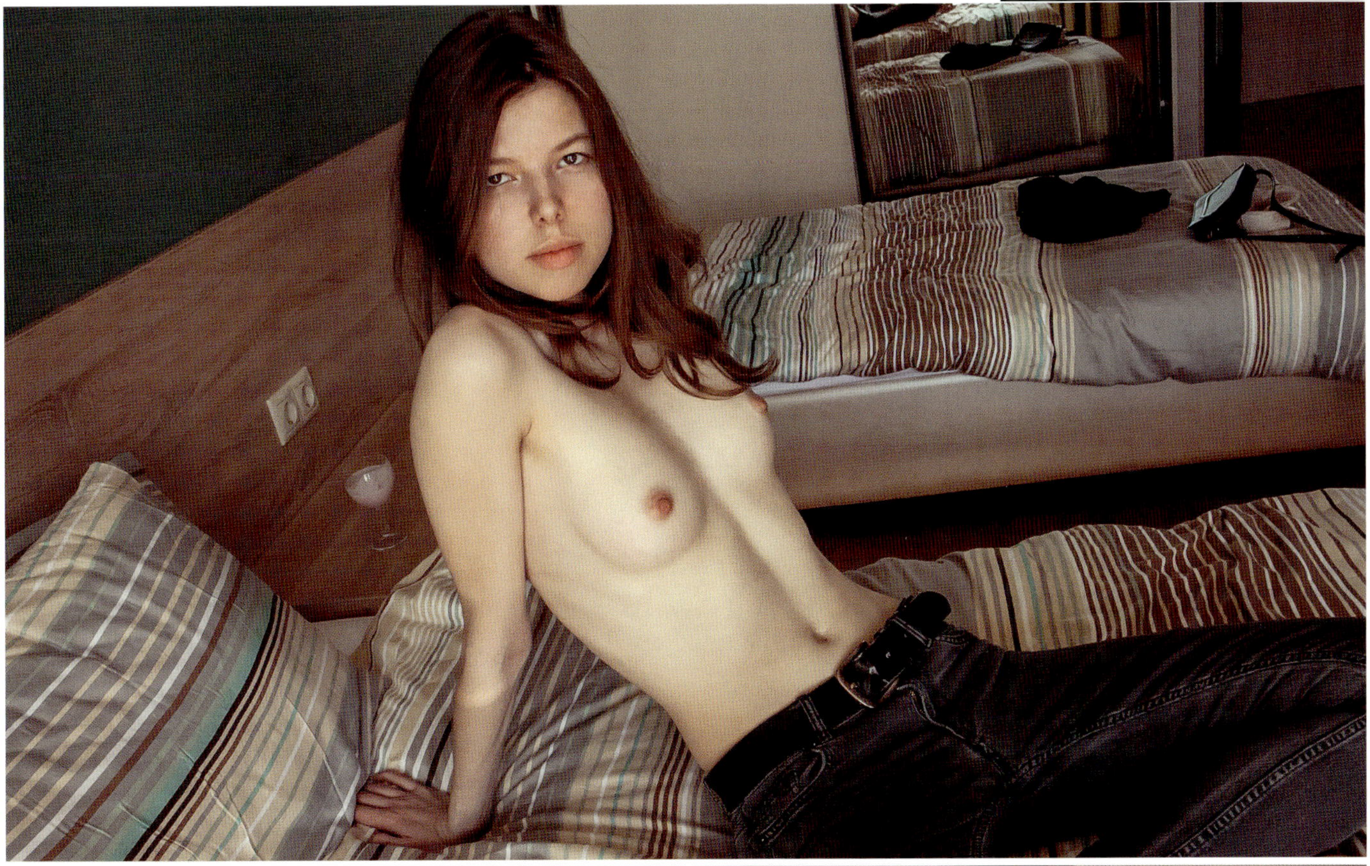

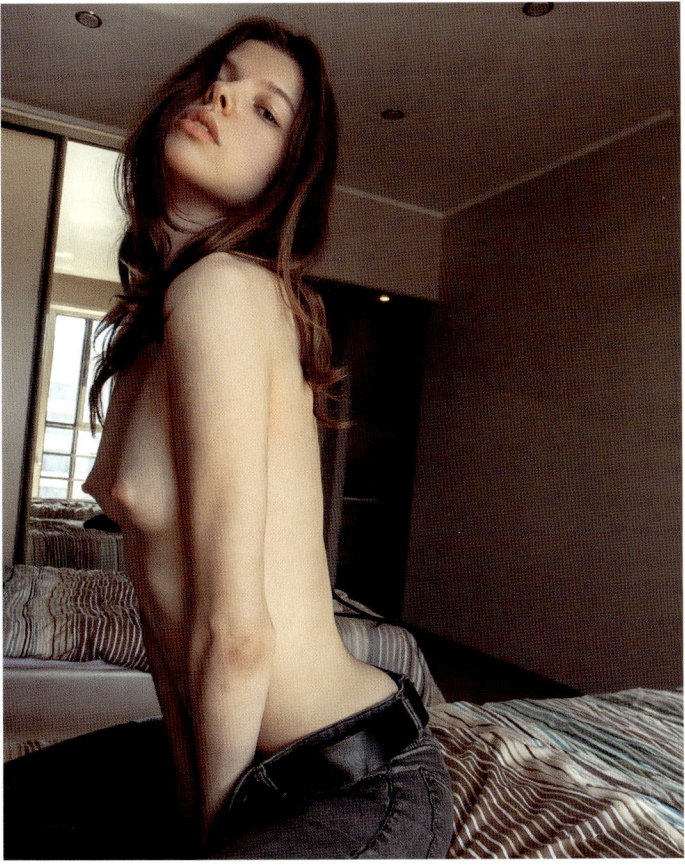

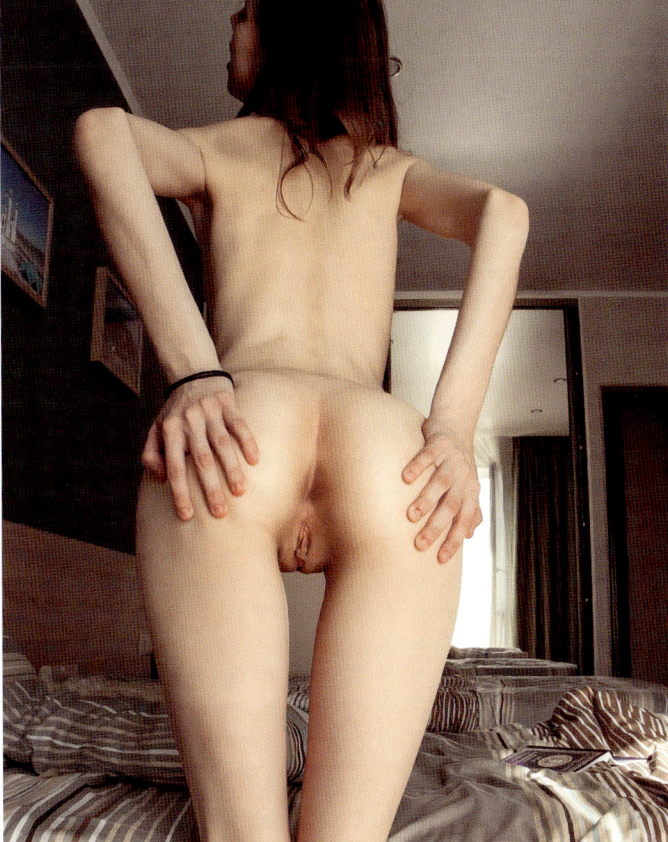

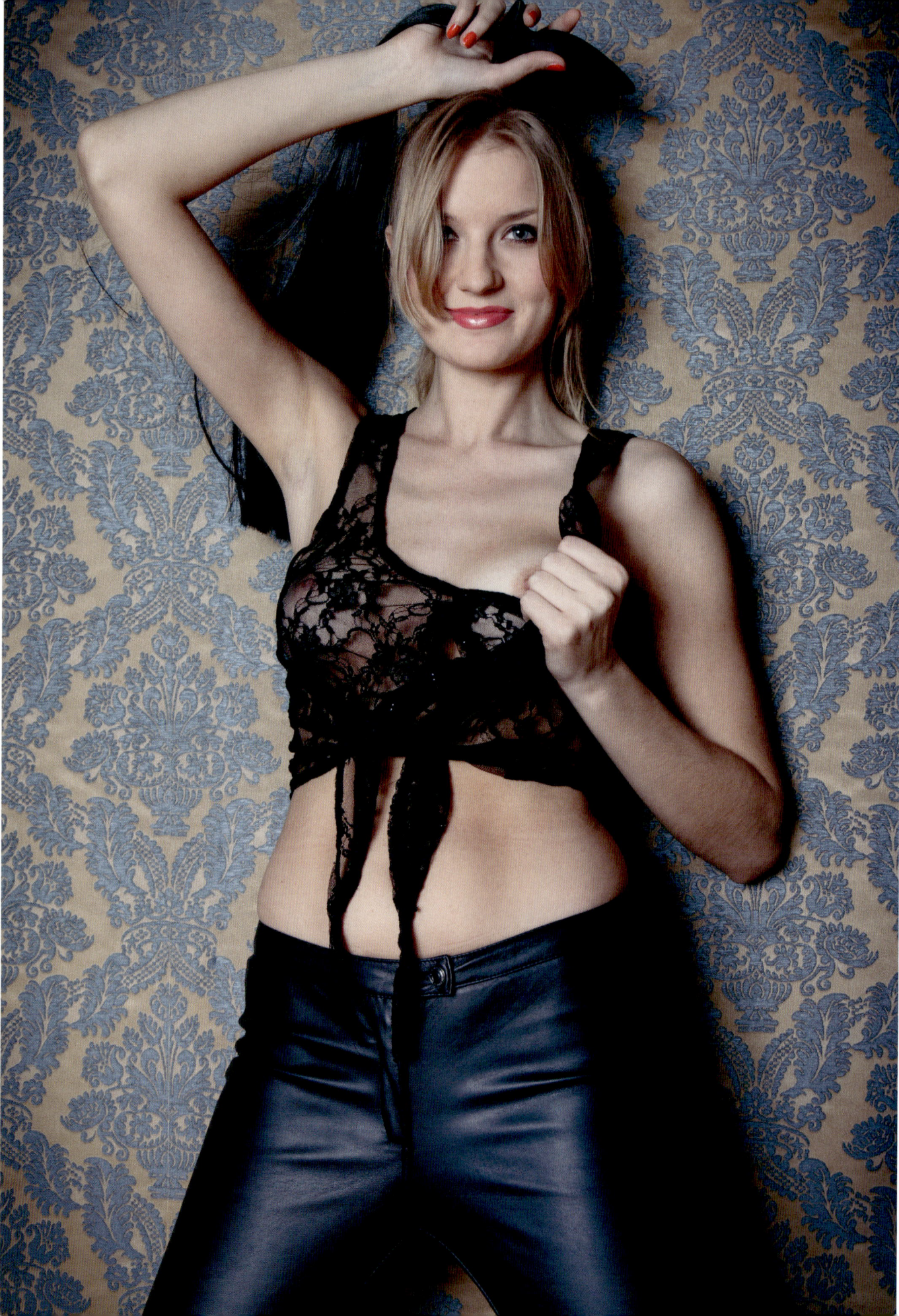

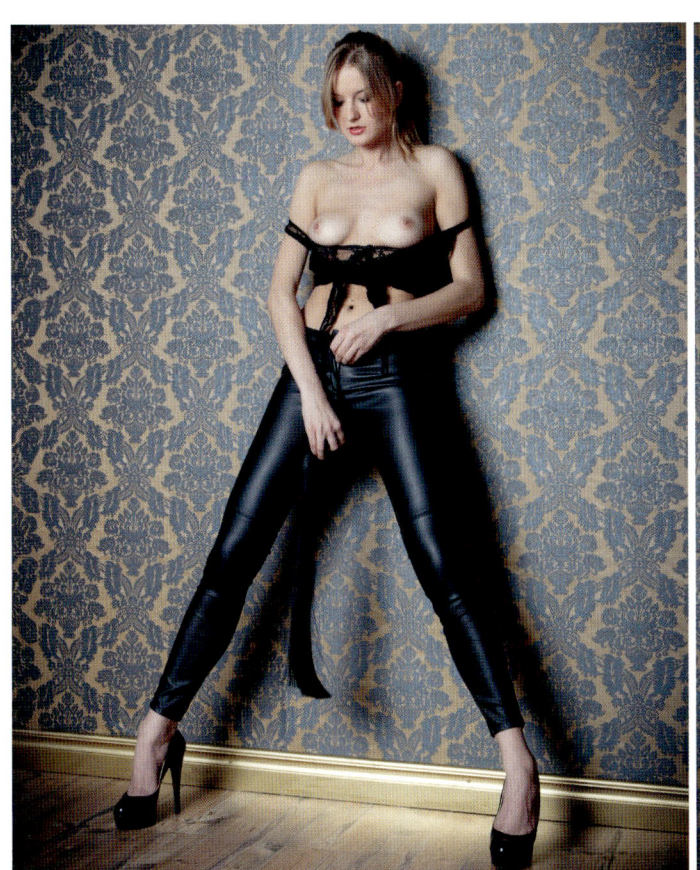

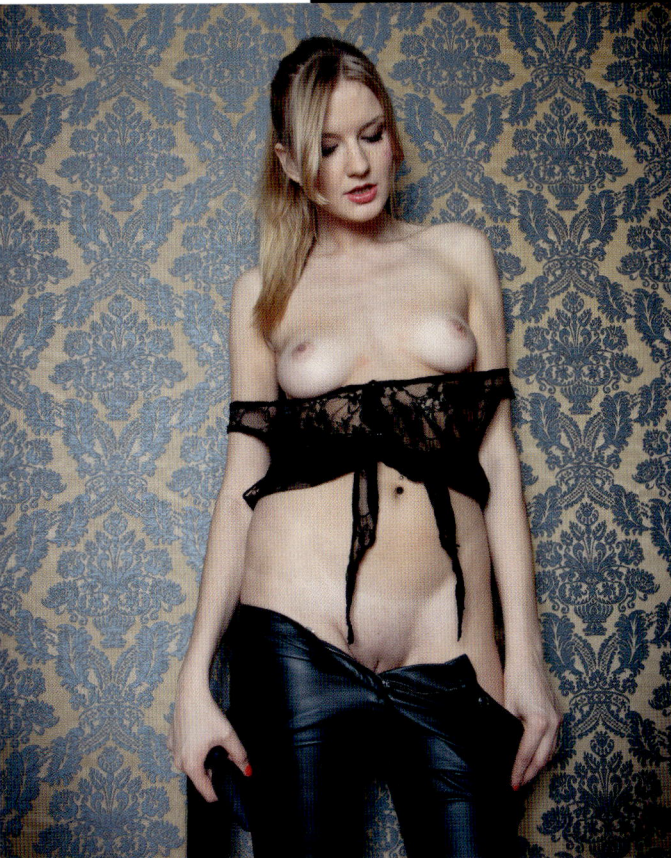

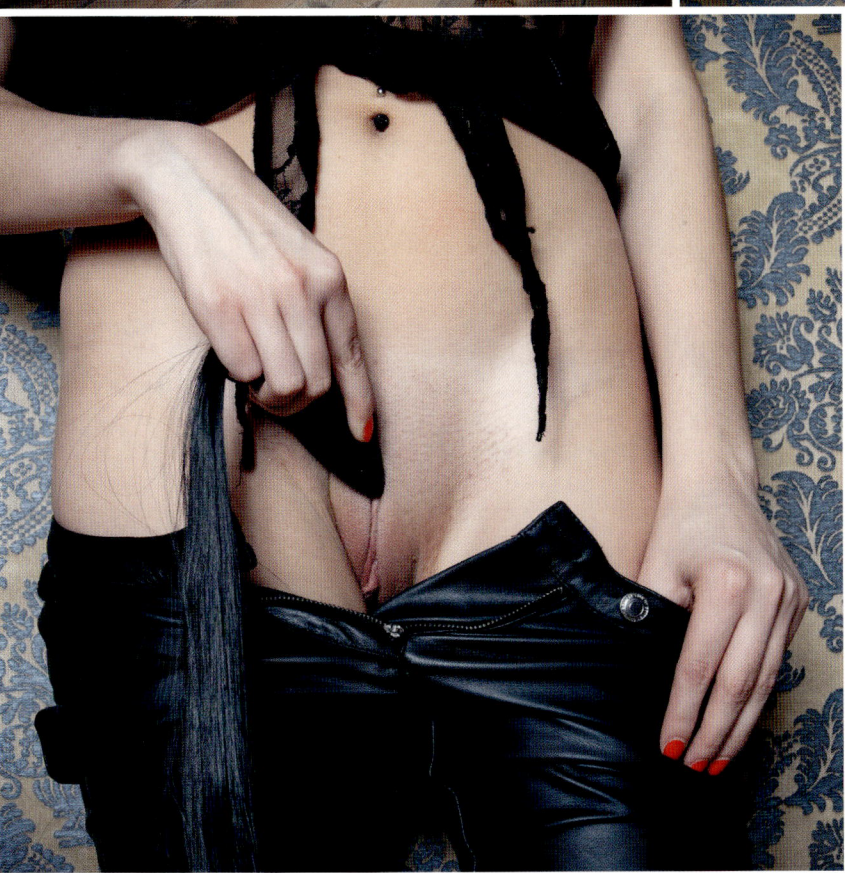

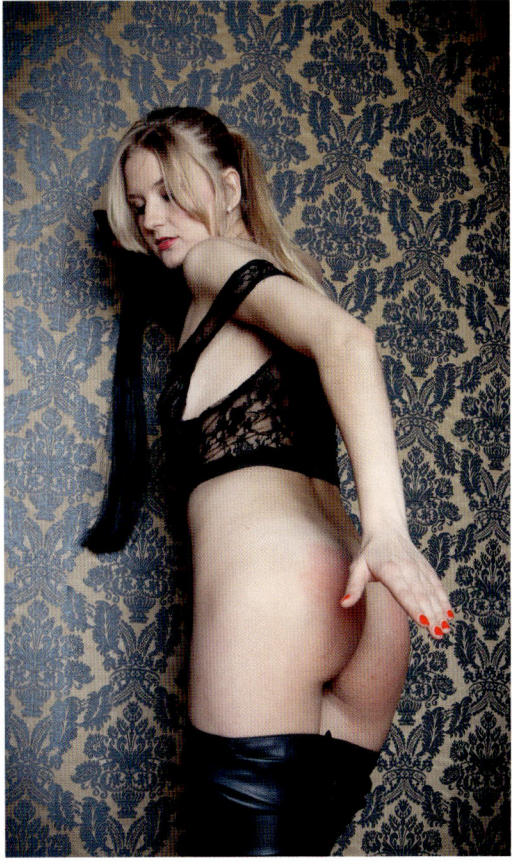

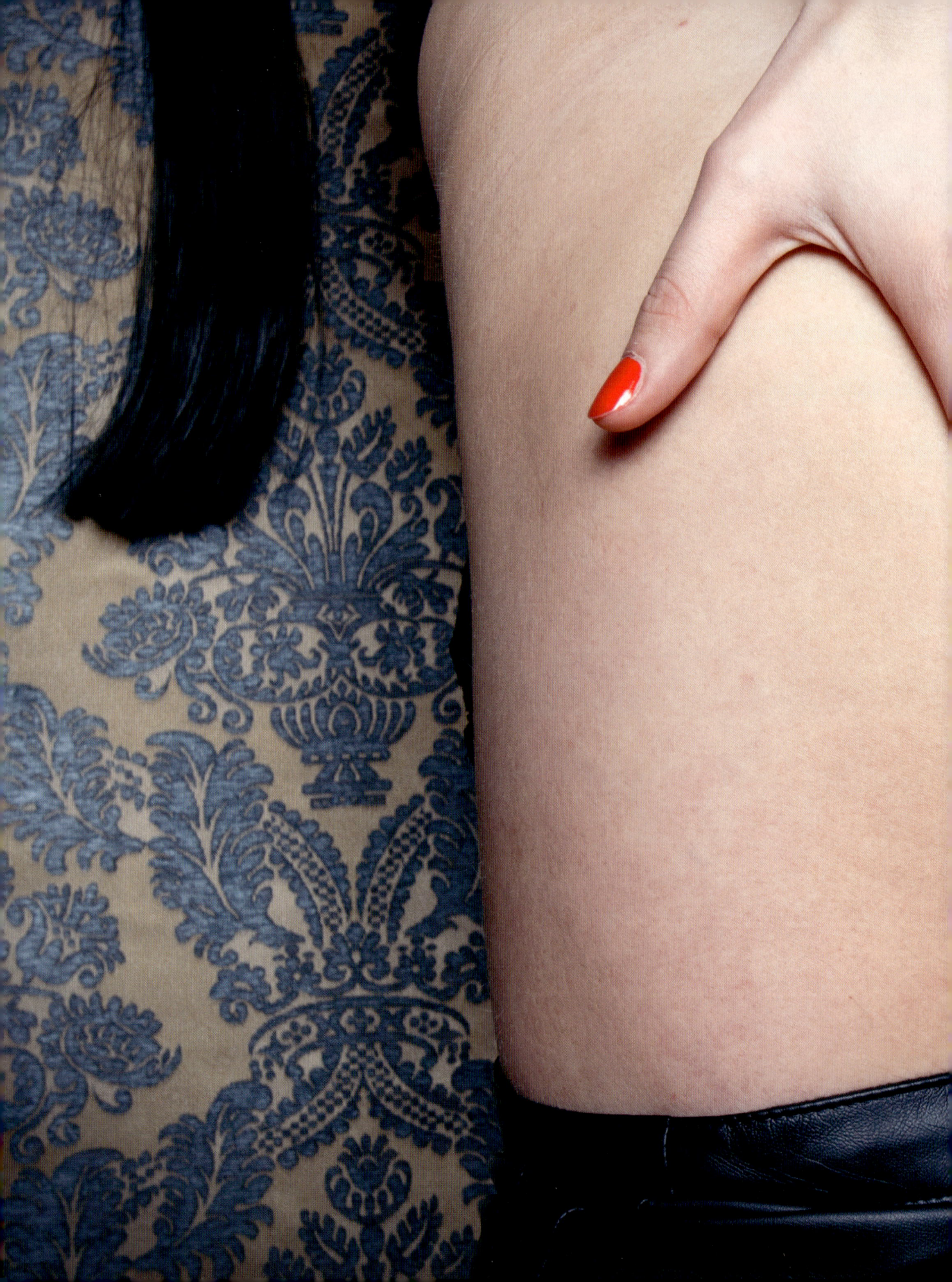

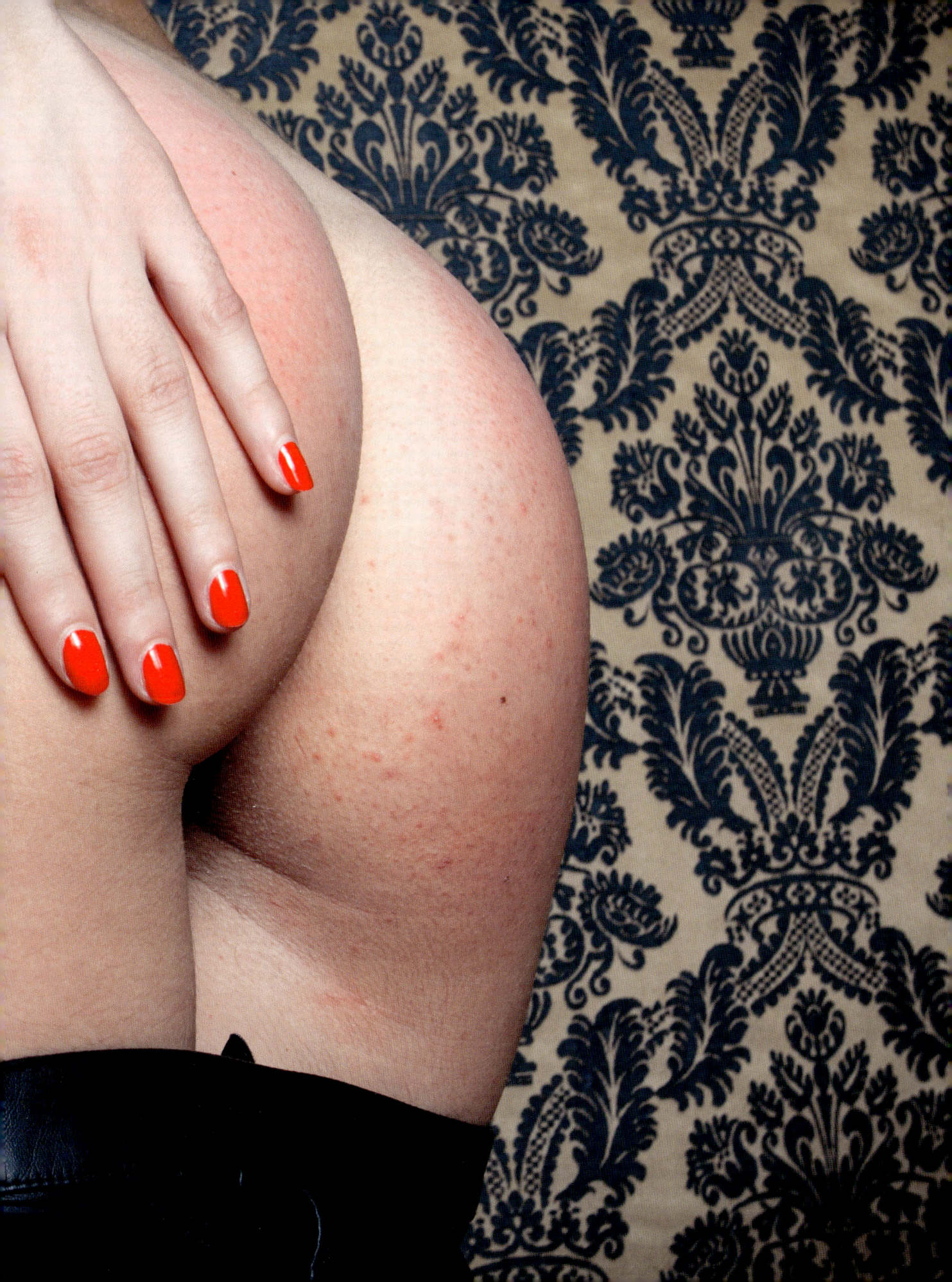

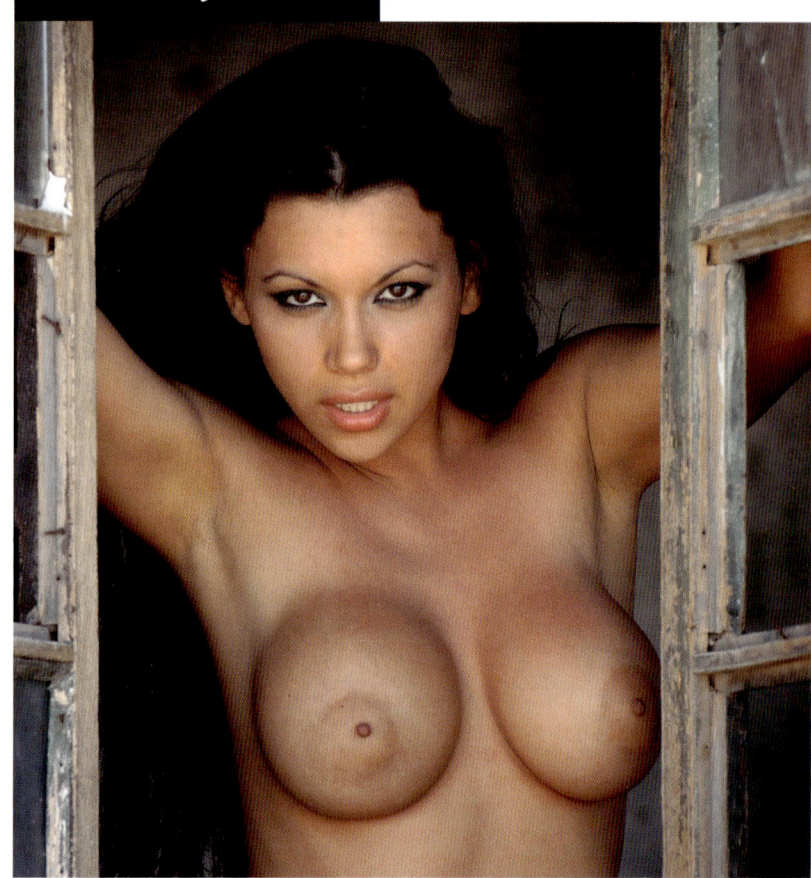
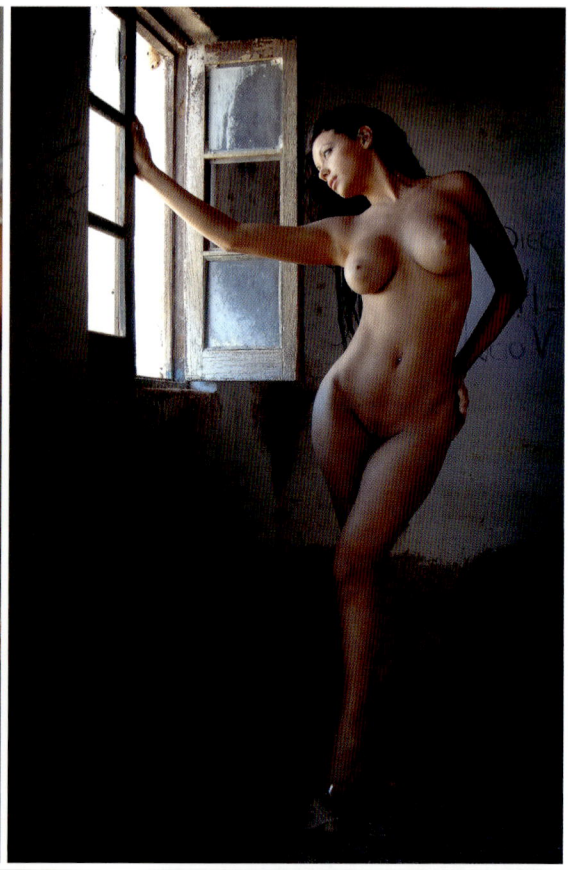
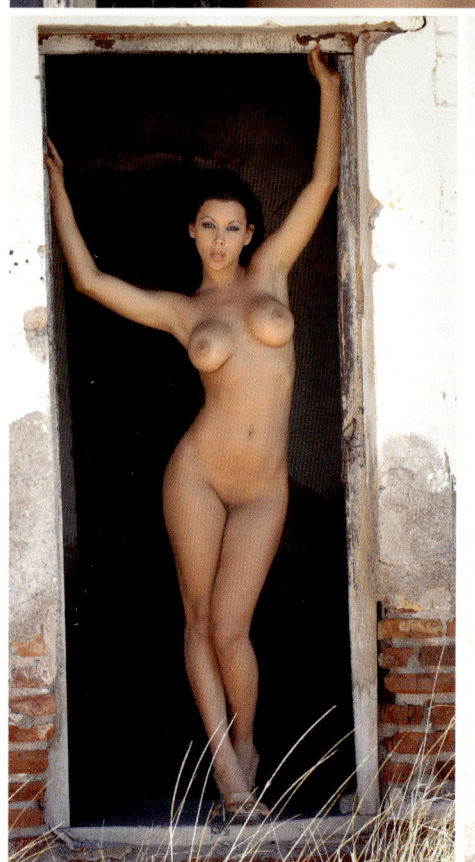
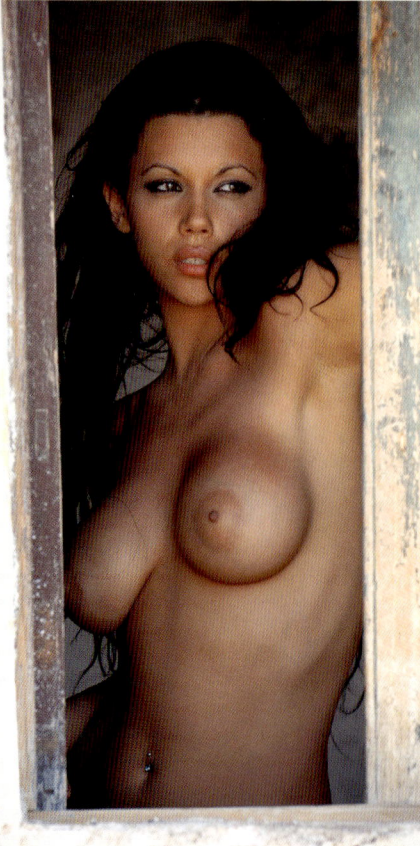
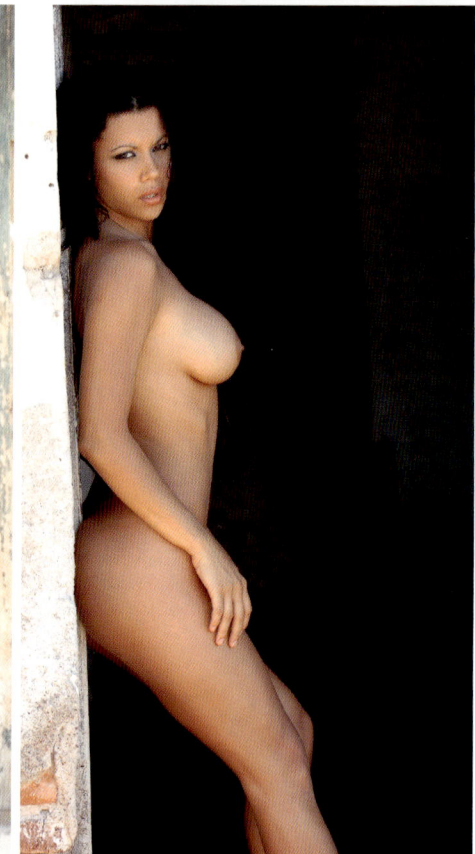

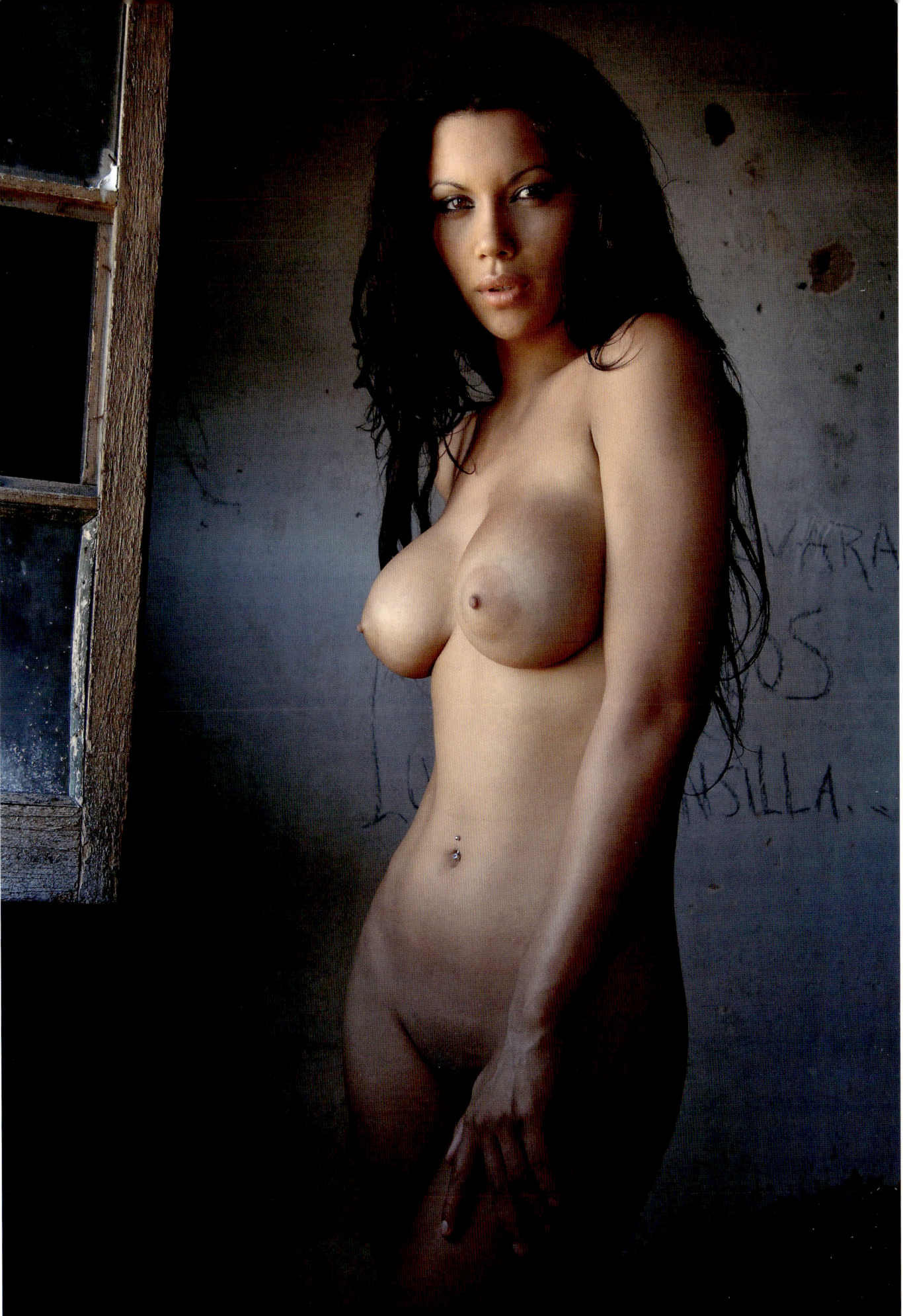

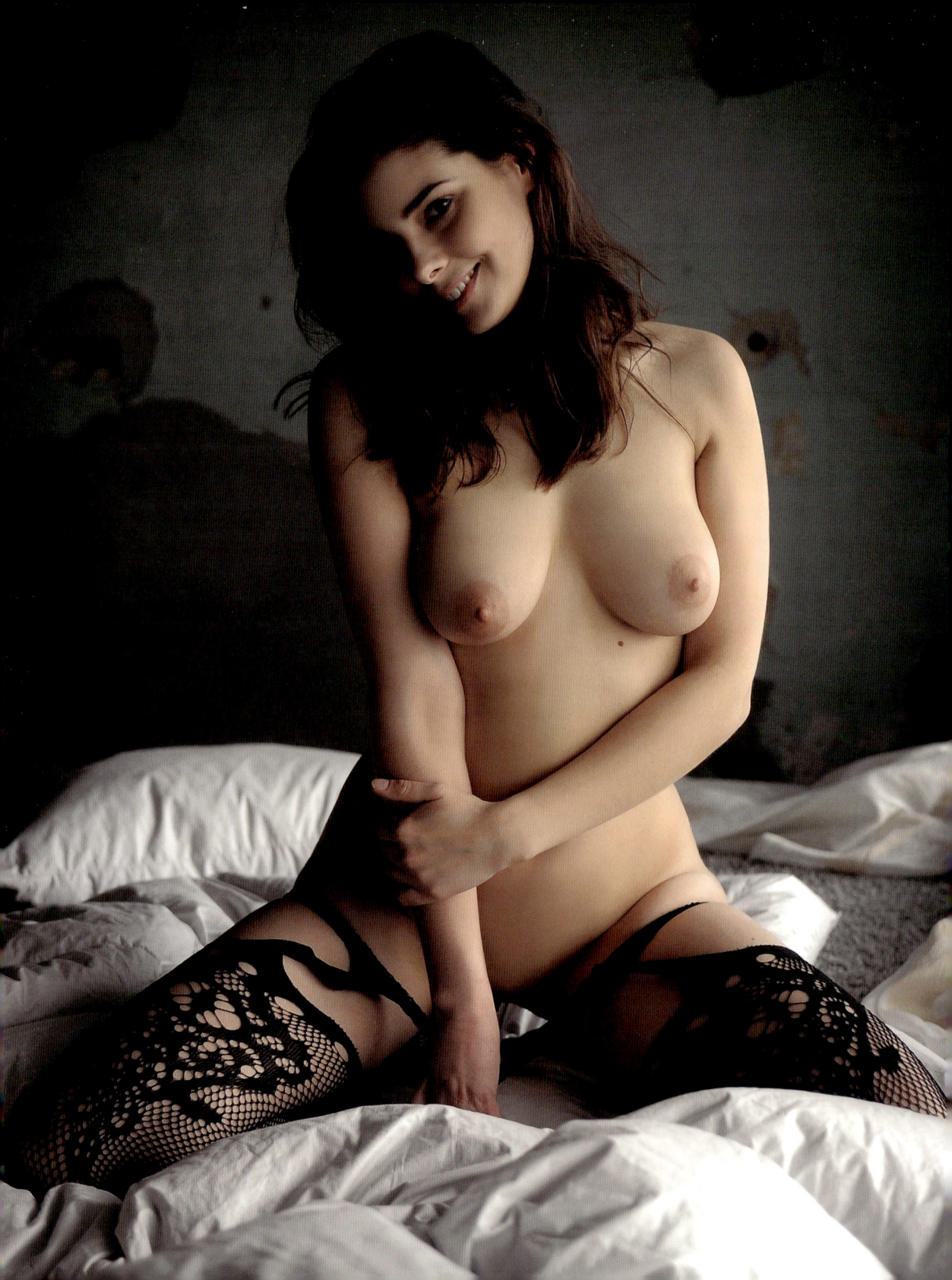

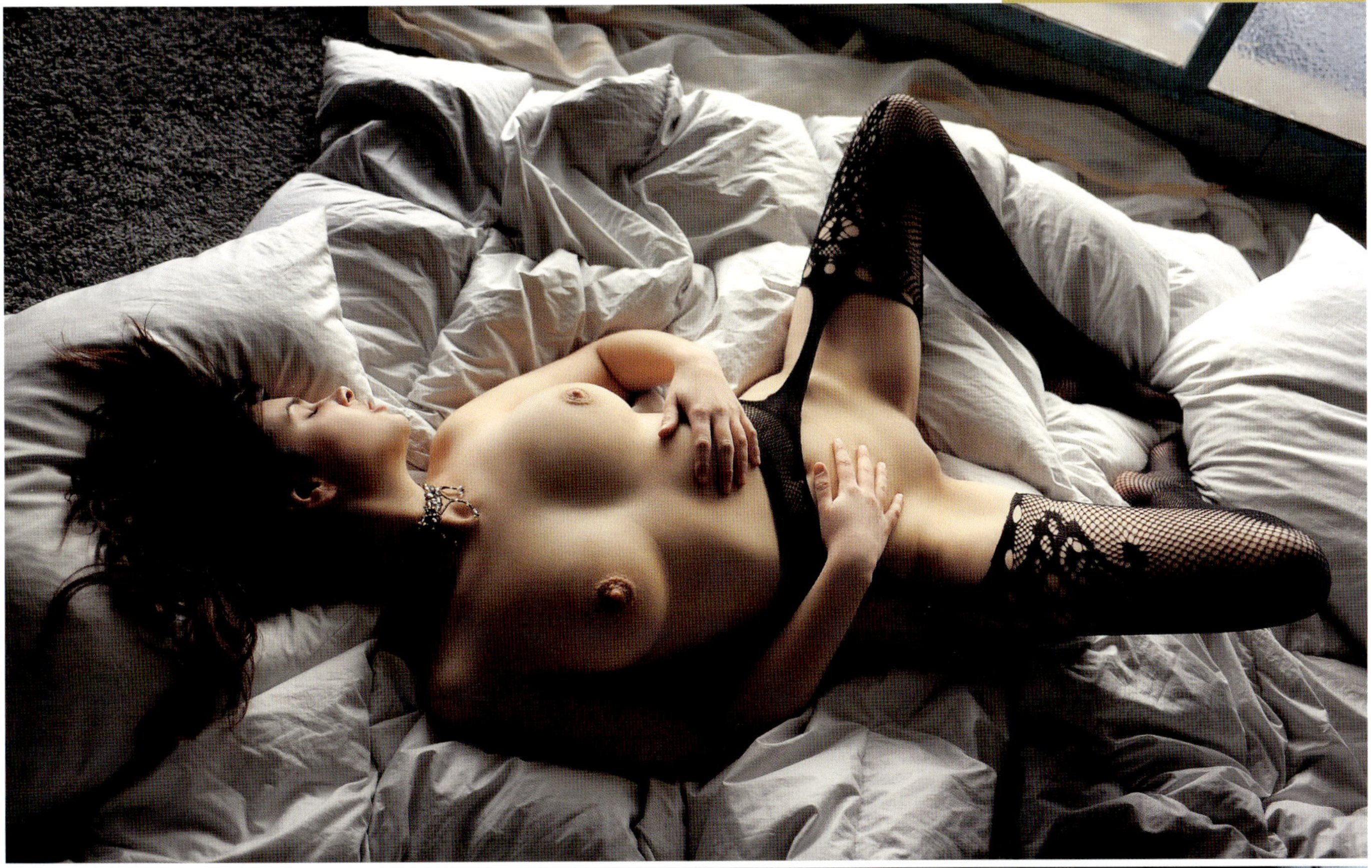

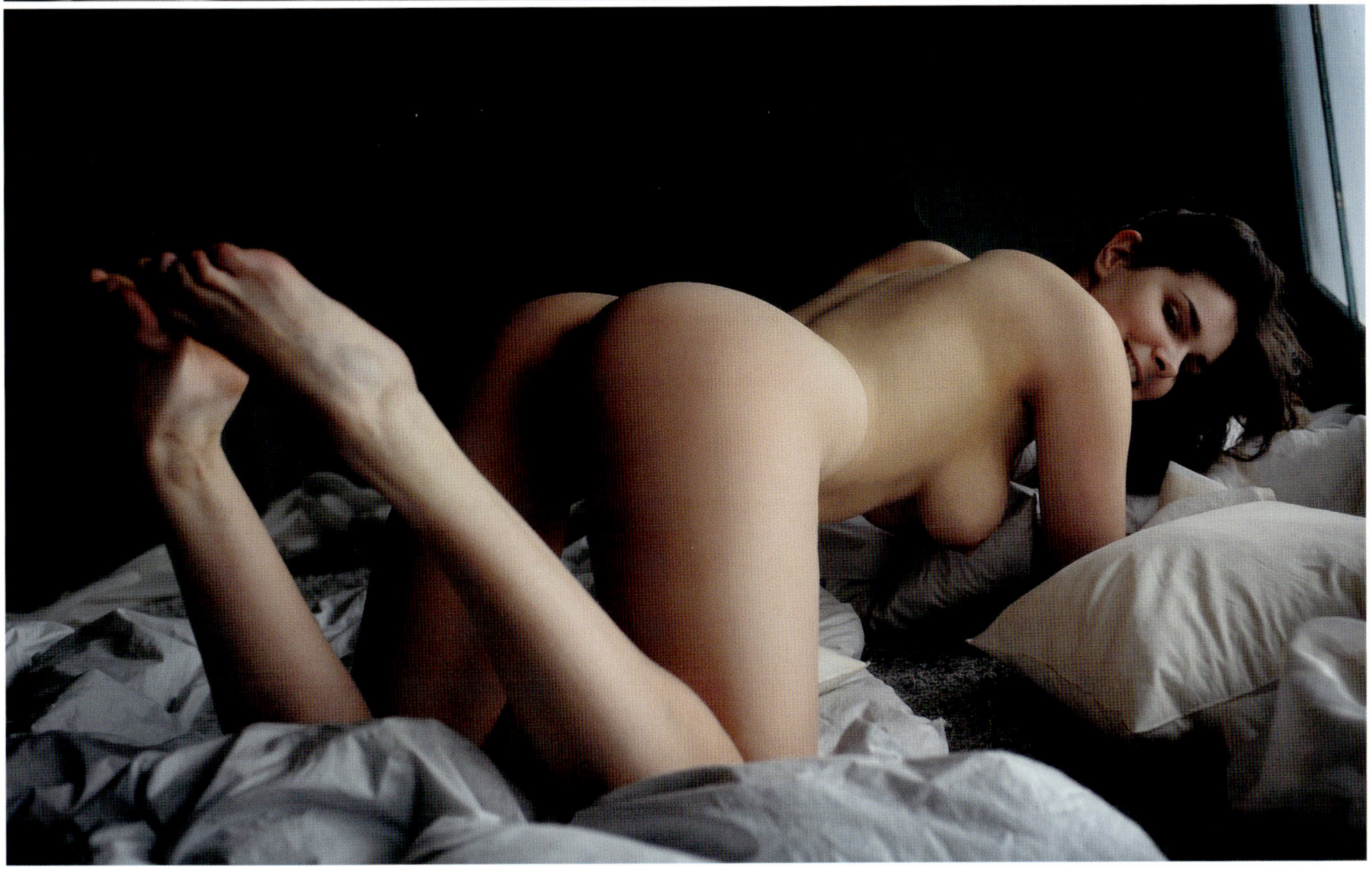

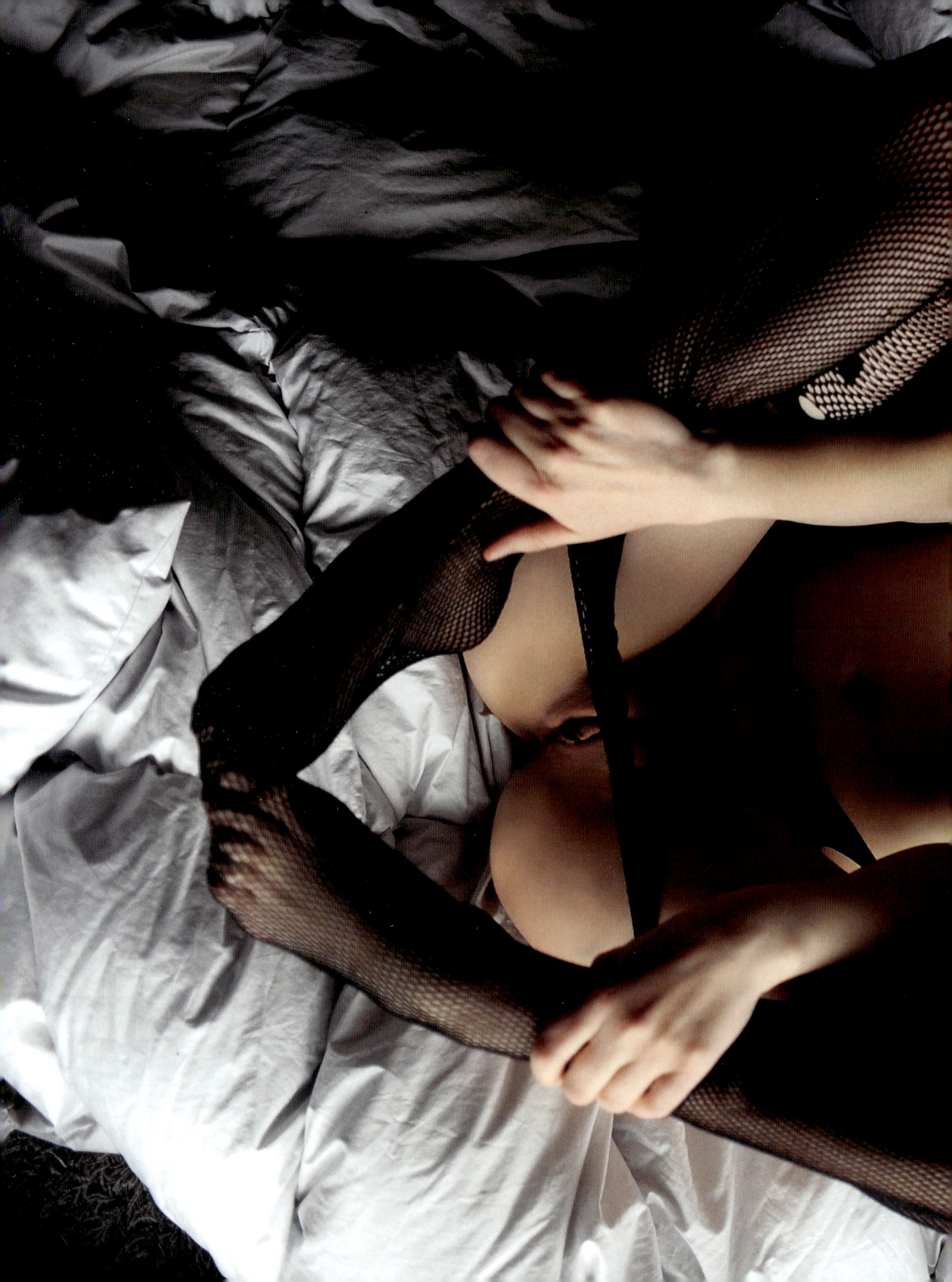

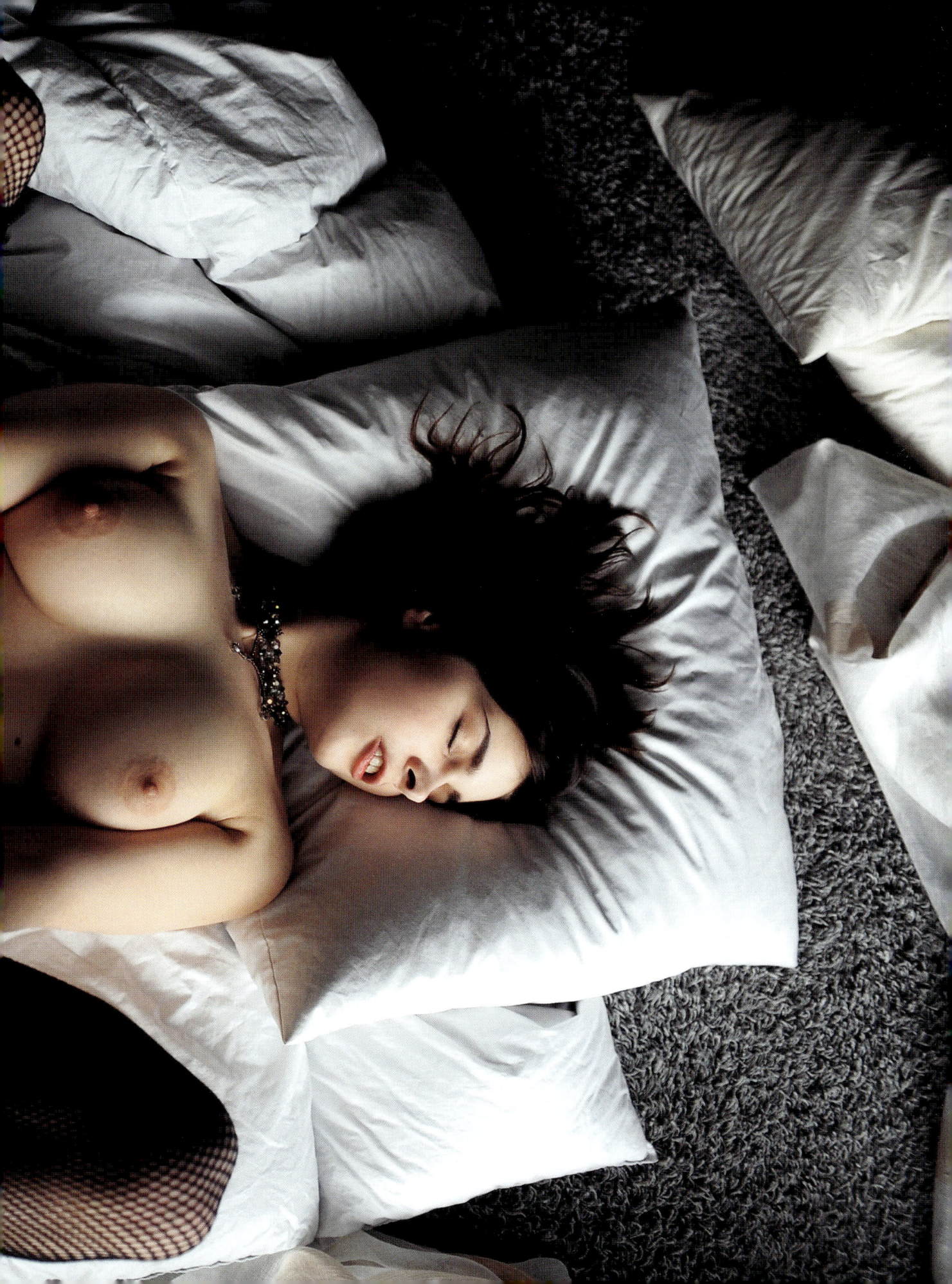

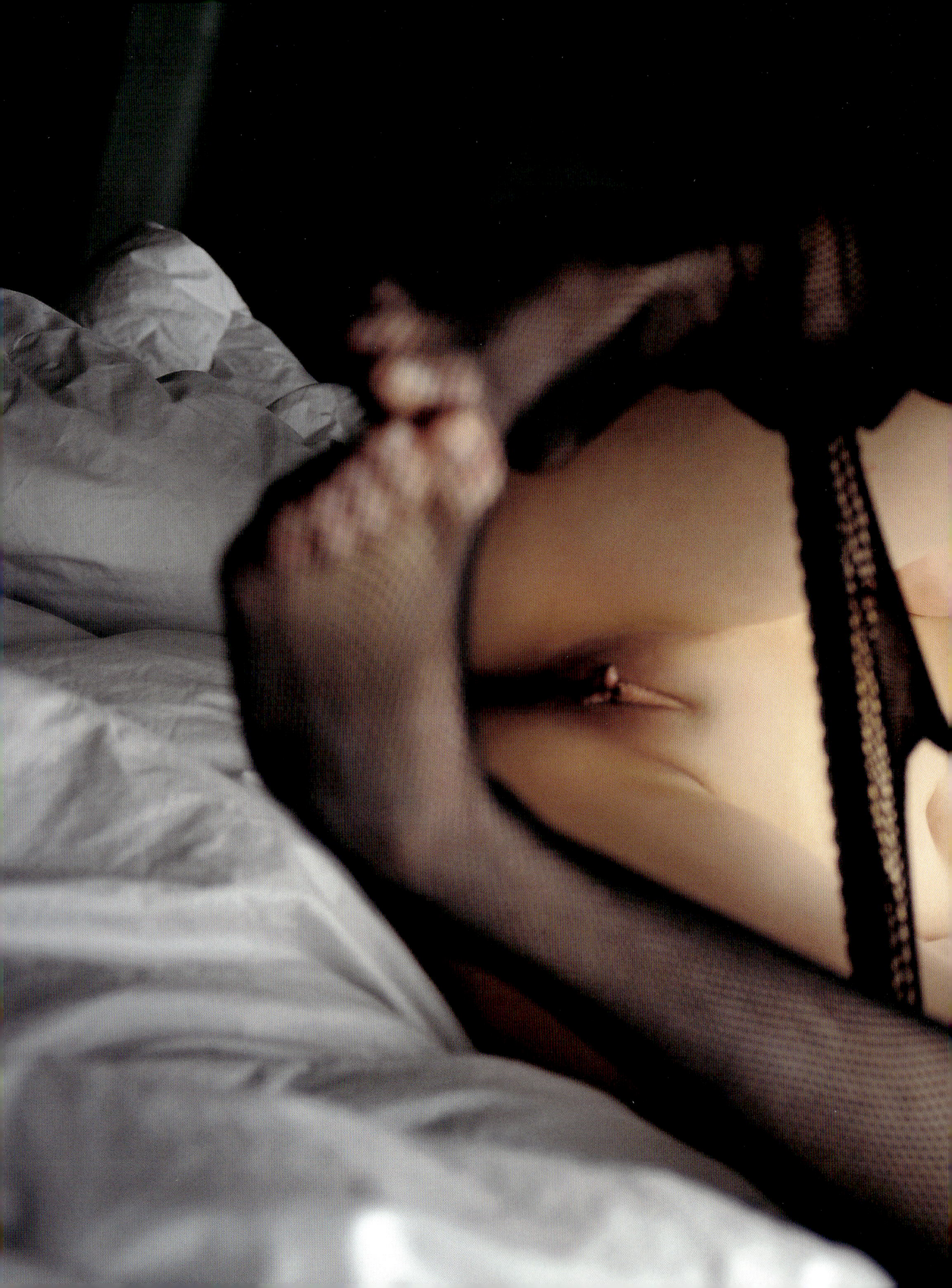

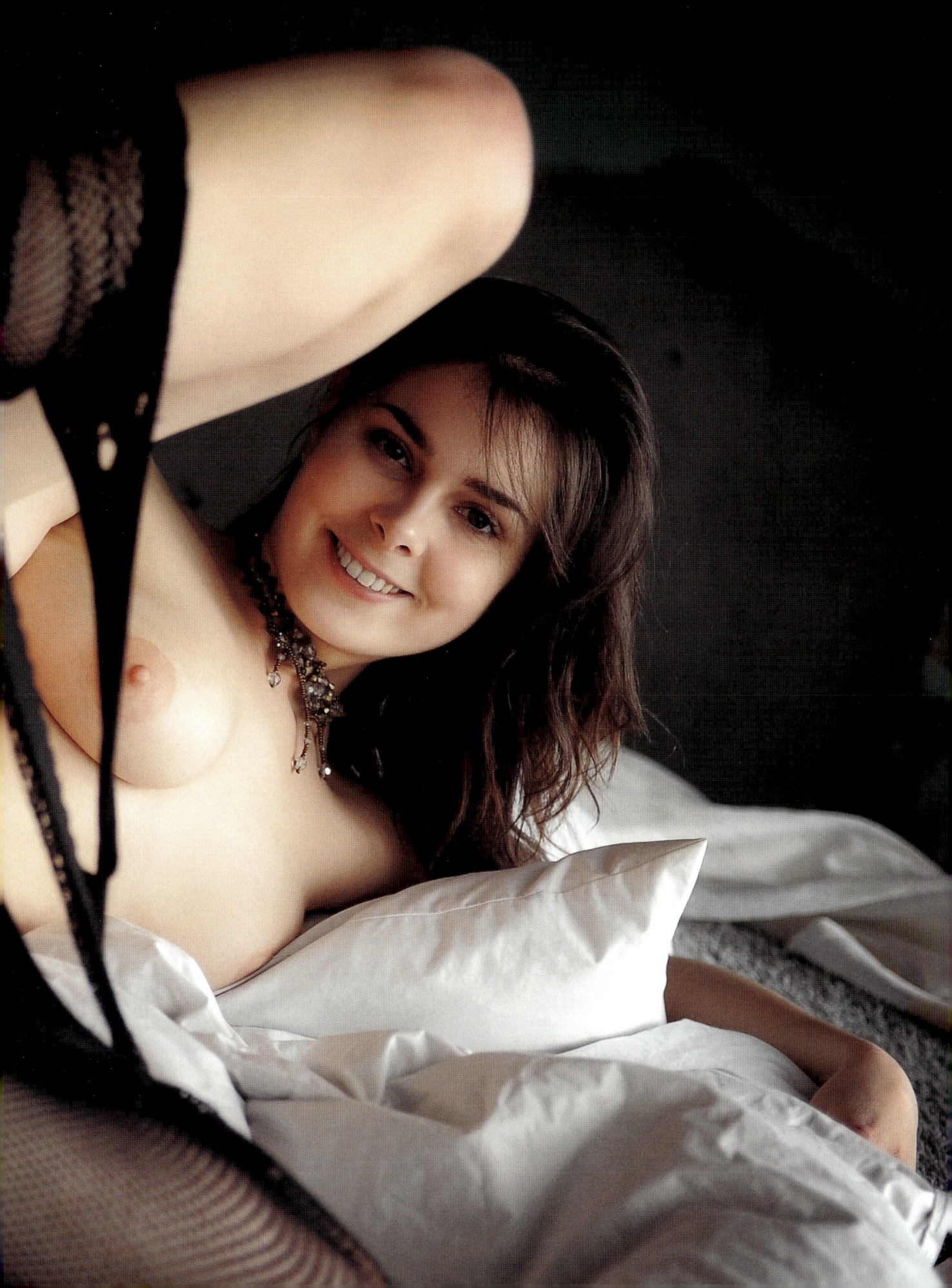

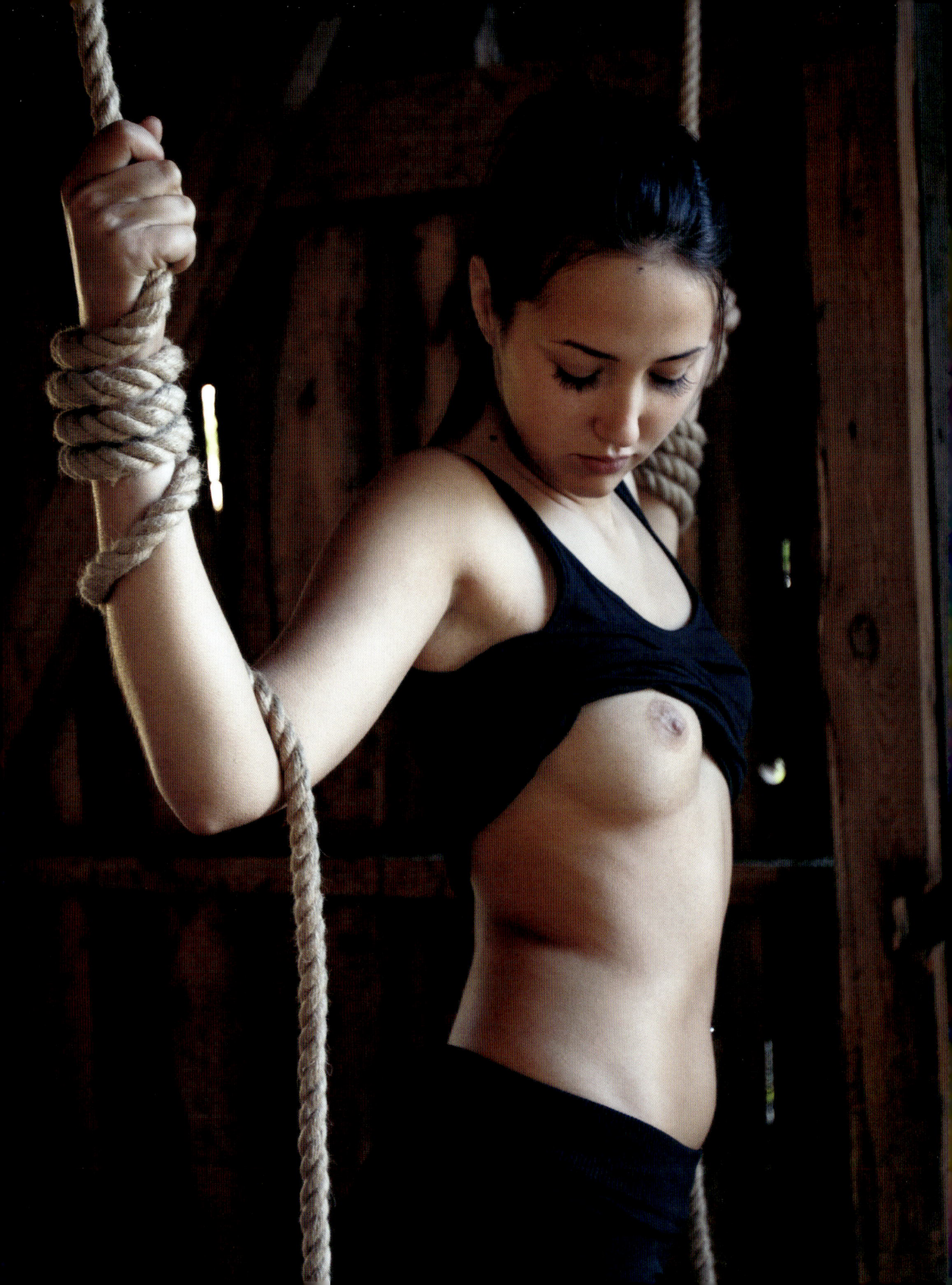

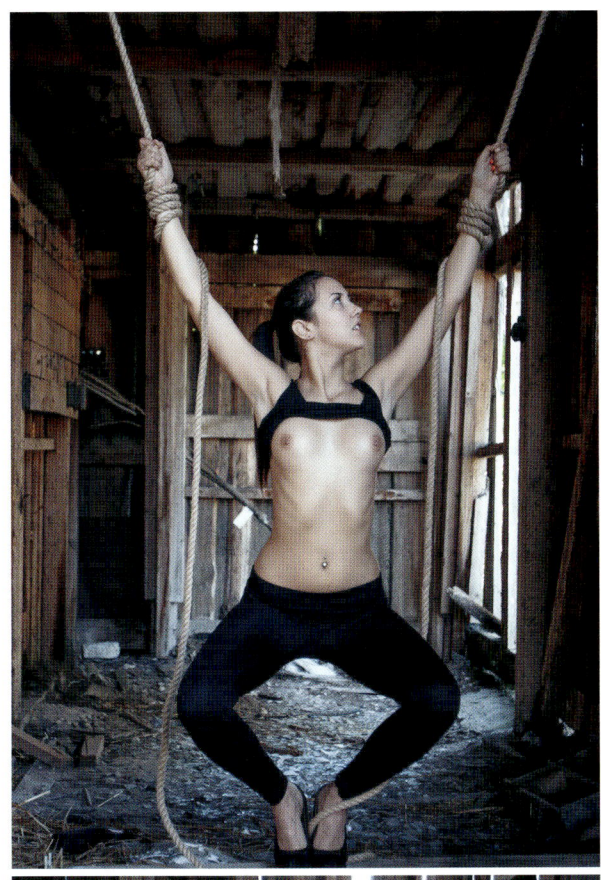

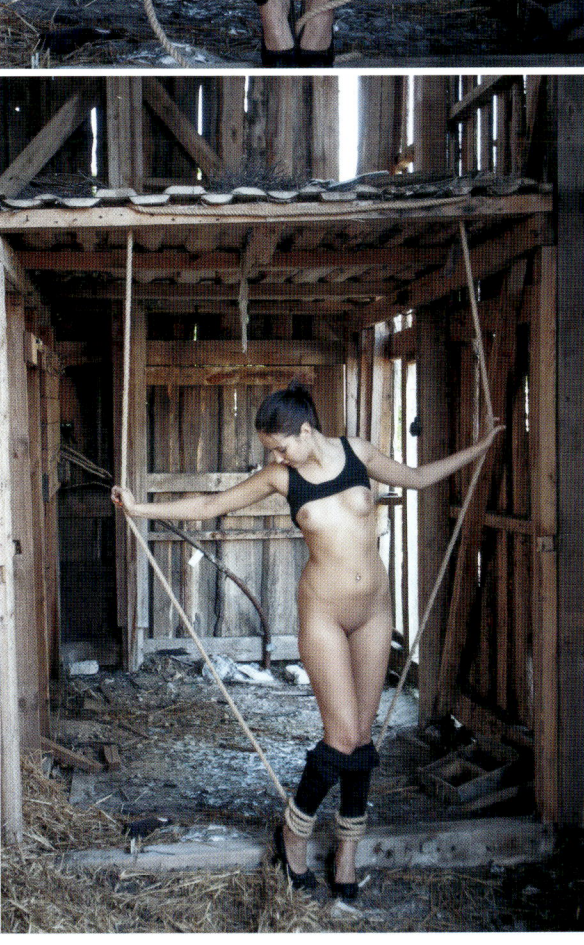

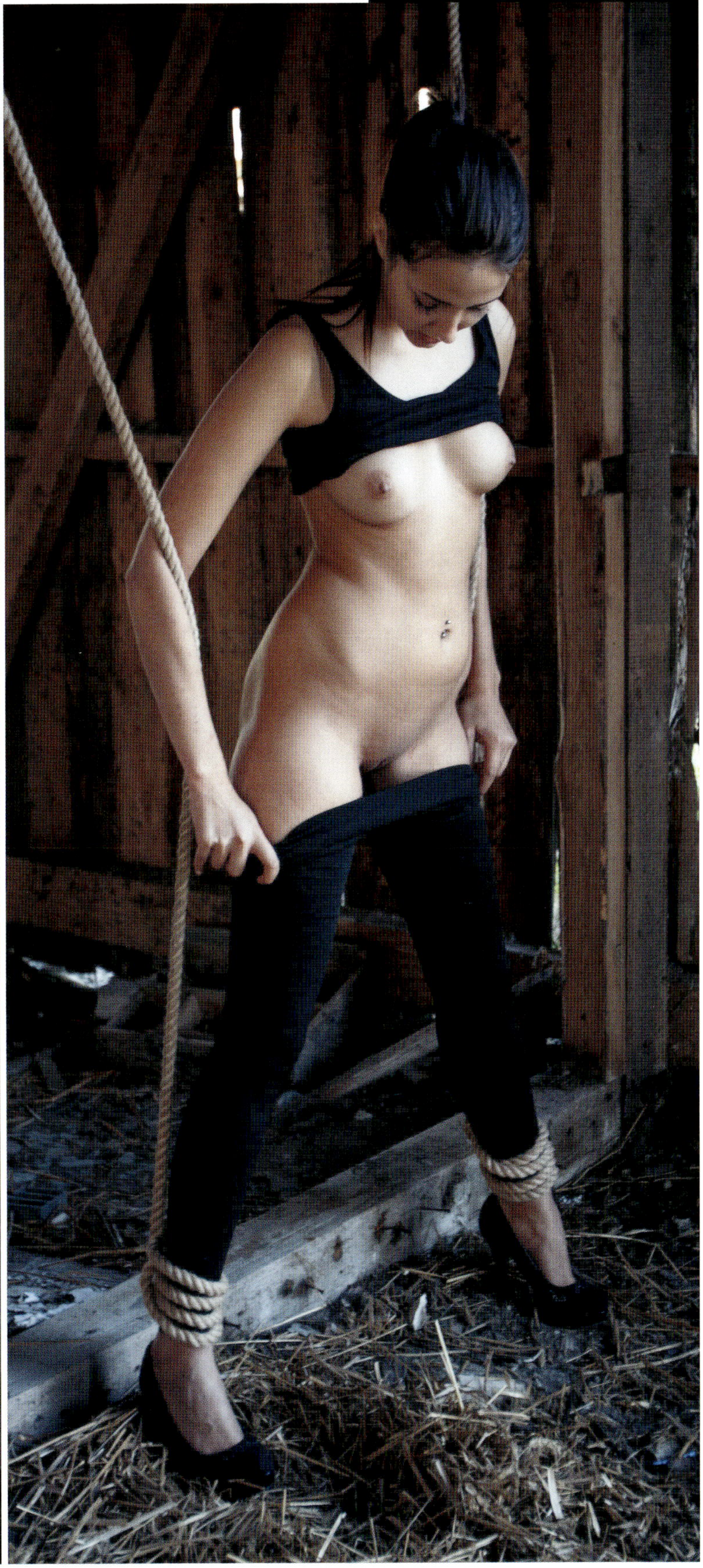

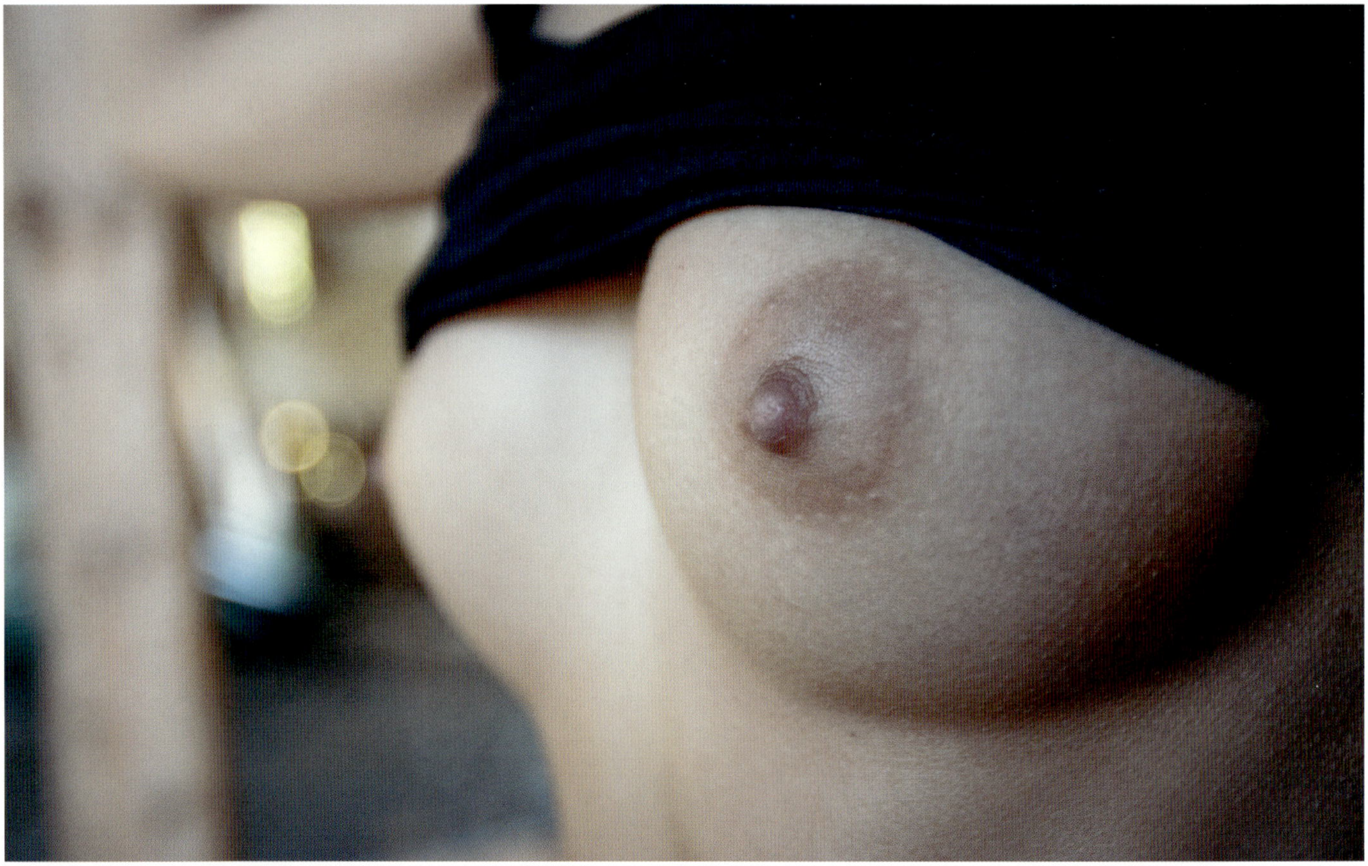

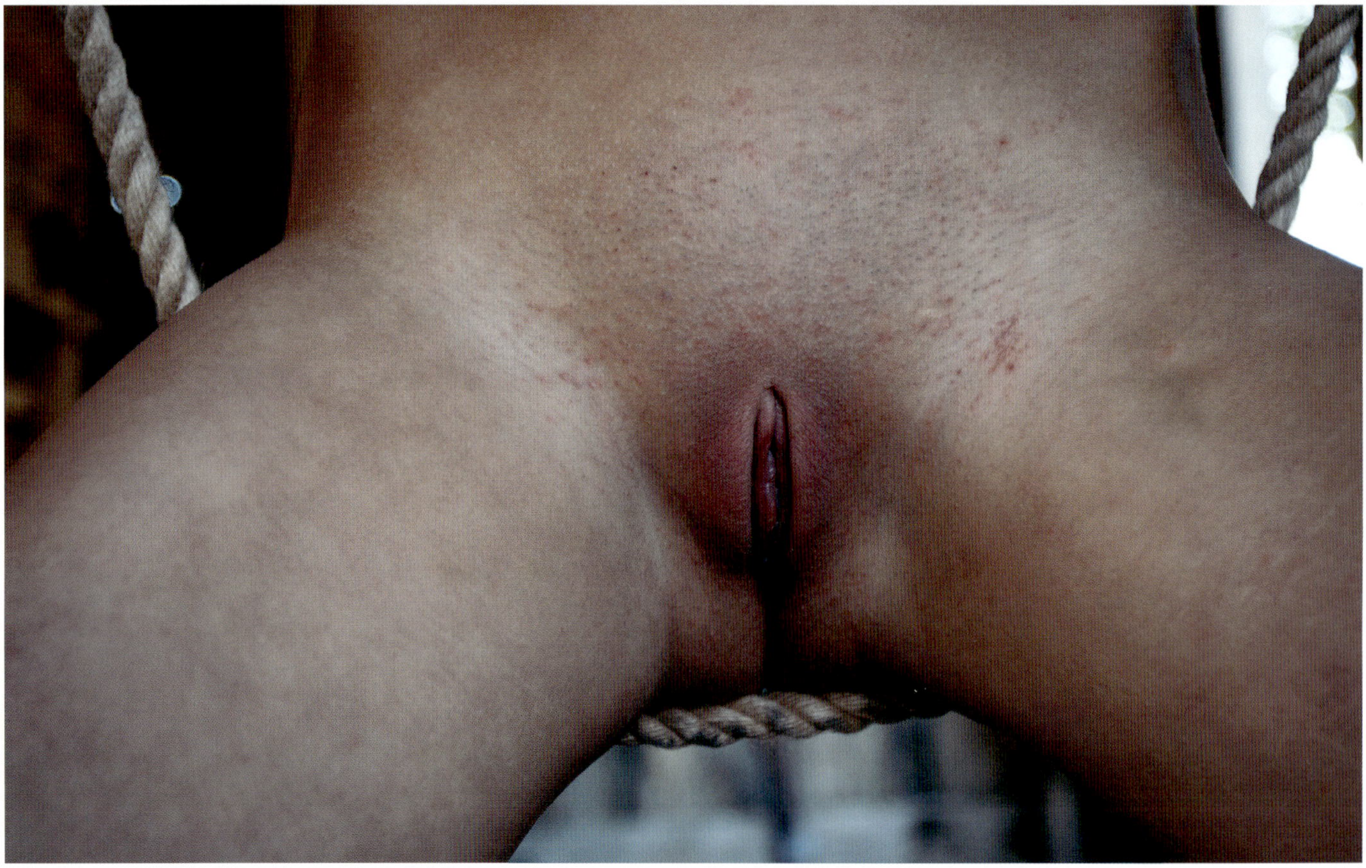

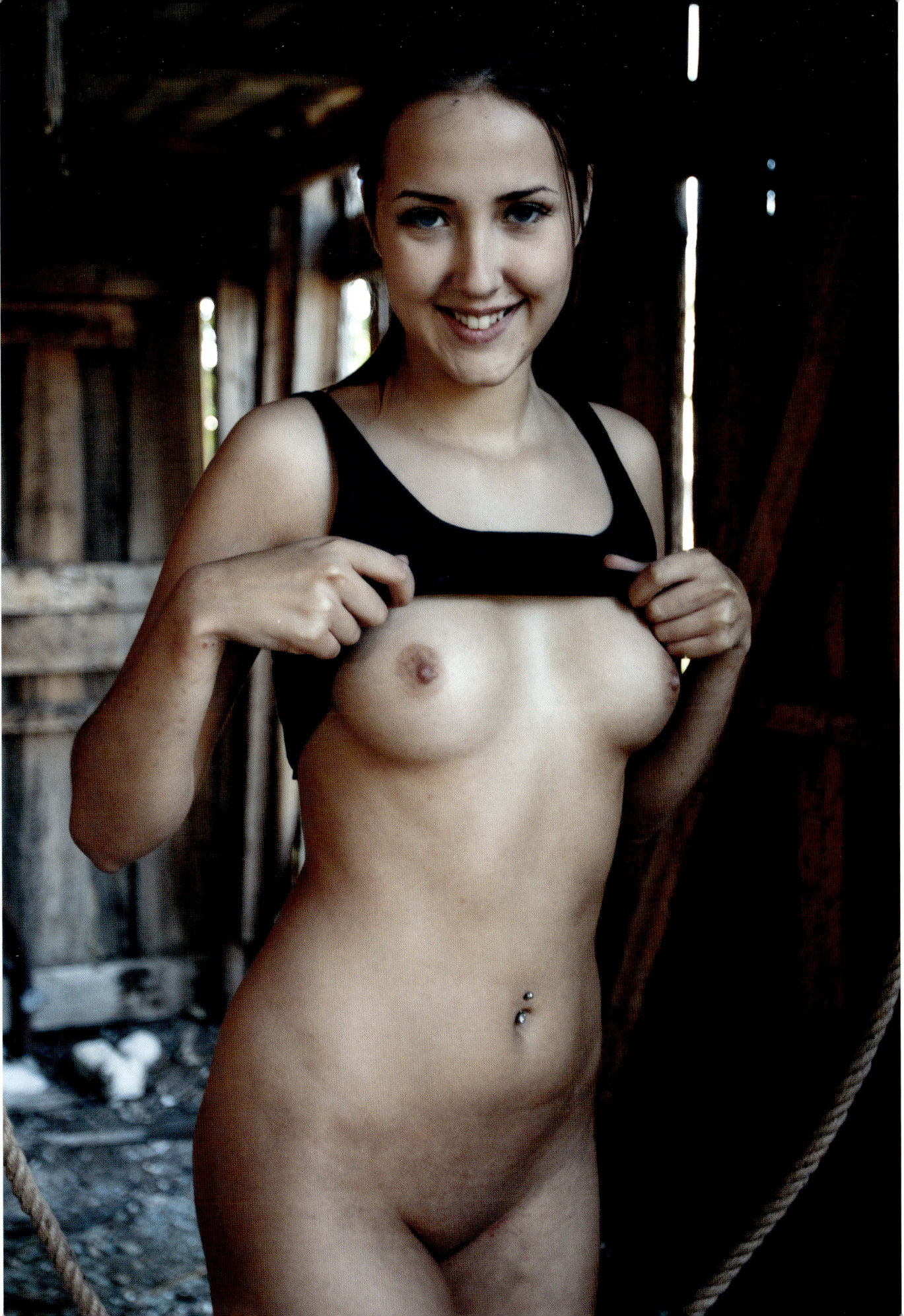

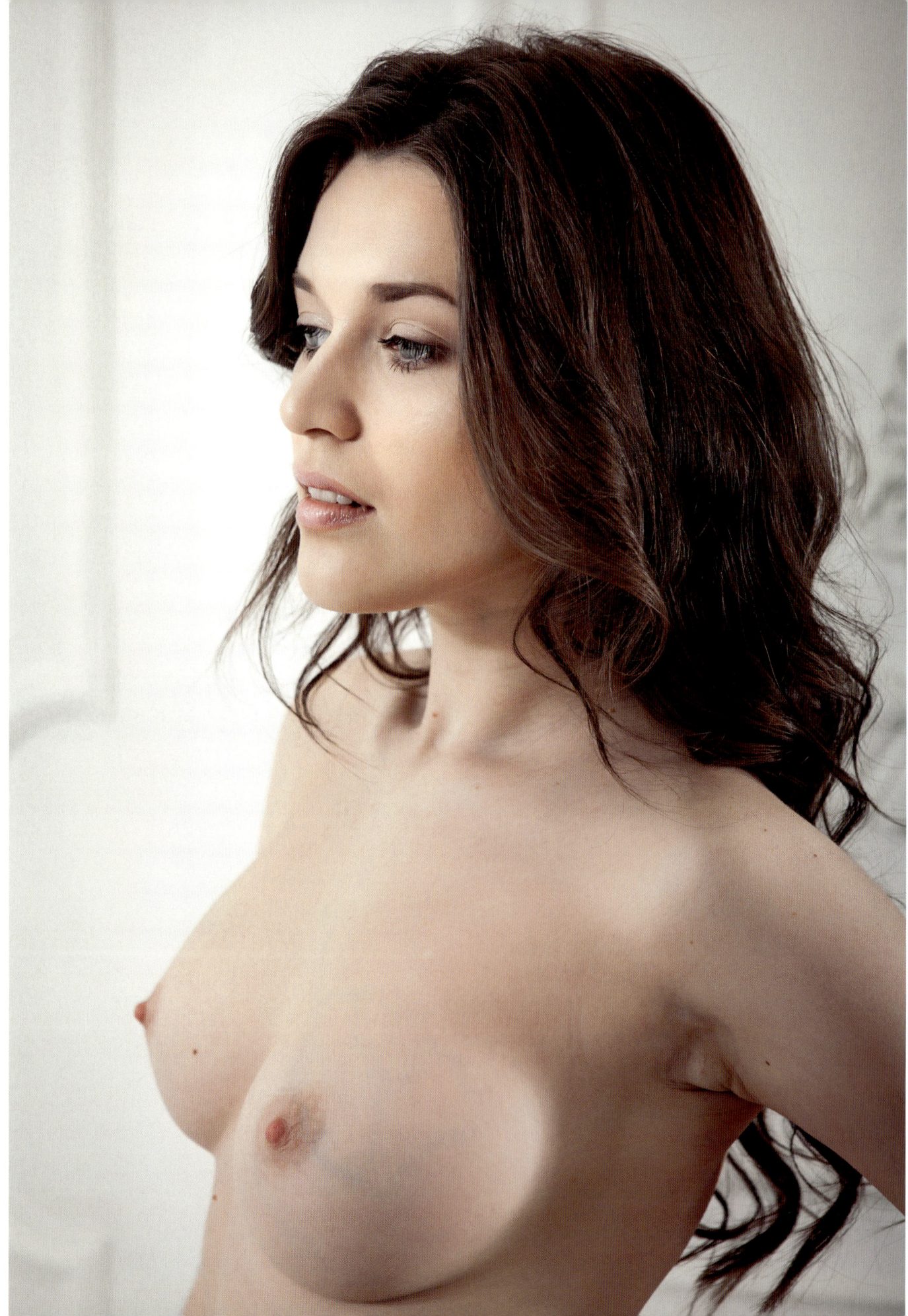

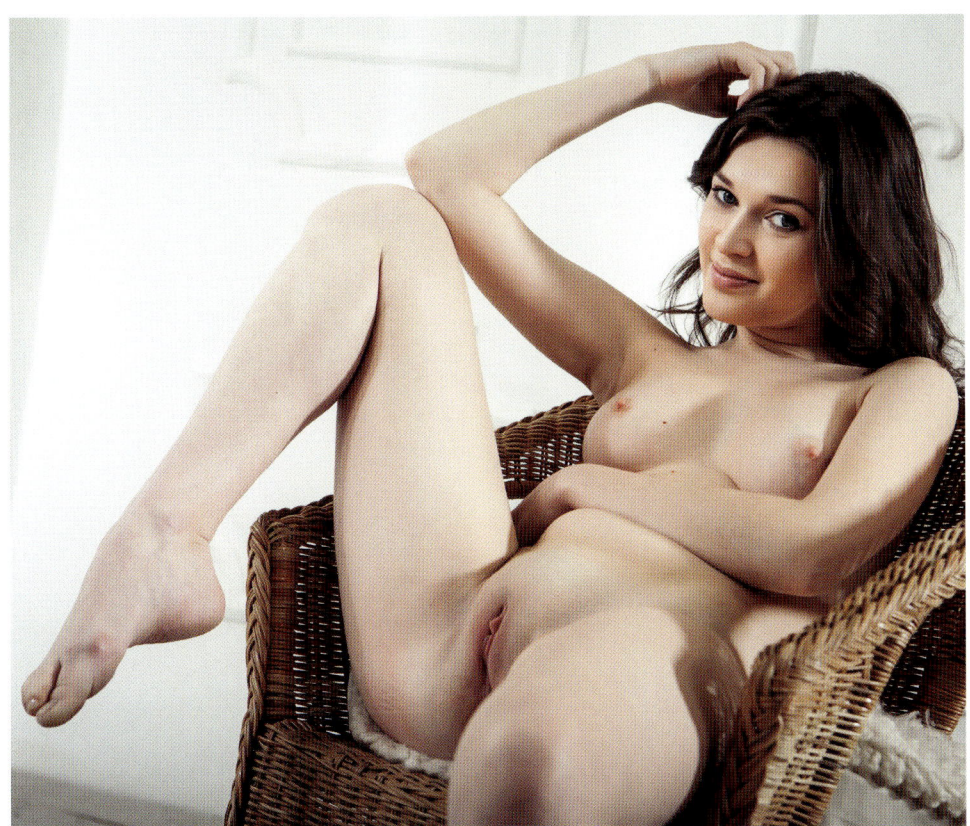

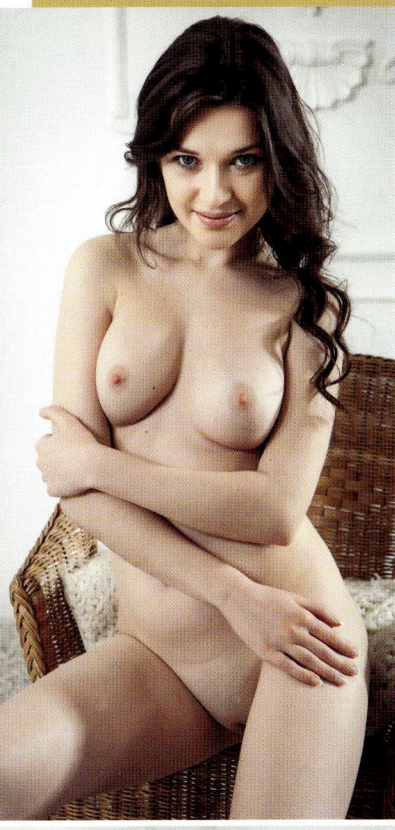

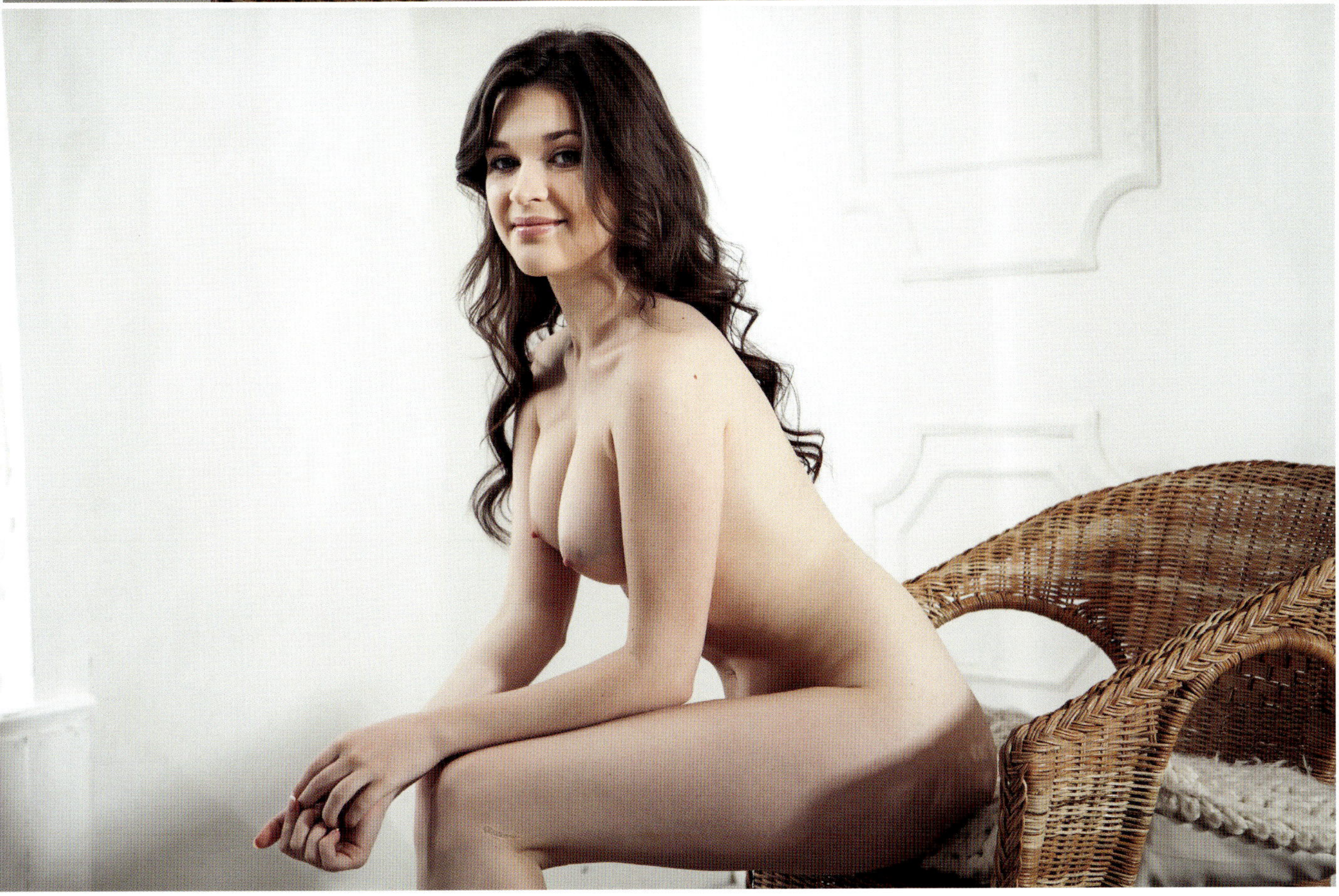

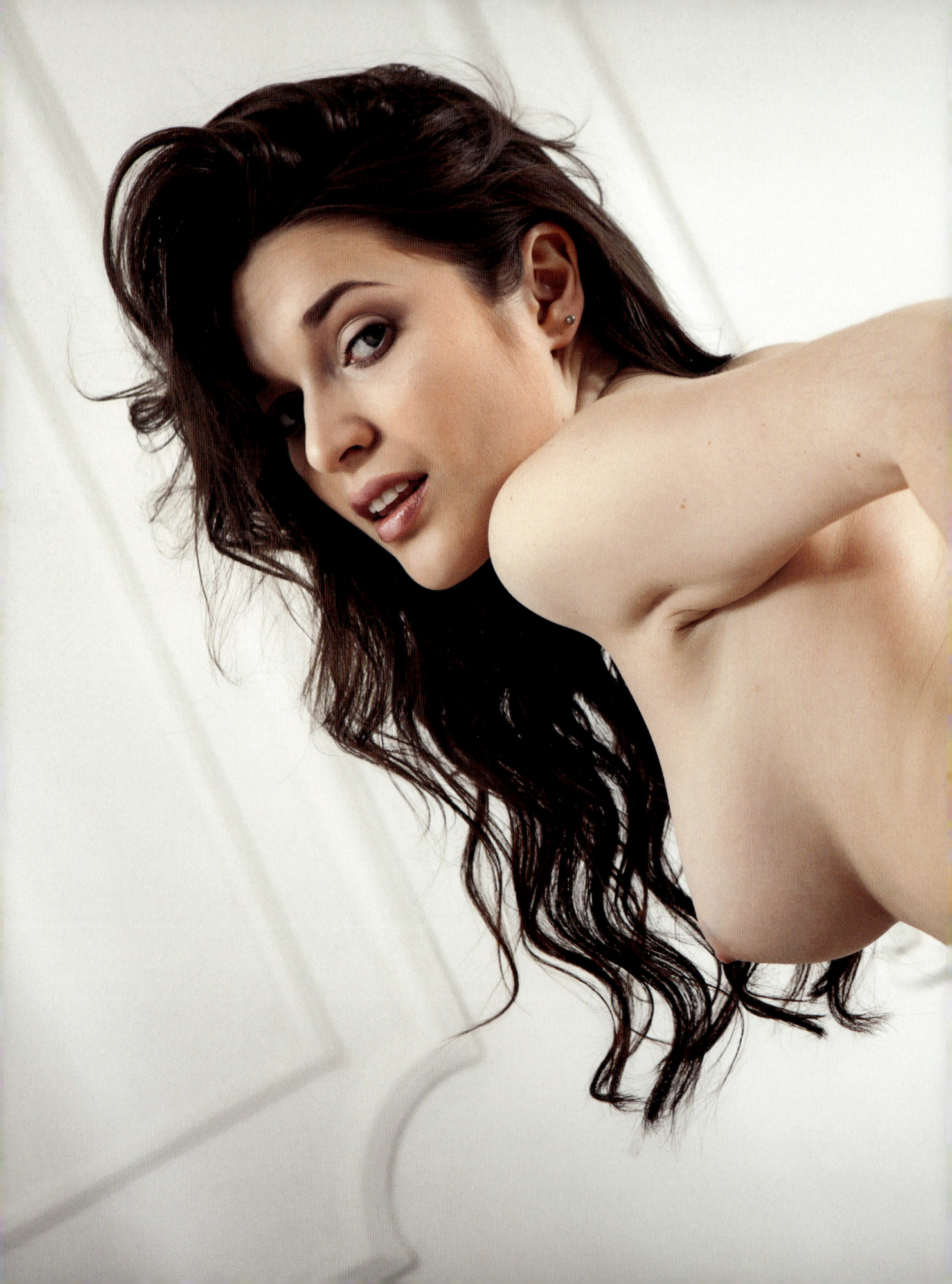

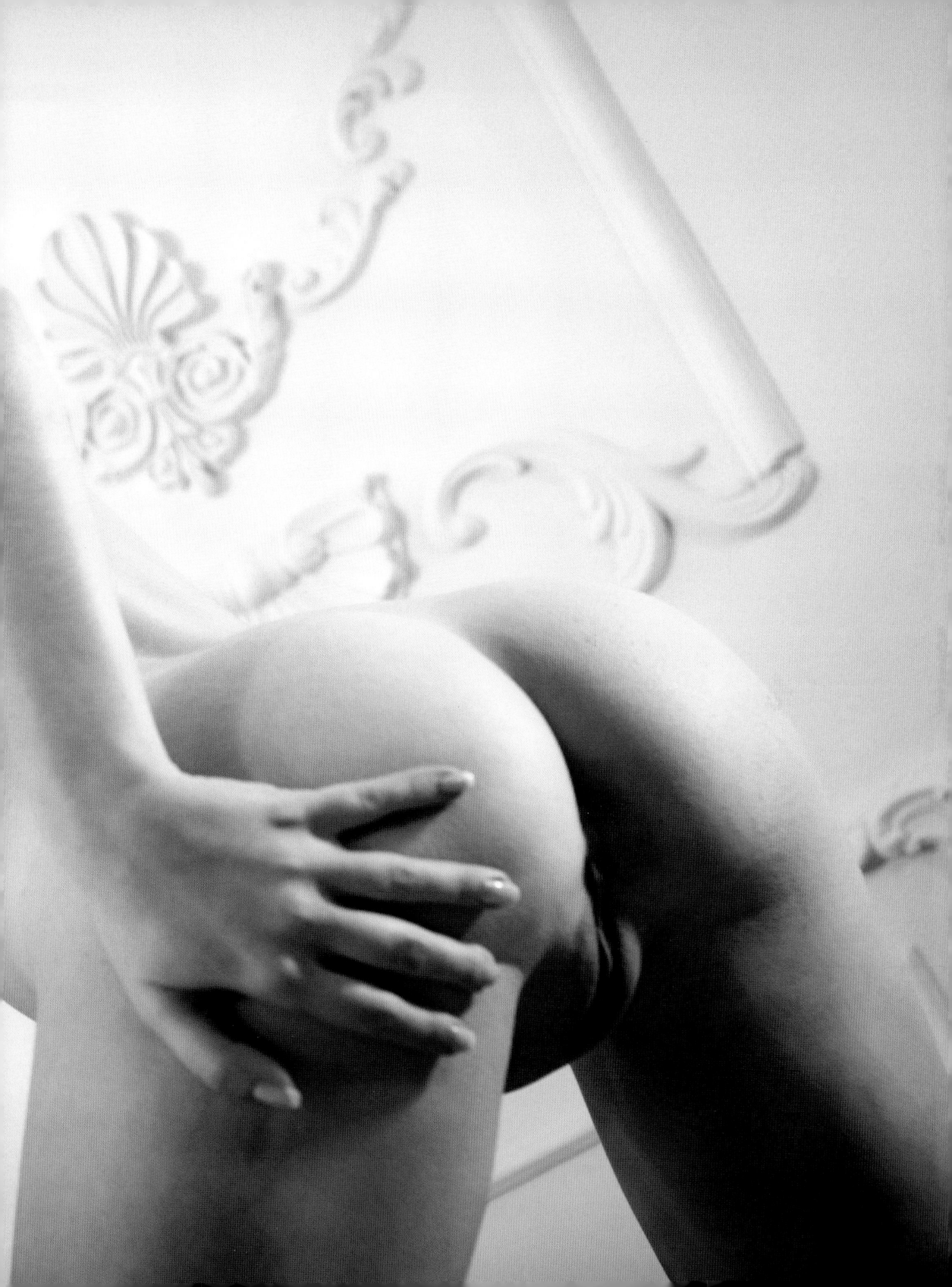

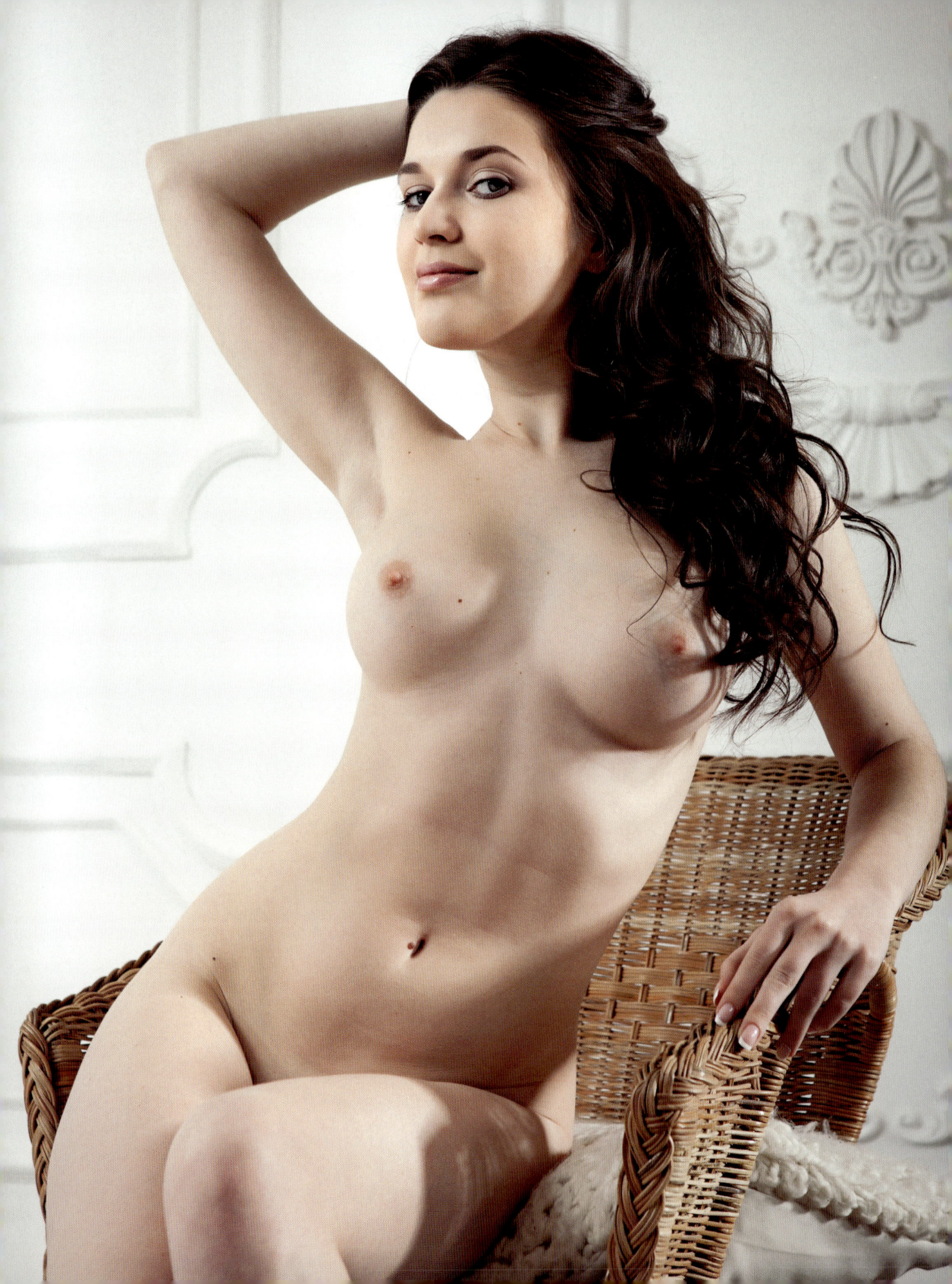

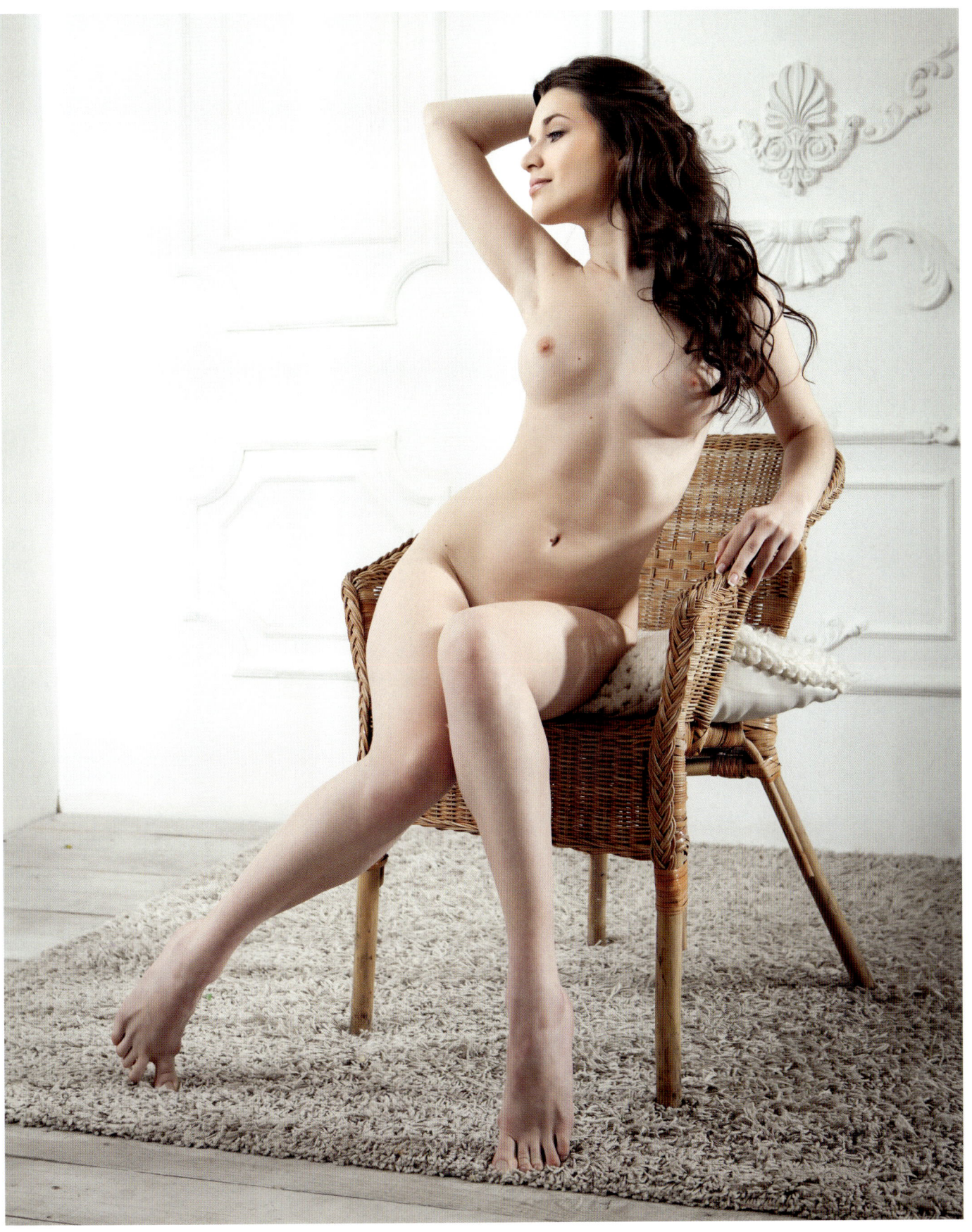

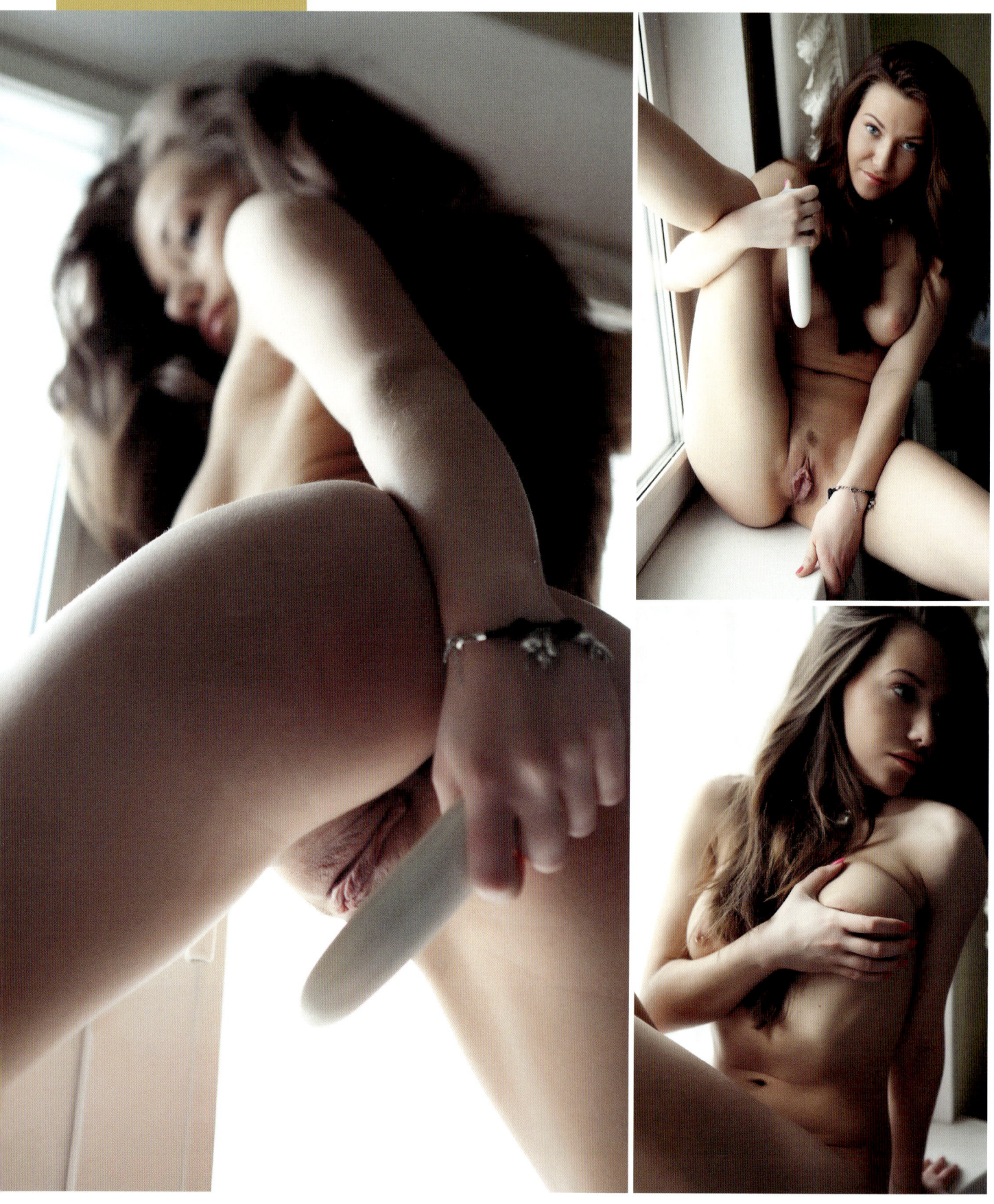

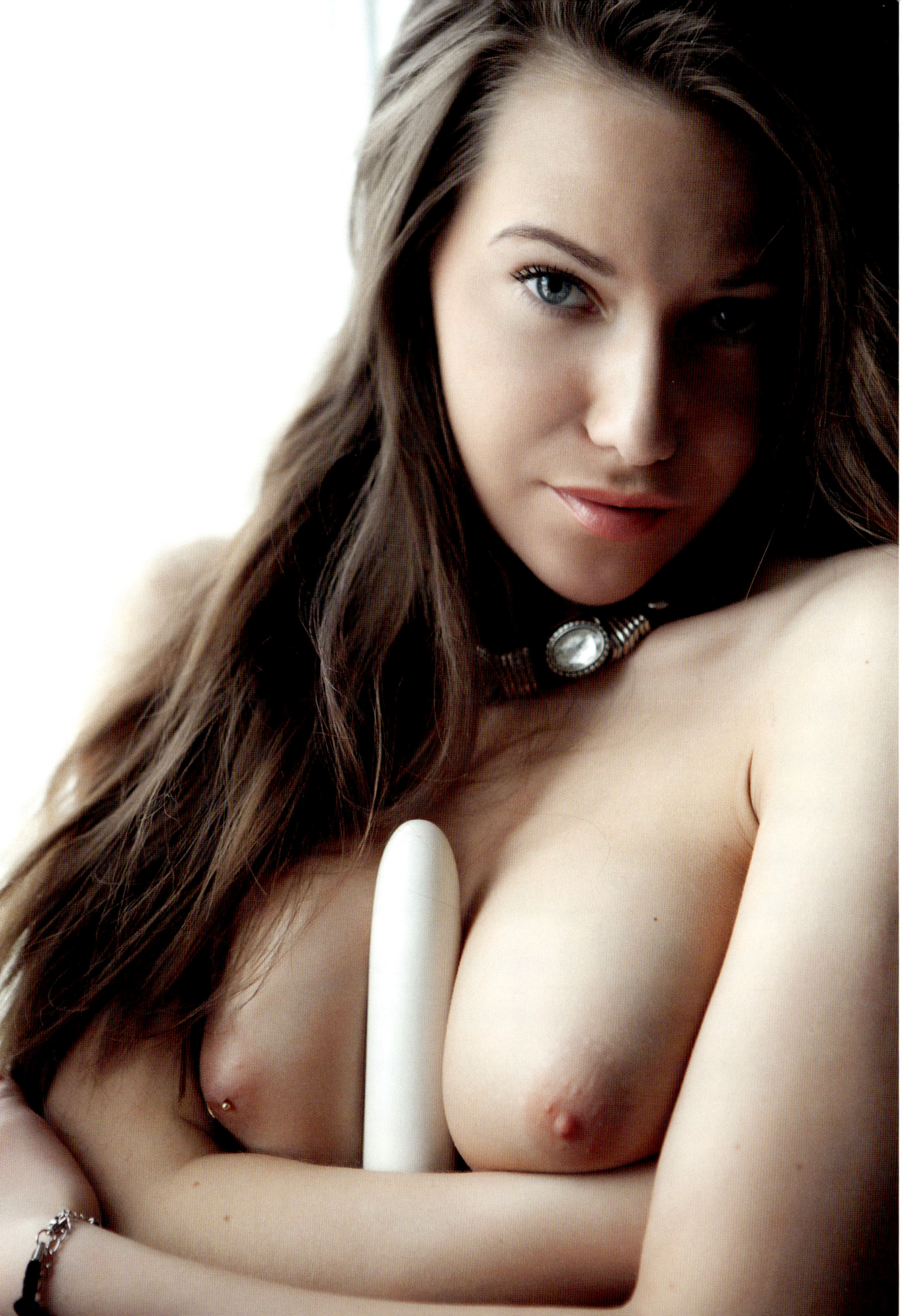

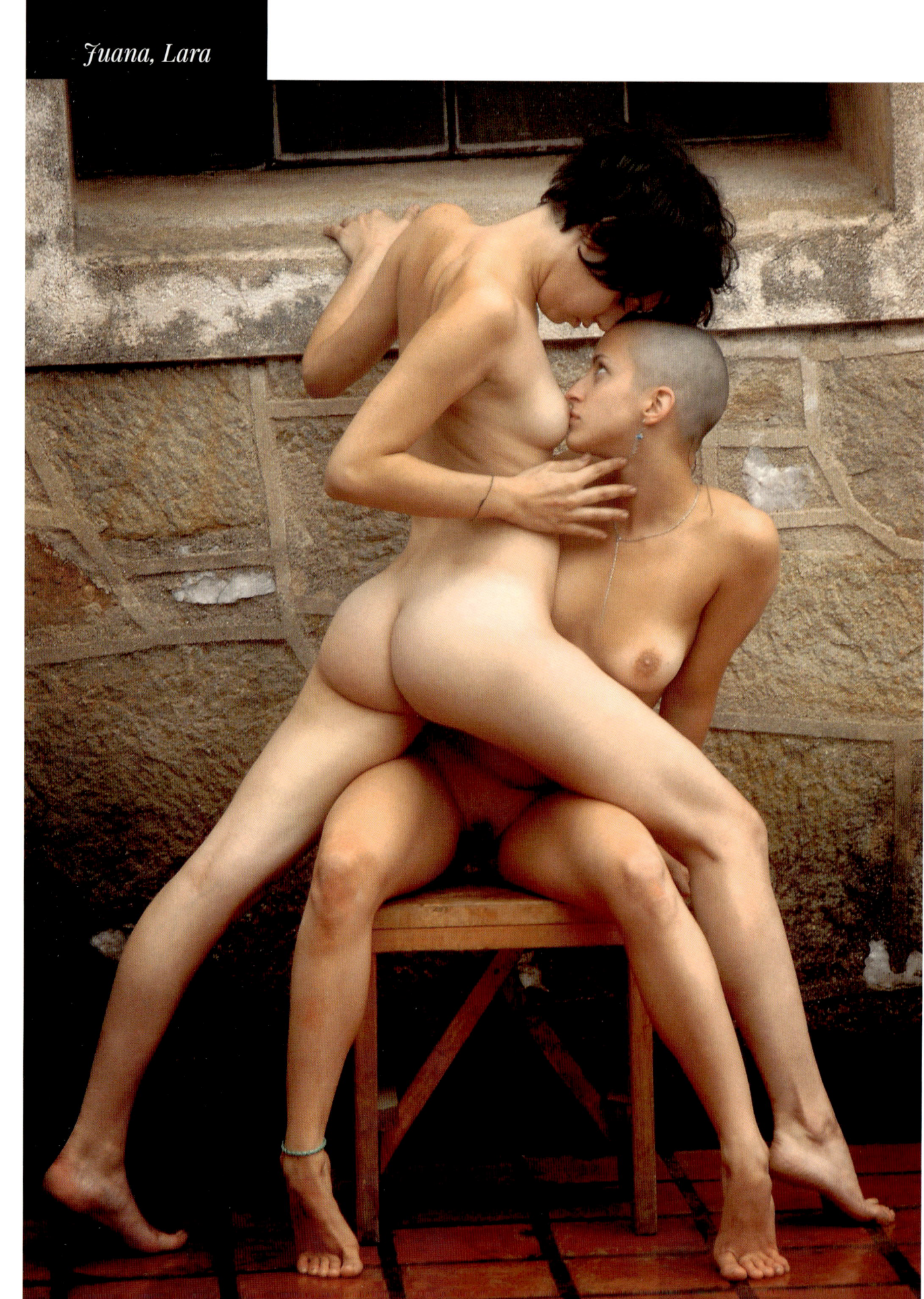

Juana, Lara

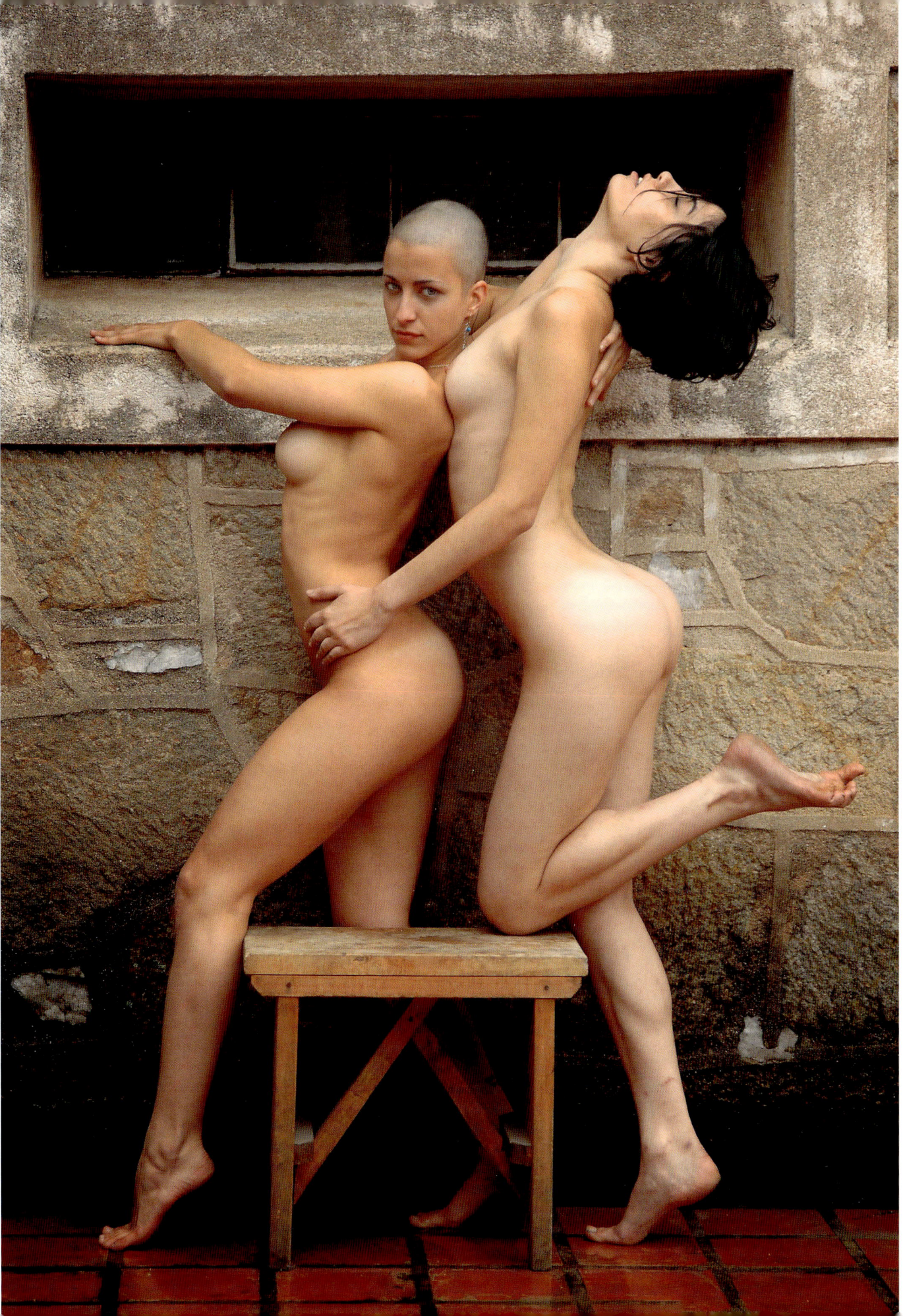

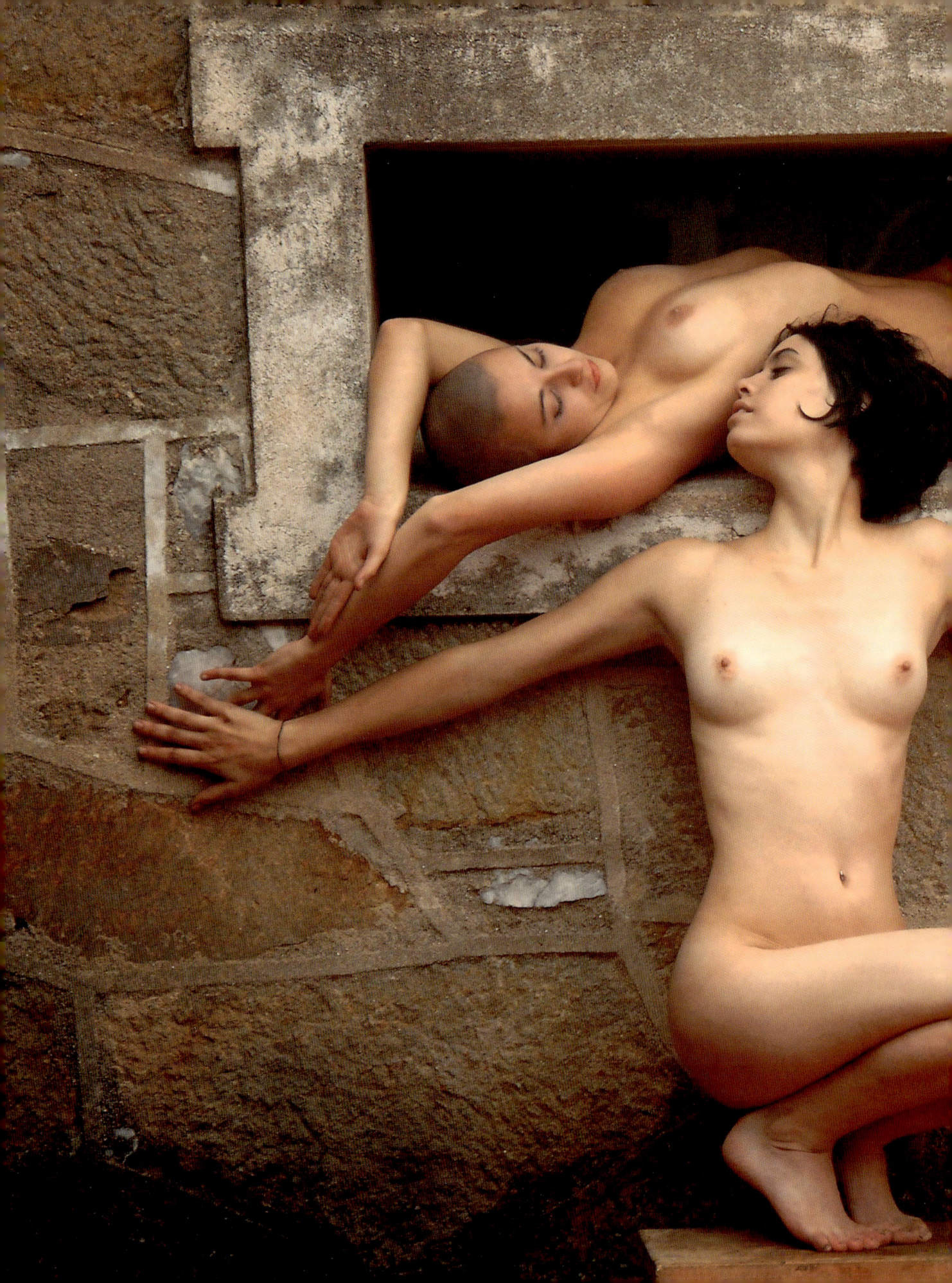

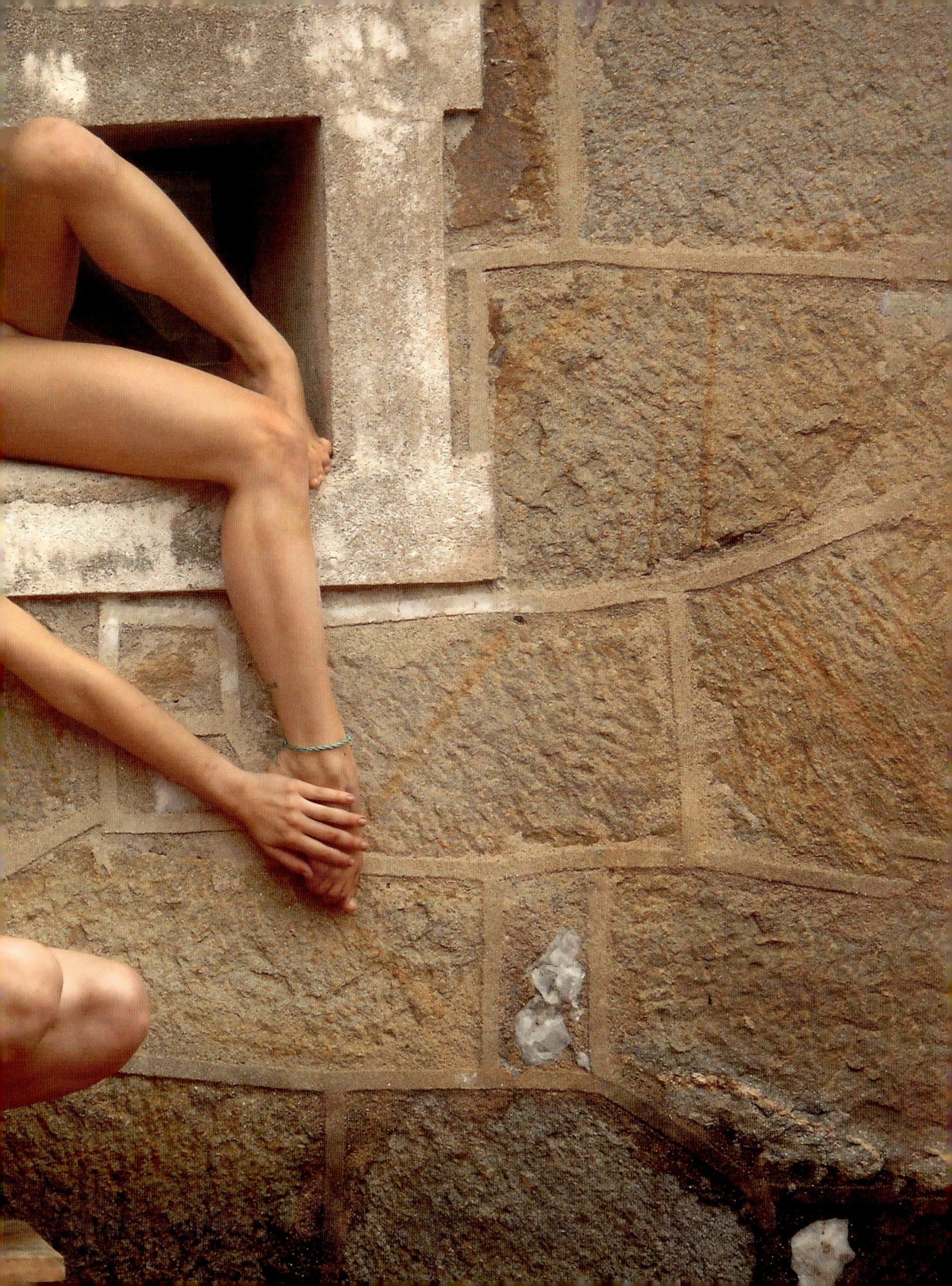

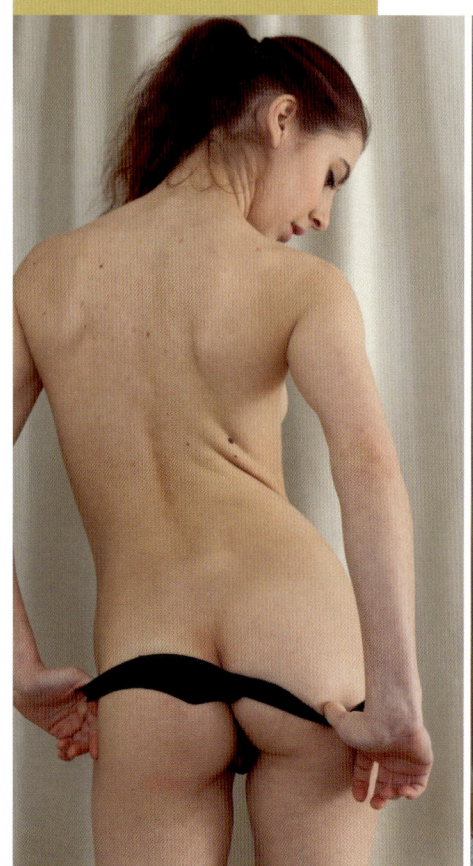
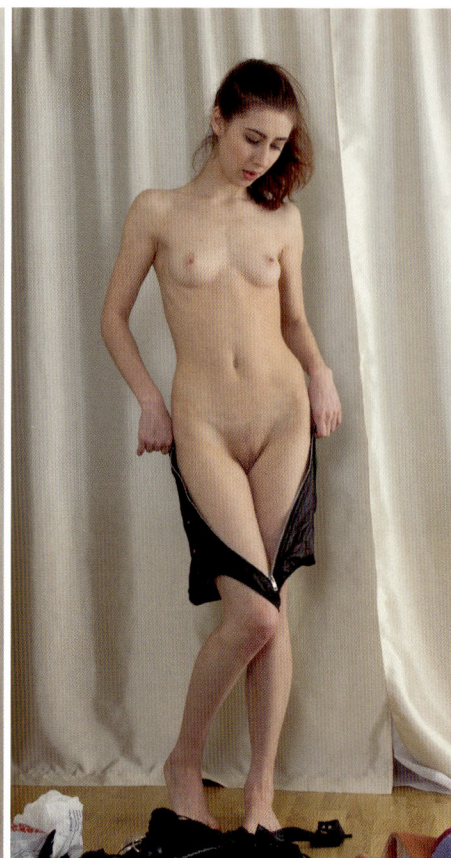
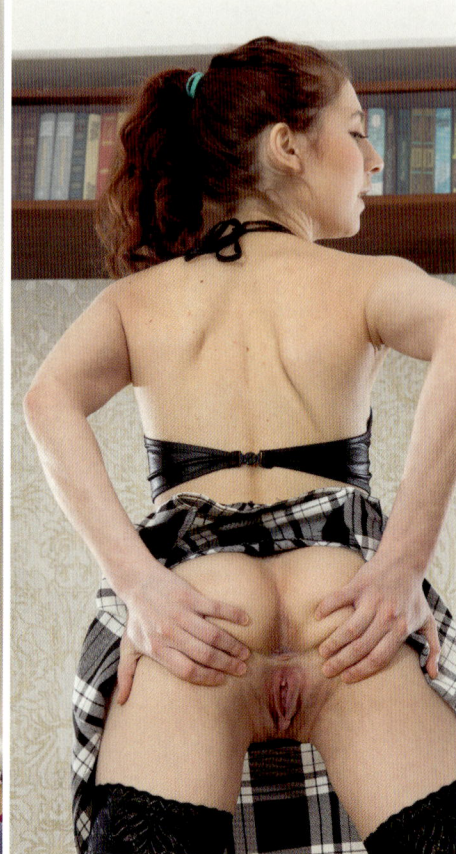

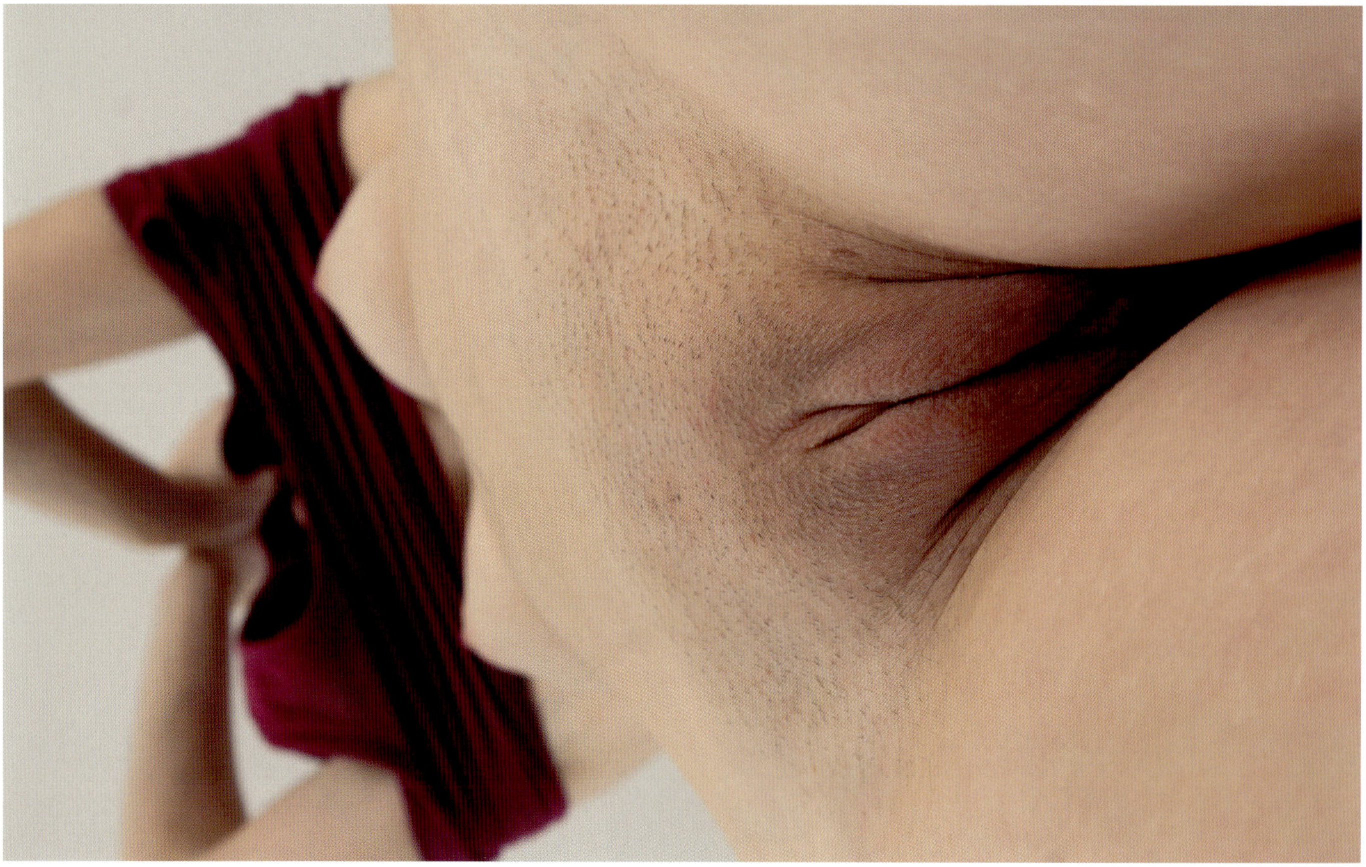

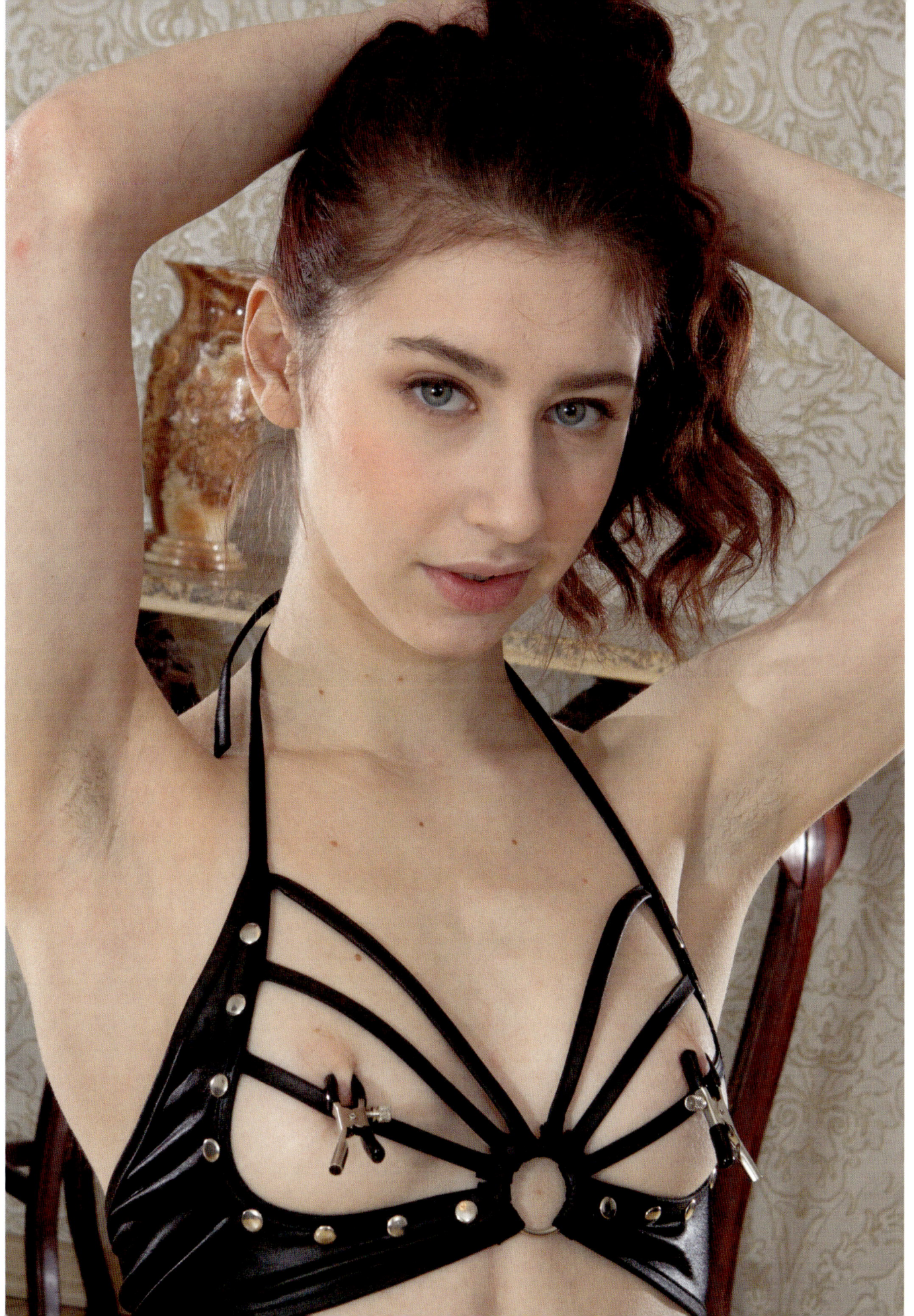

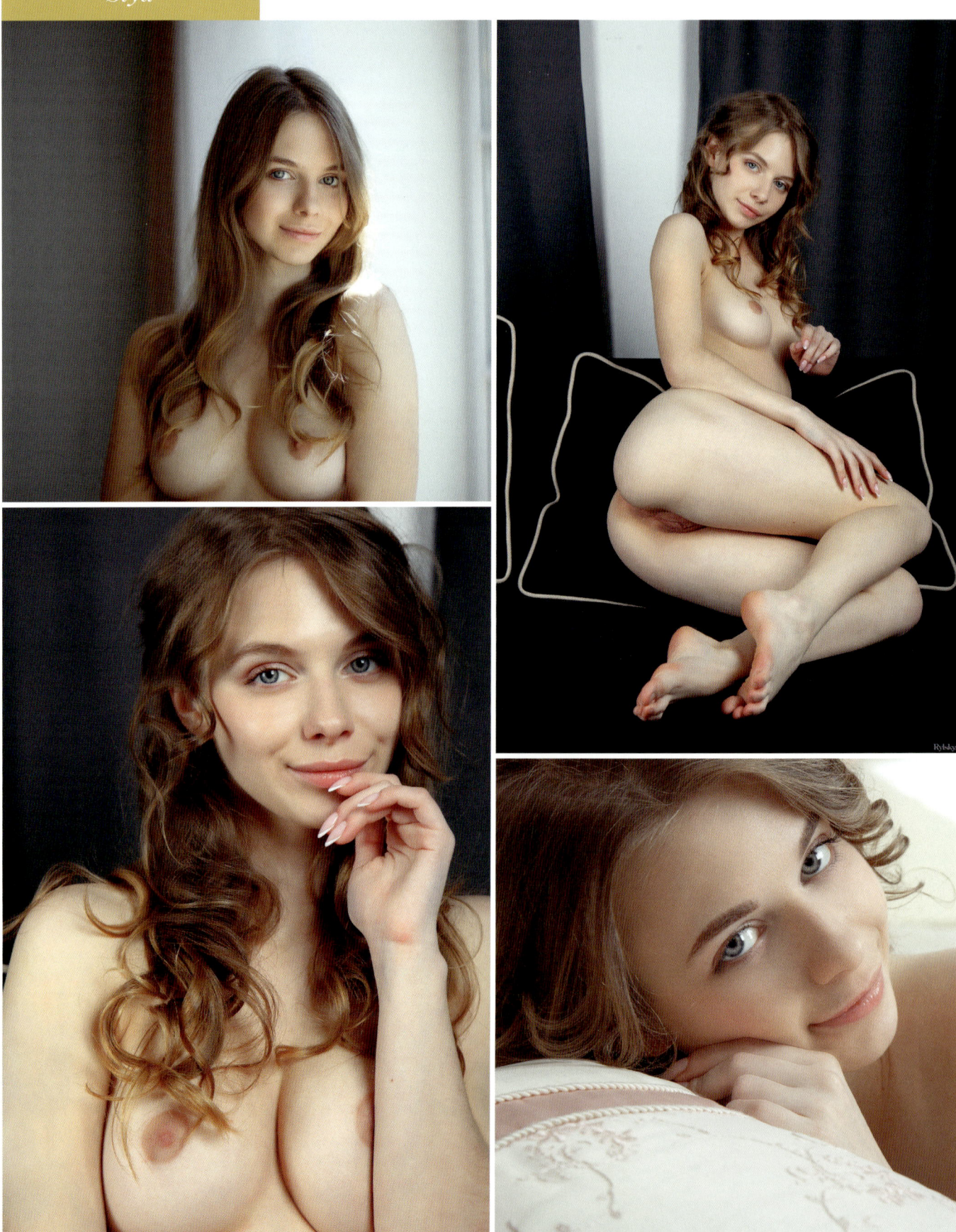

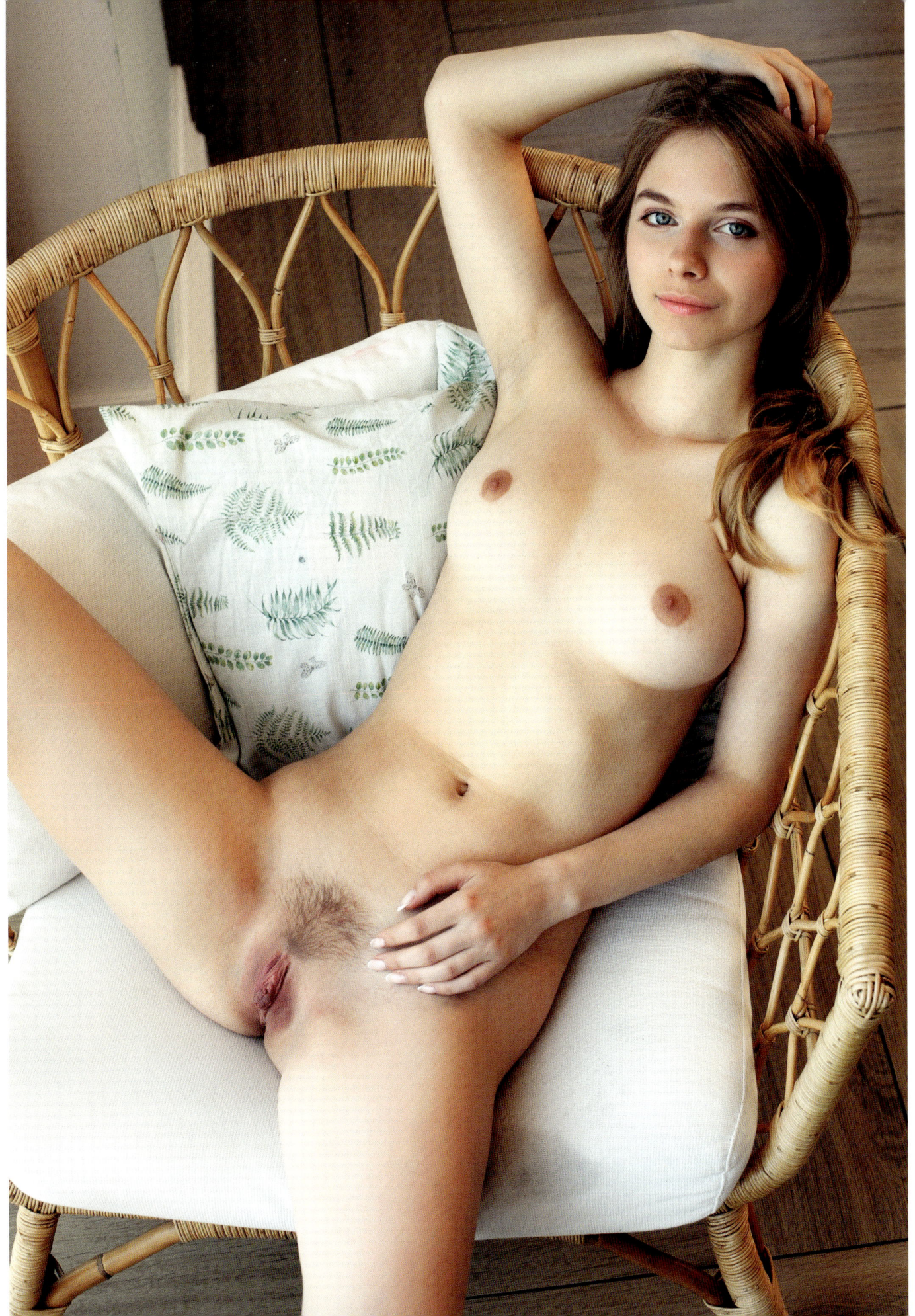

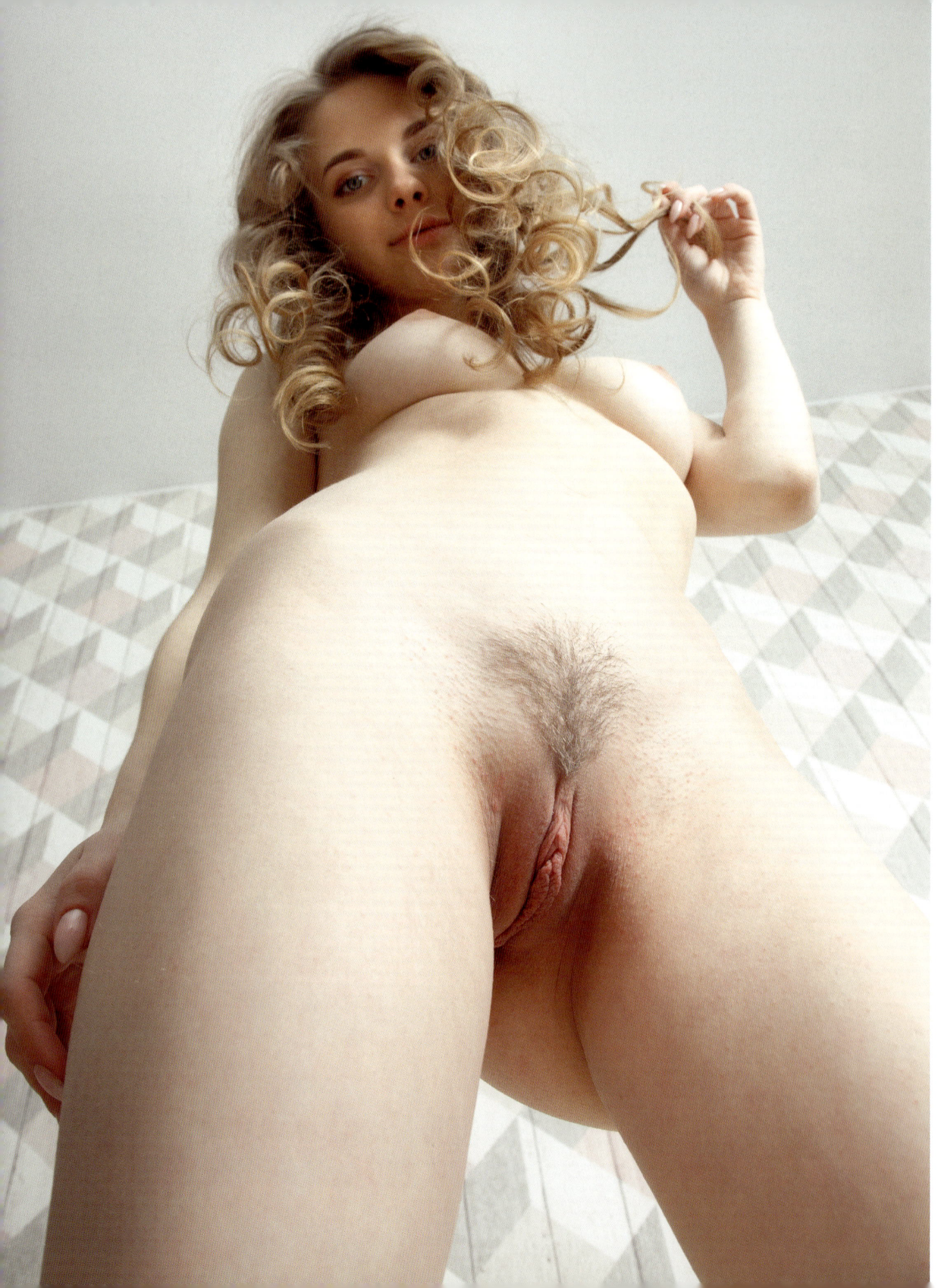

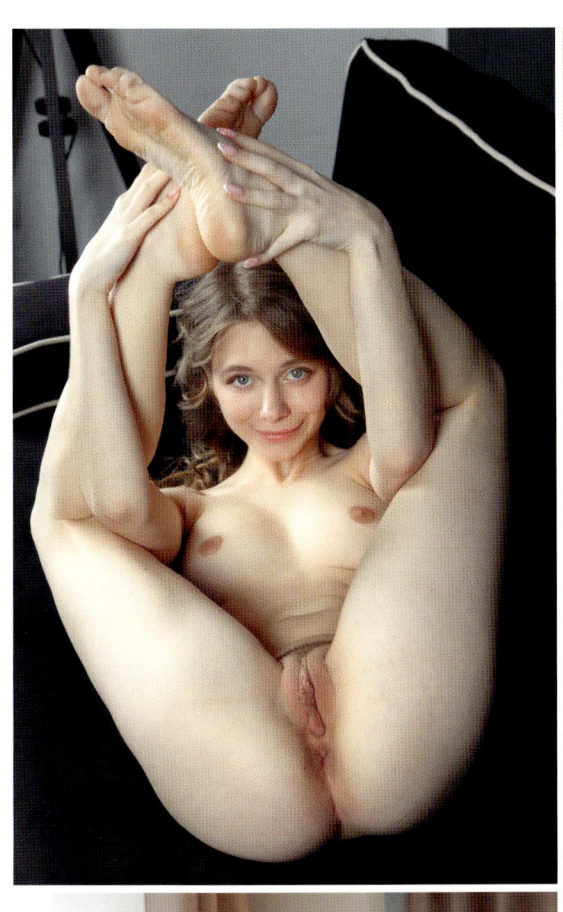
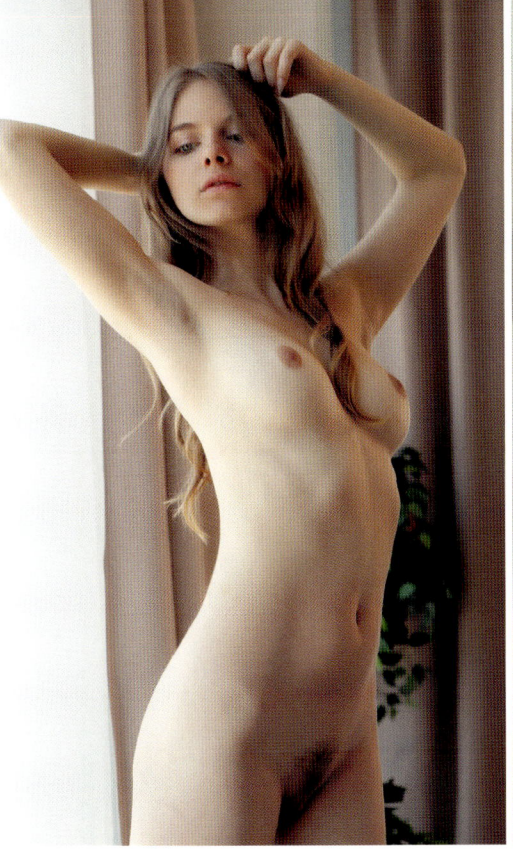

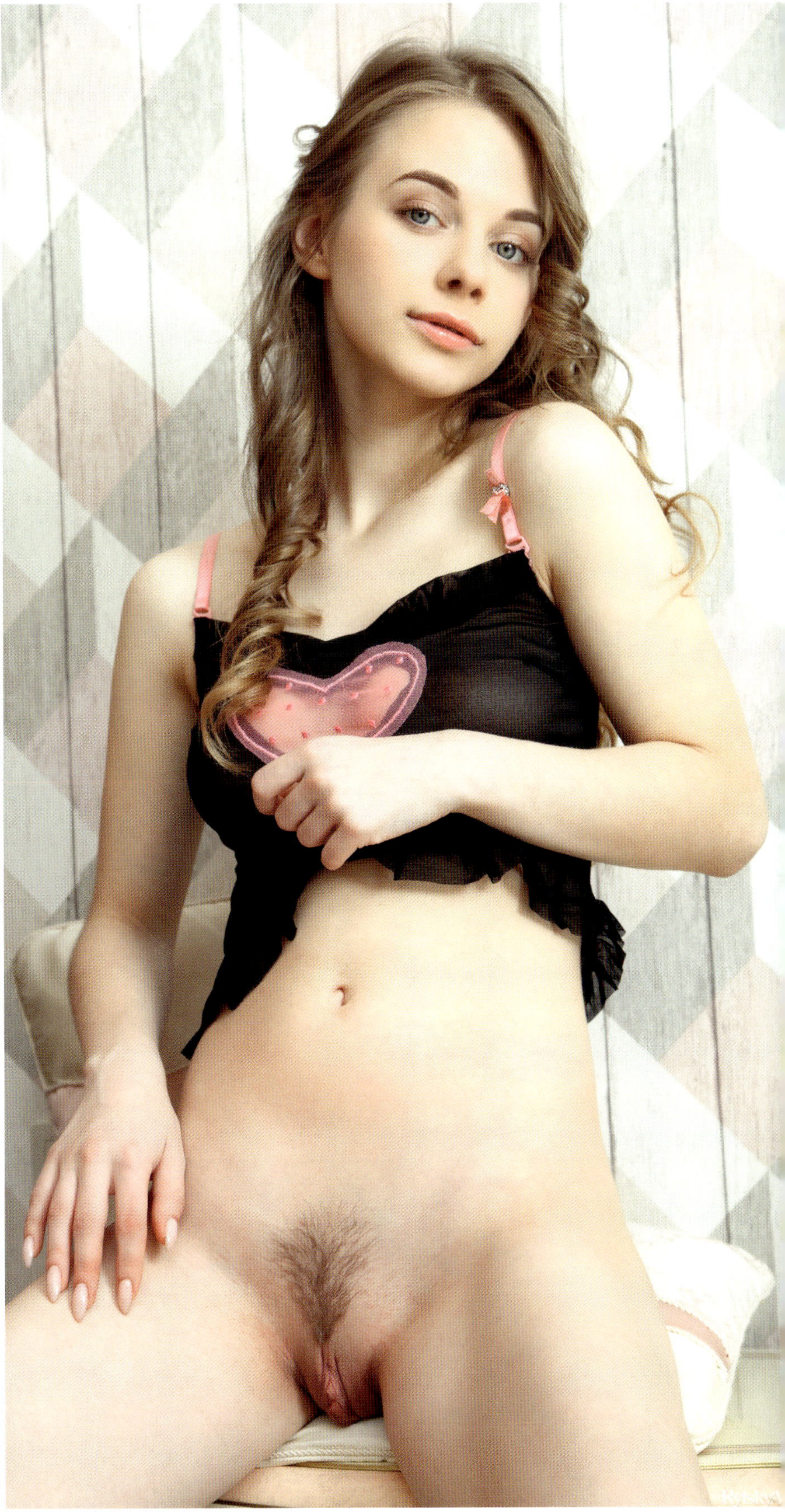

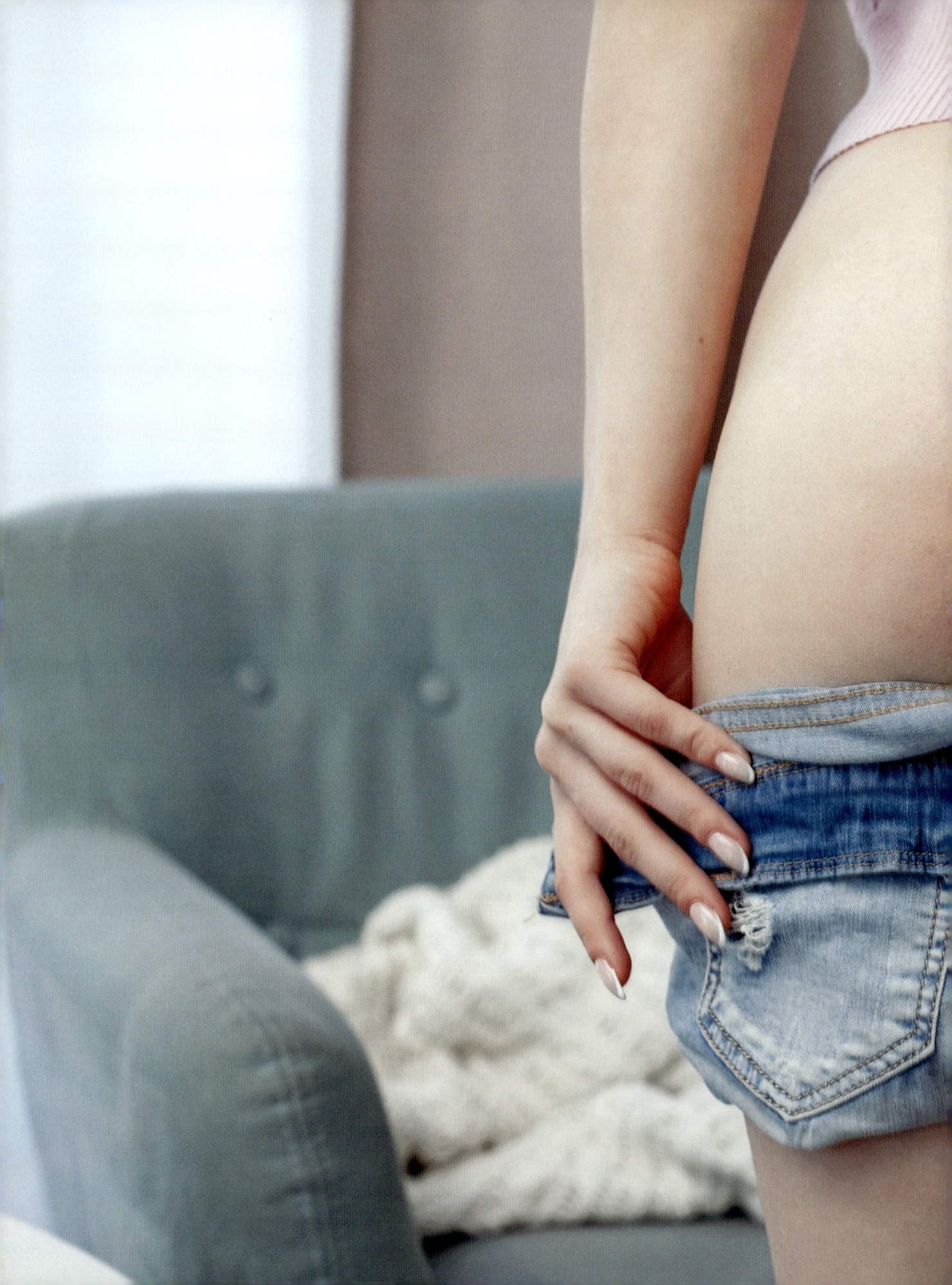

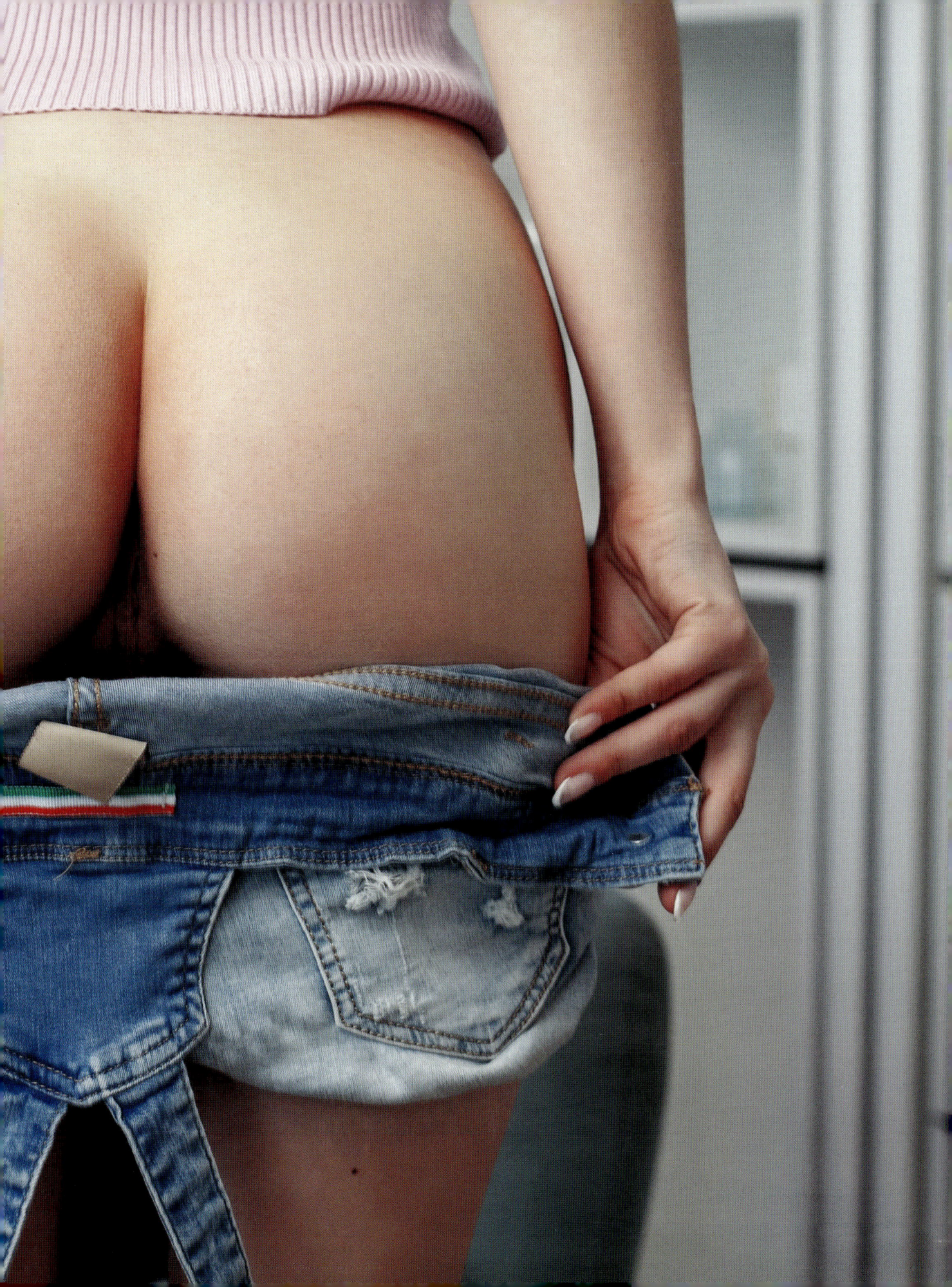

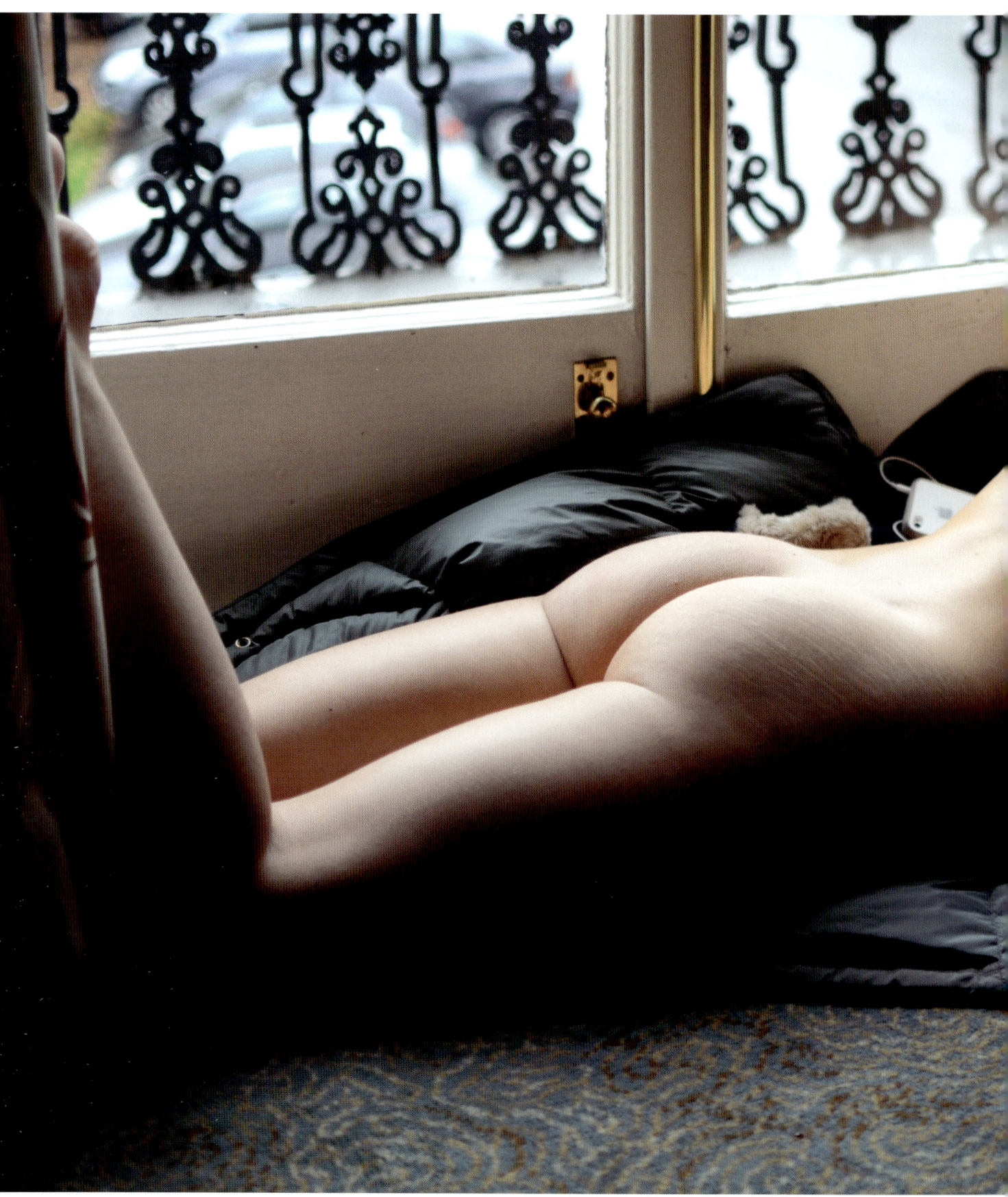

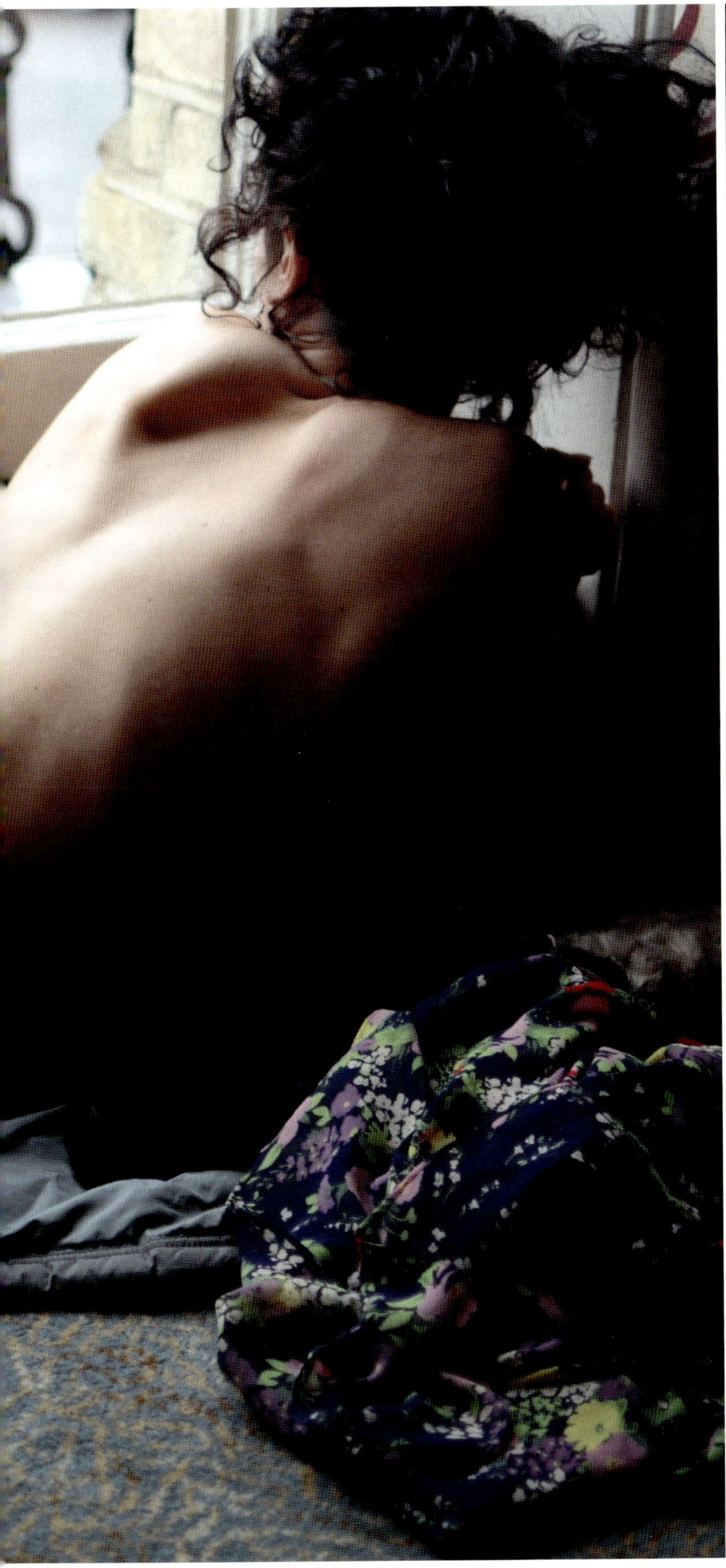

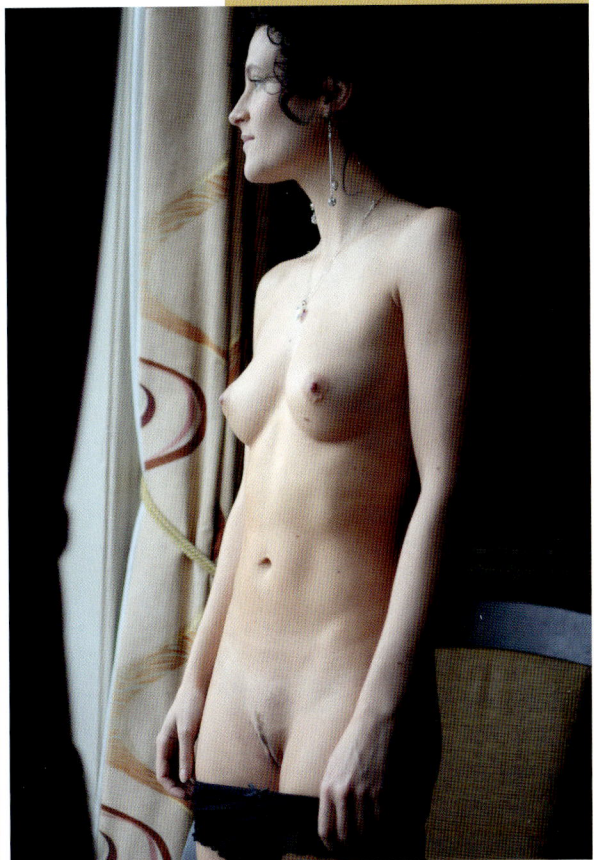

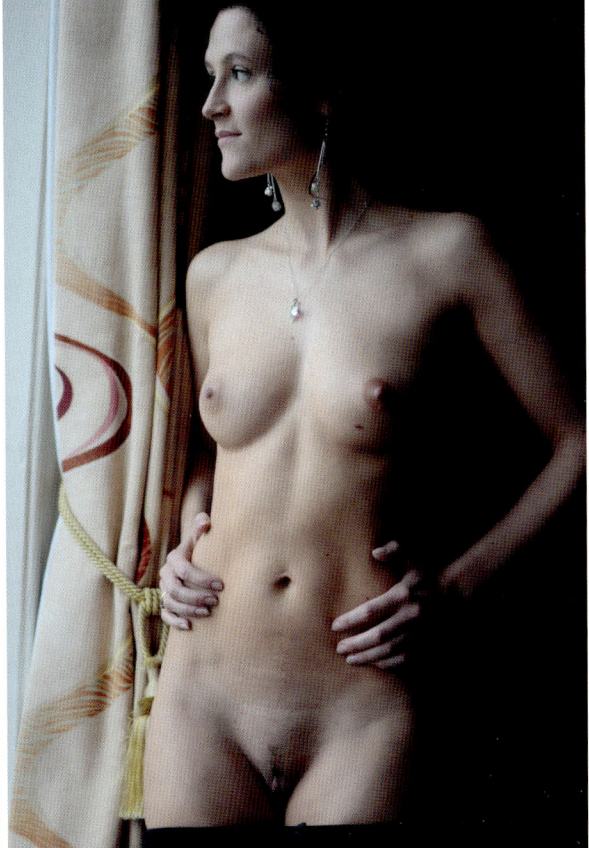

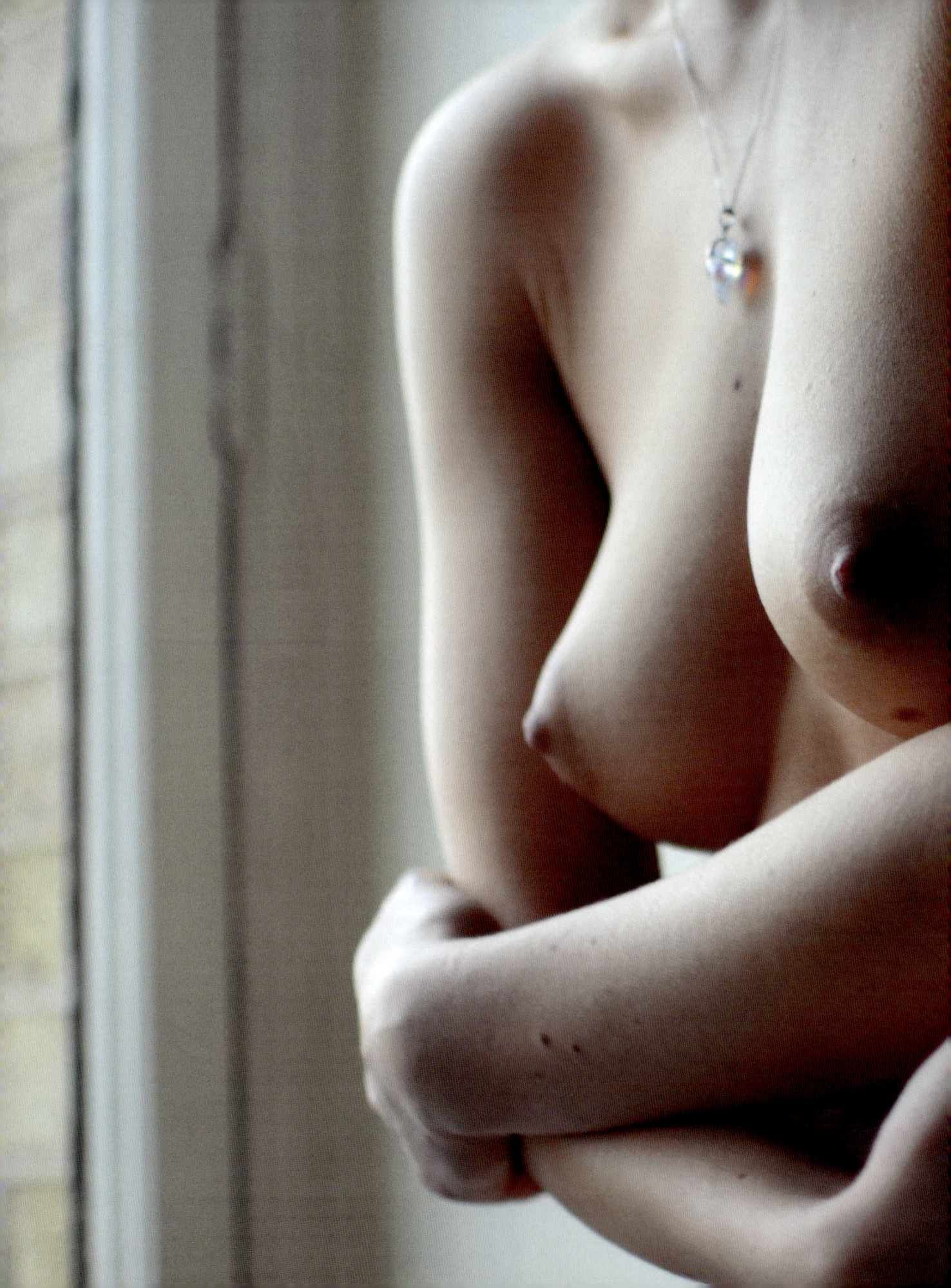

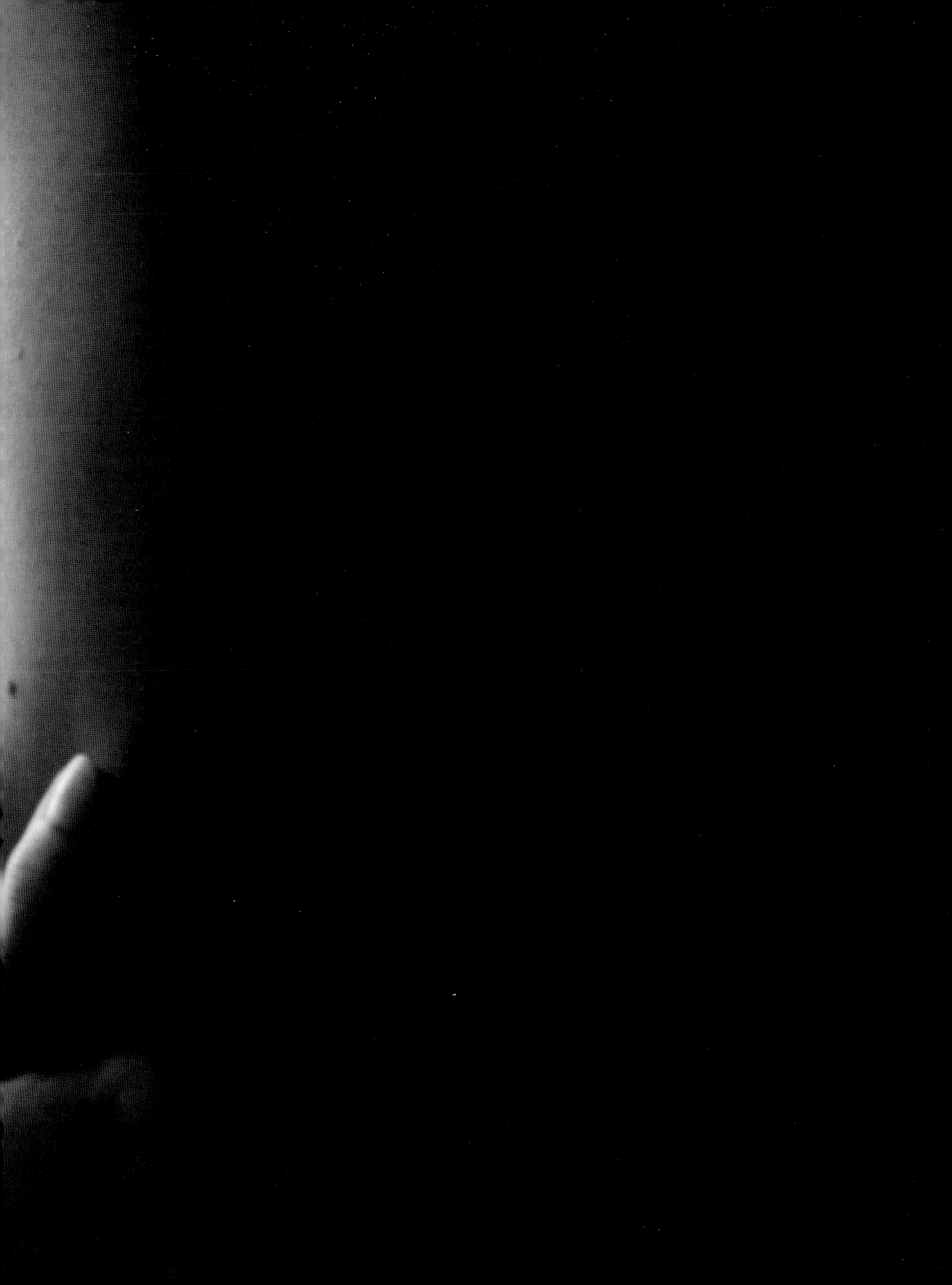

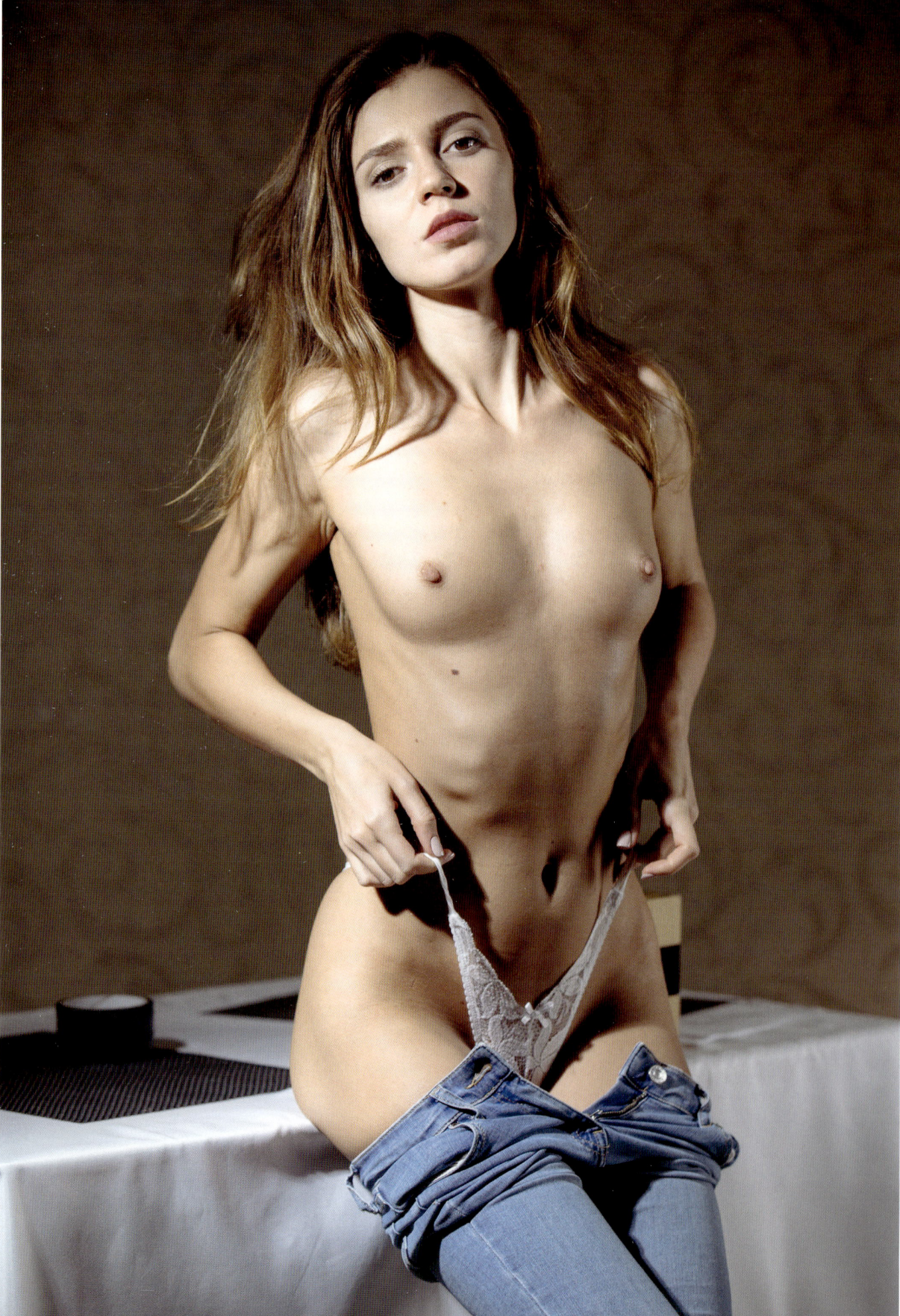

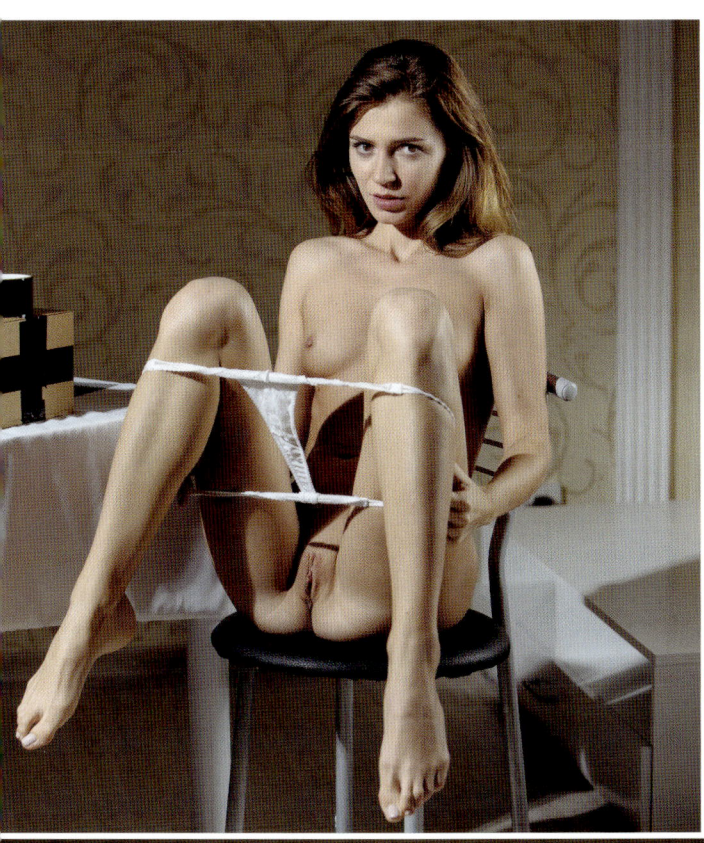

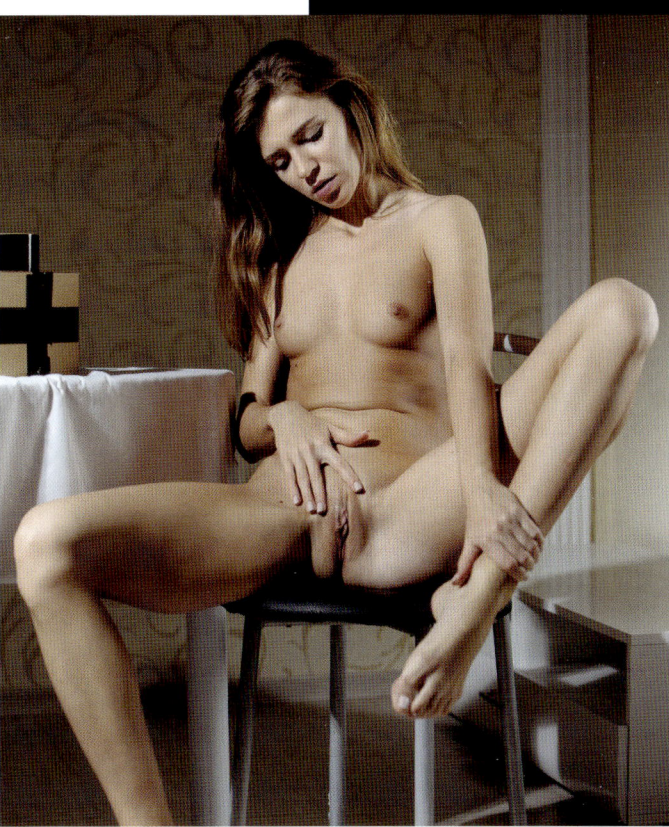

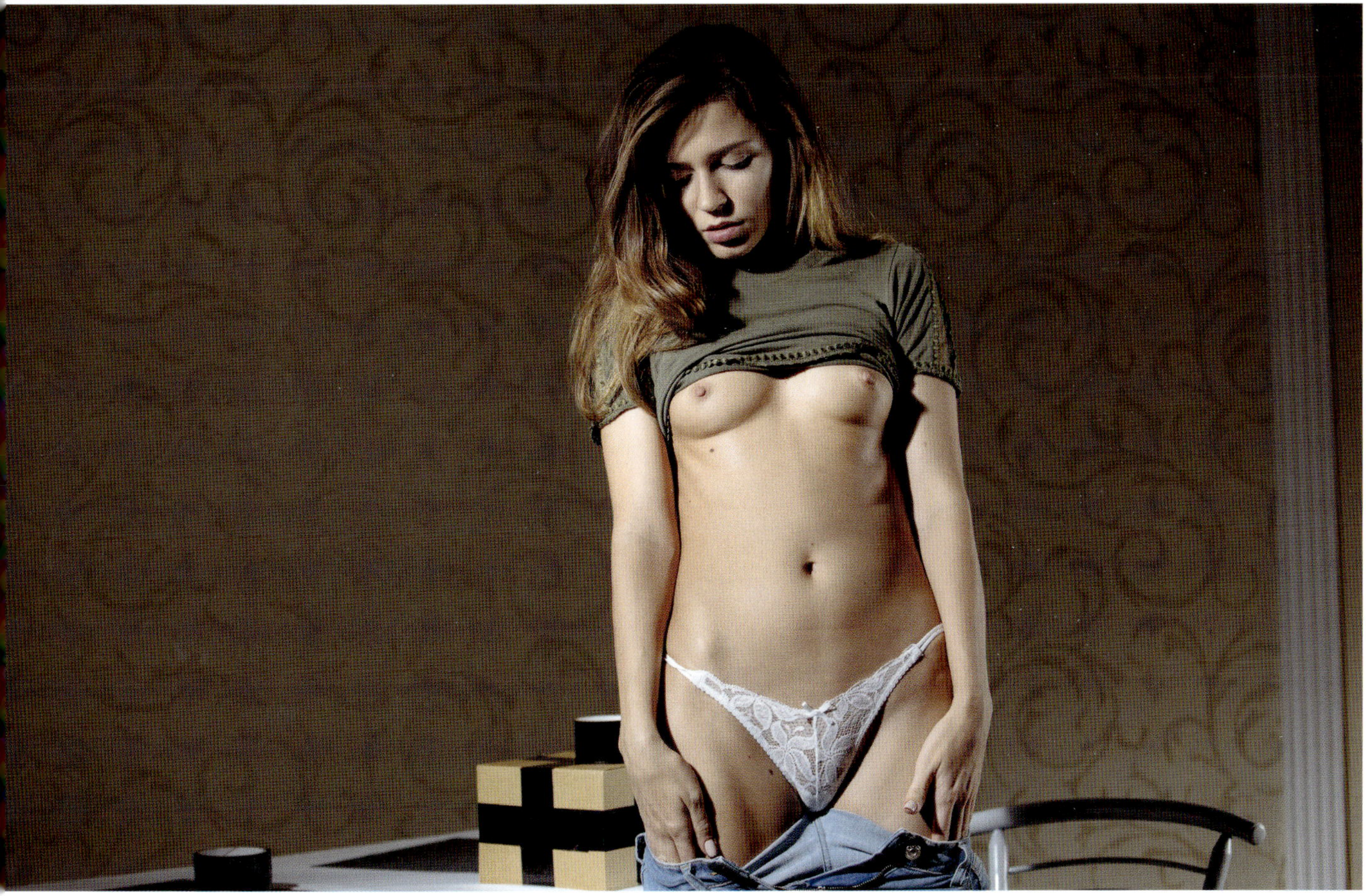

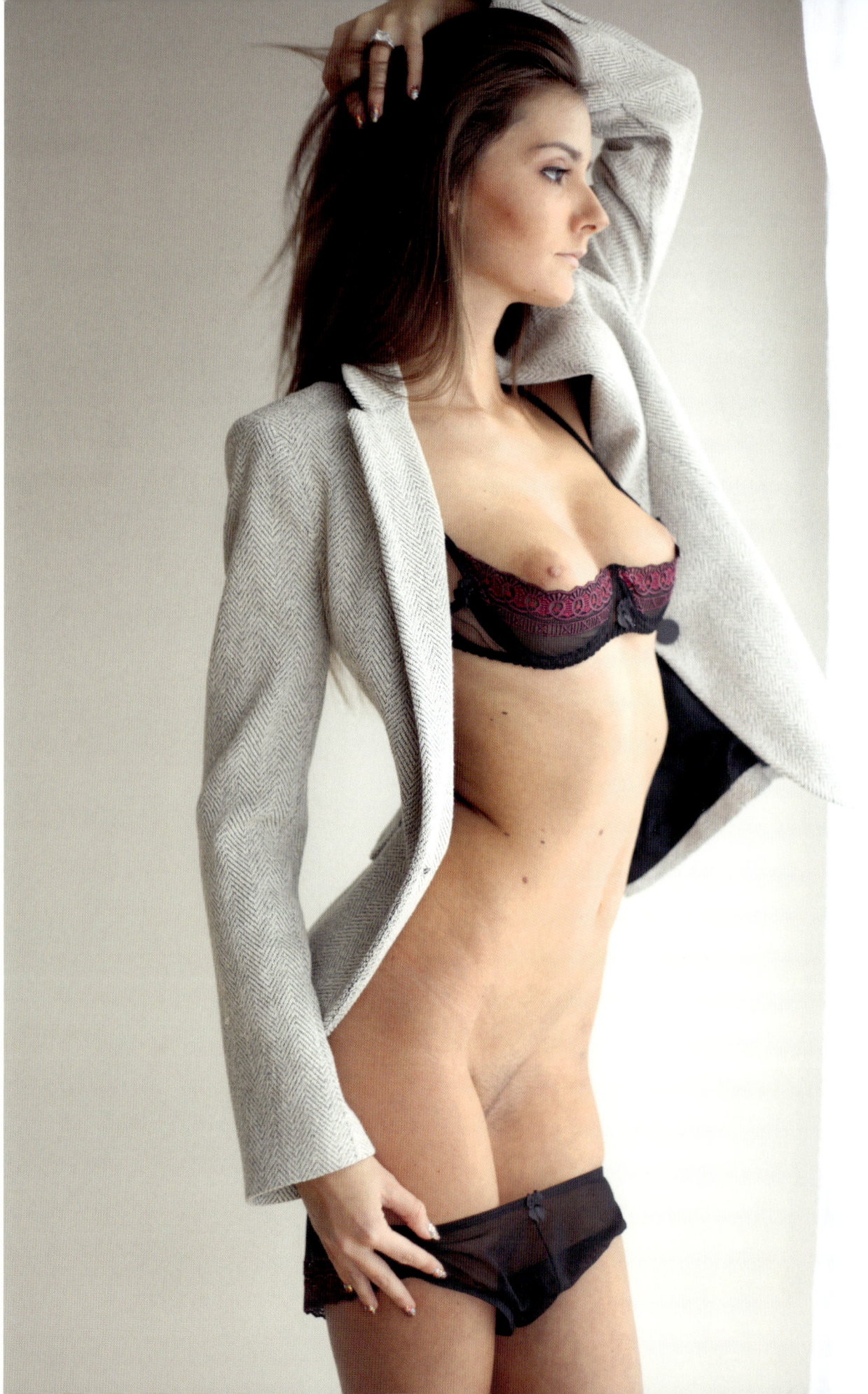

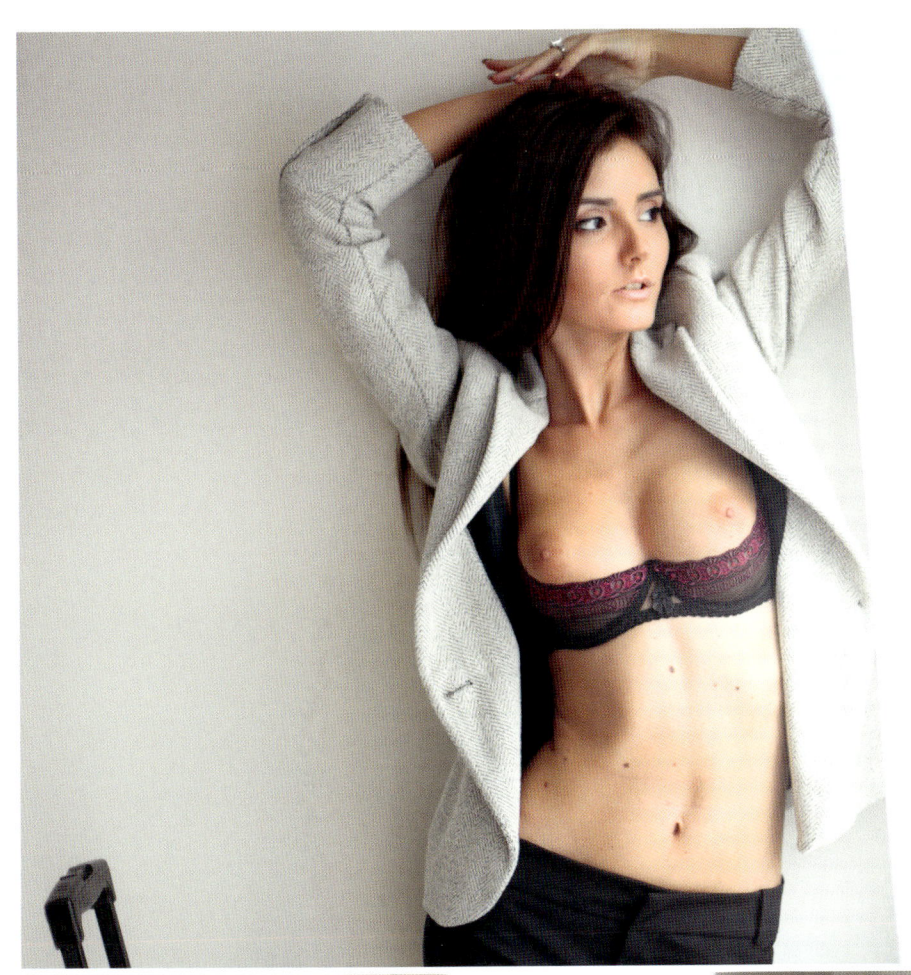

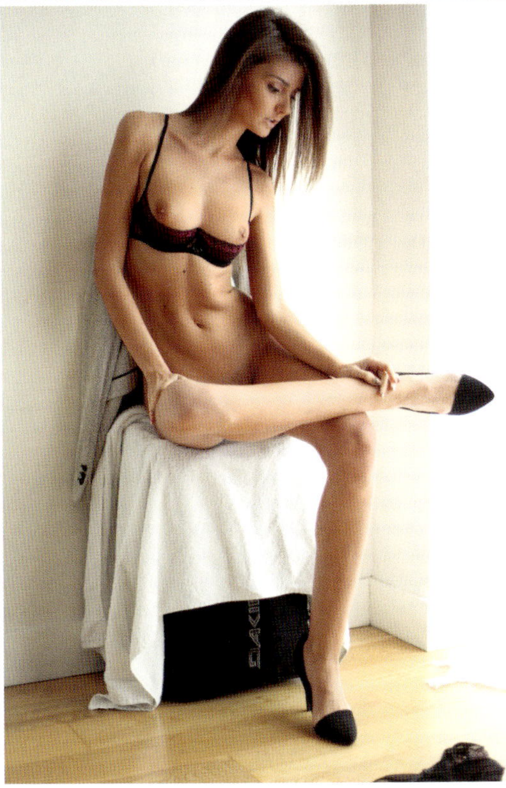

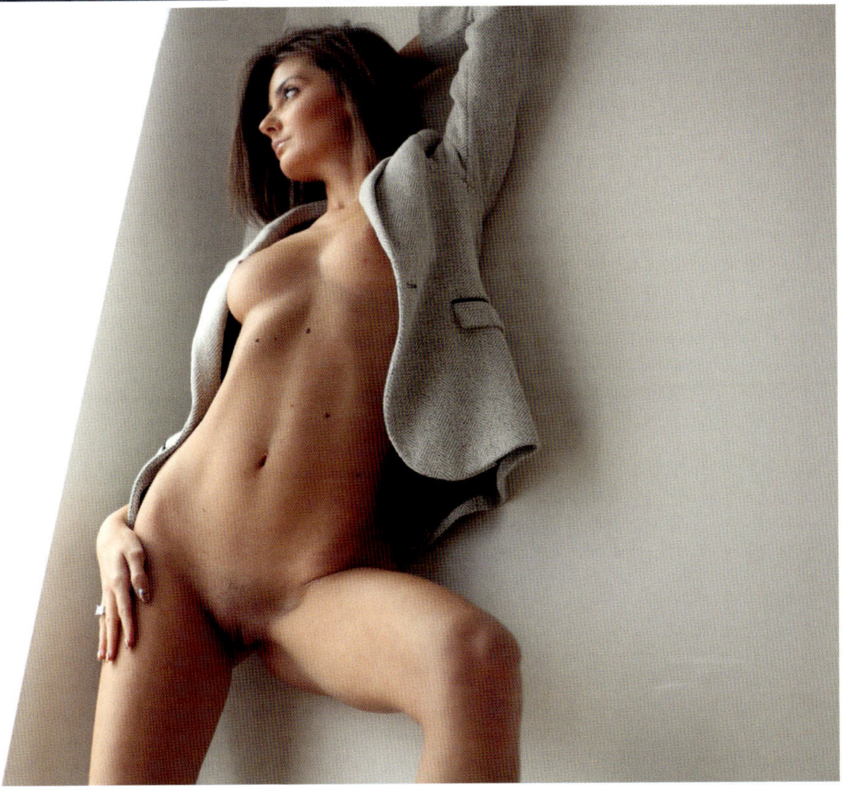

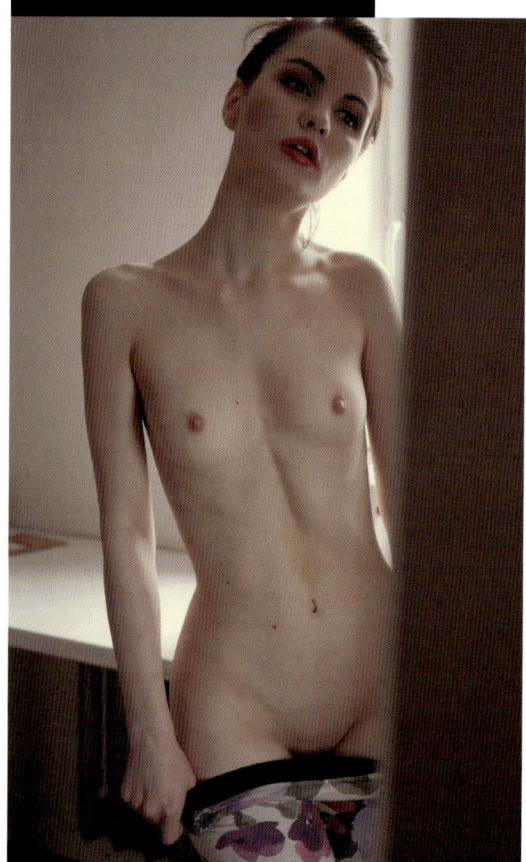
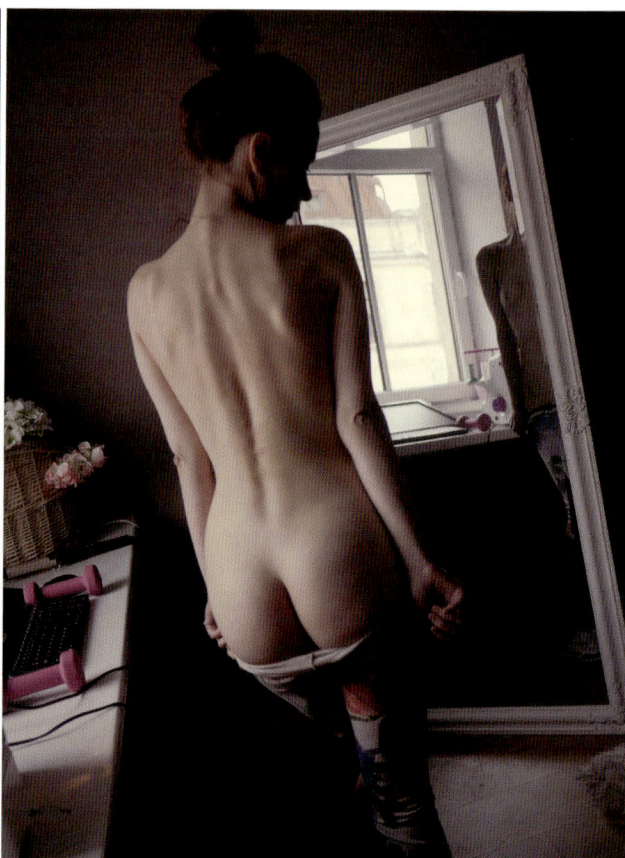
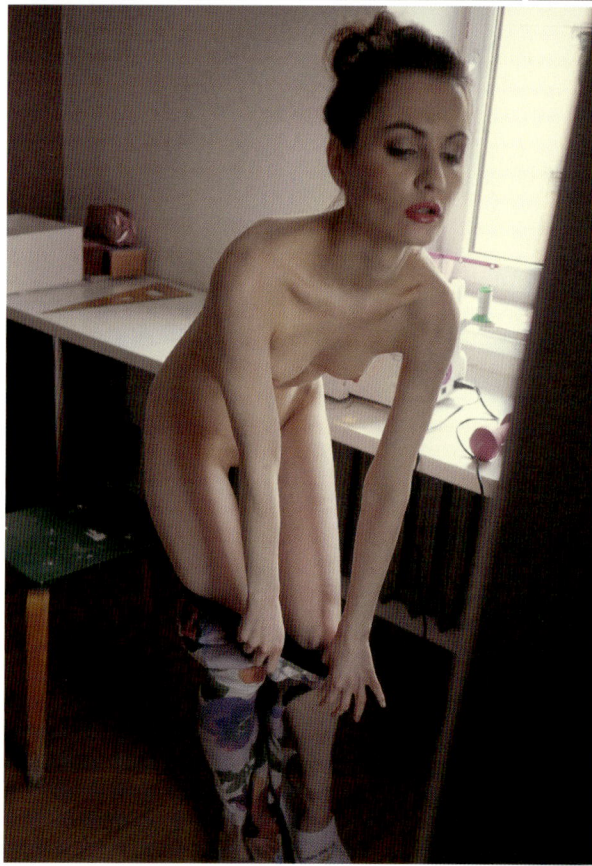
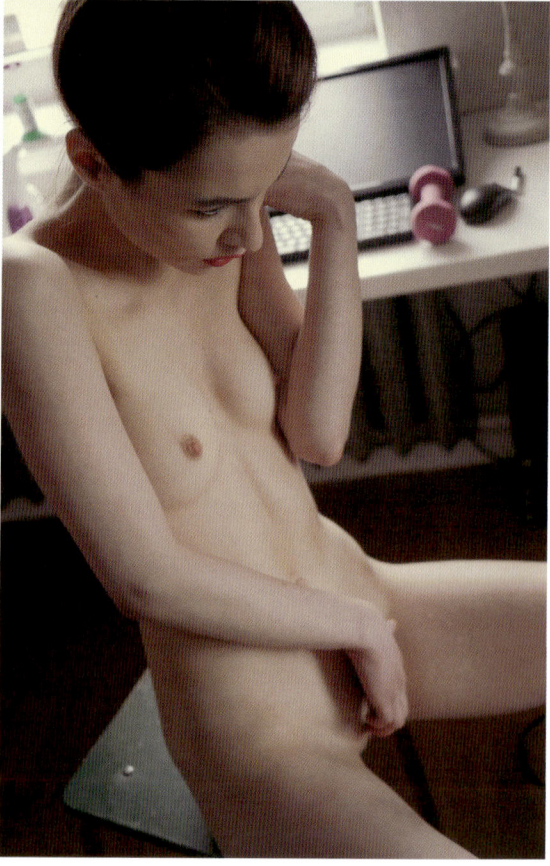

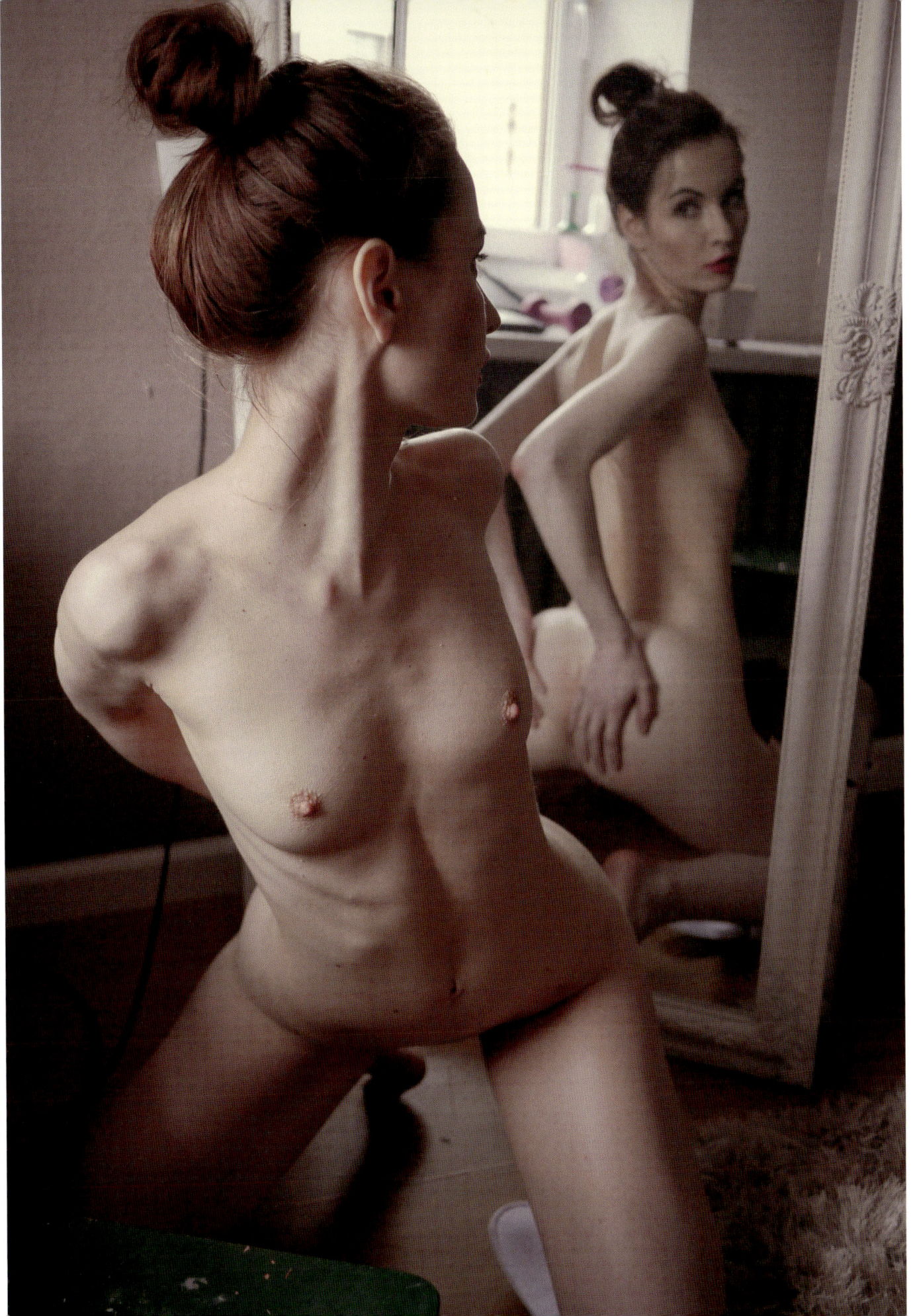

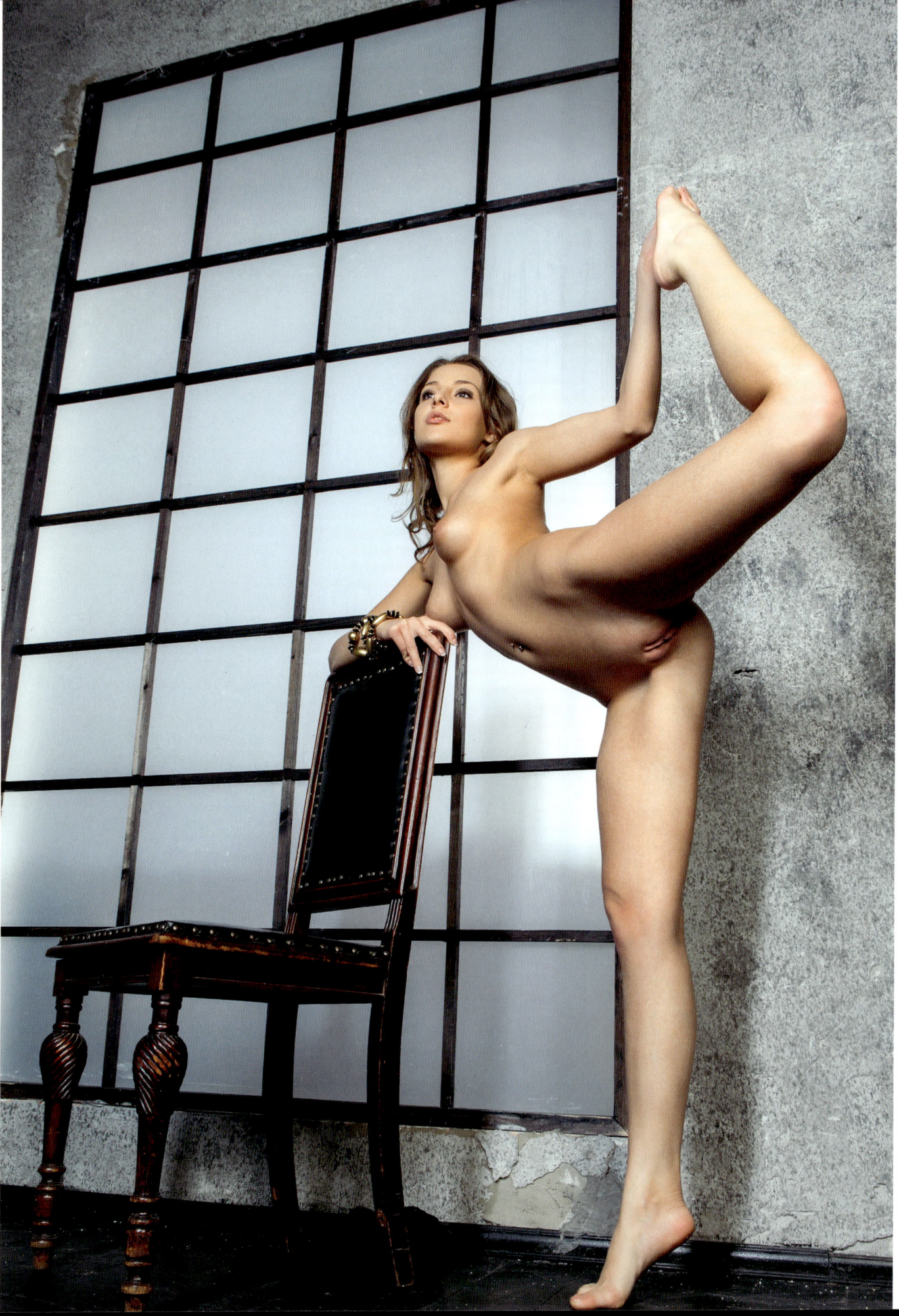

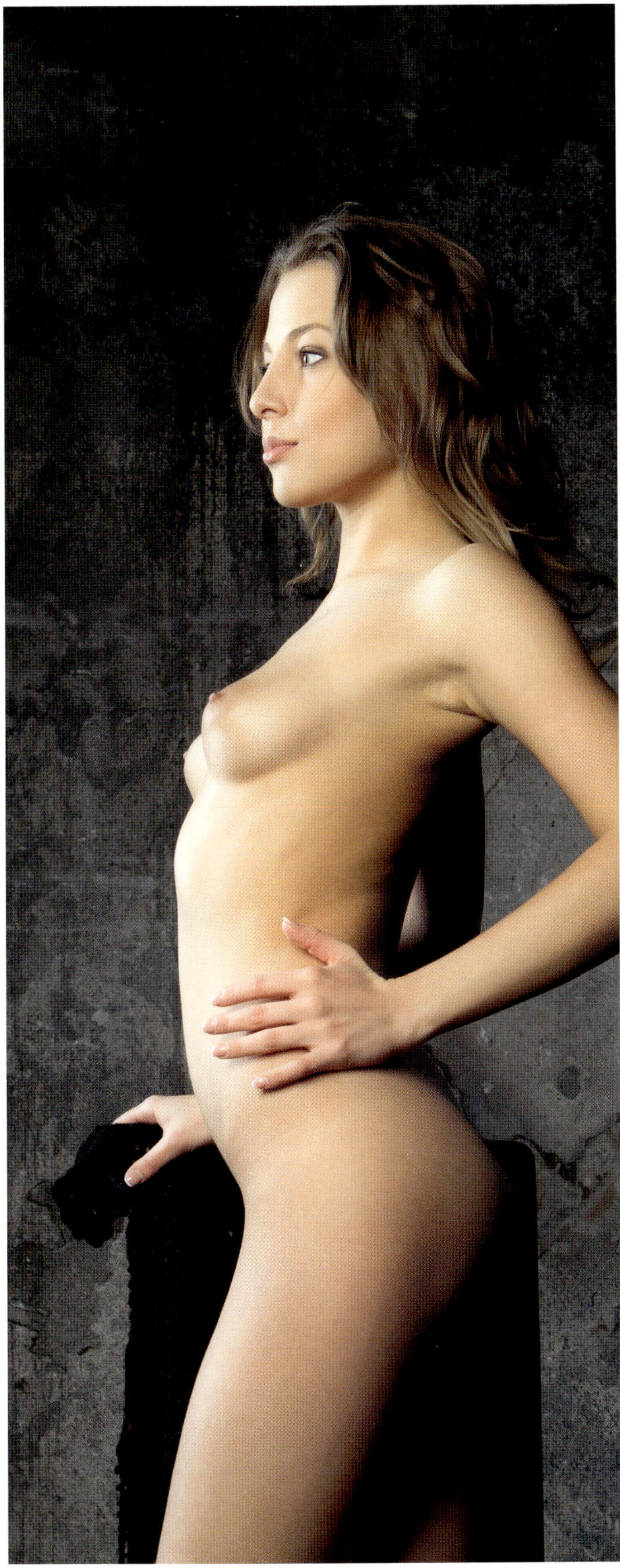

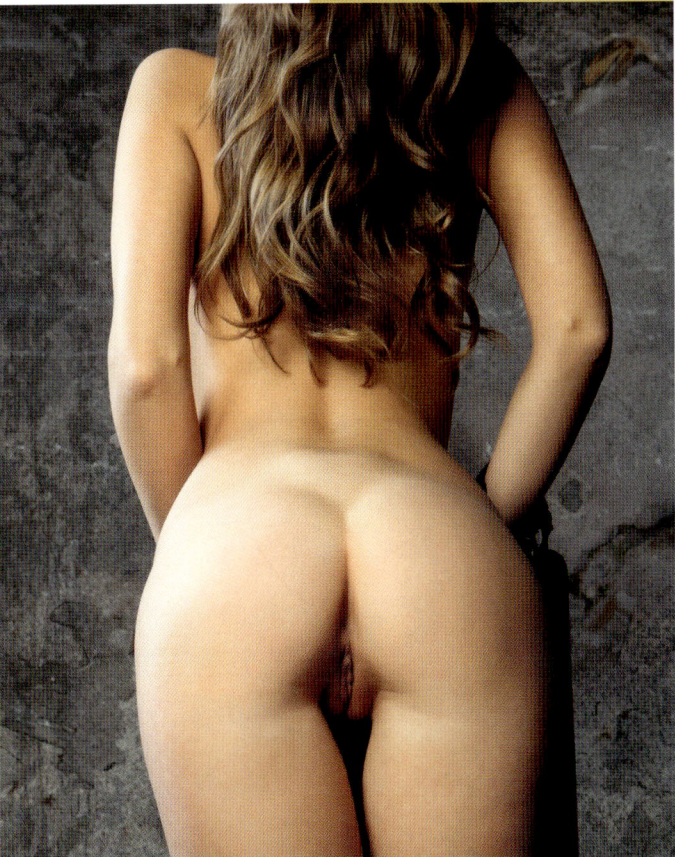

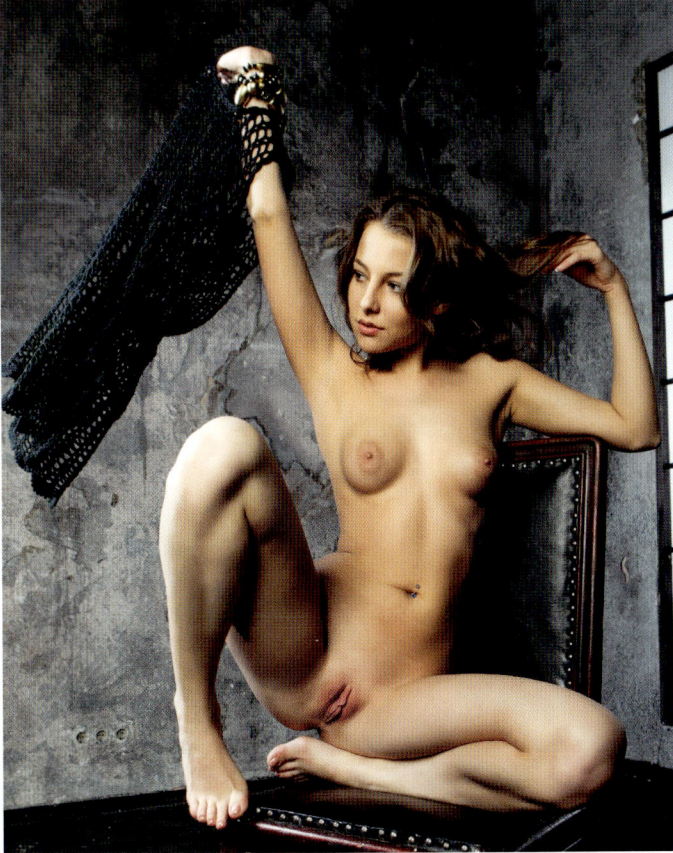

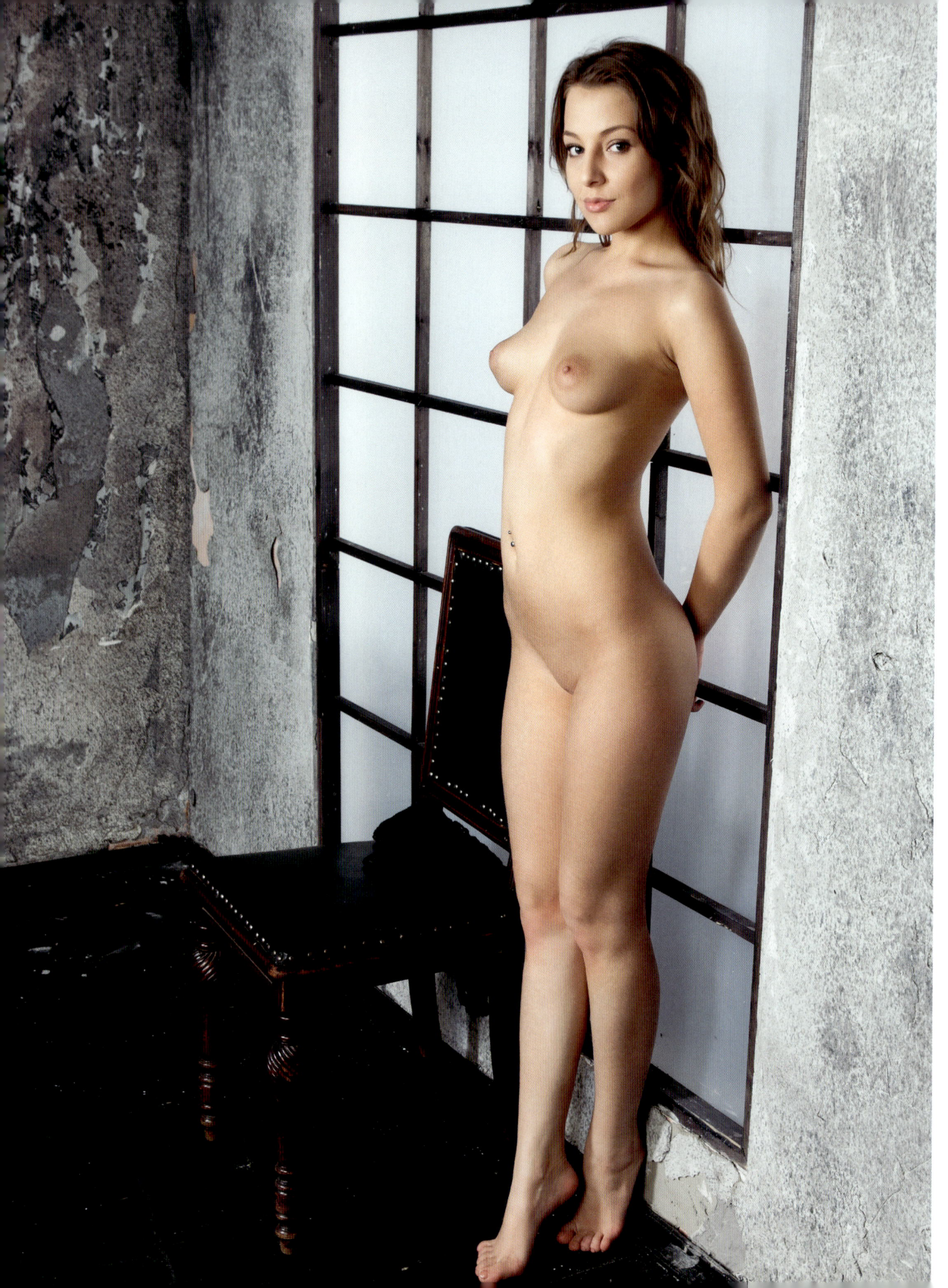

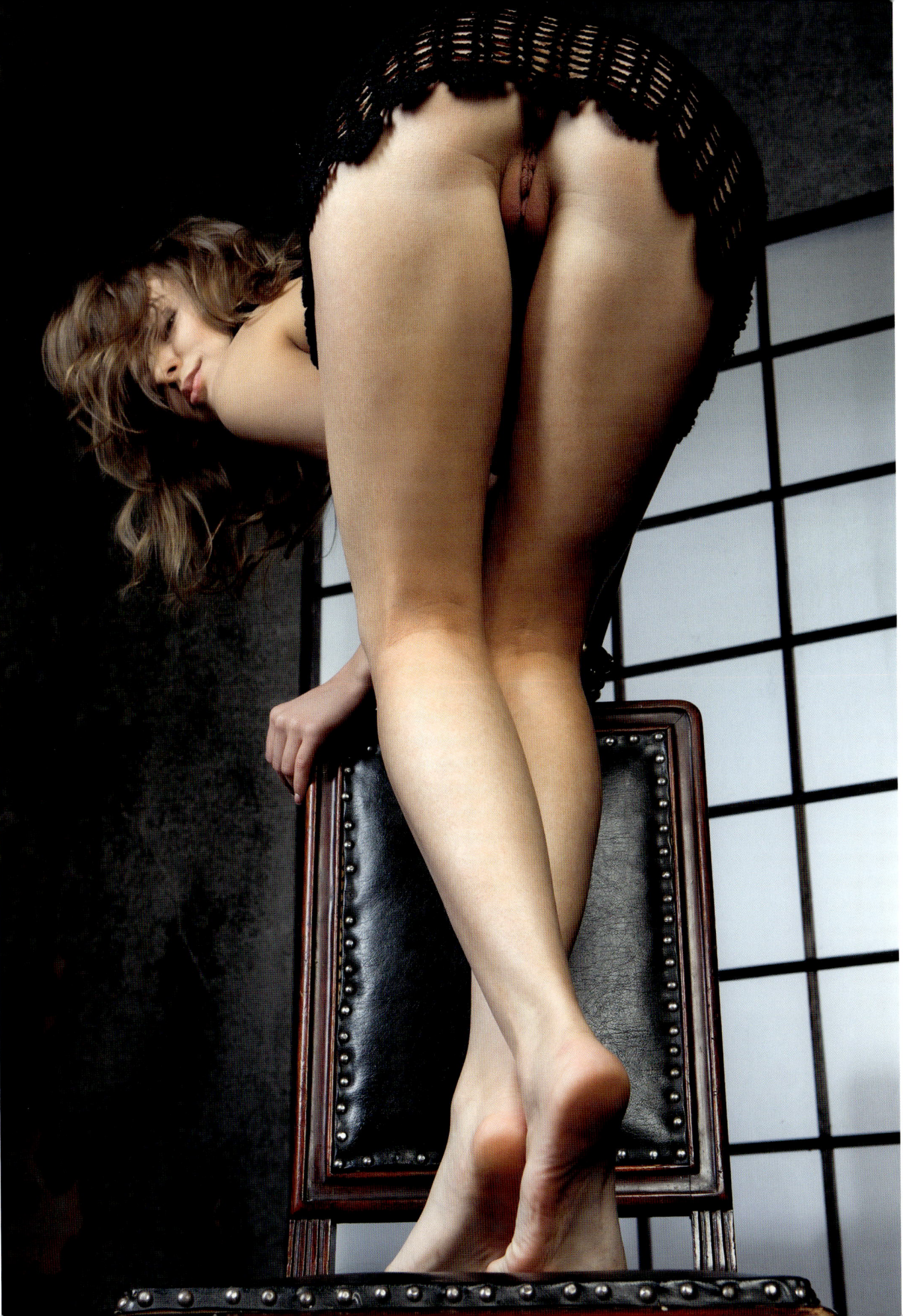

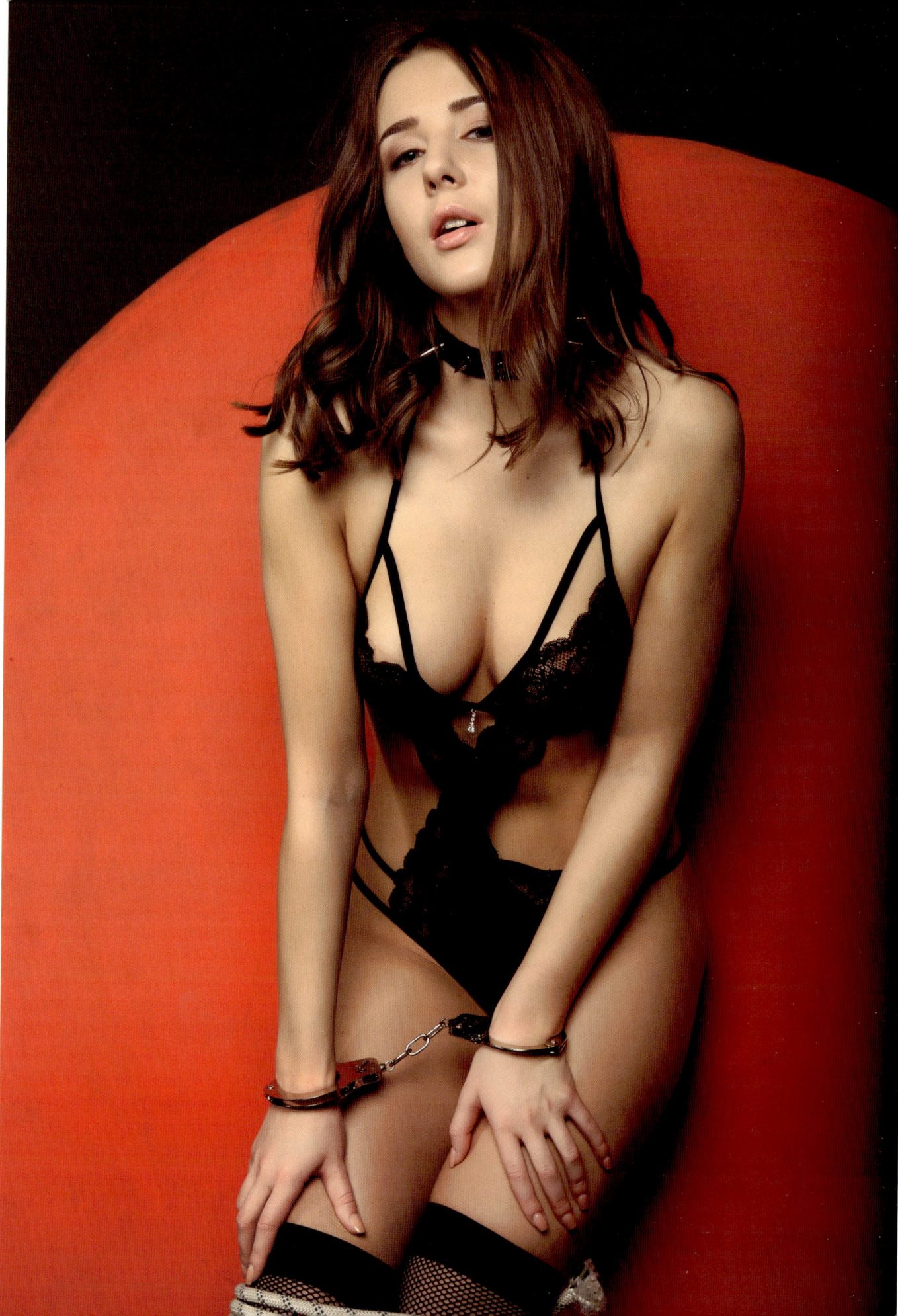

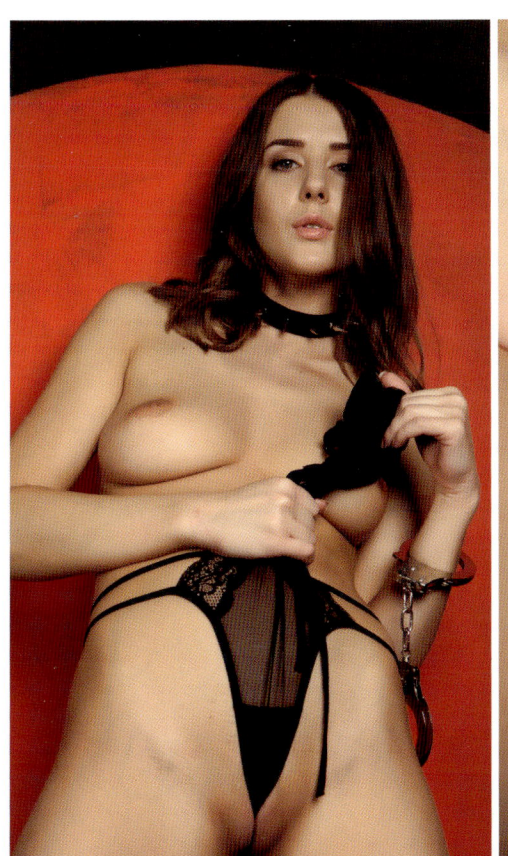
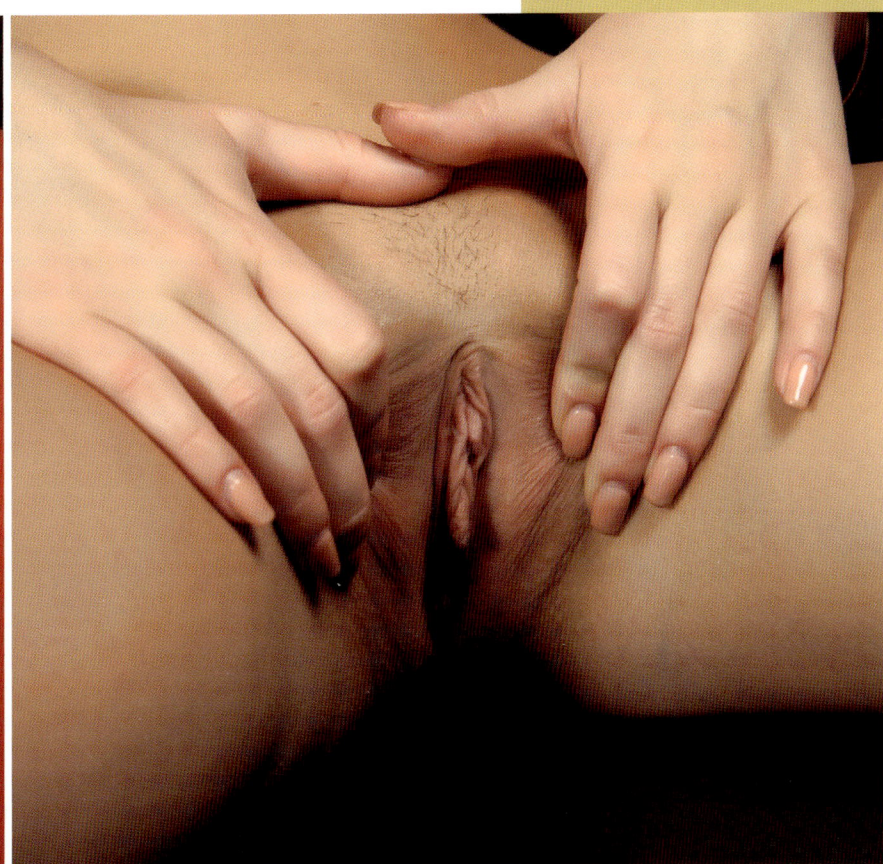

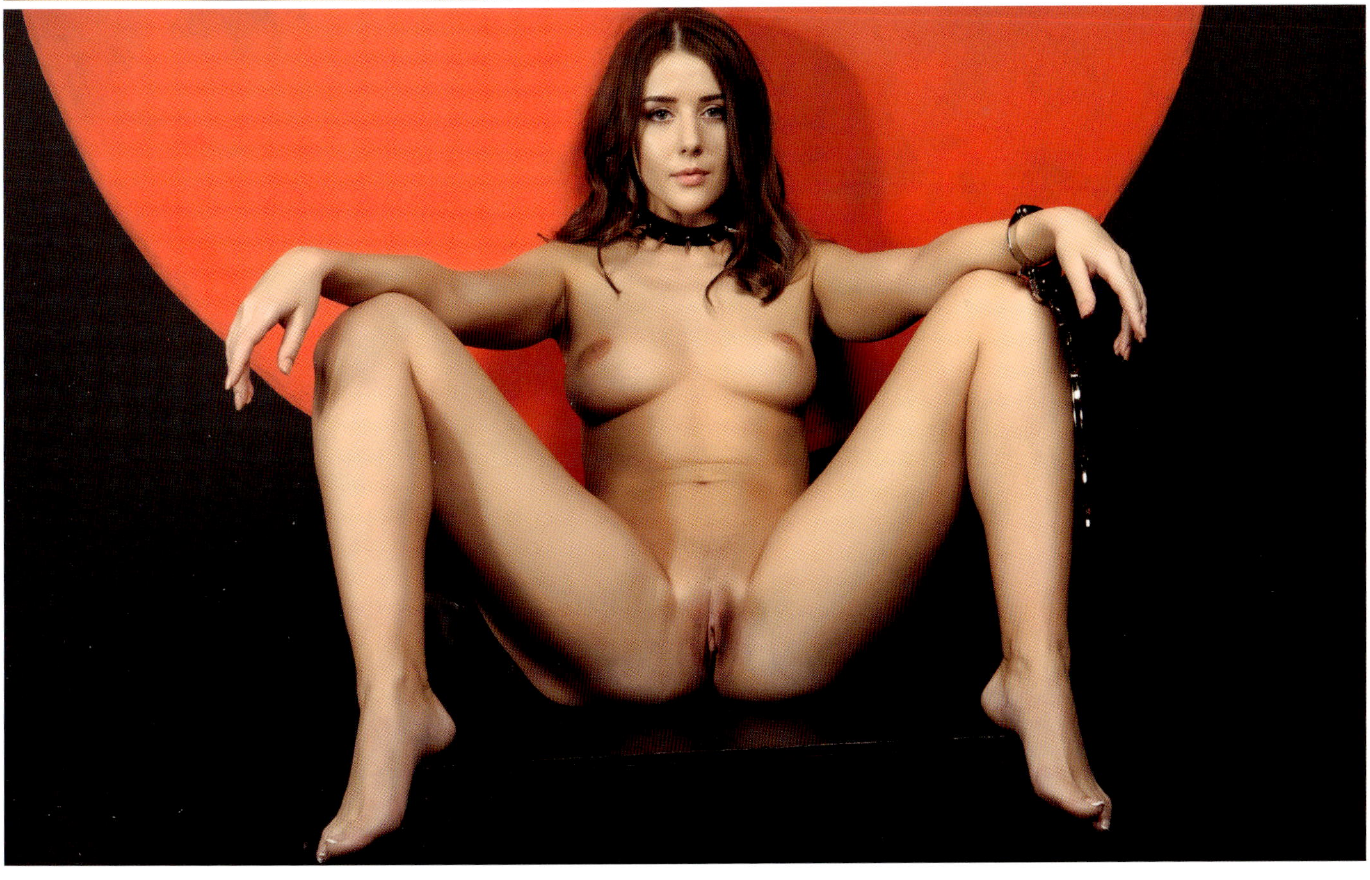

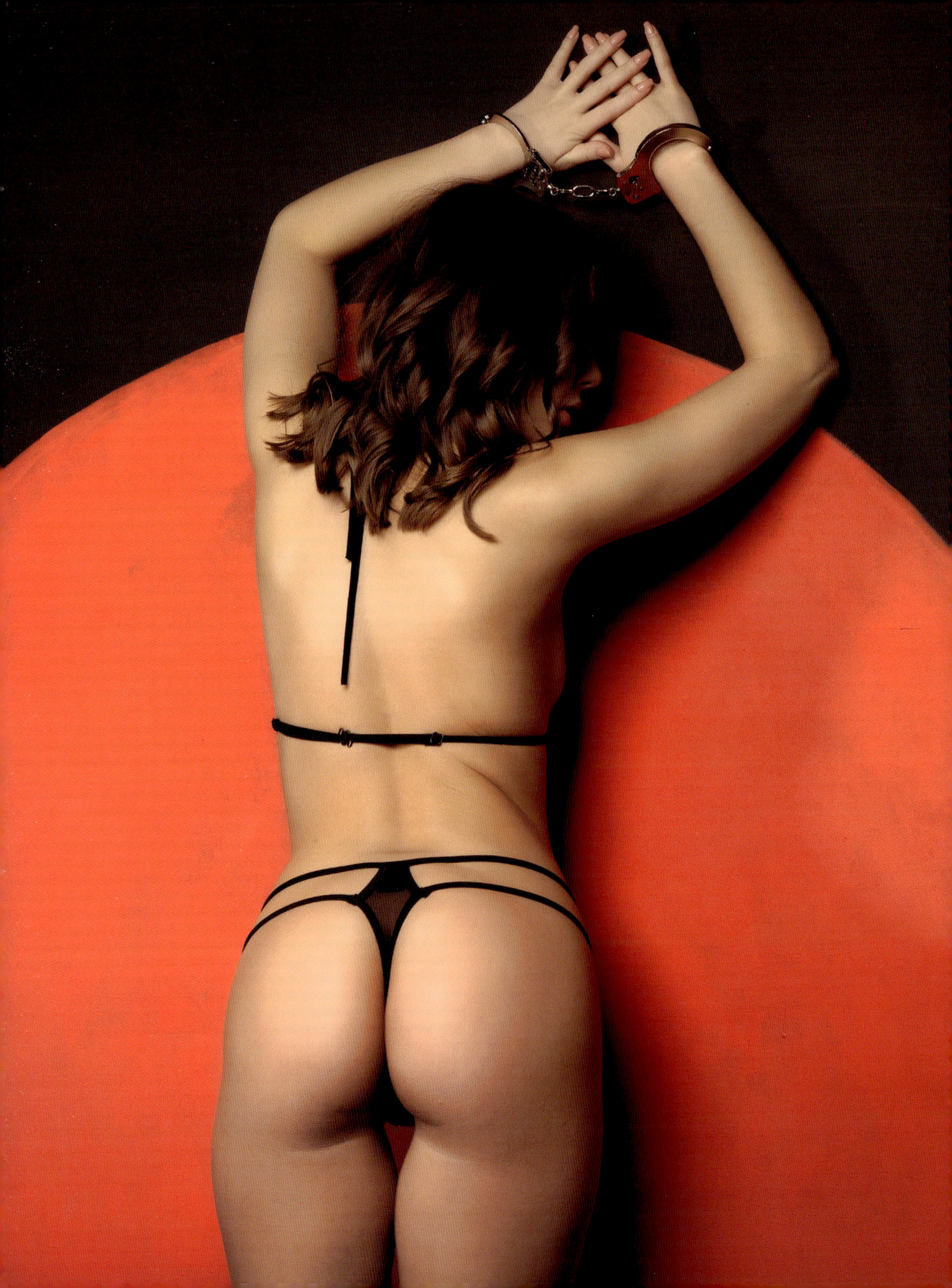

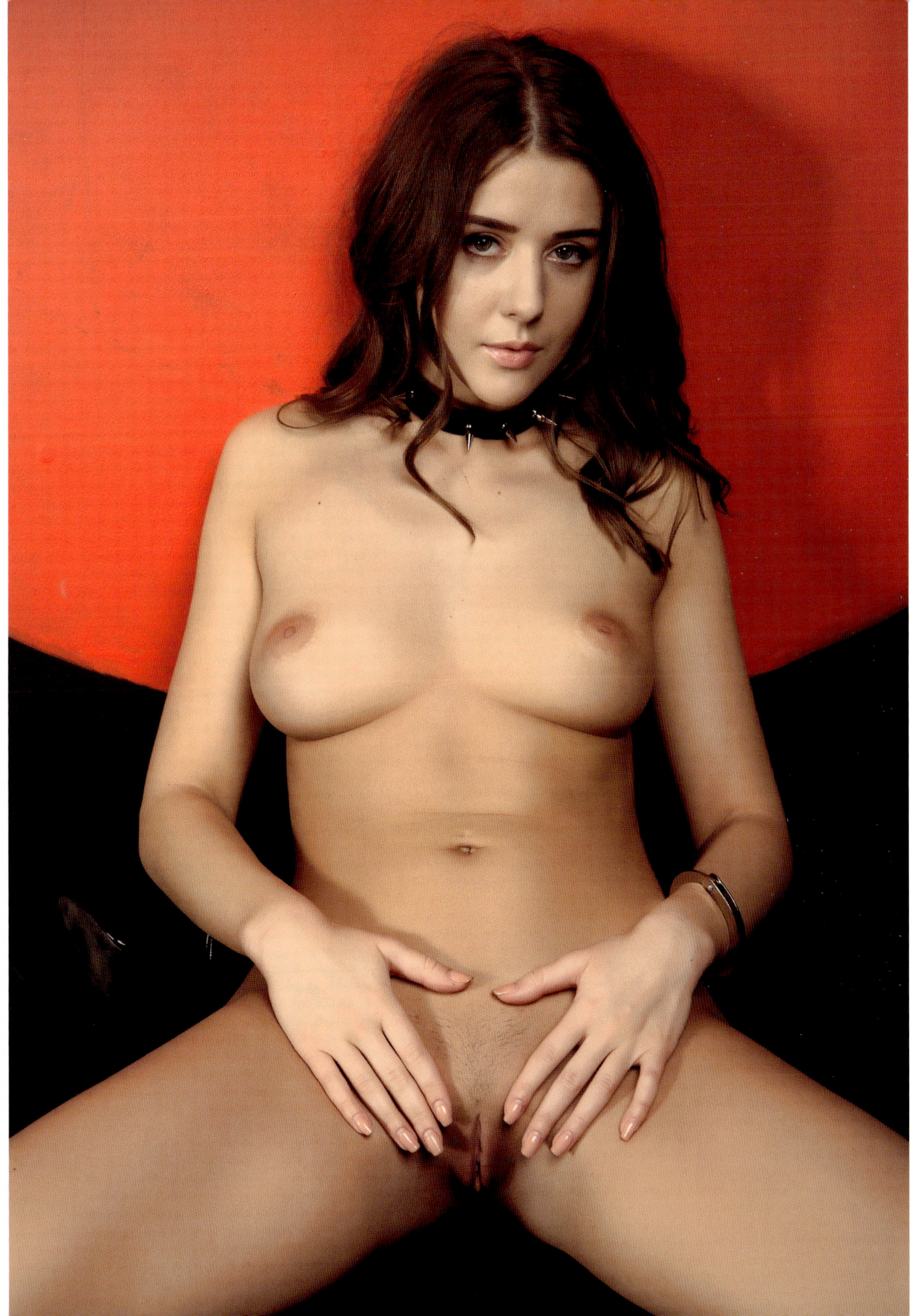

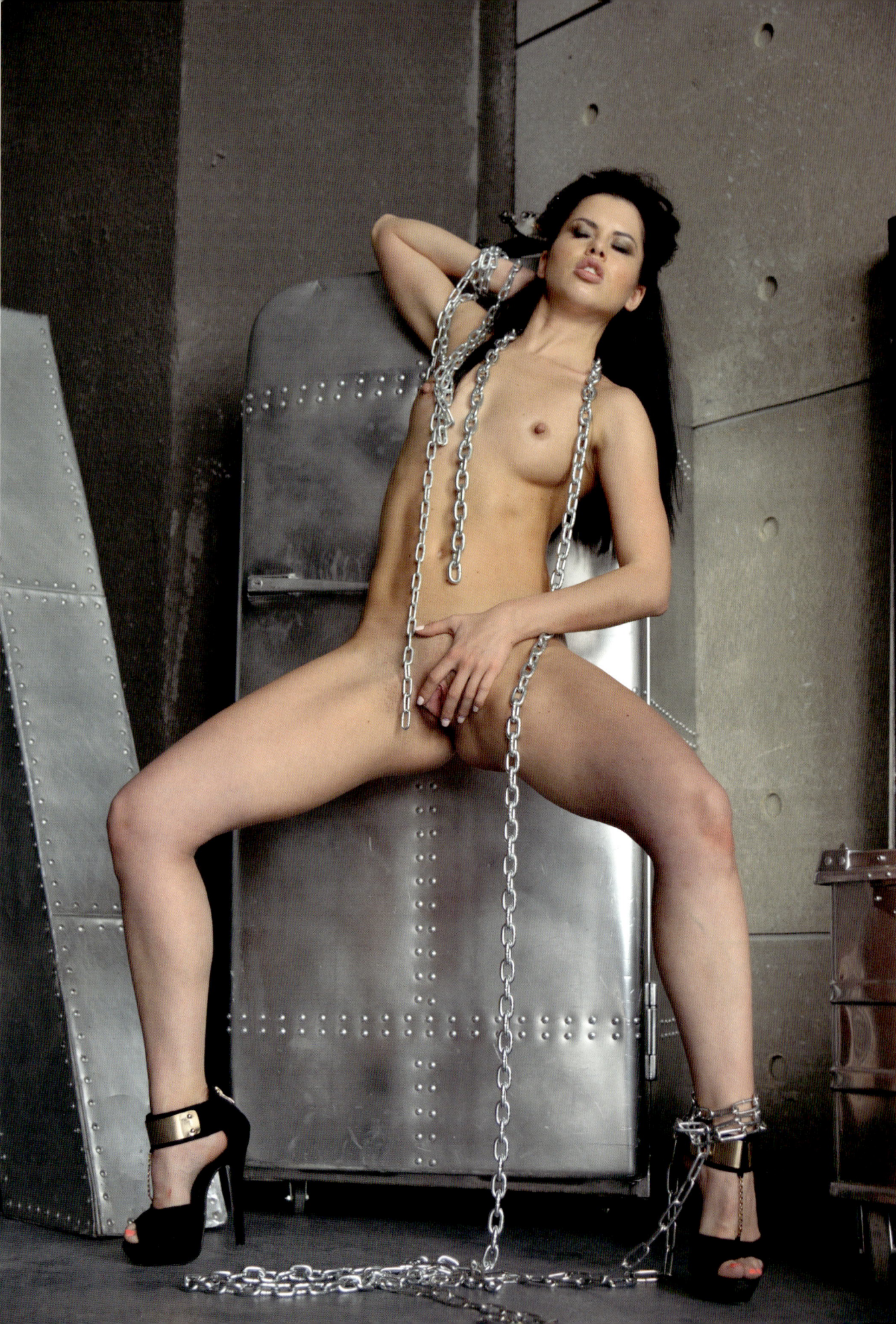

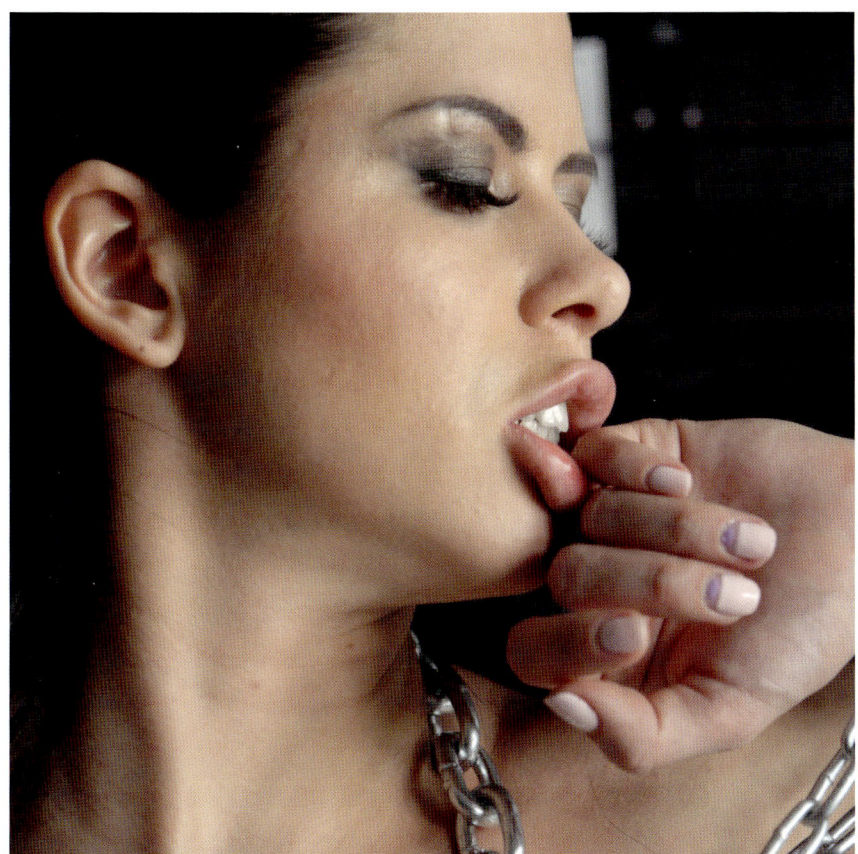

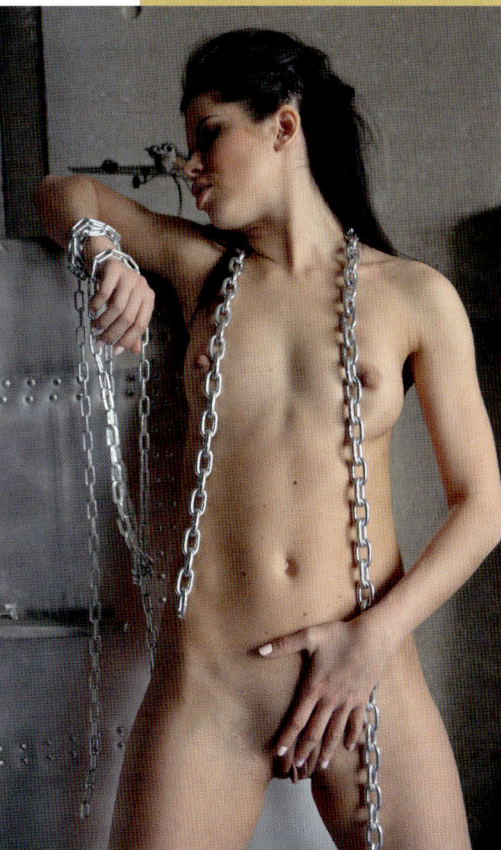

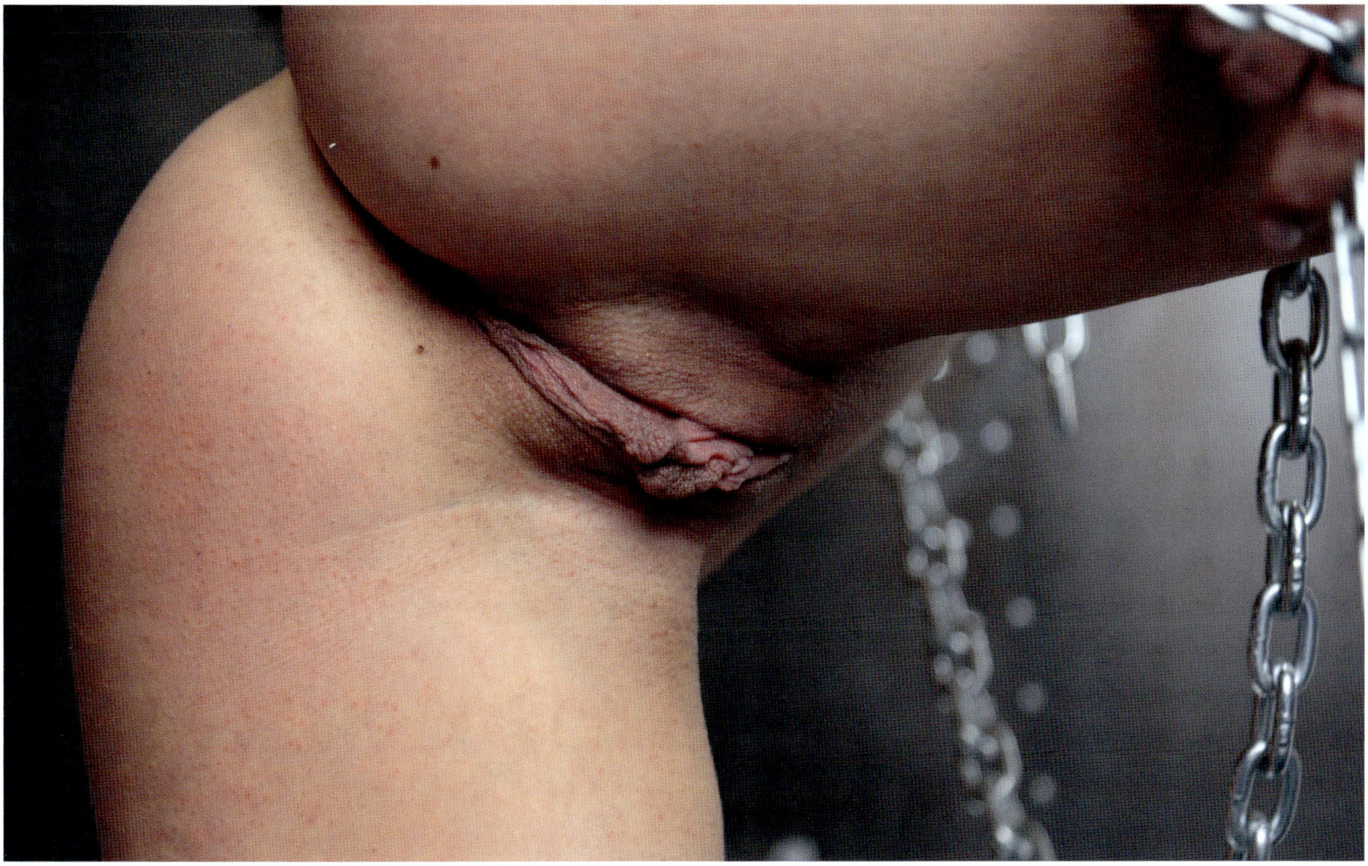

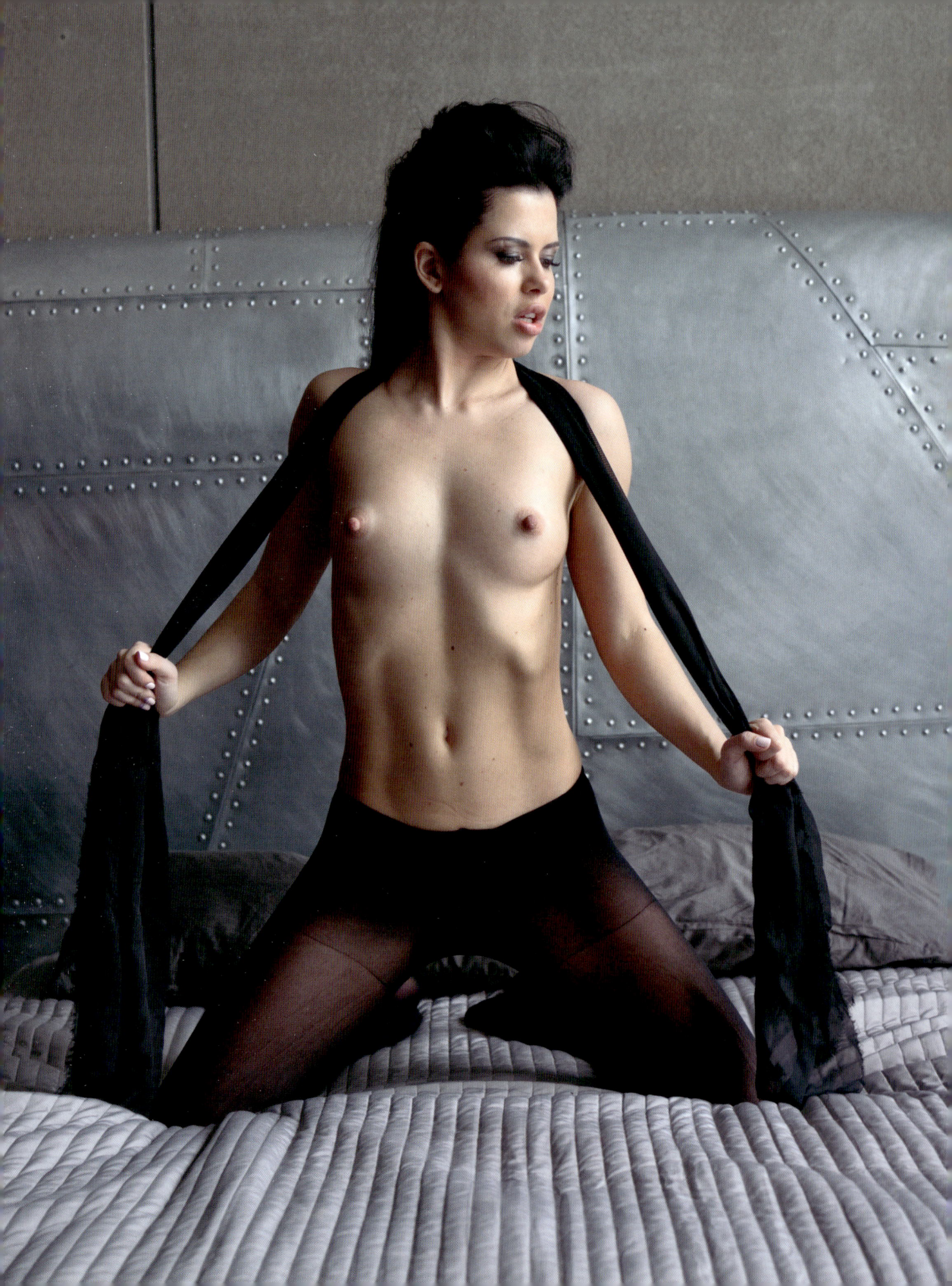

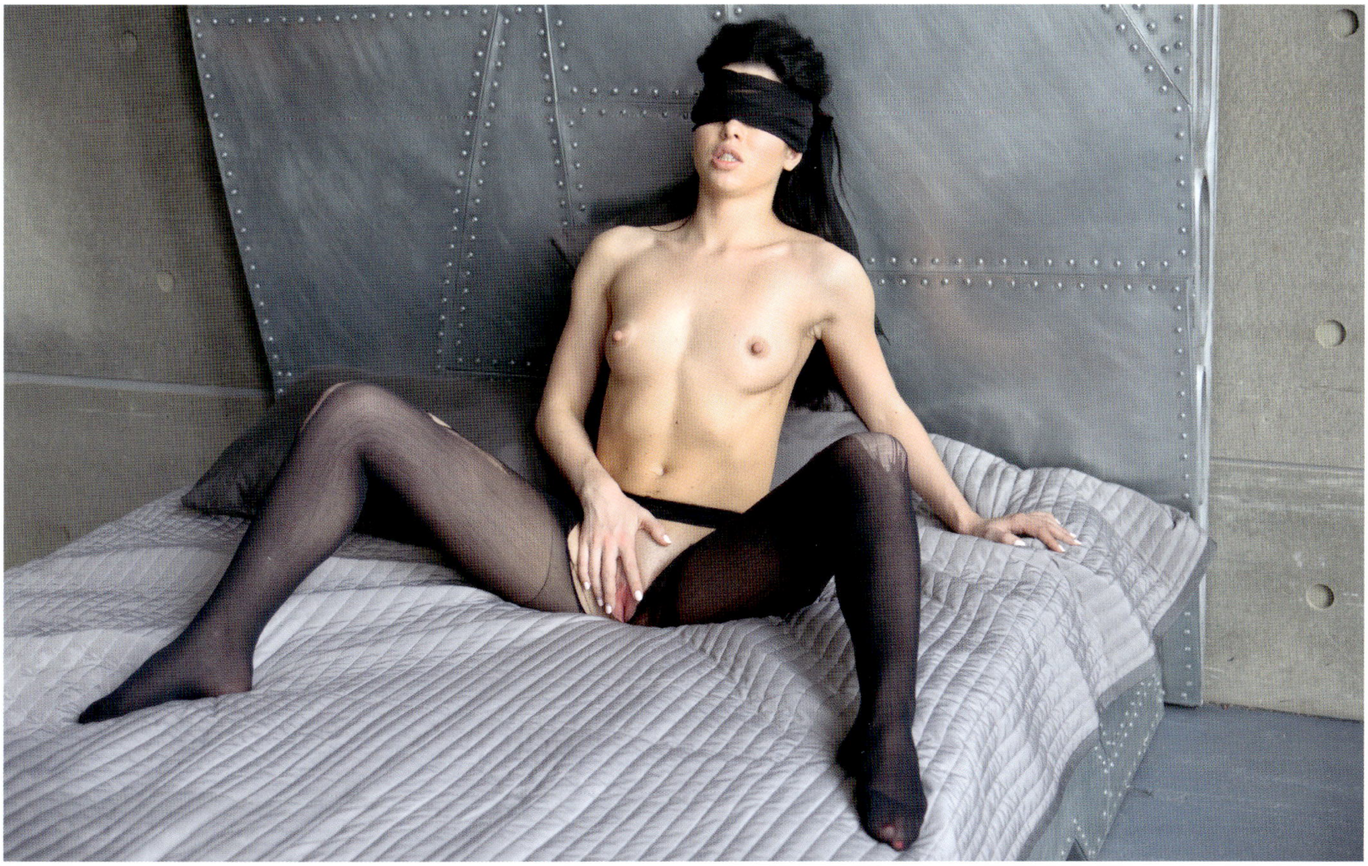

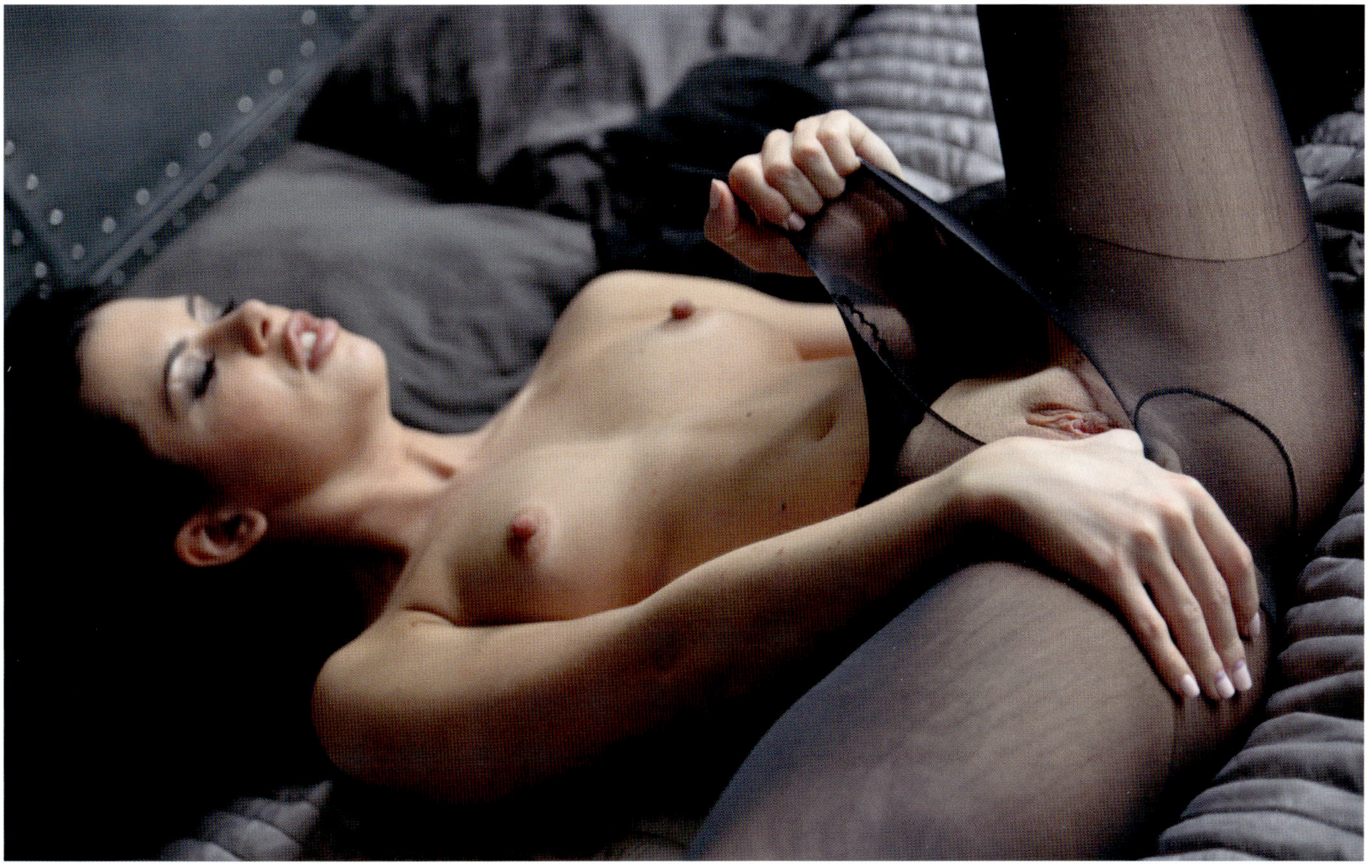

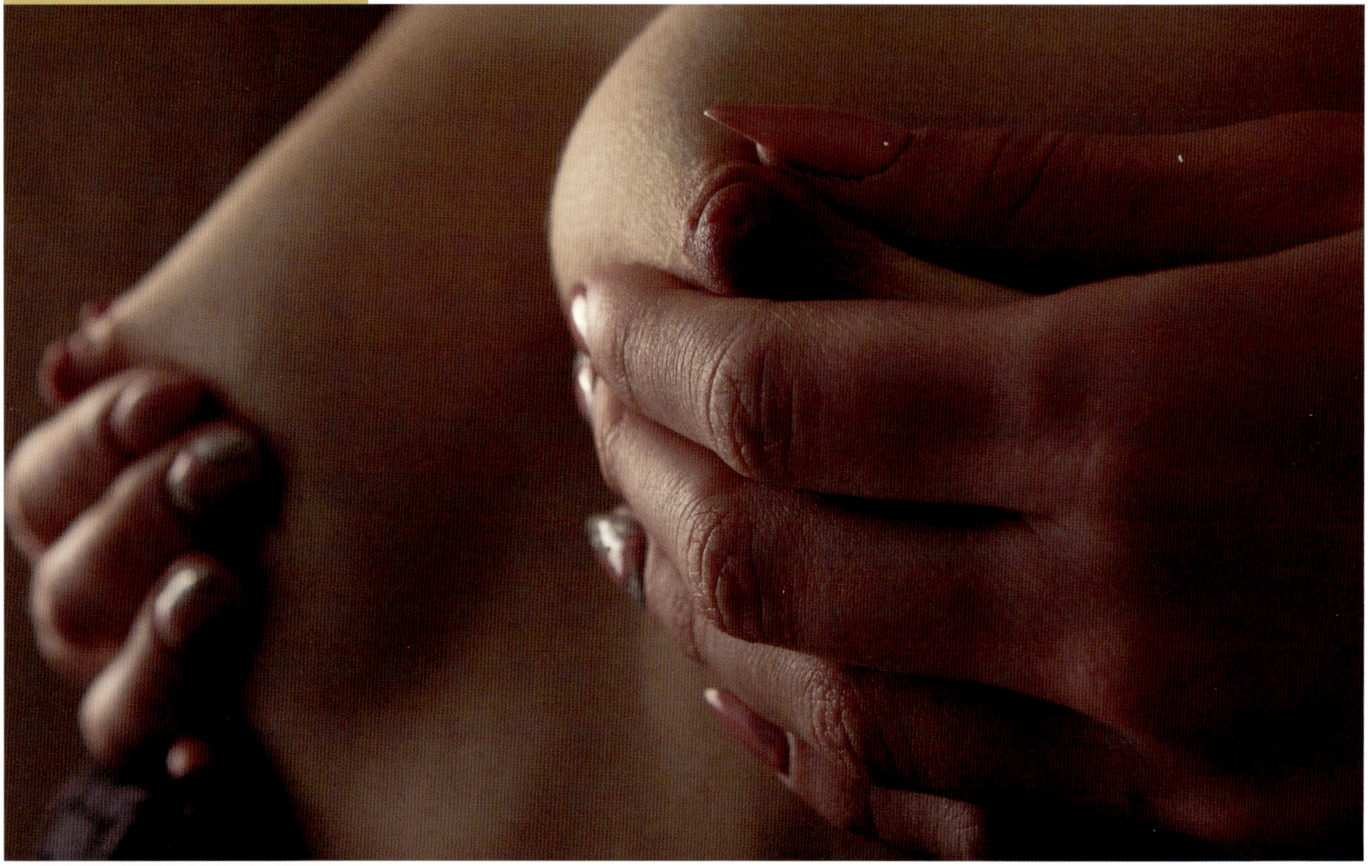

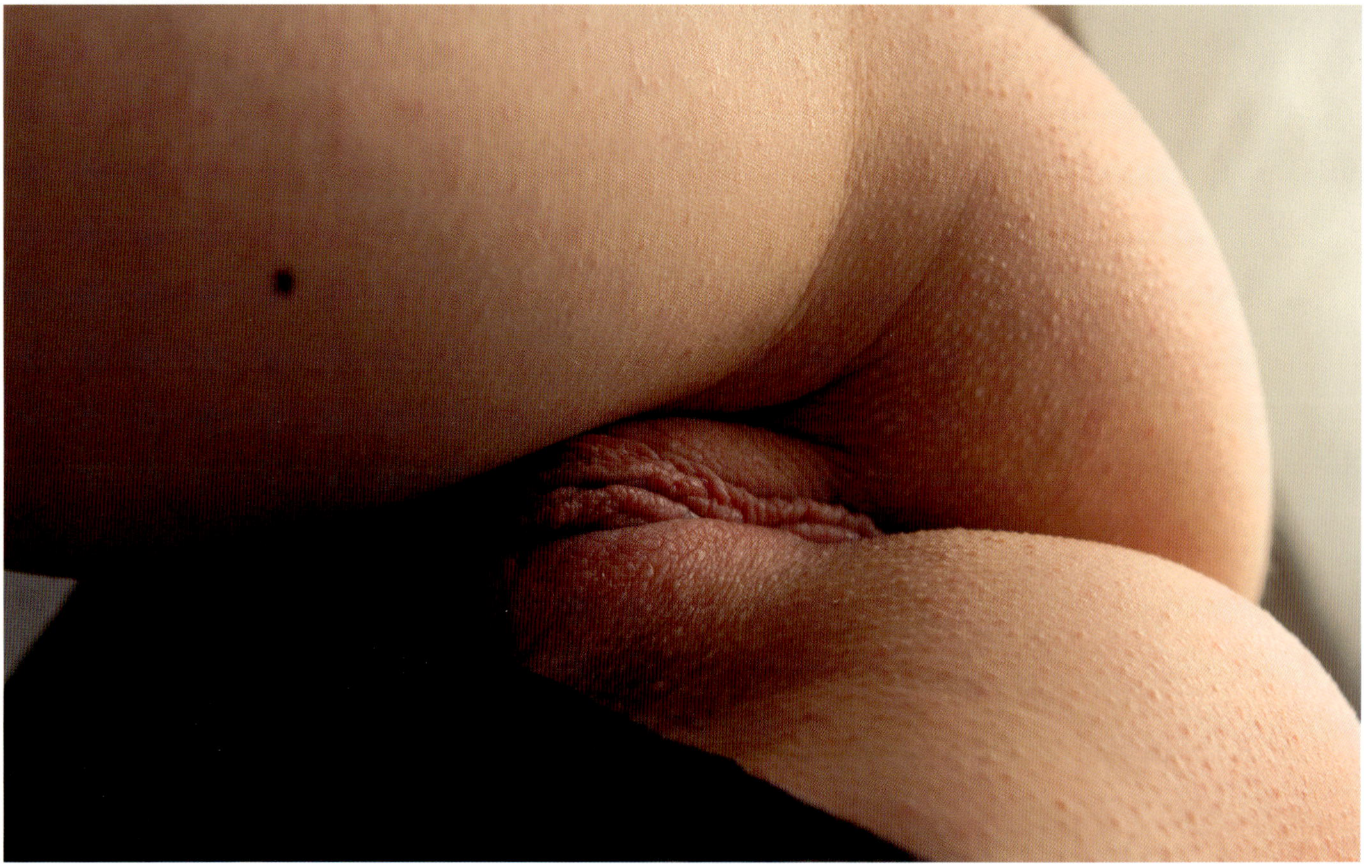

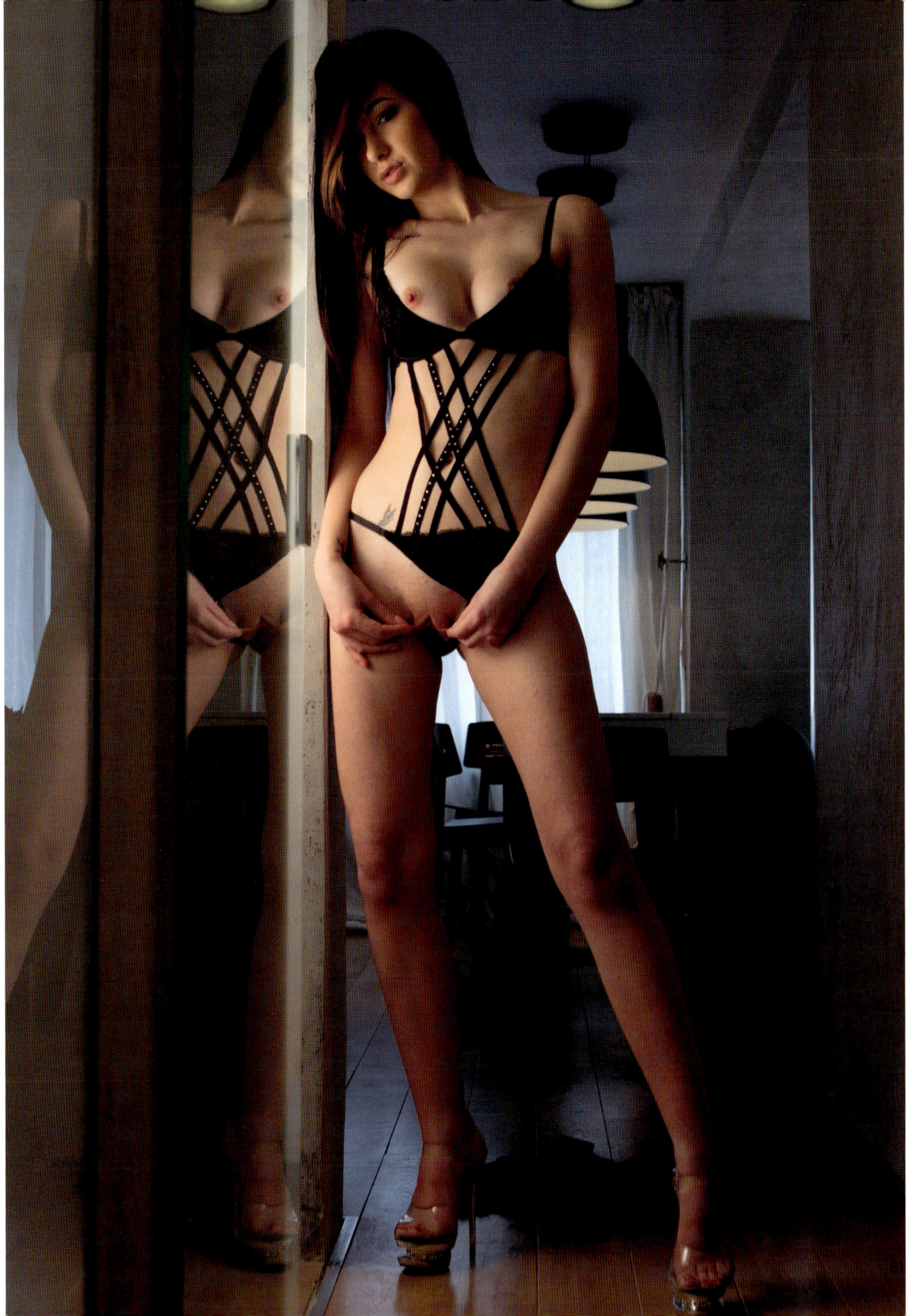

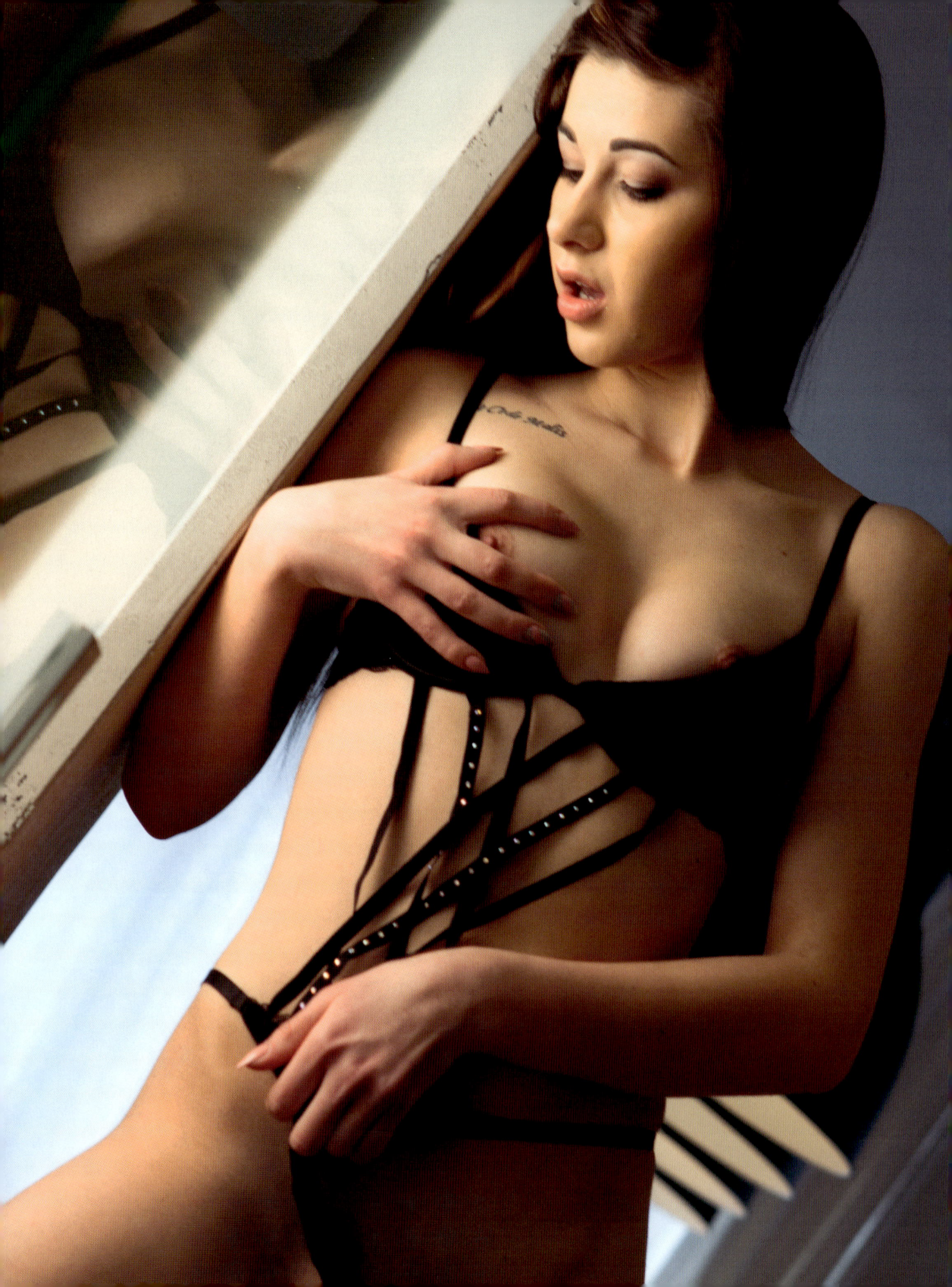

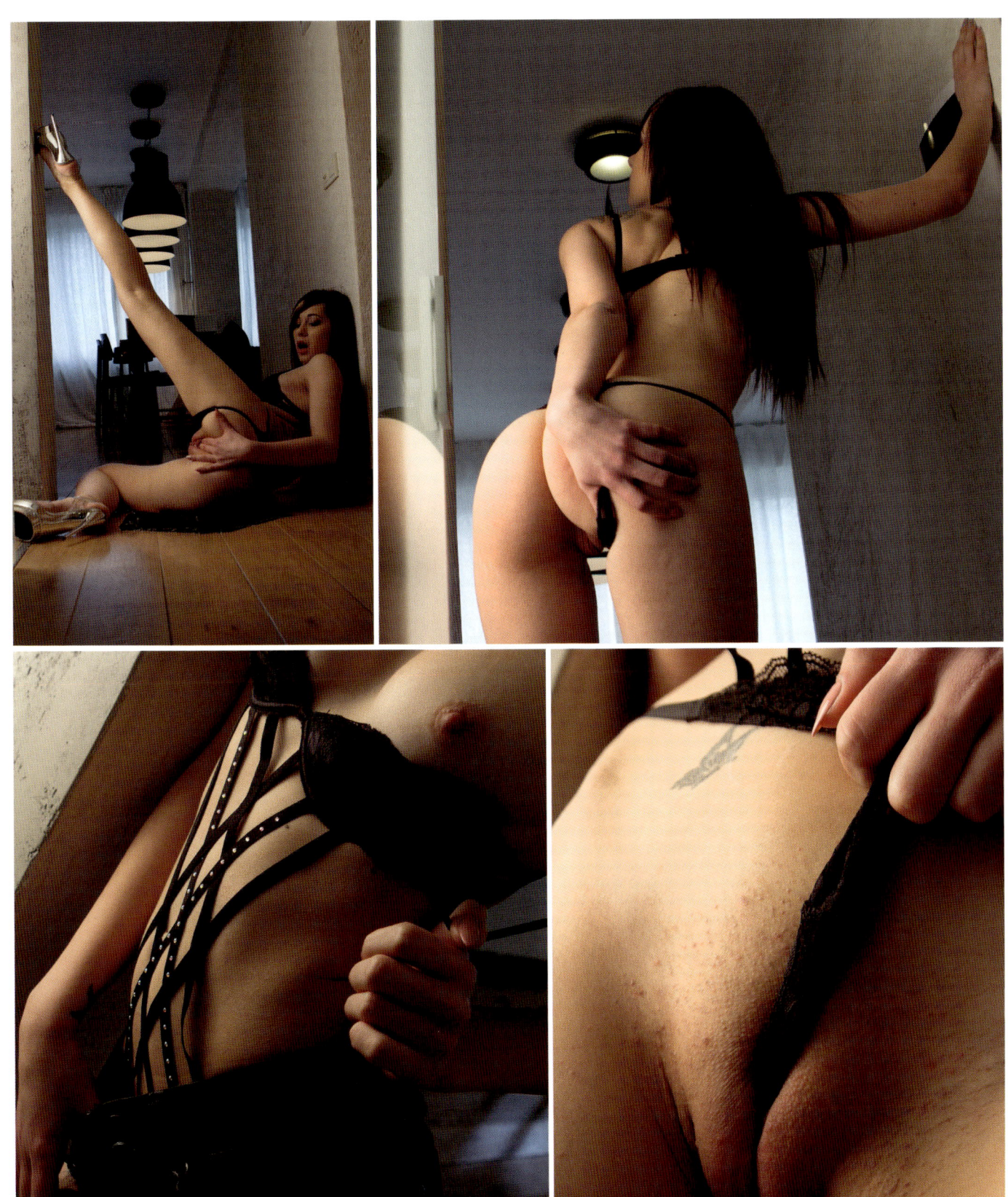

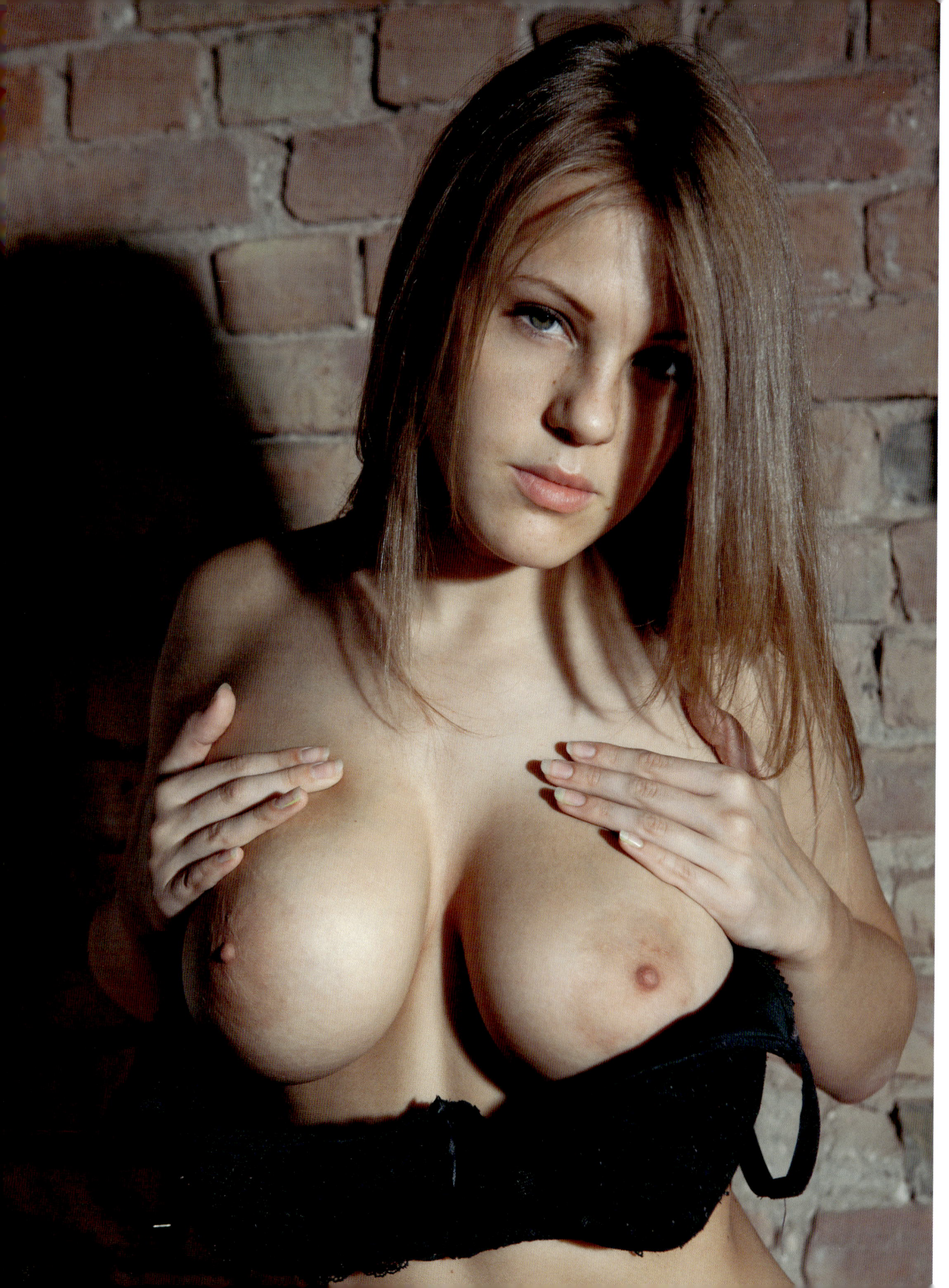

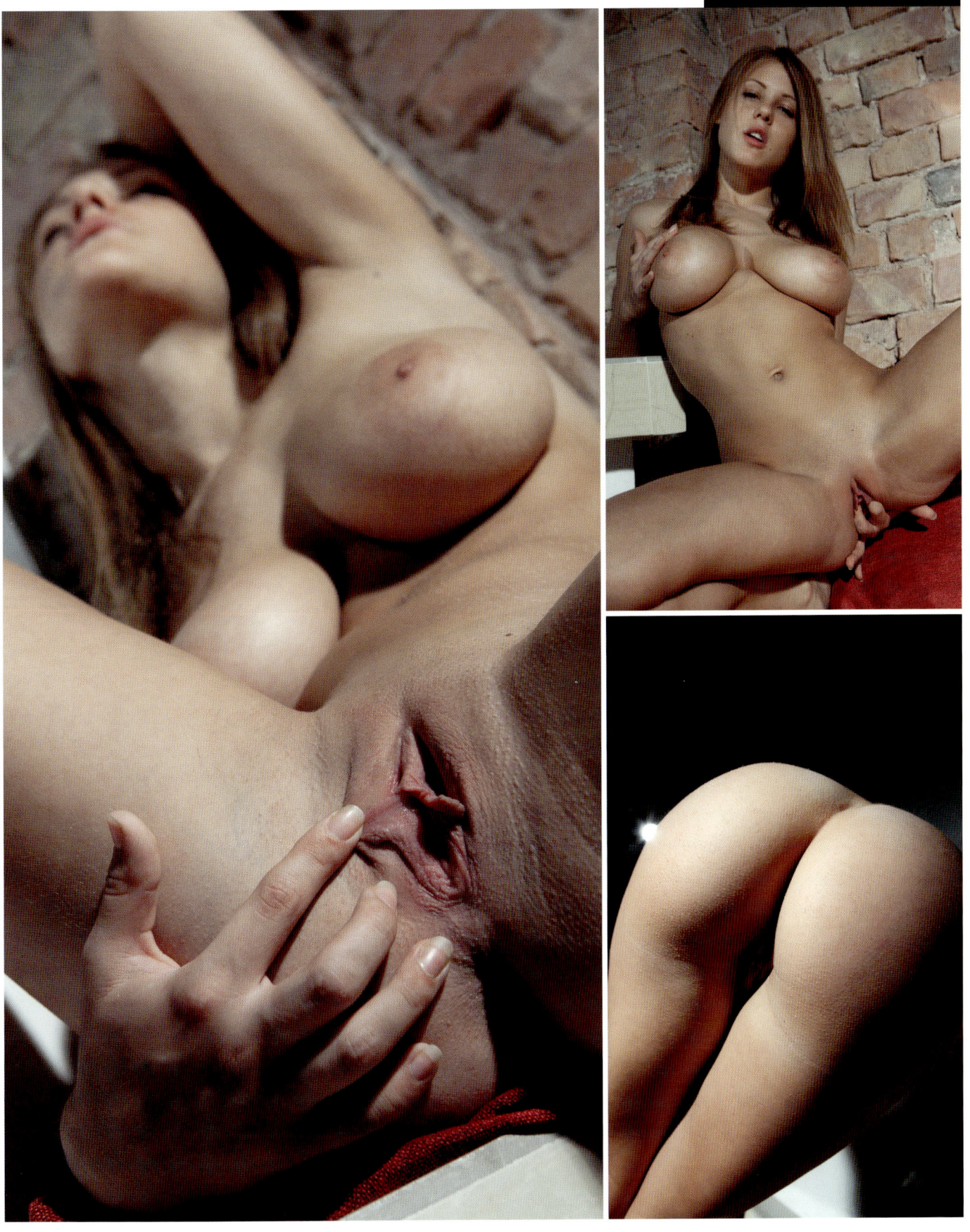

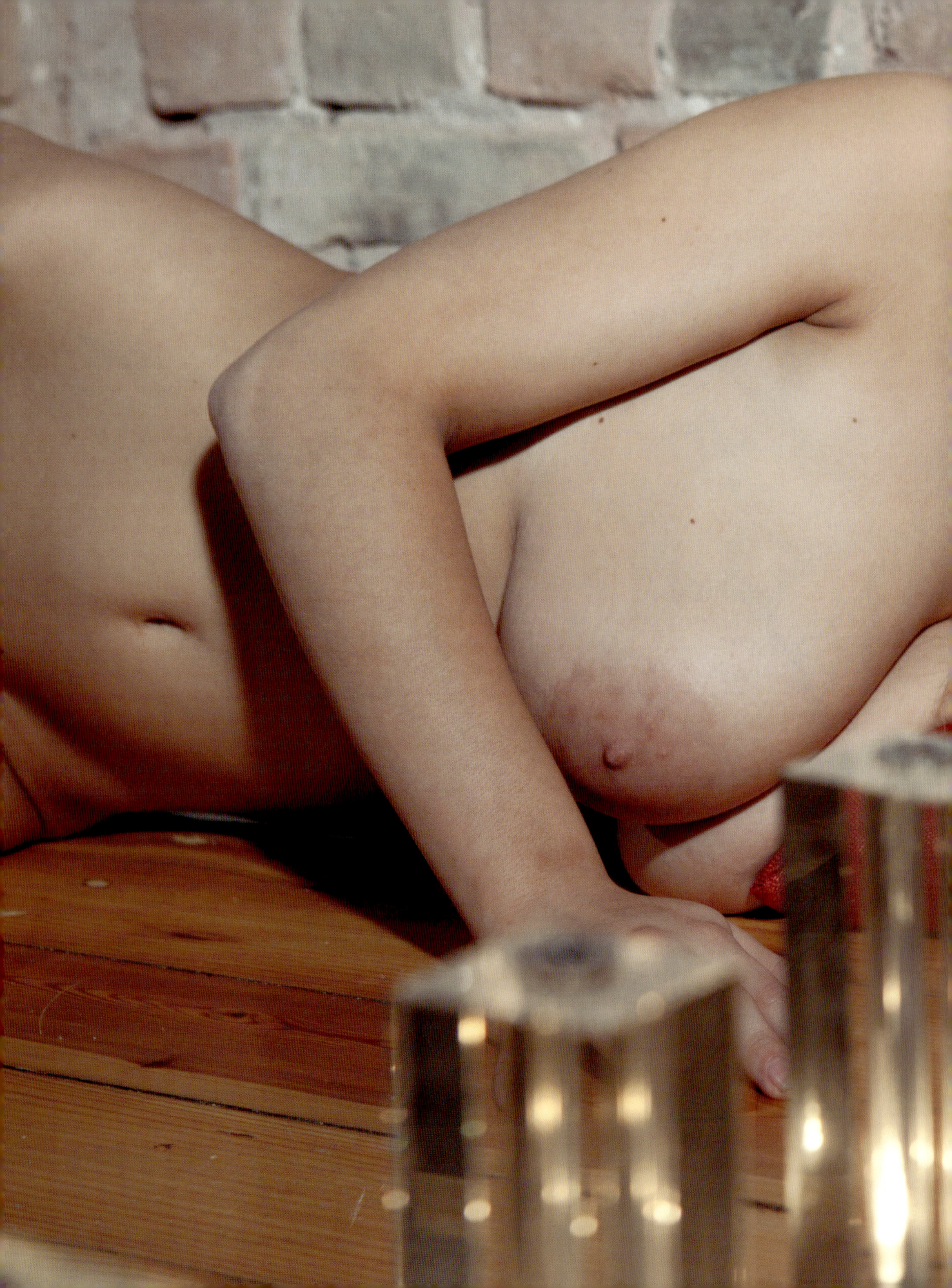

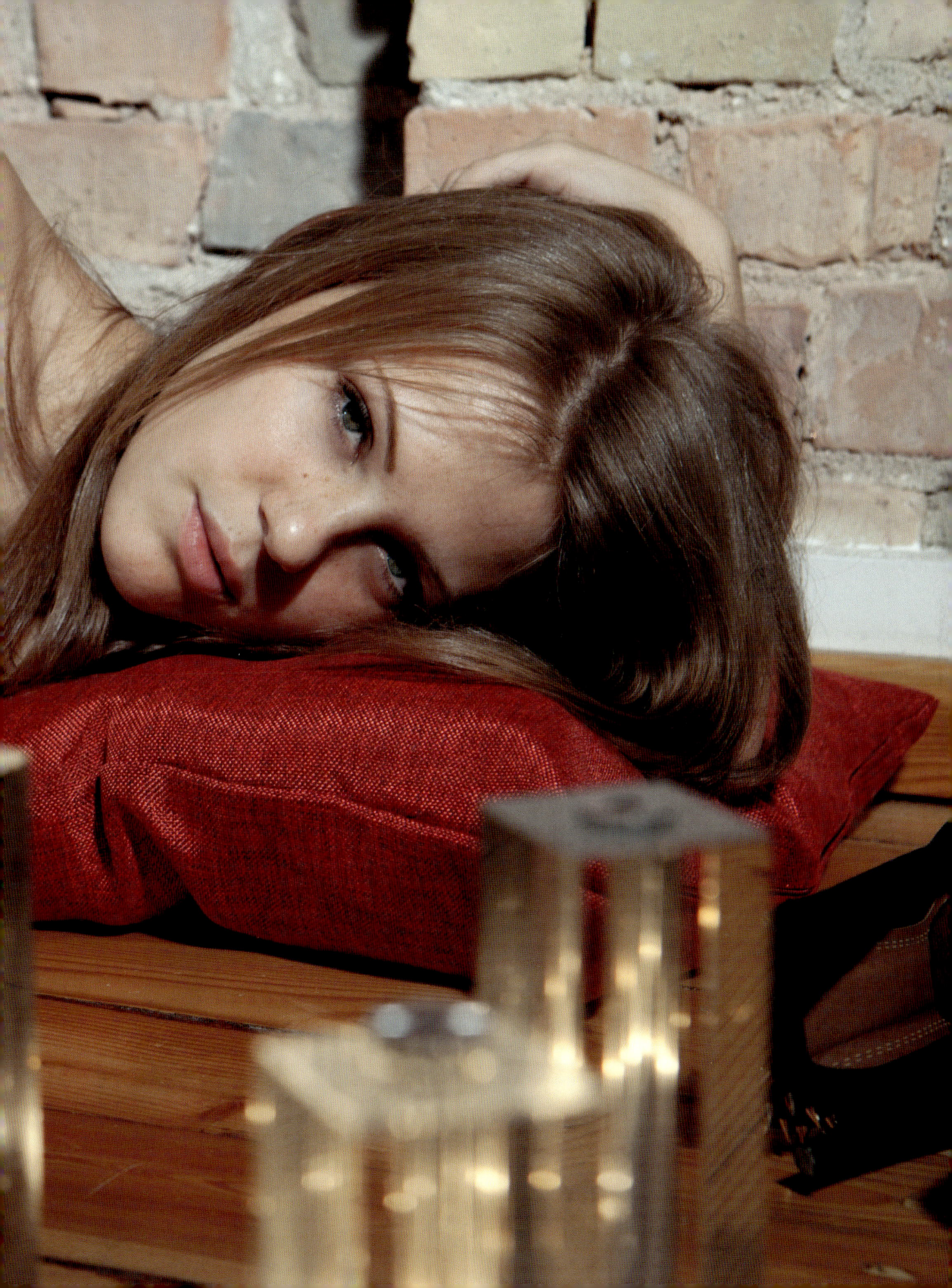

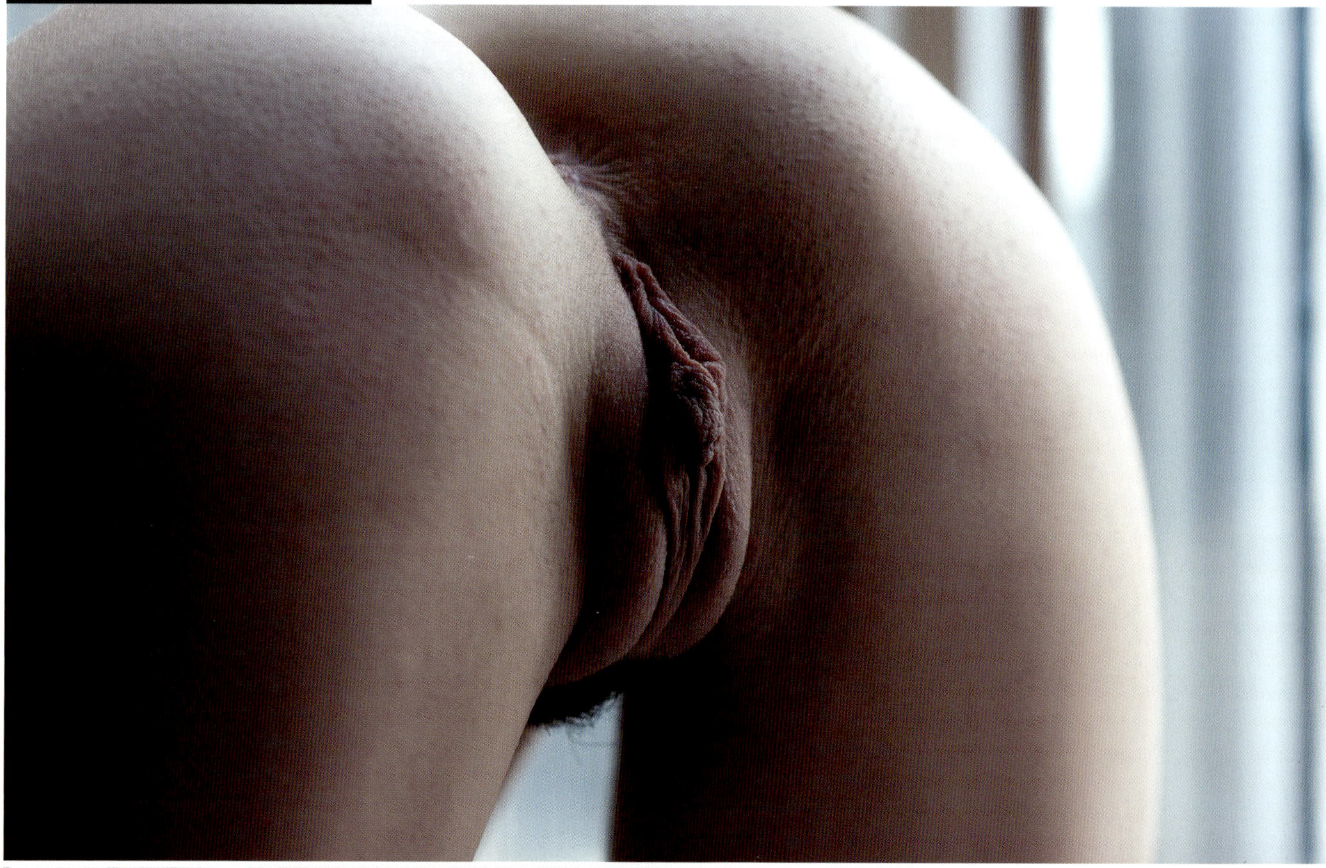

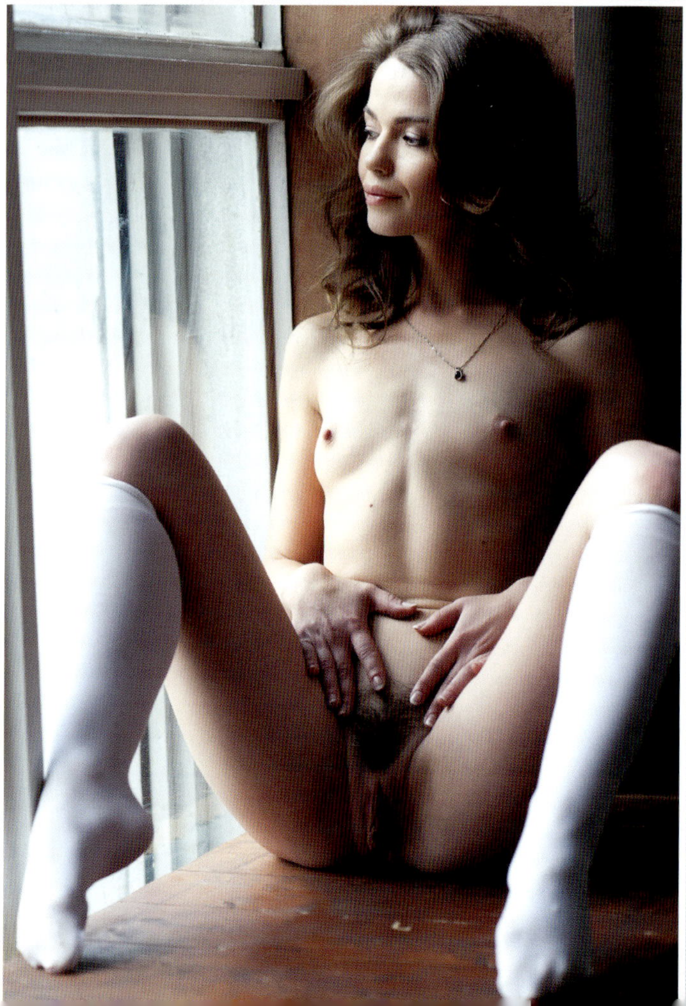

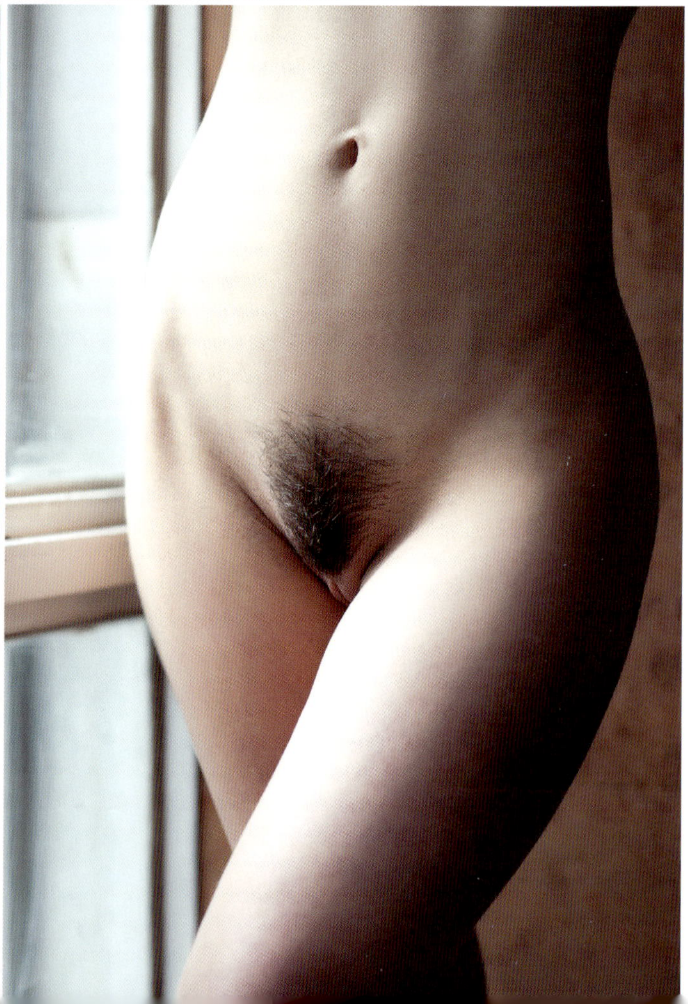

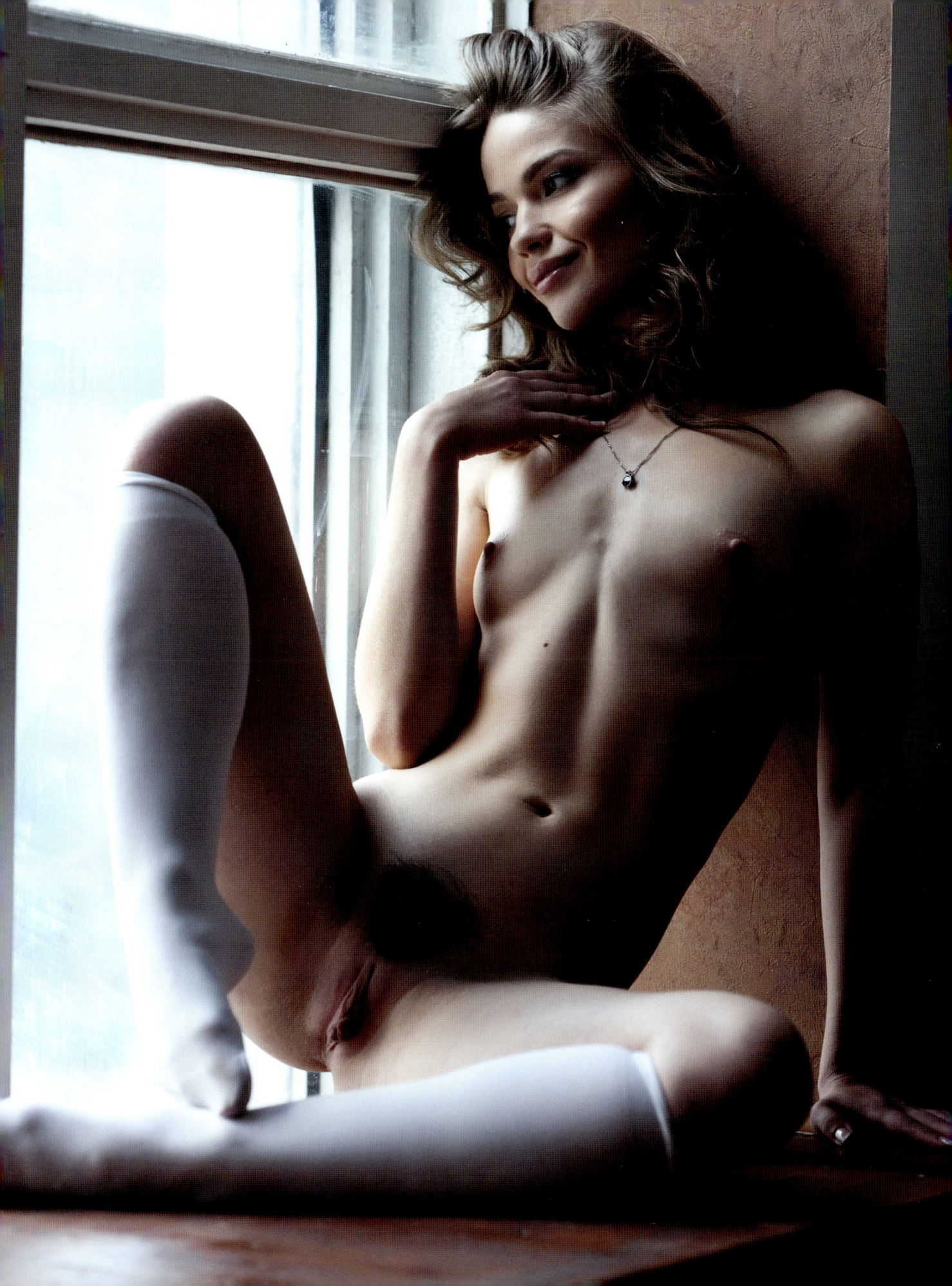

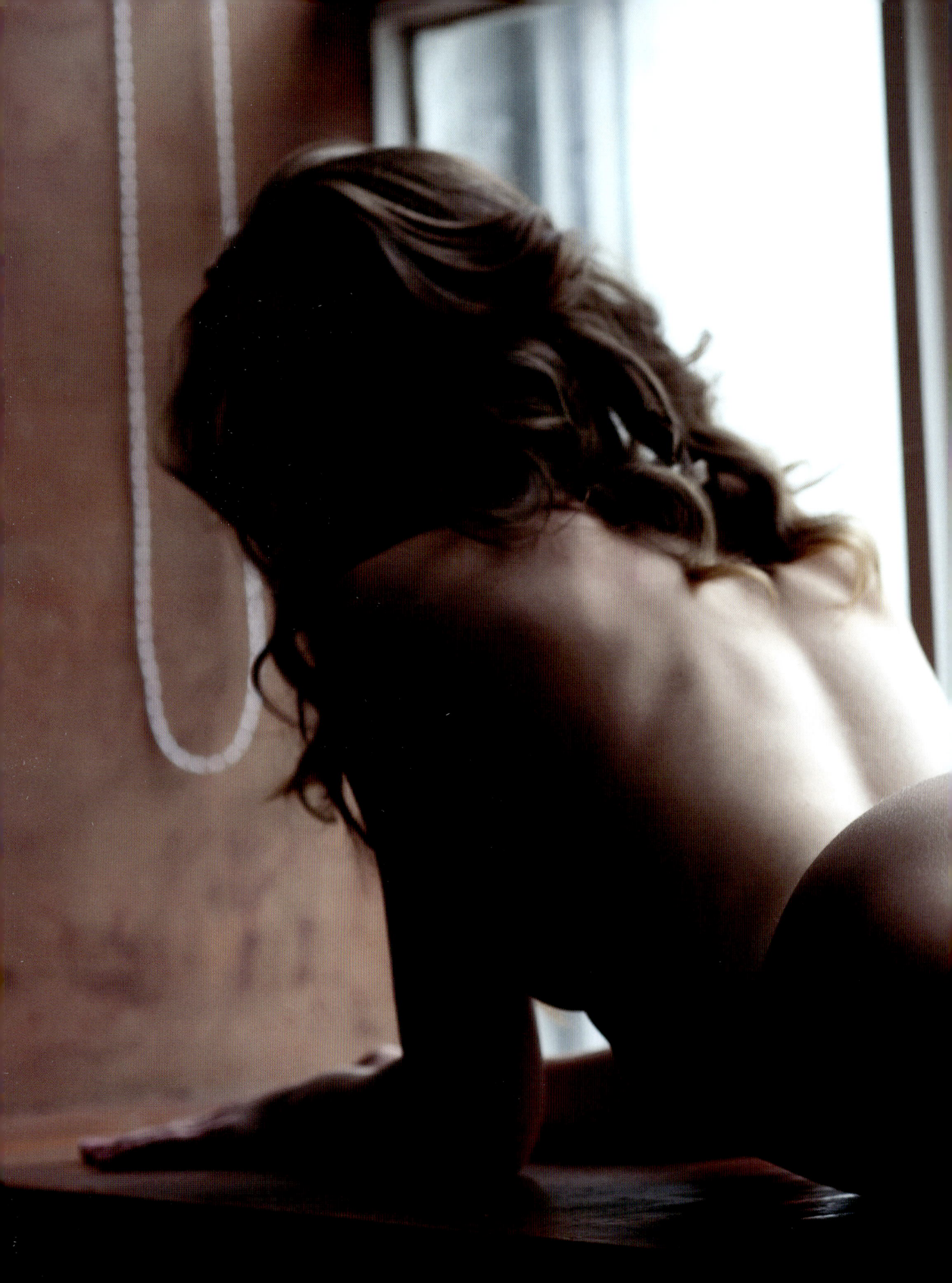

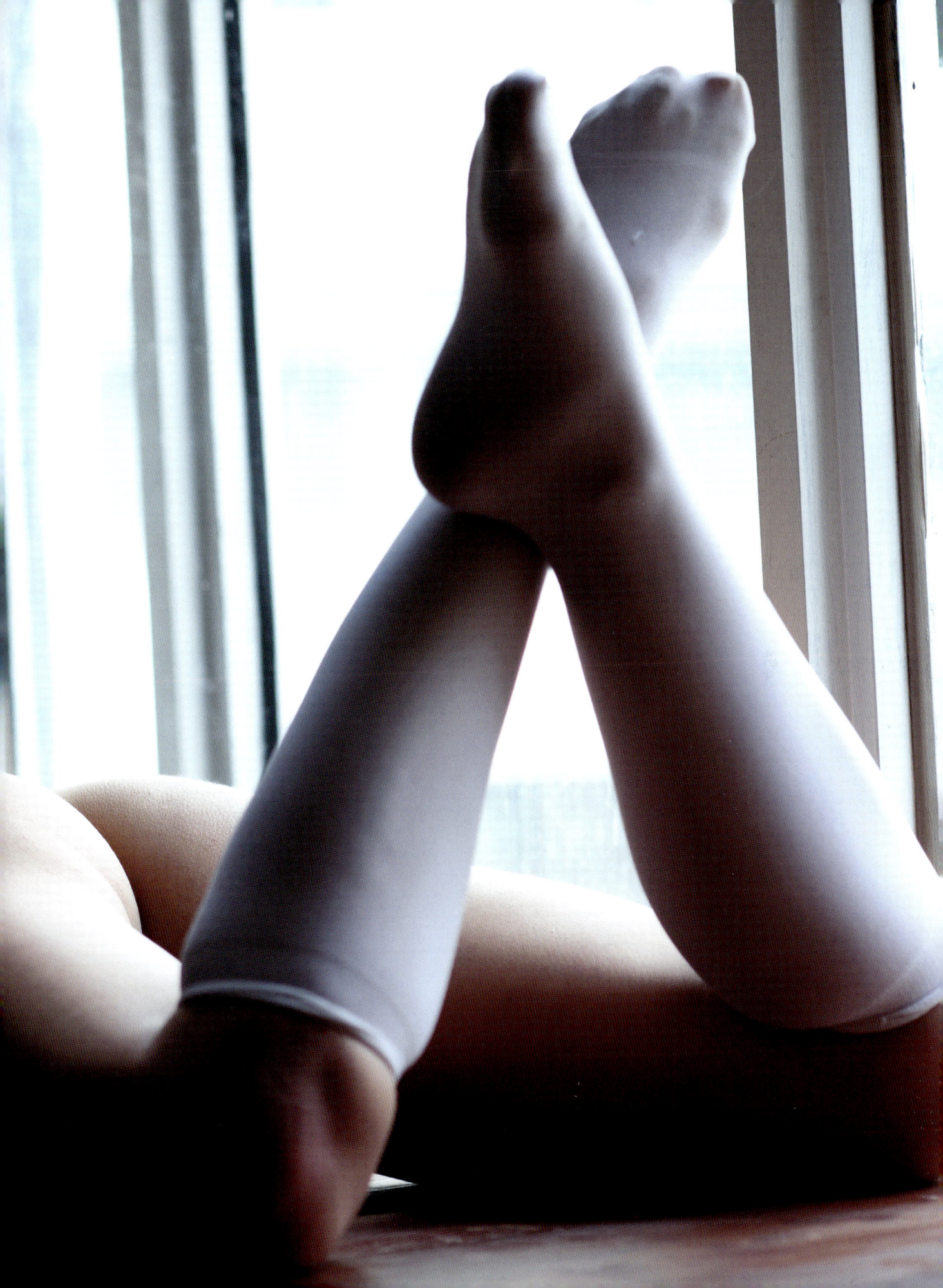

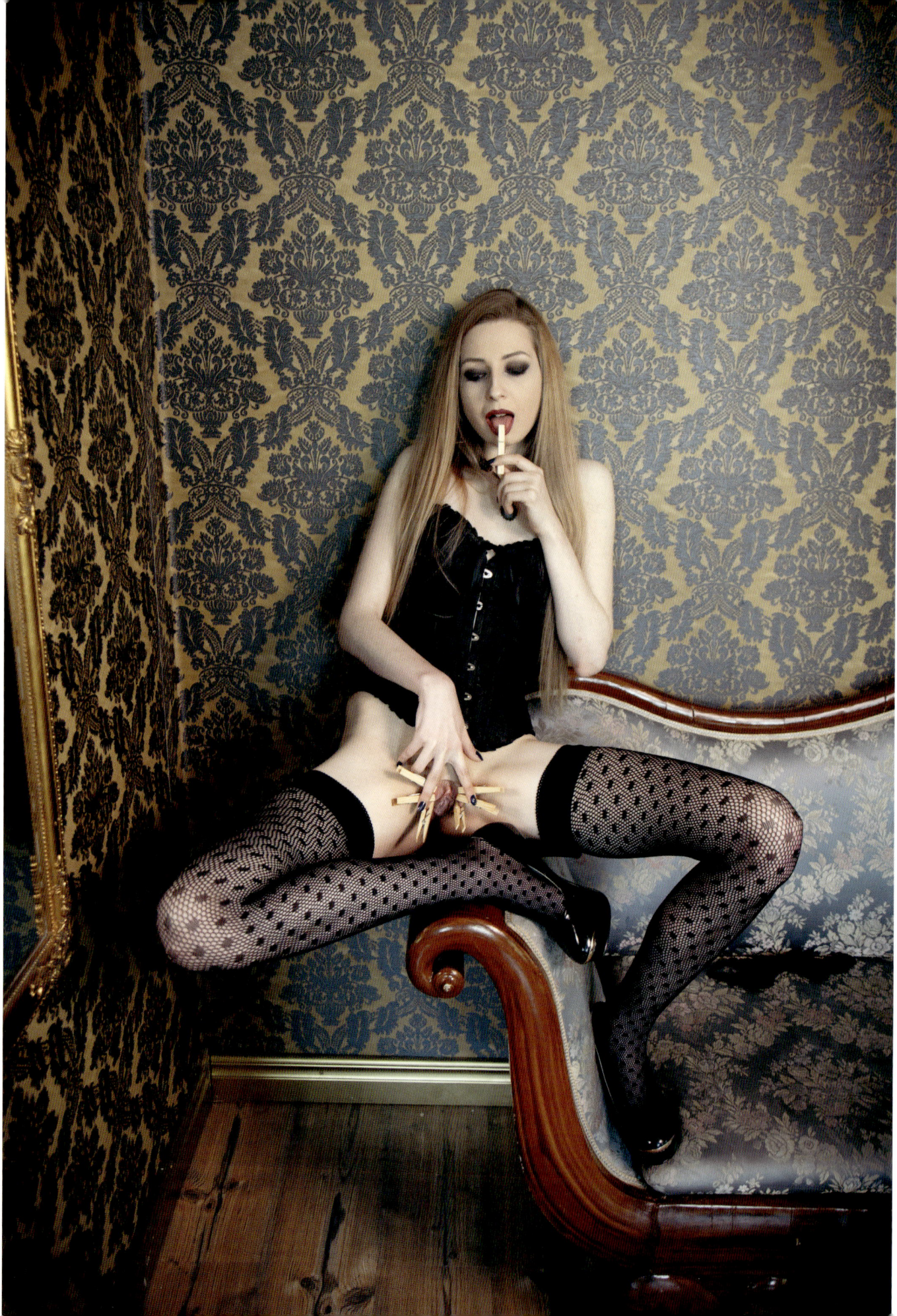

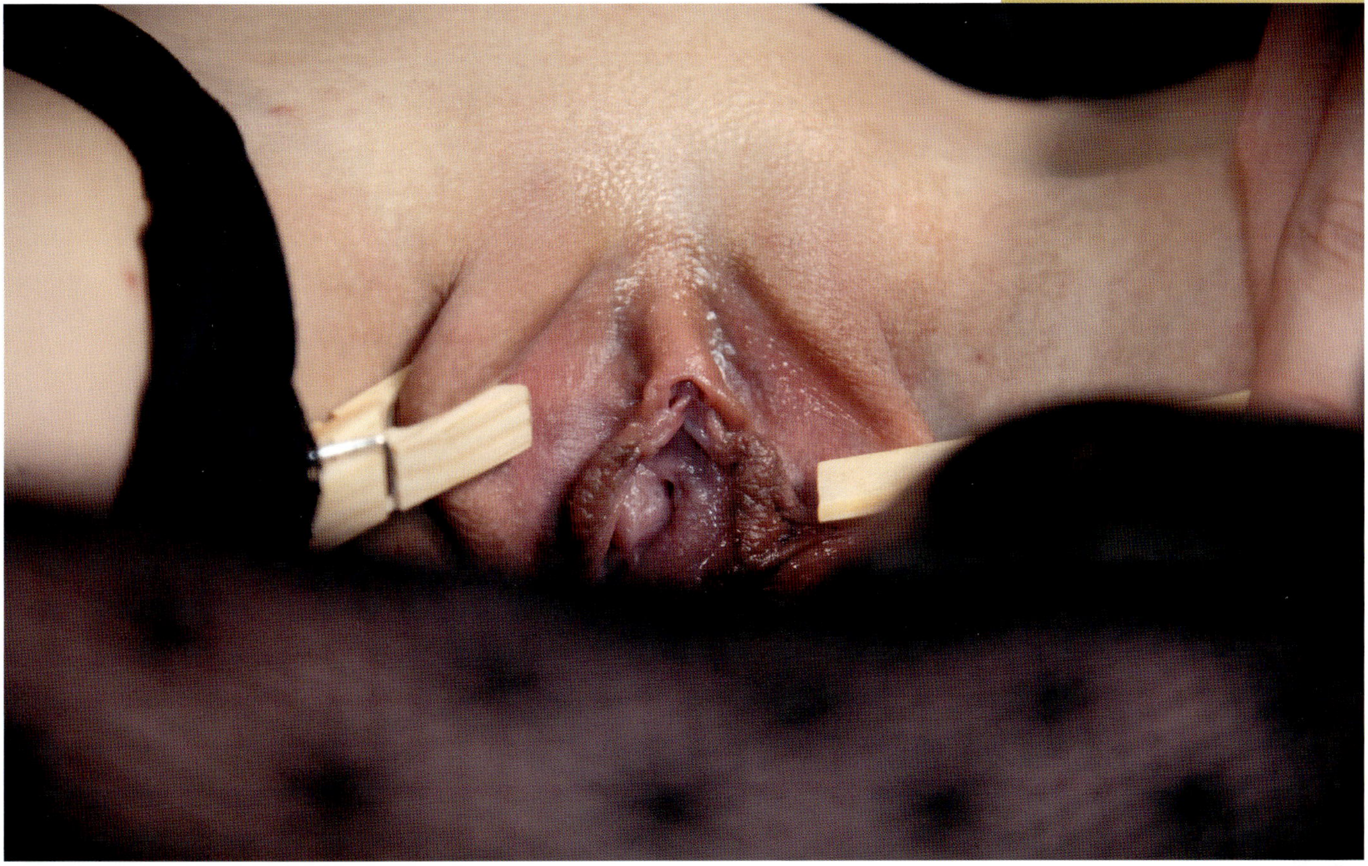

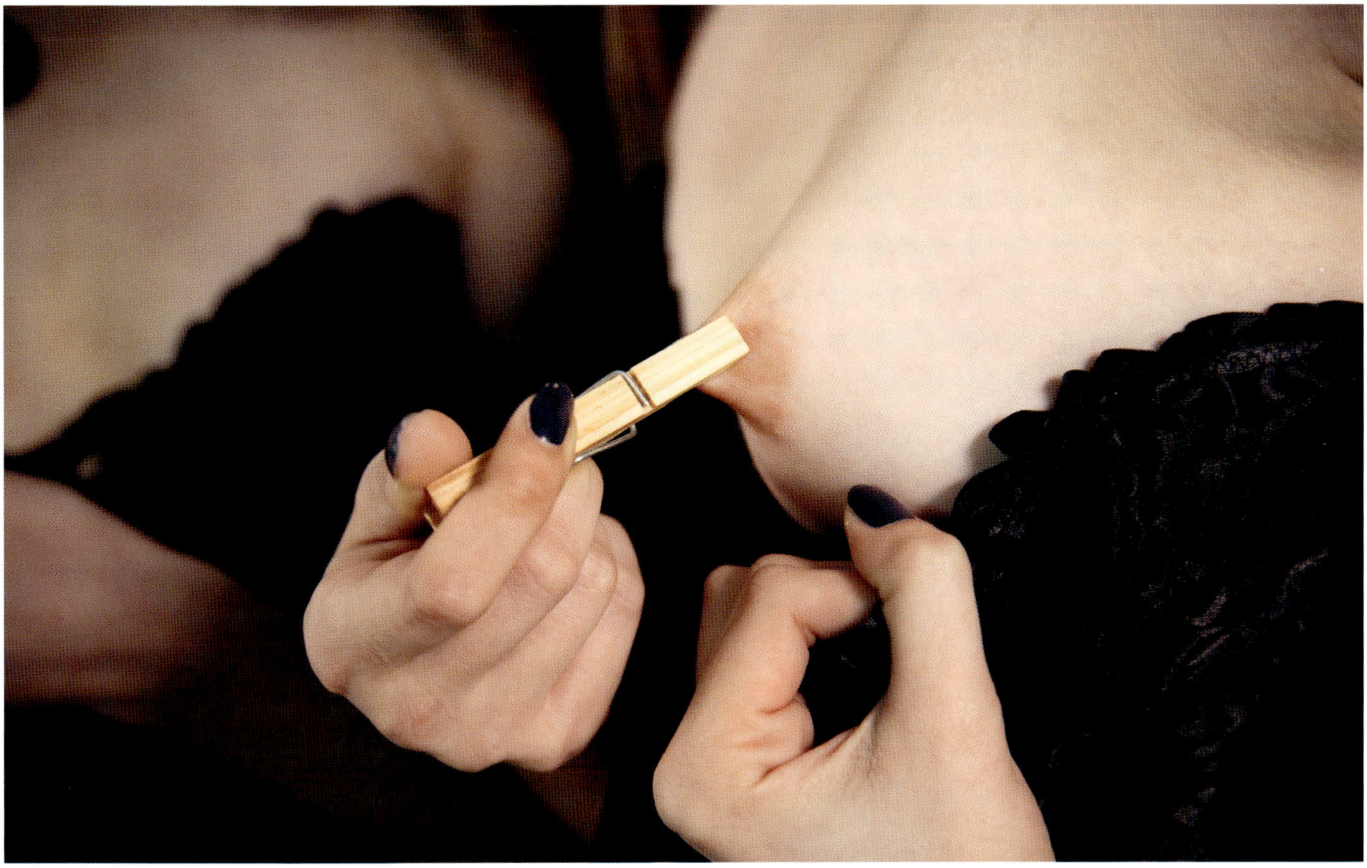

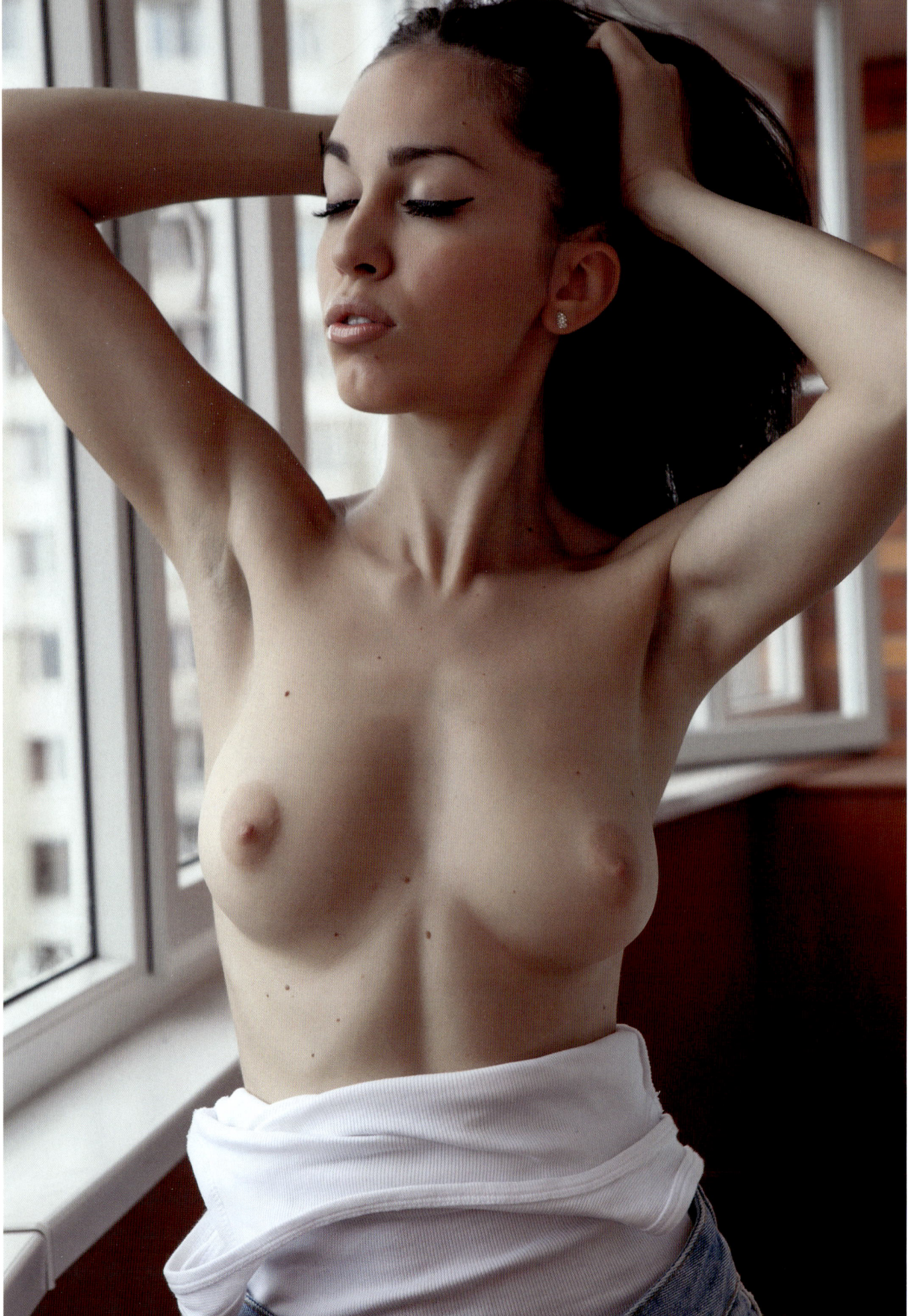

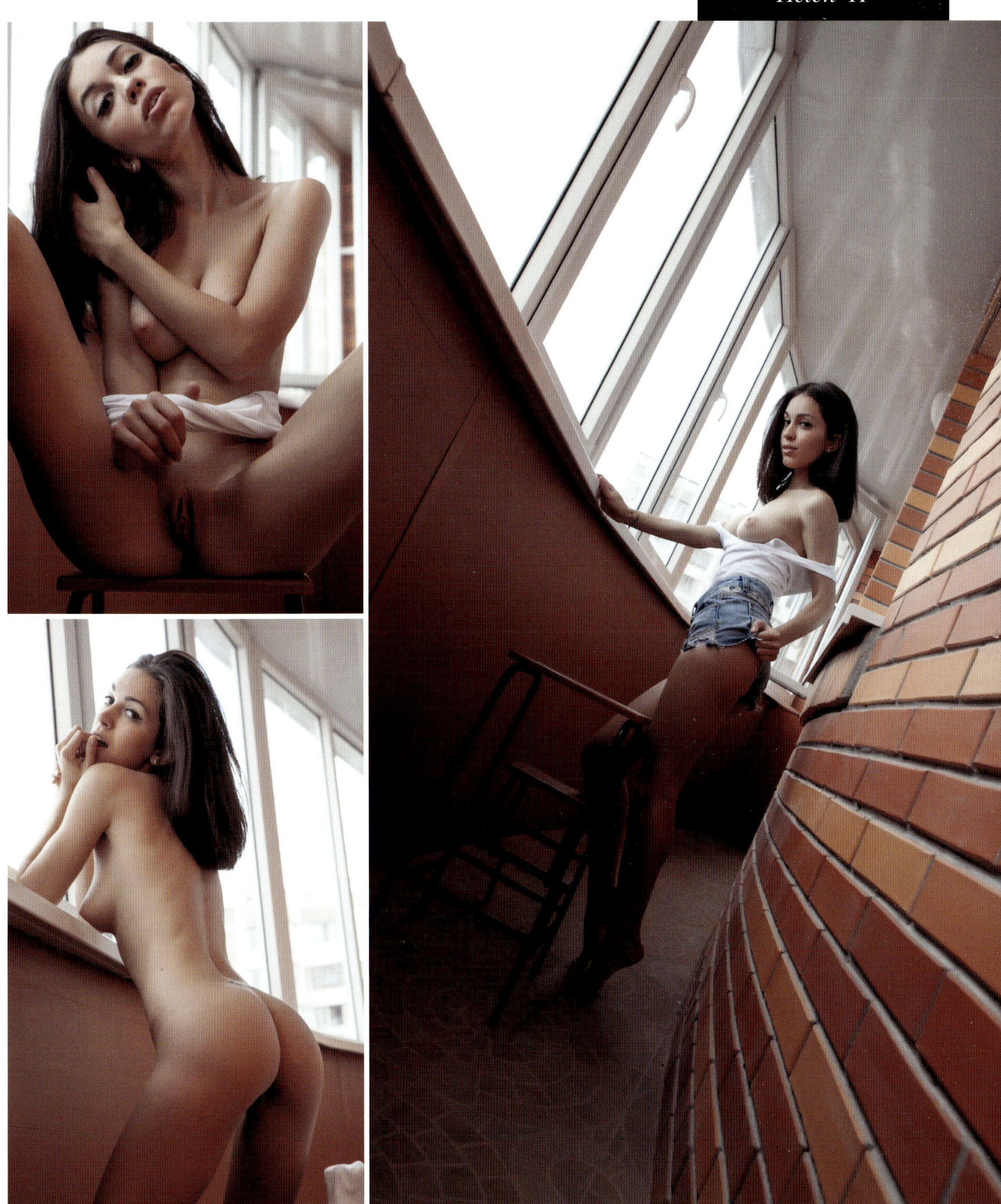

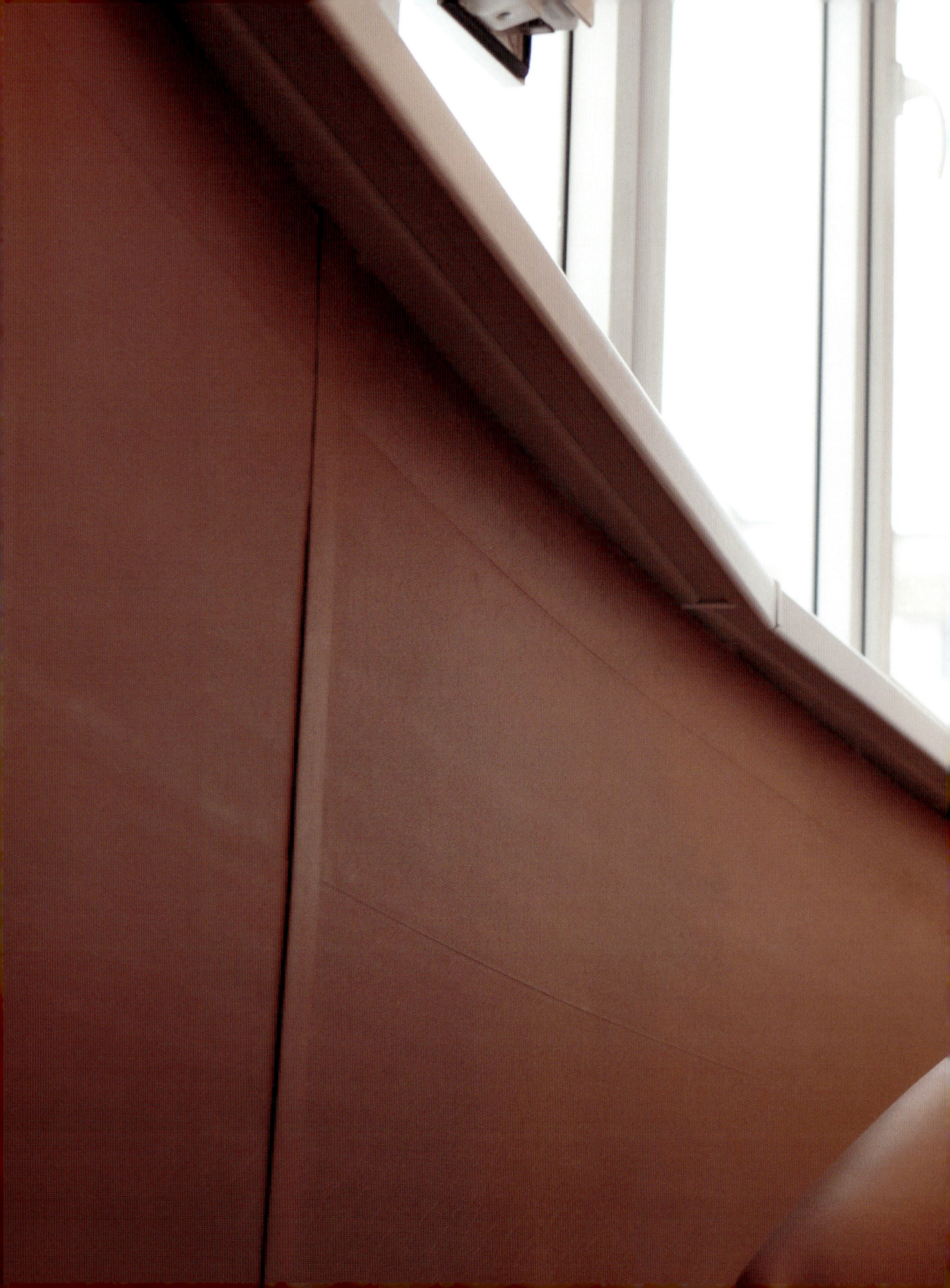

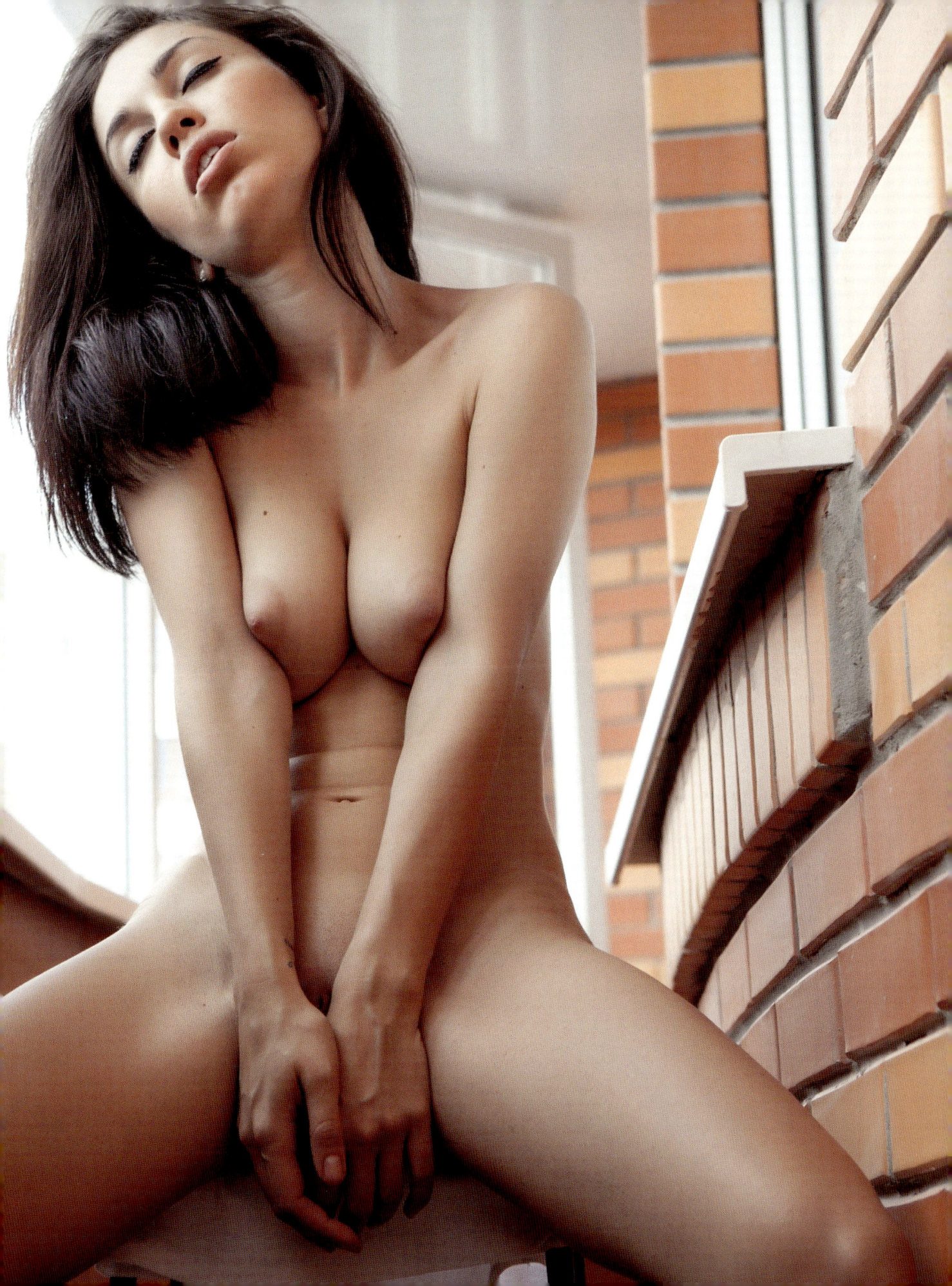

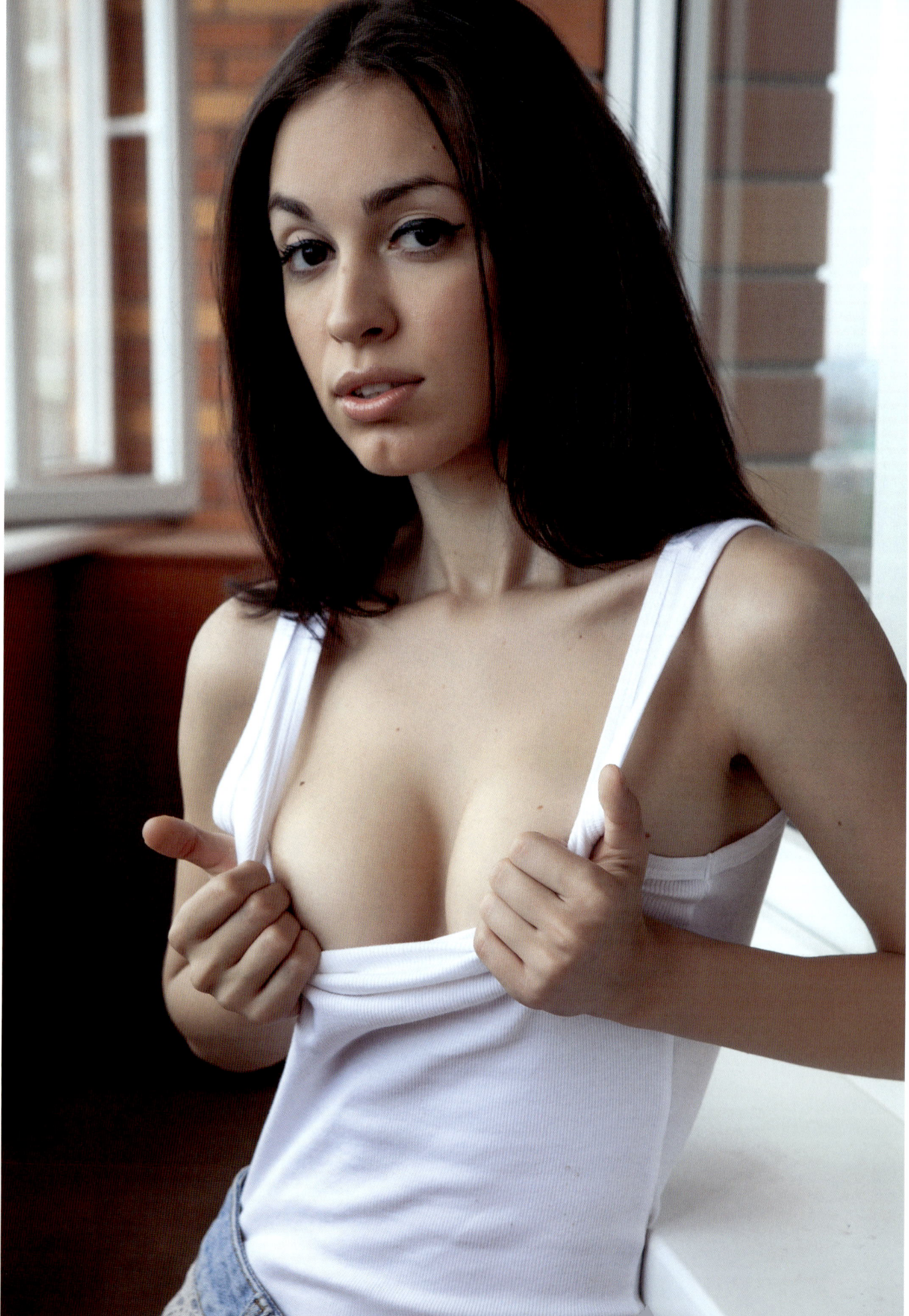

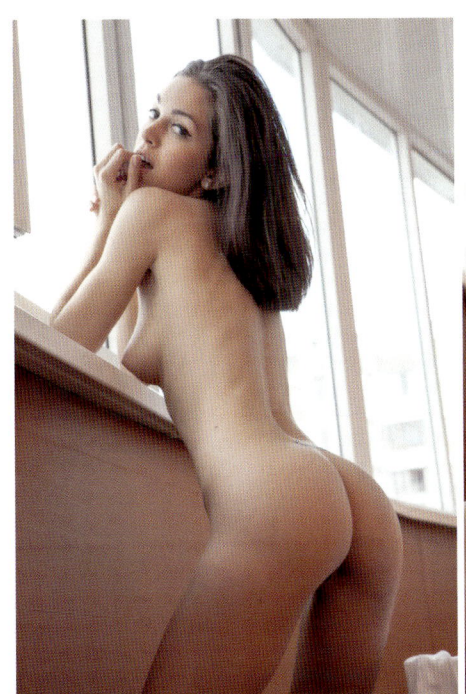
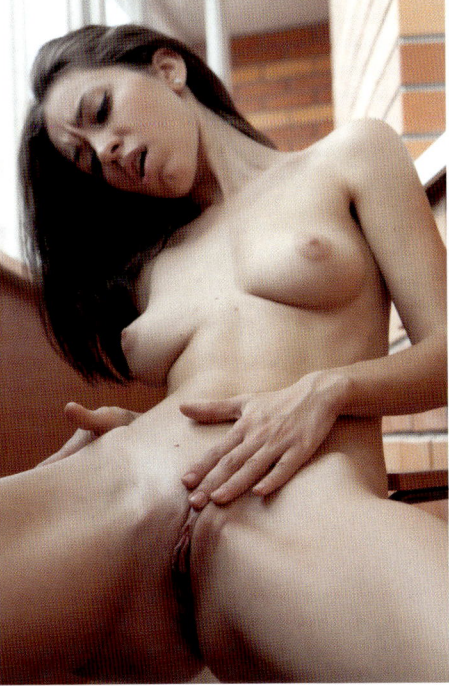
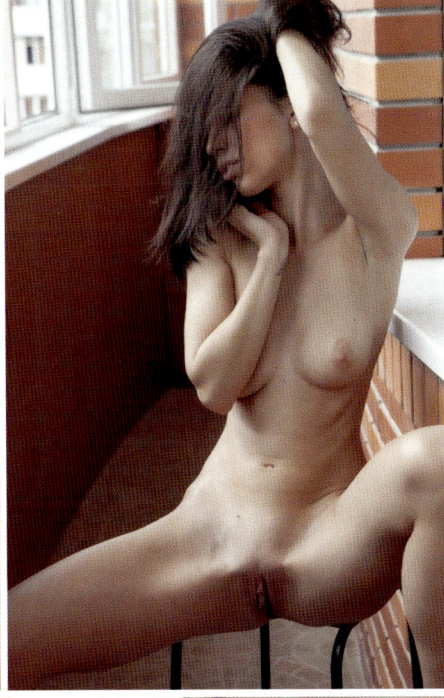
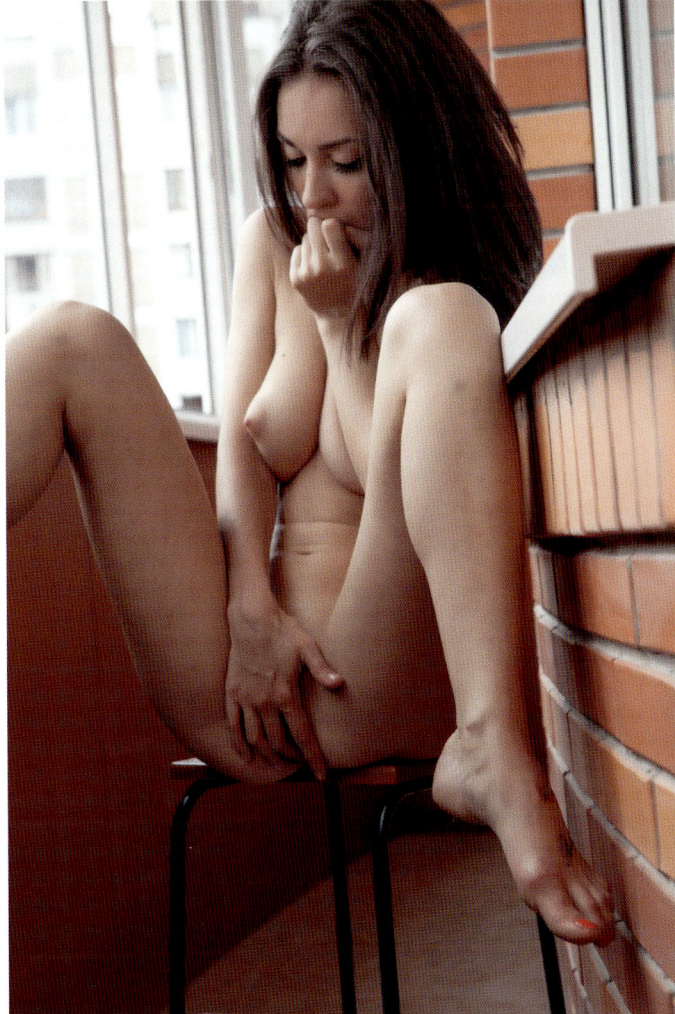
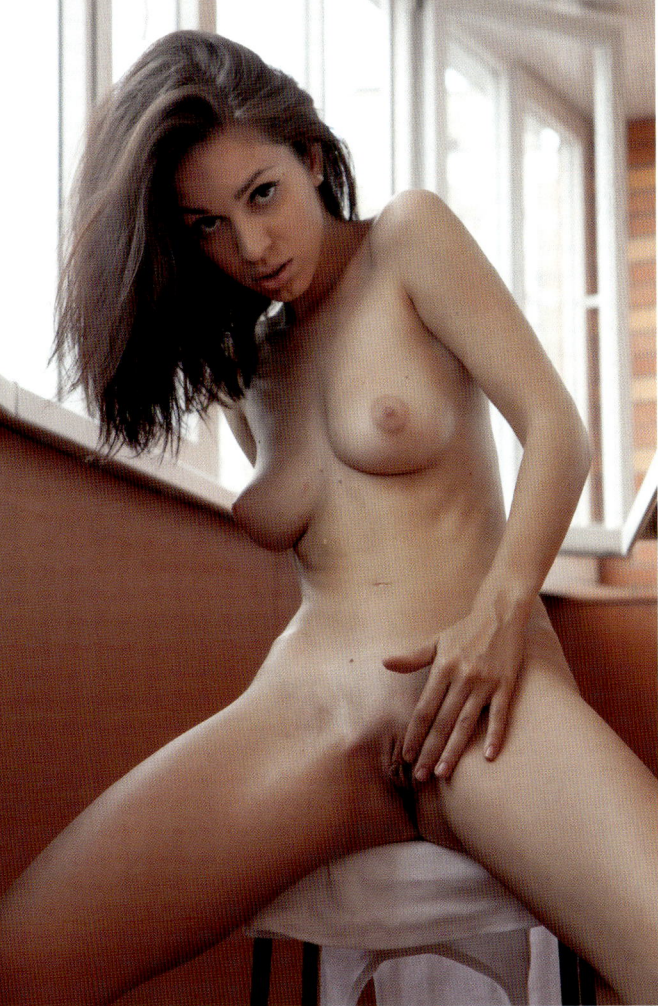

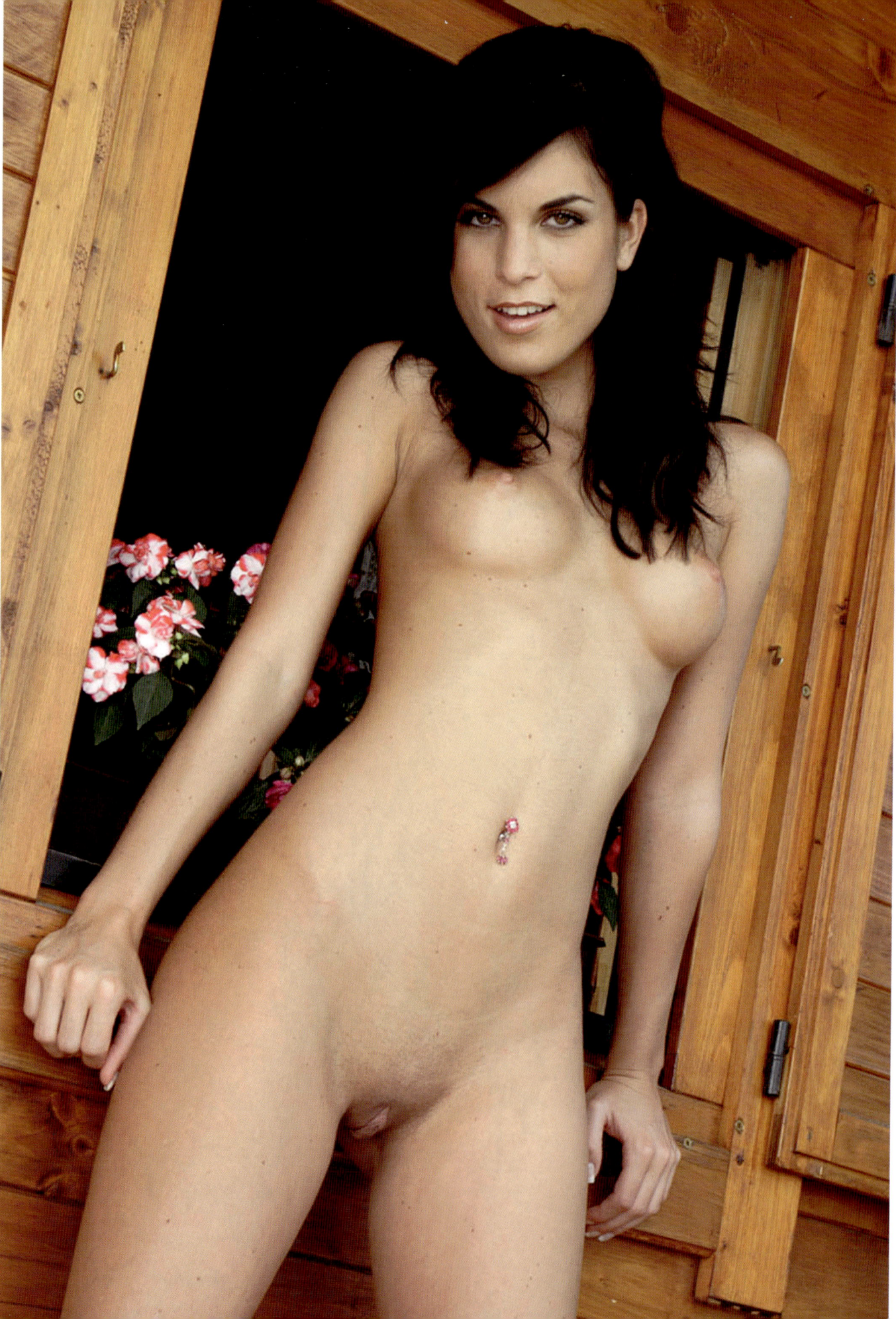

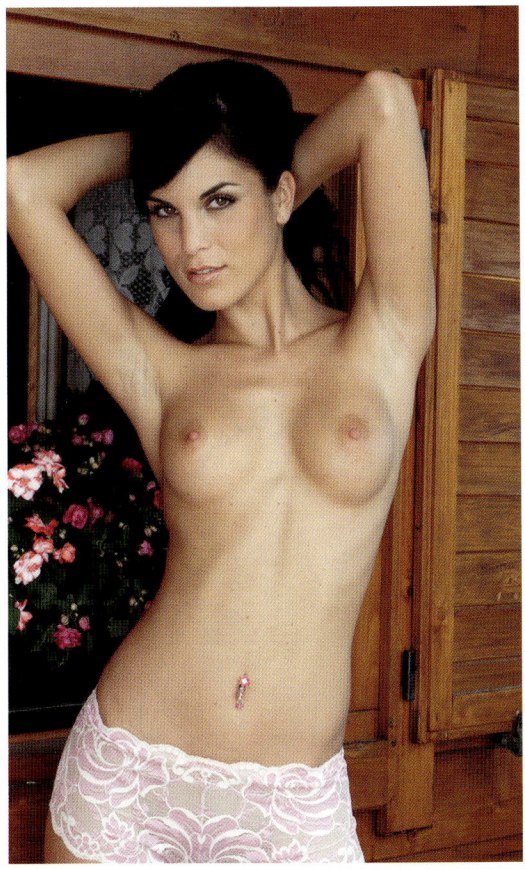
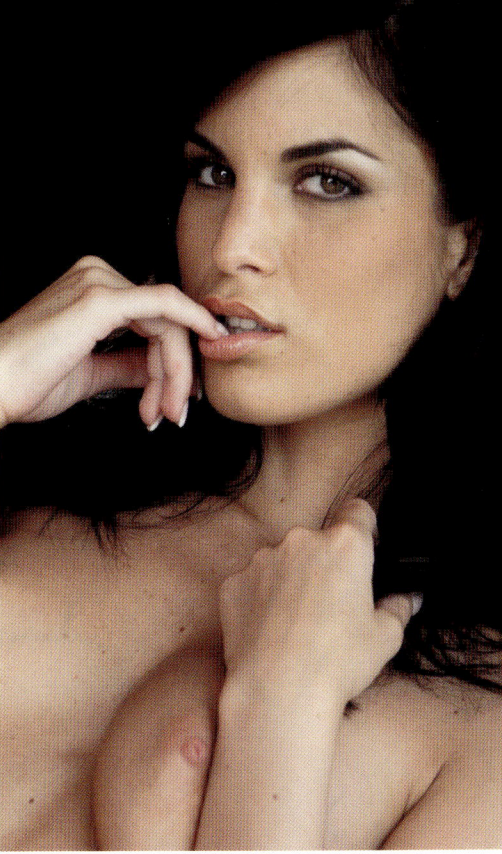

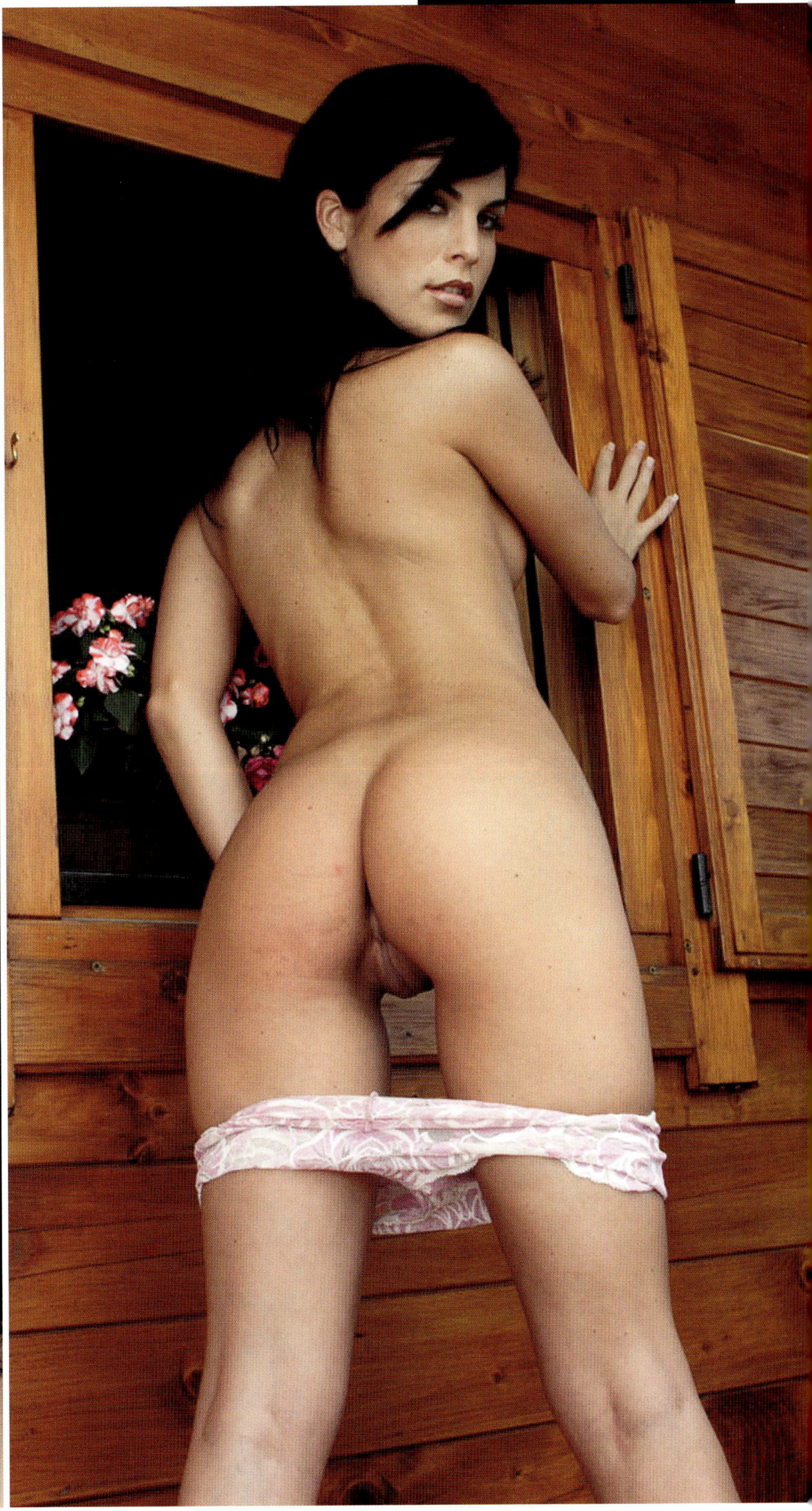

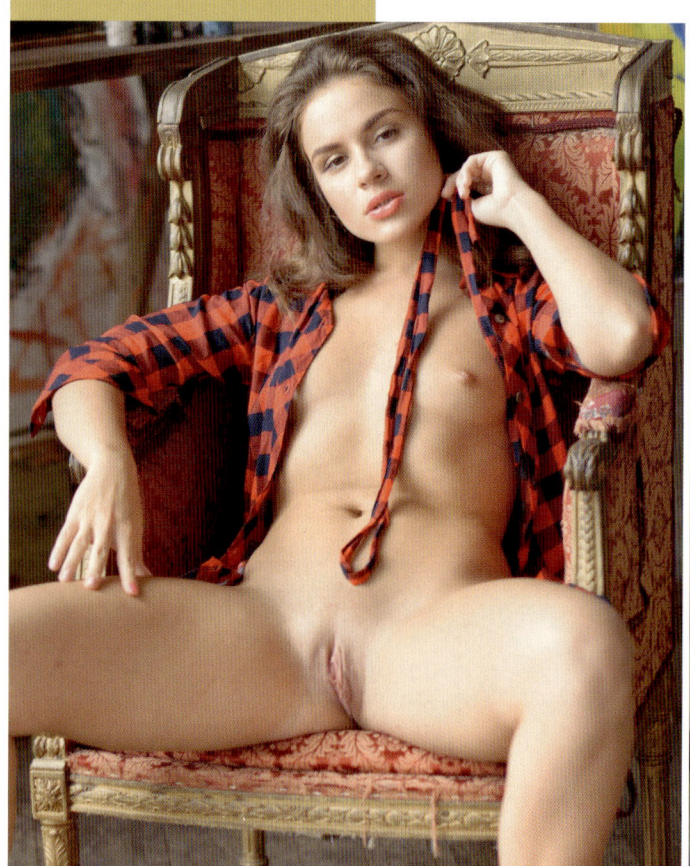
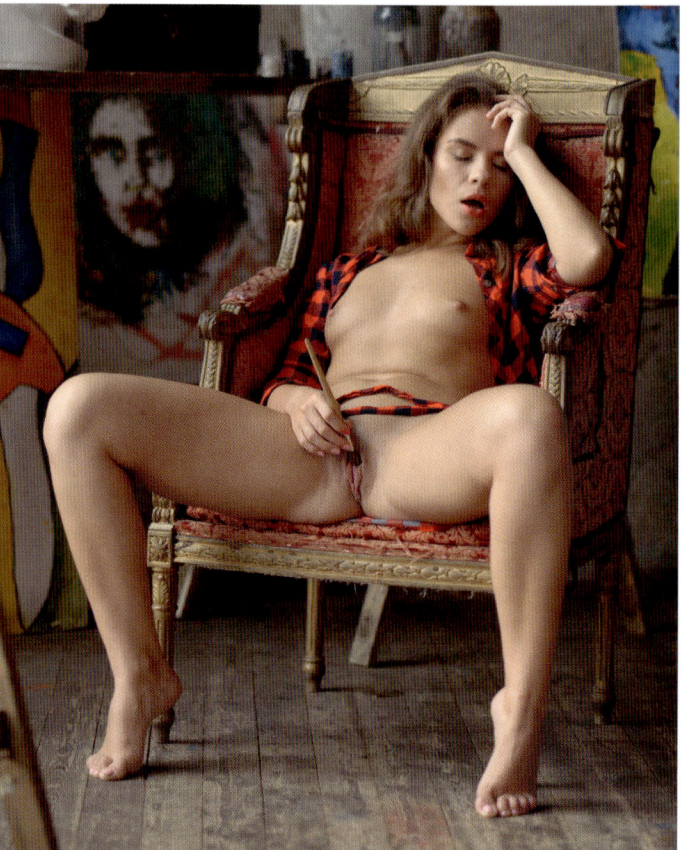

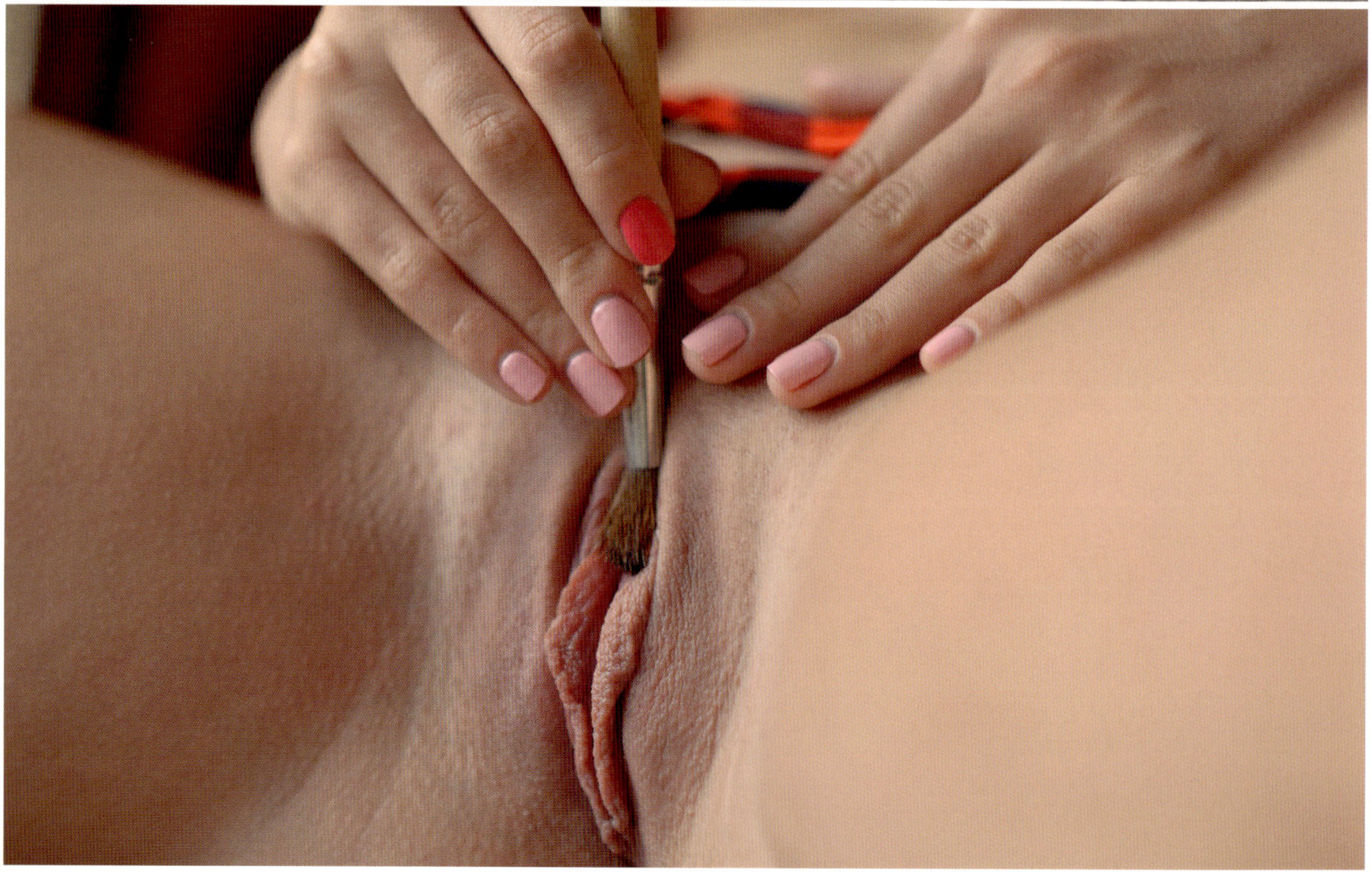

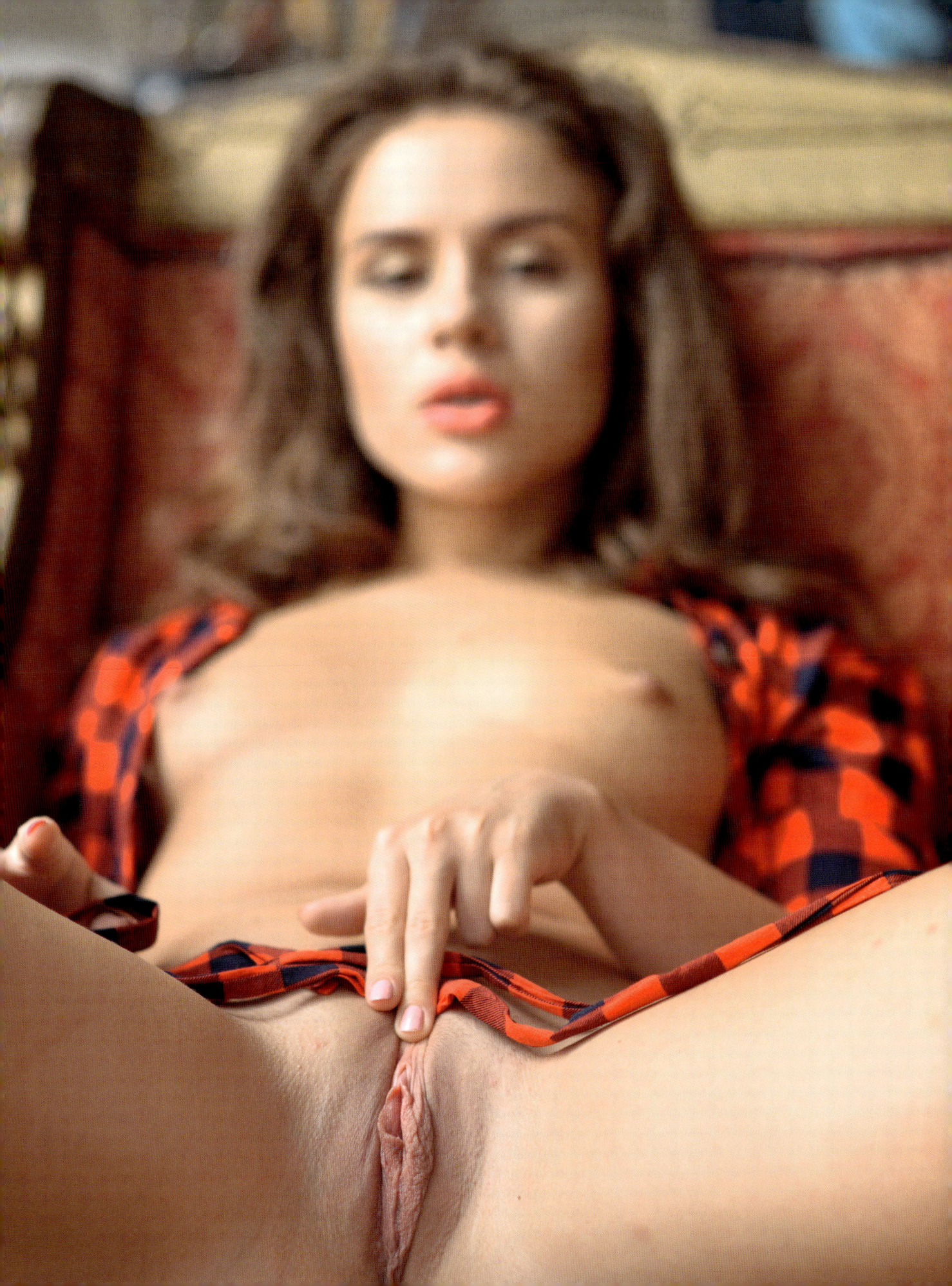

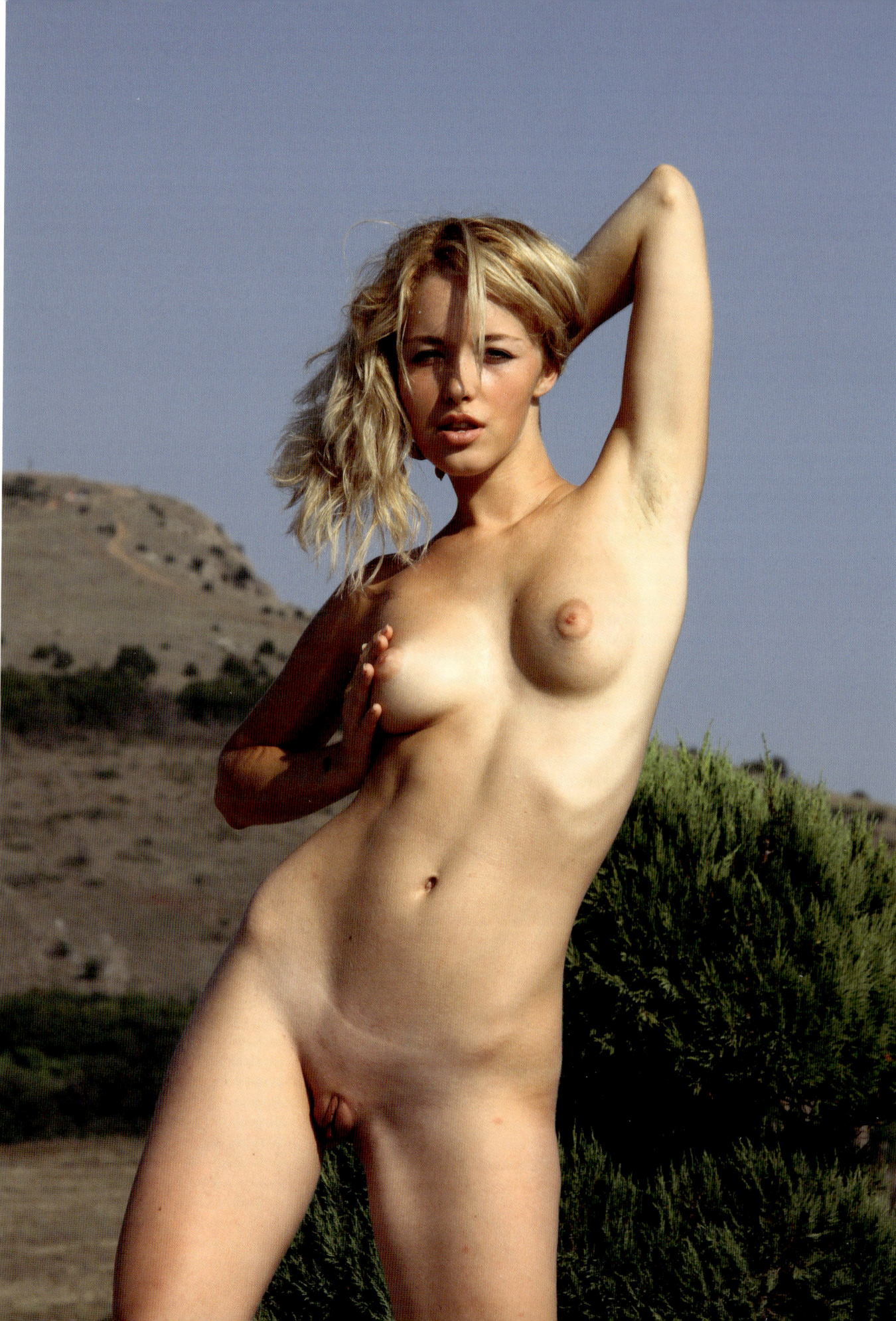

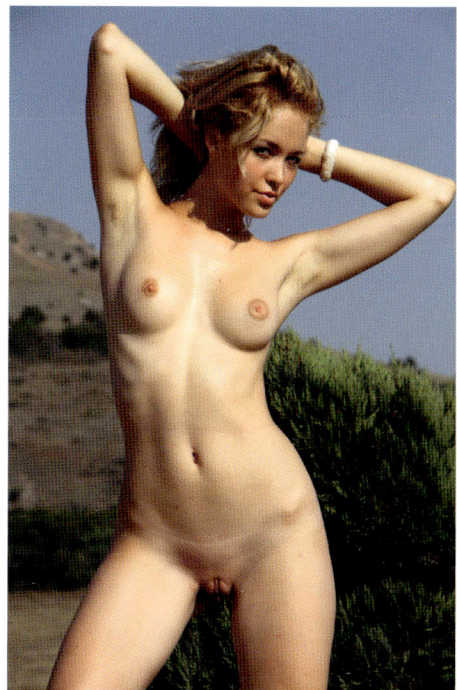
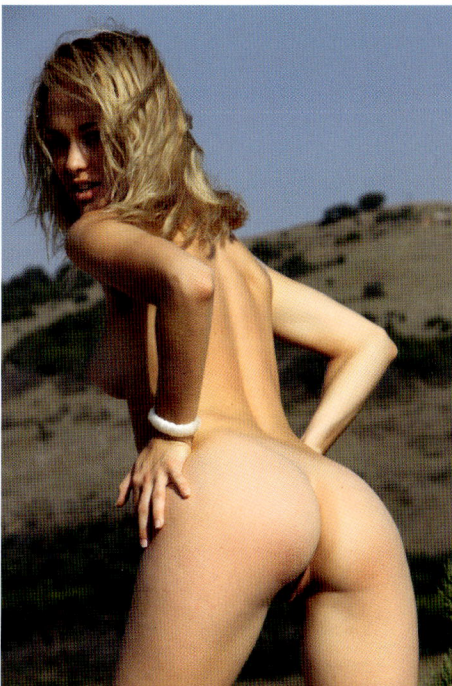
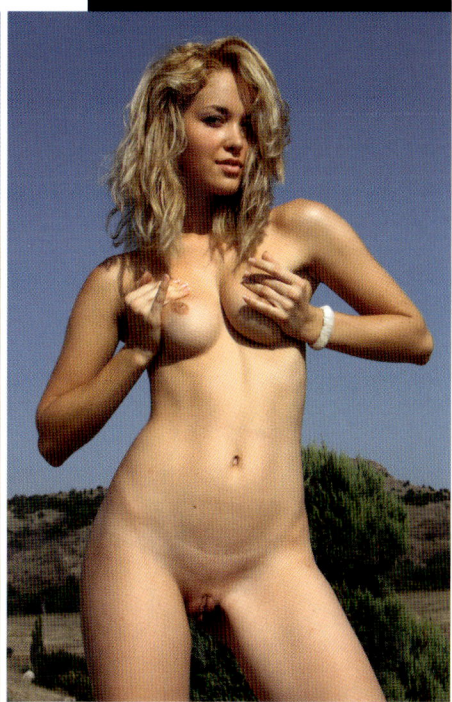
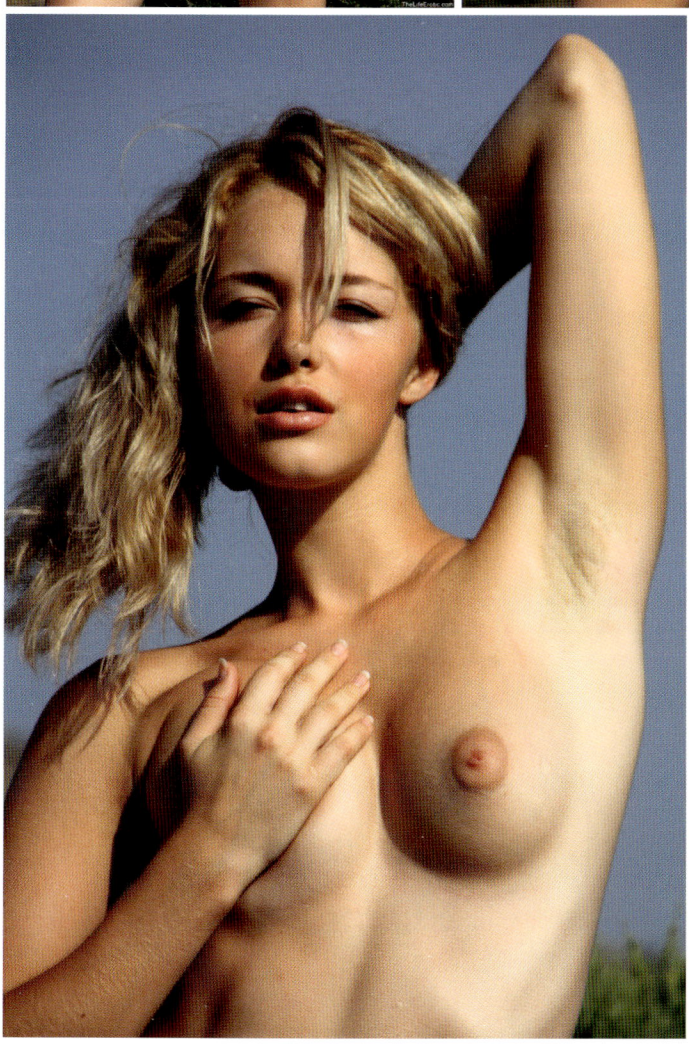
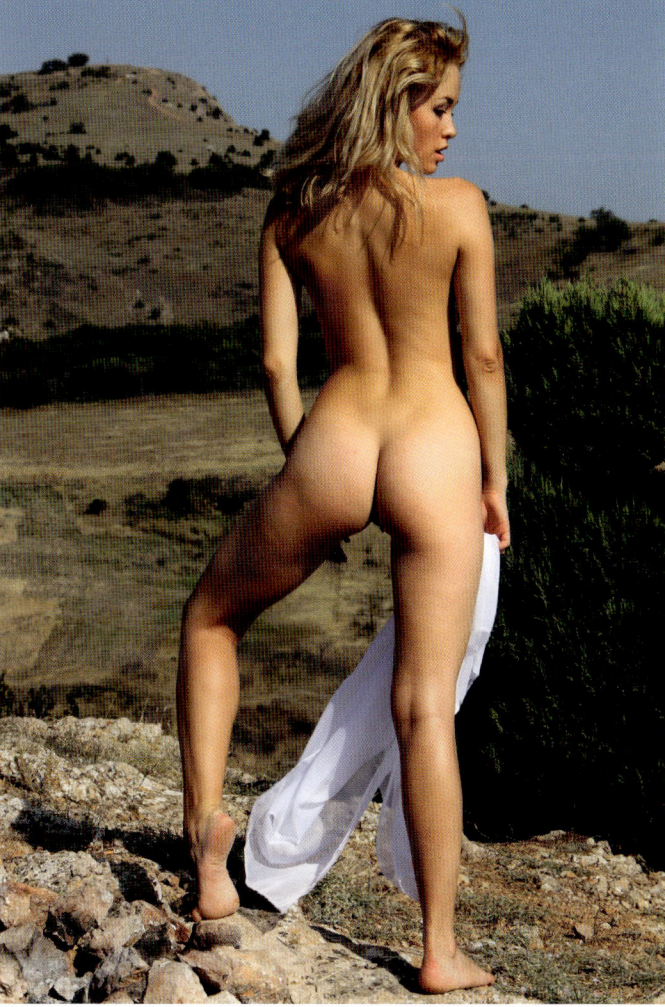

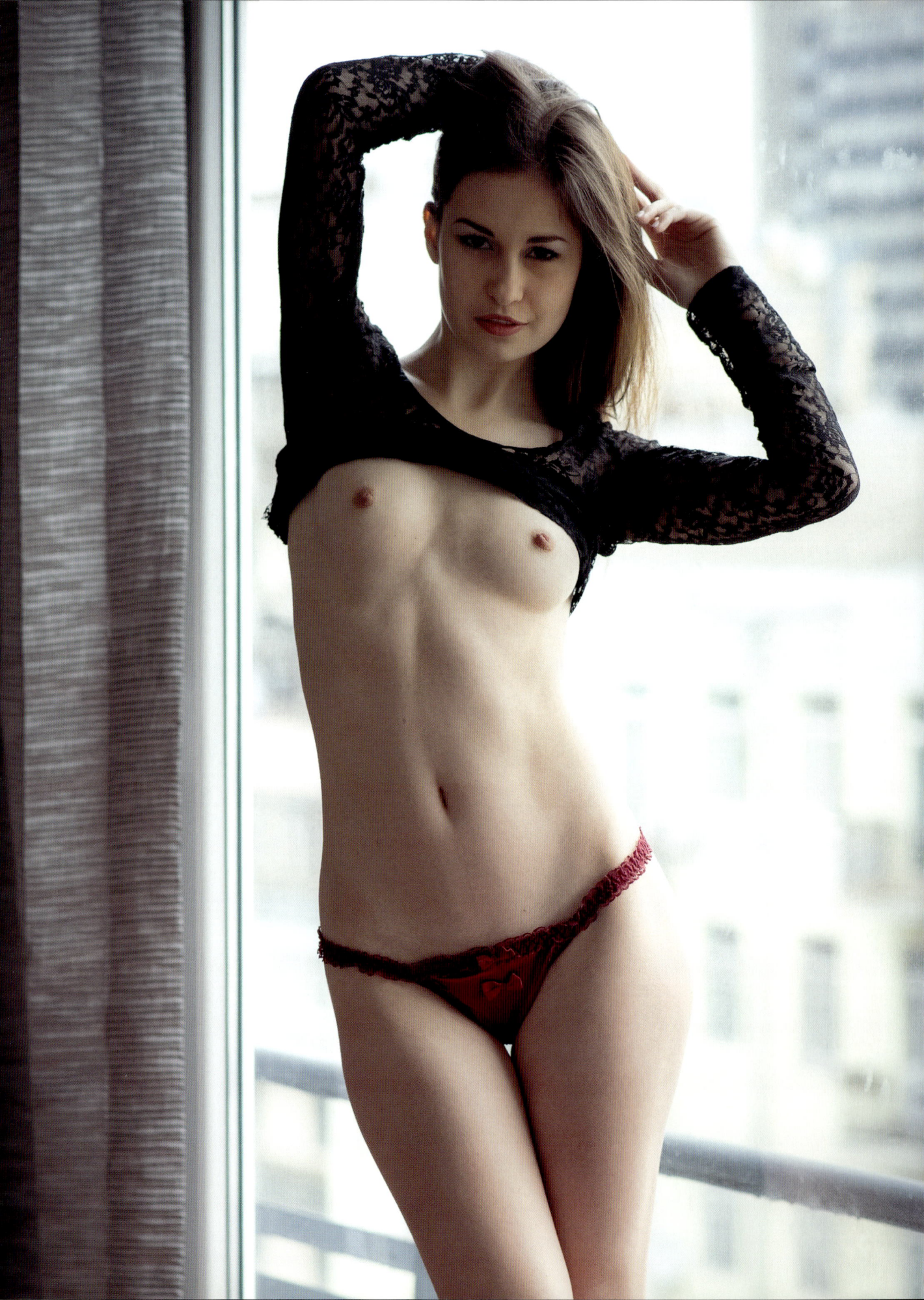

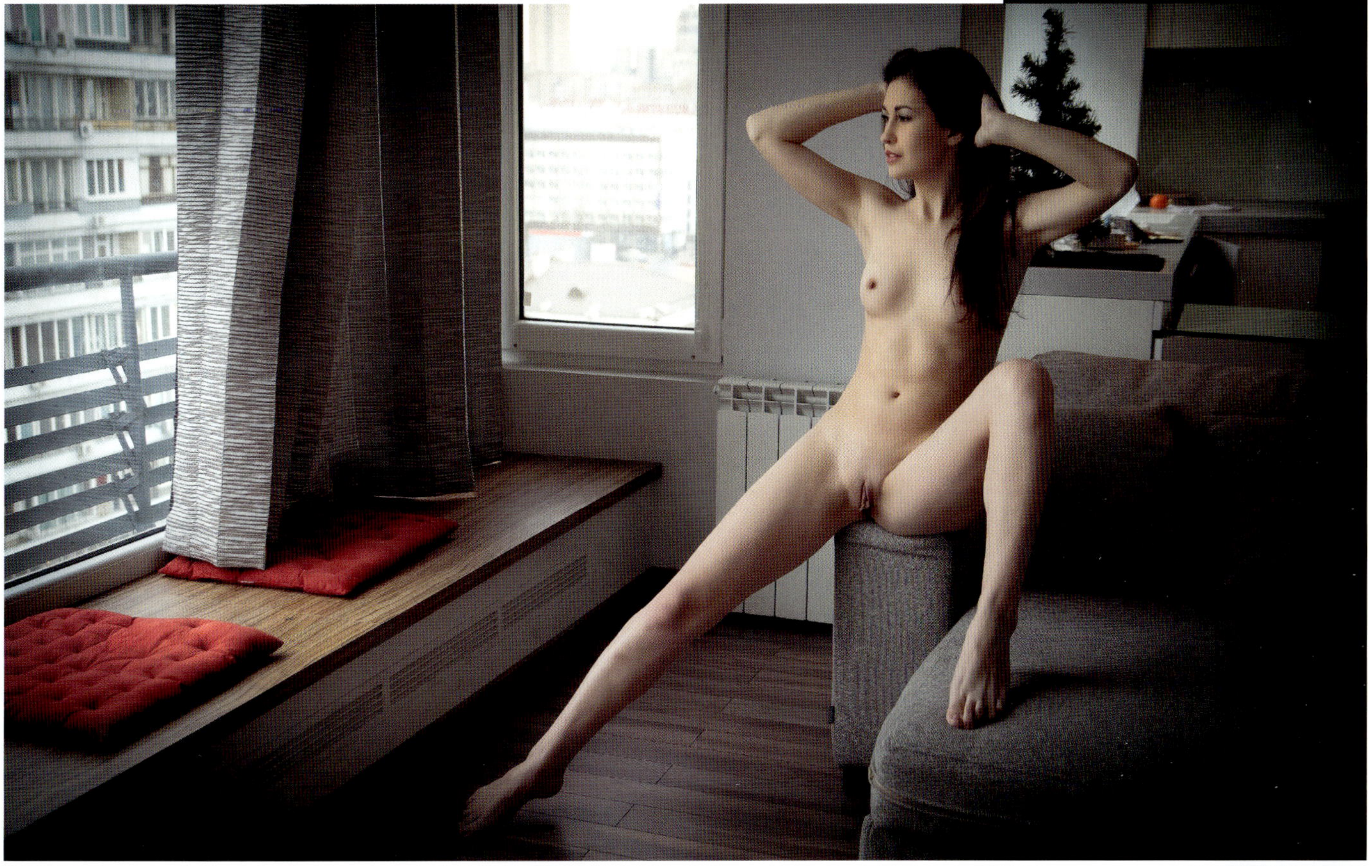

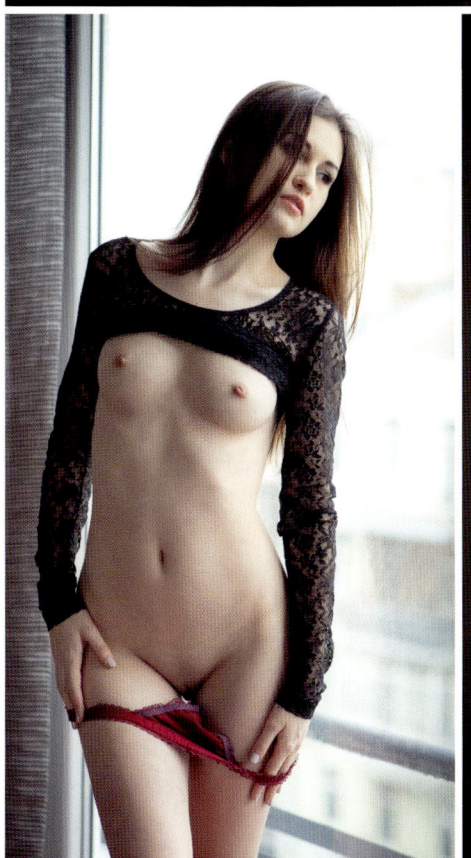

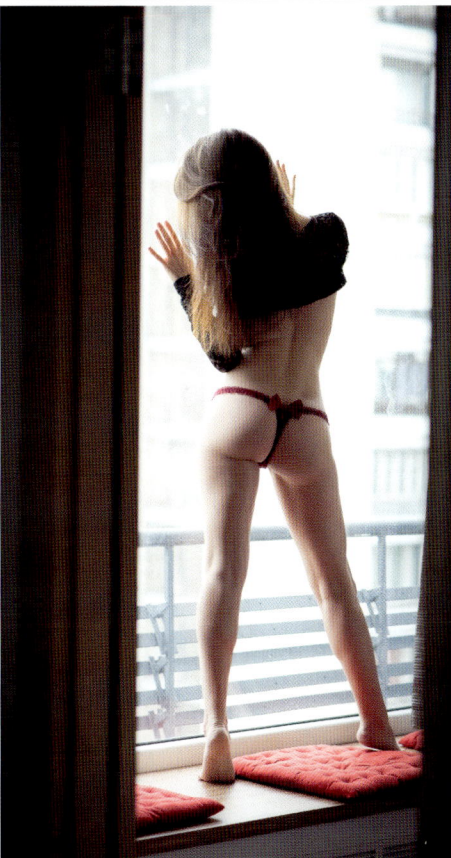

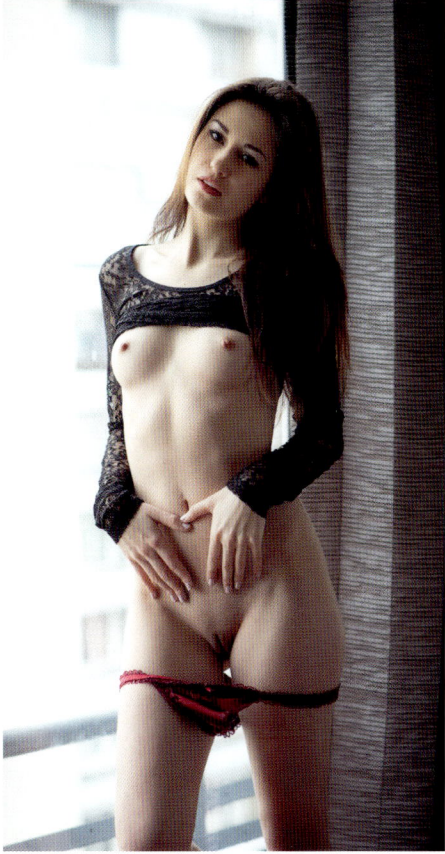

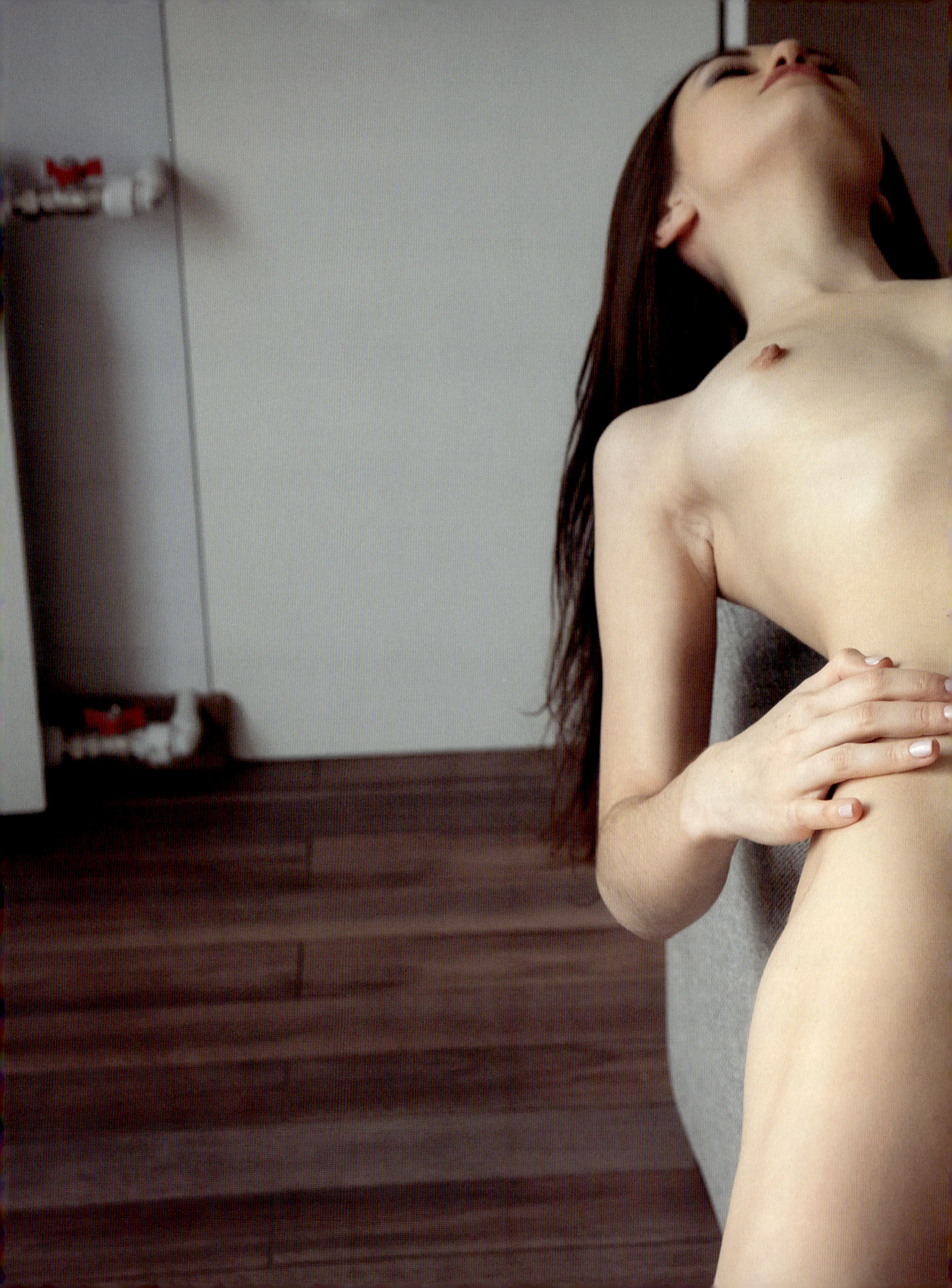

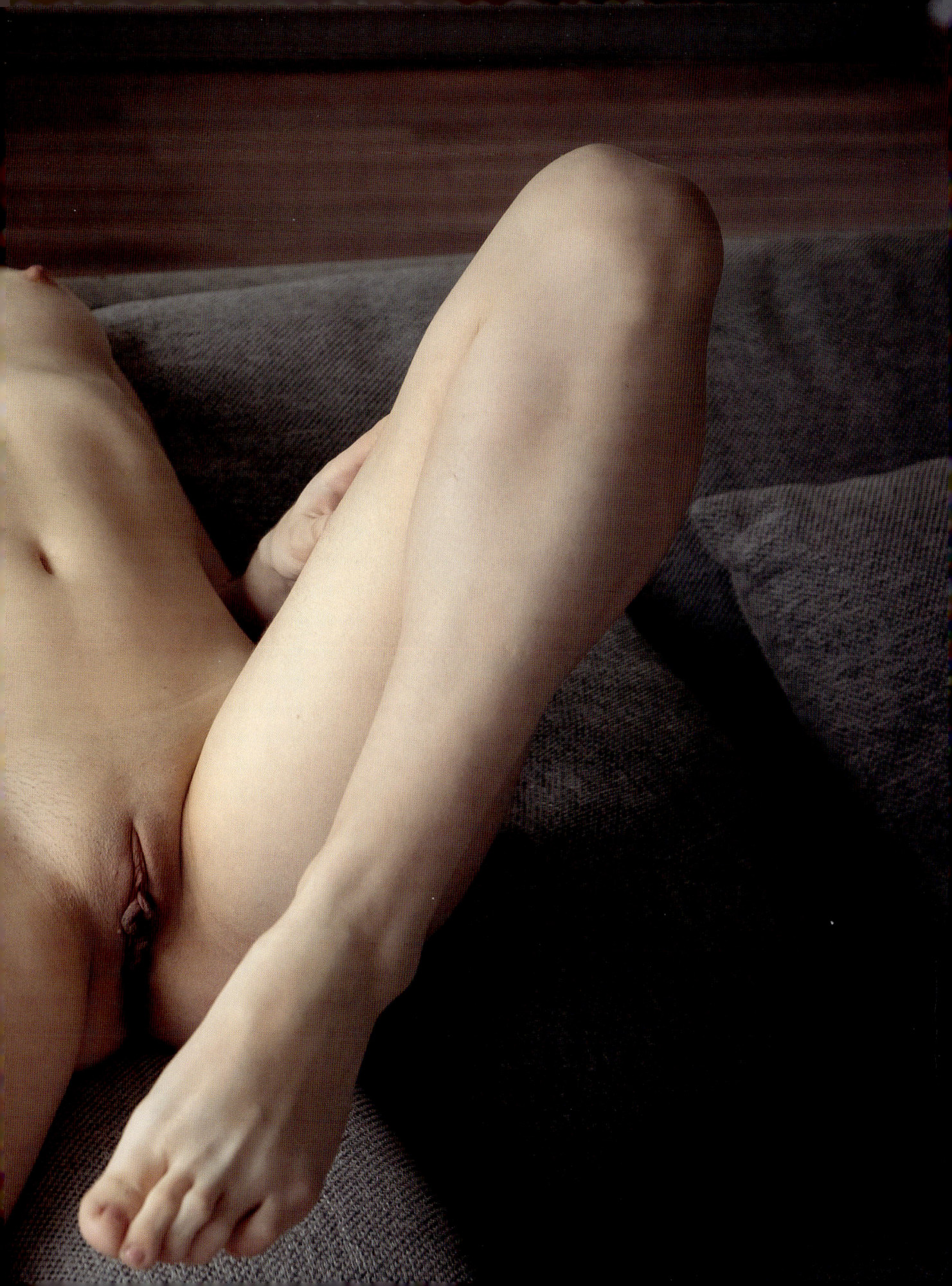

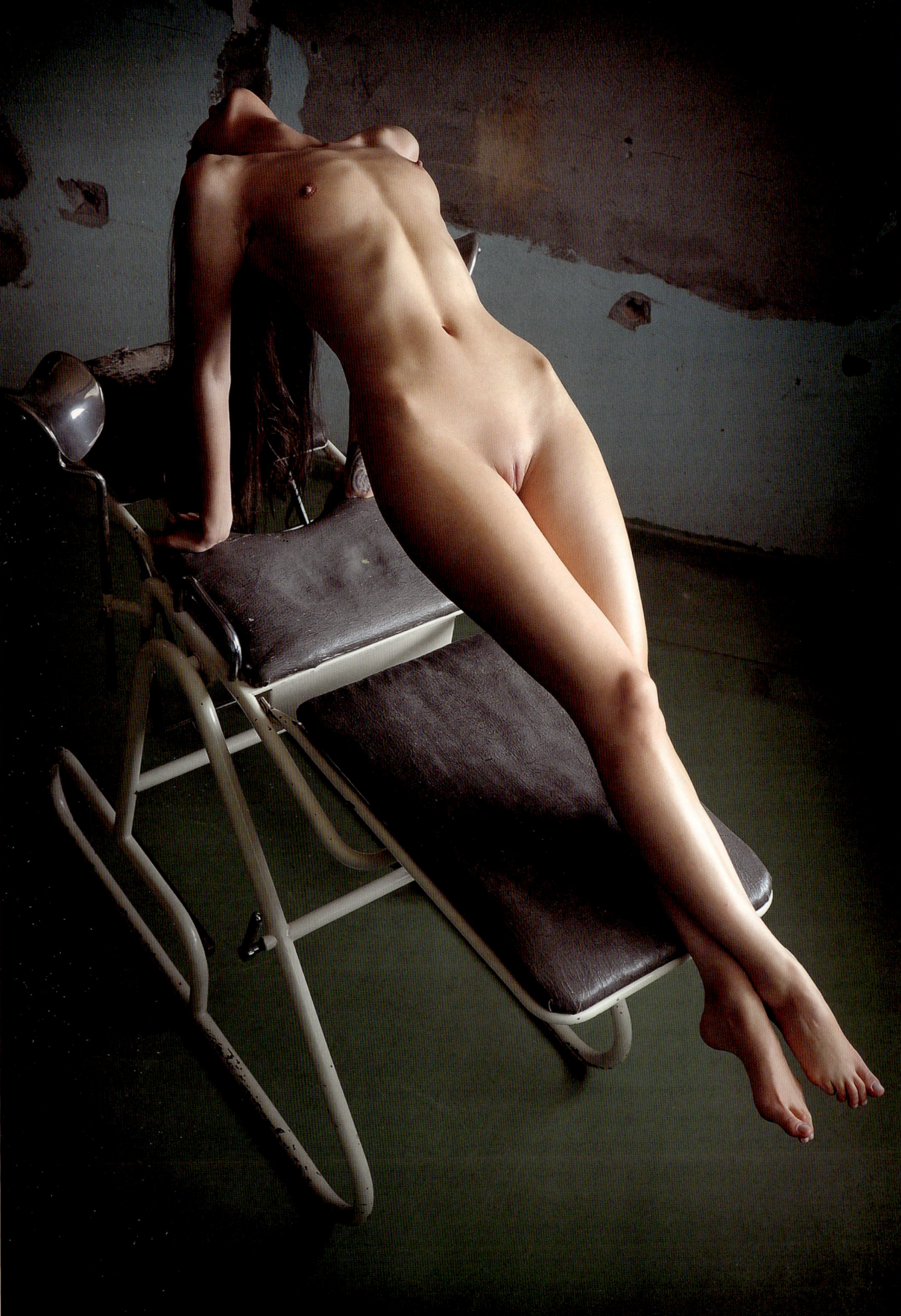

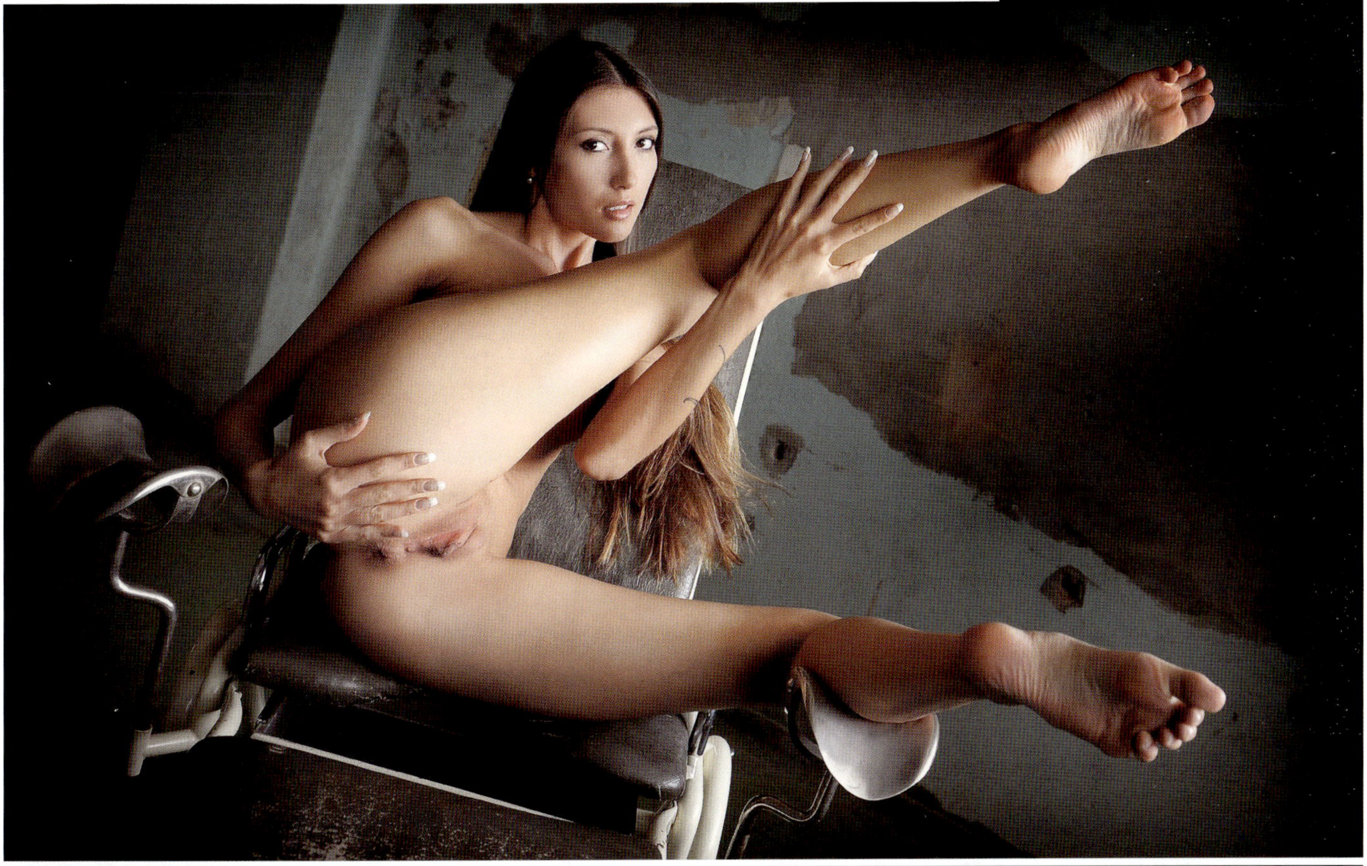

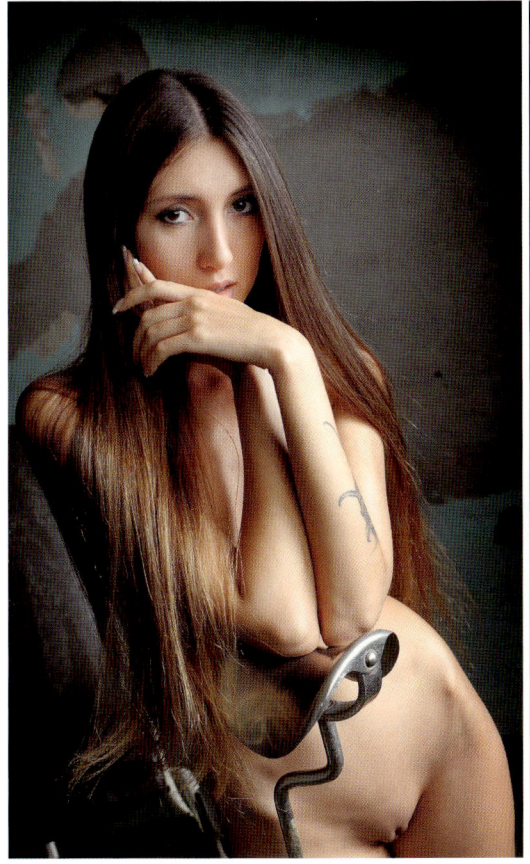

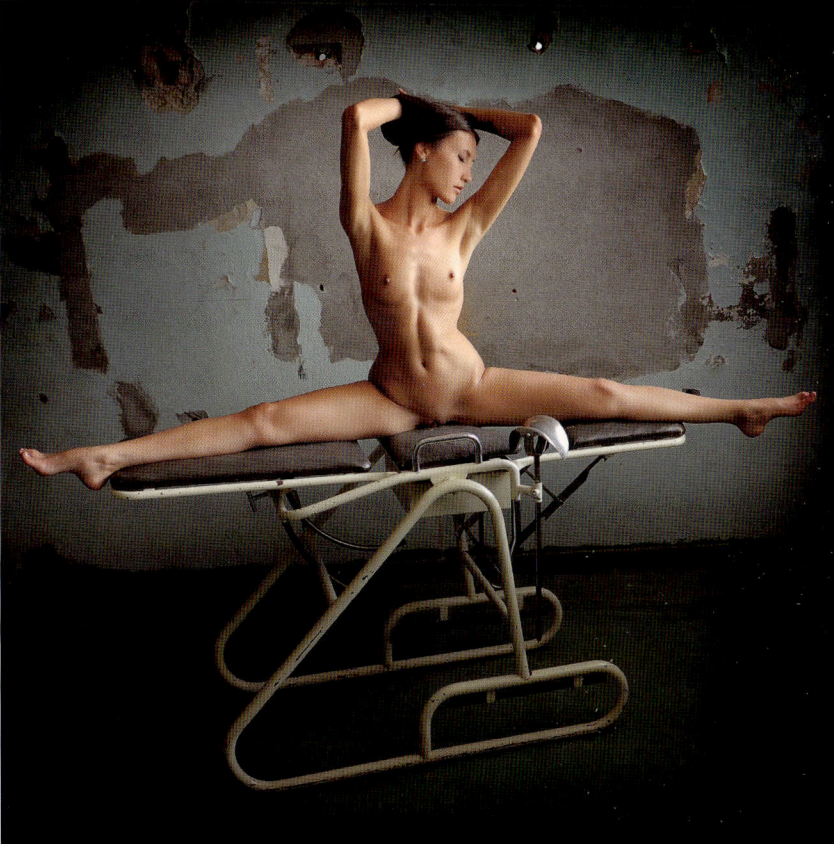

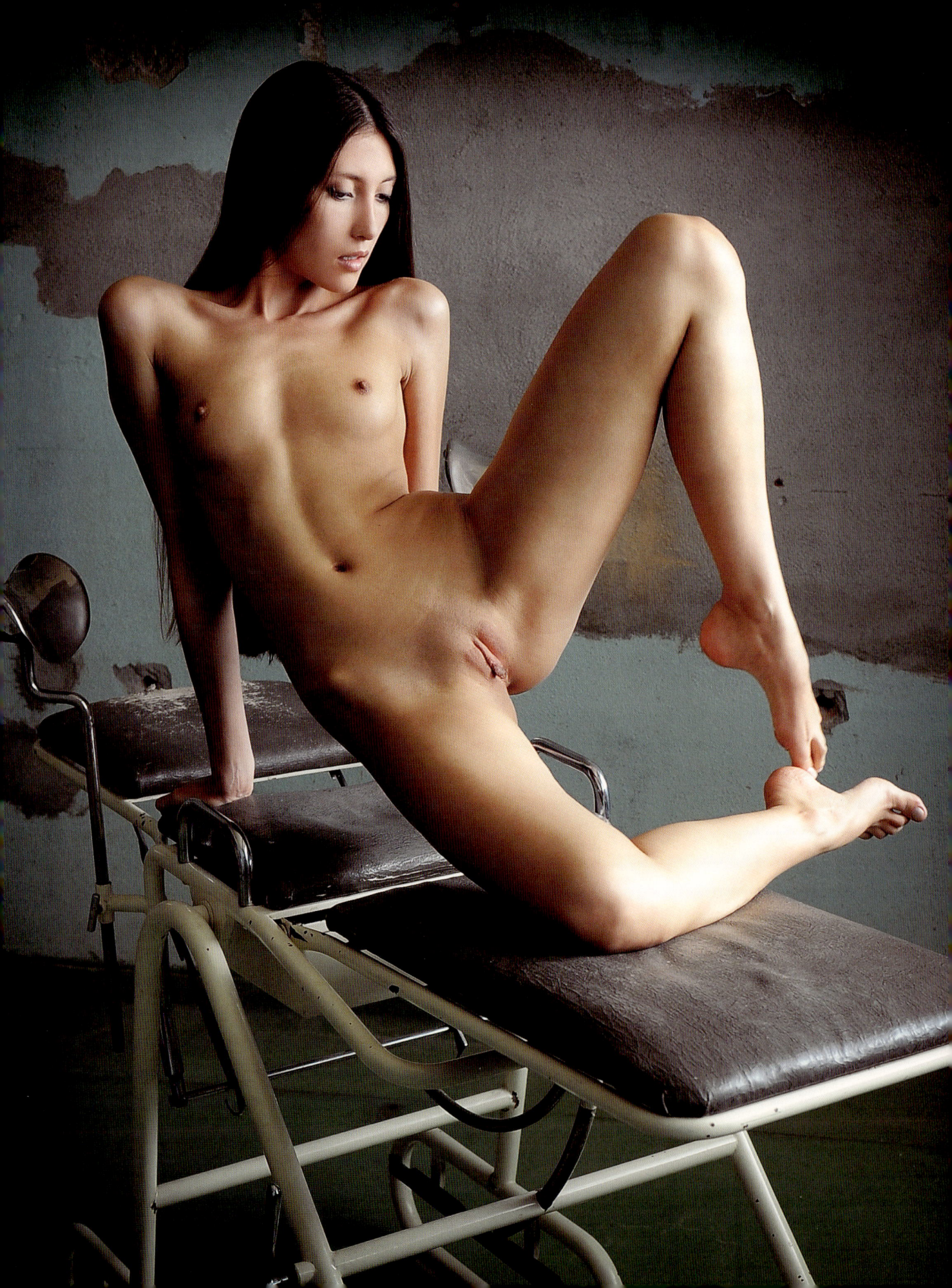

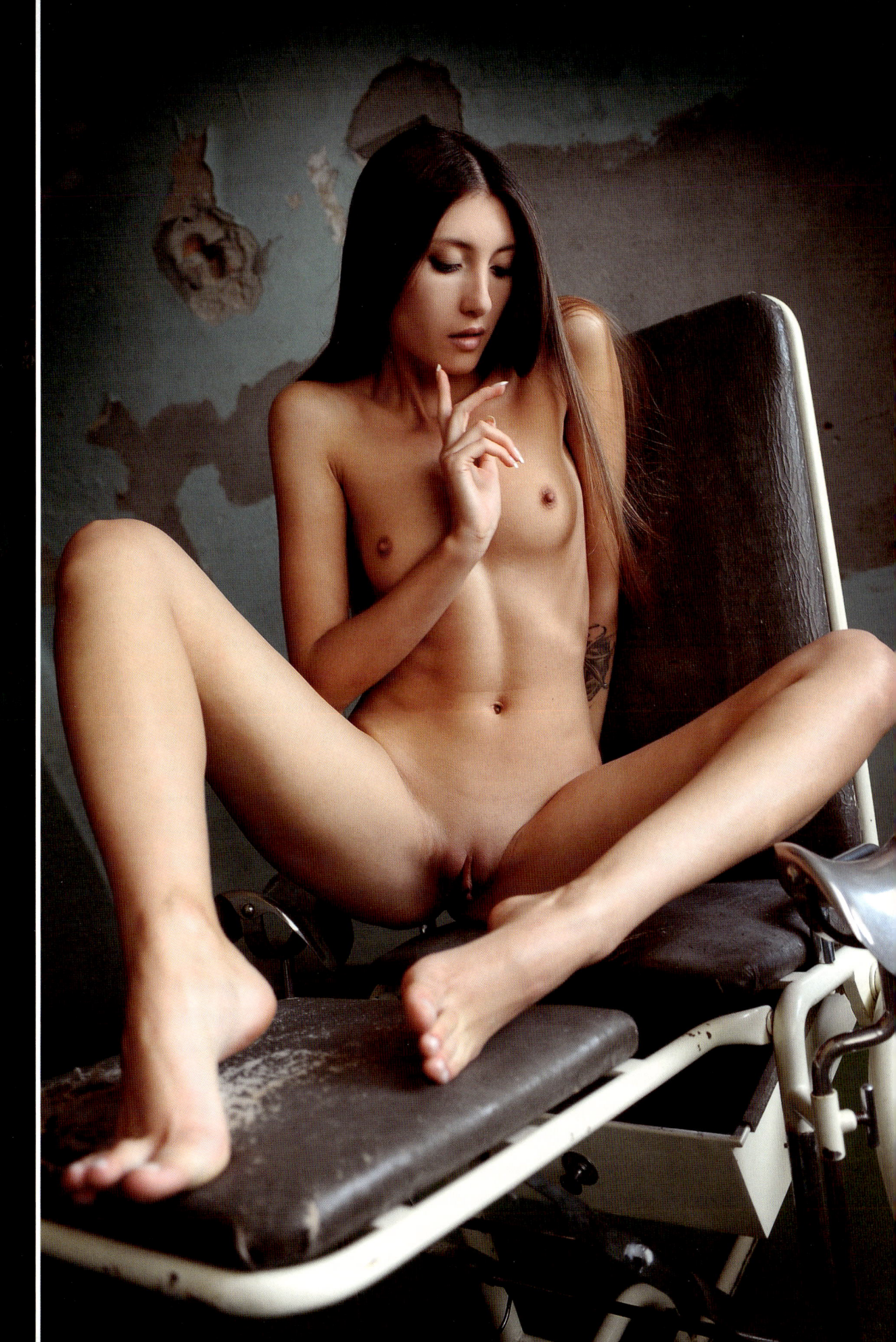

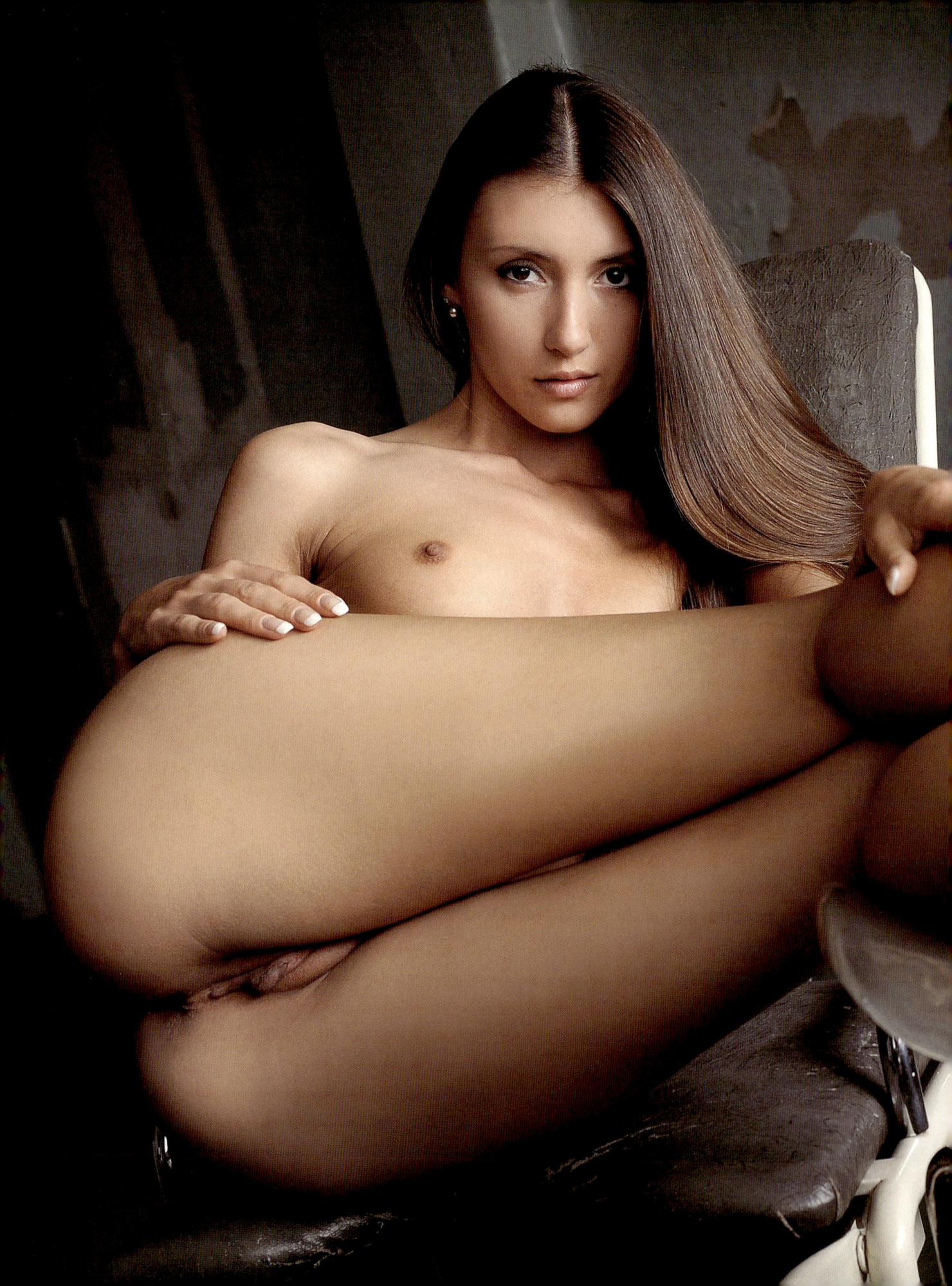

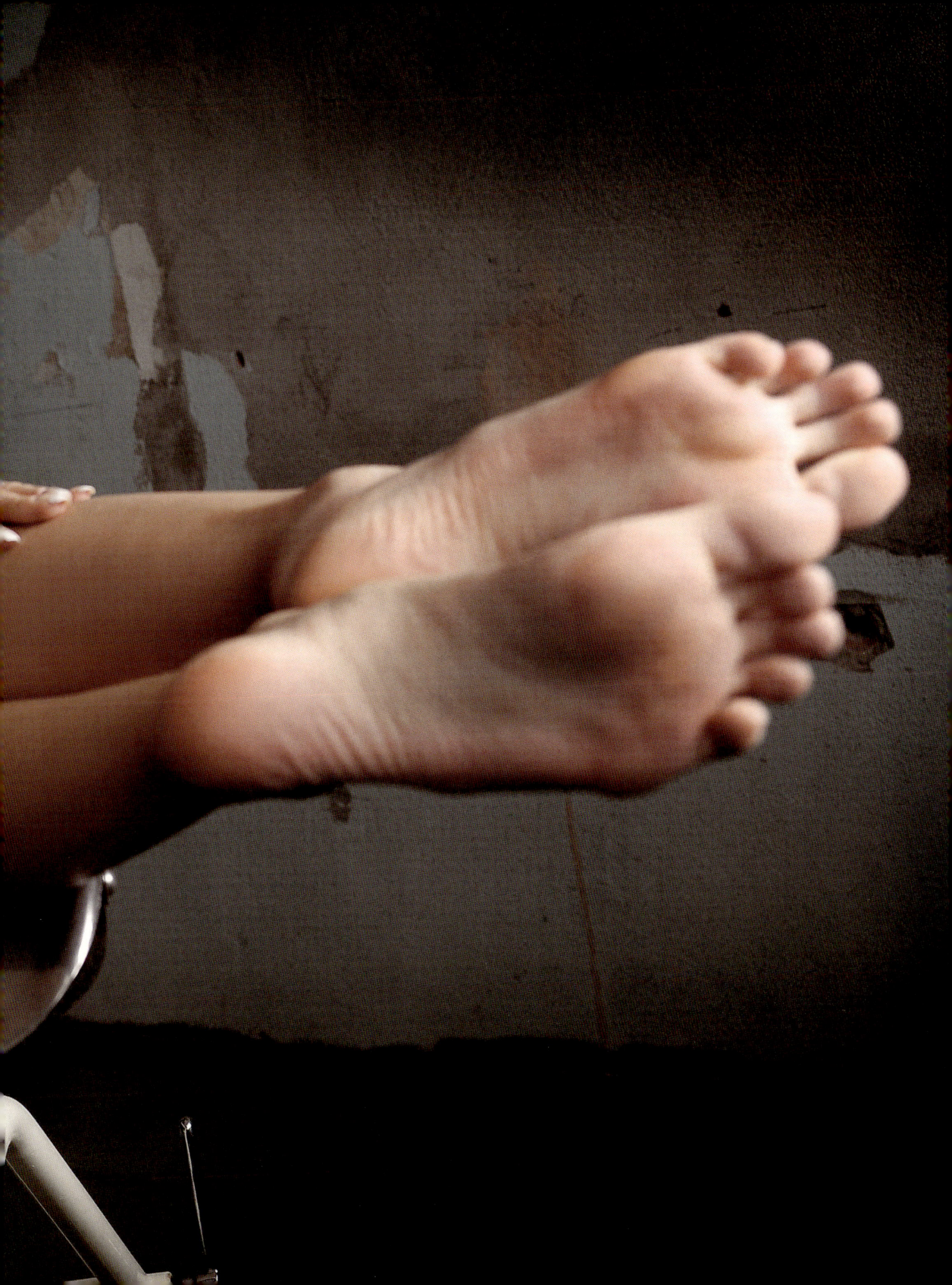

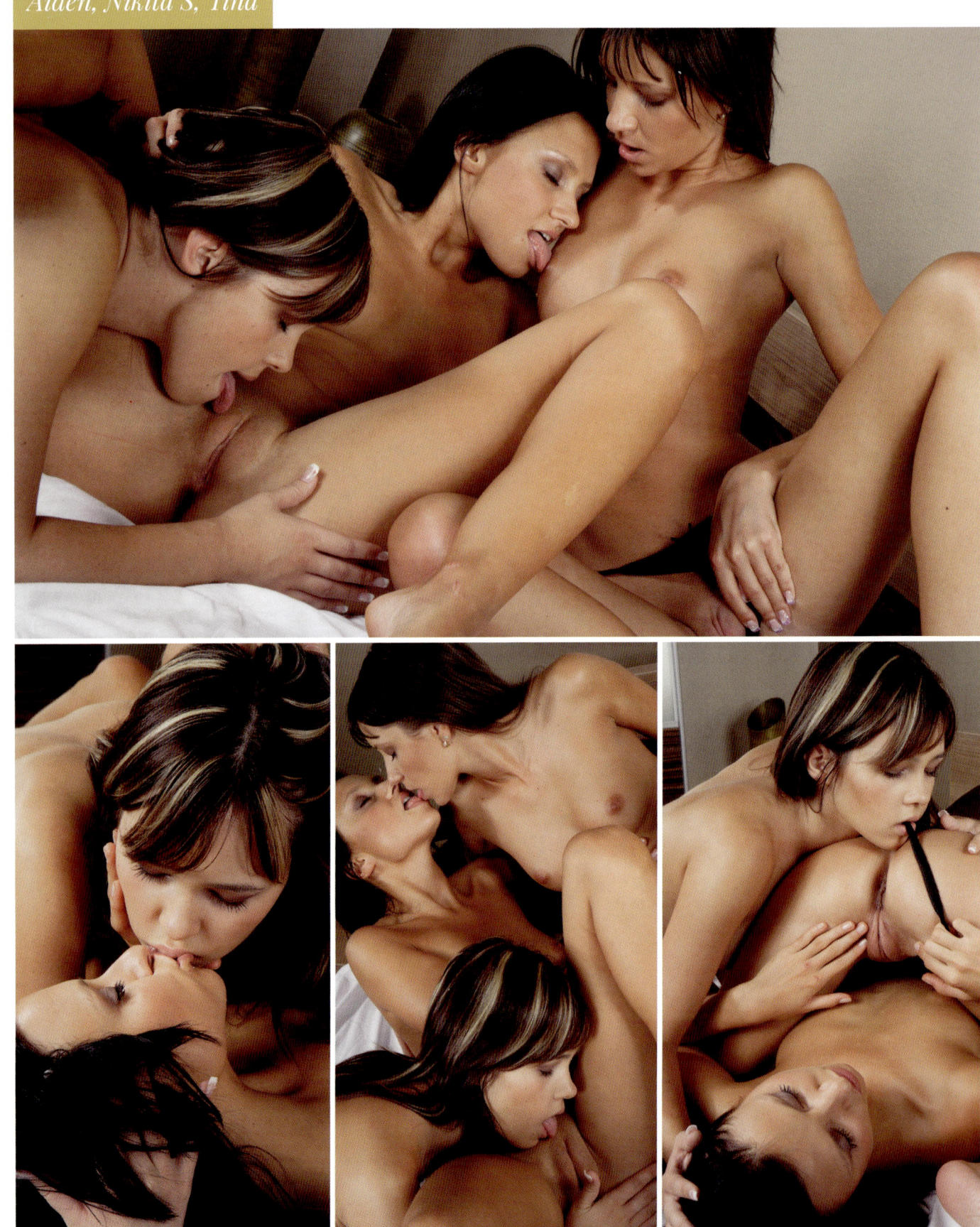

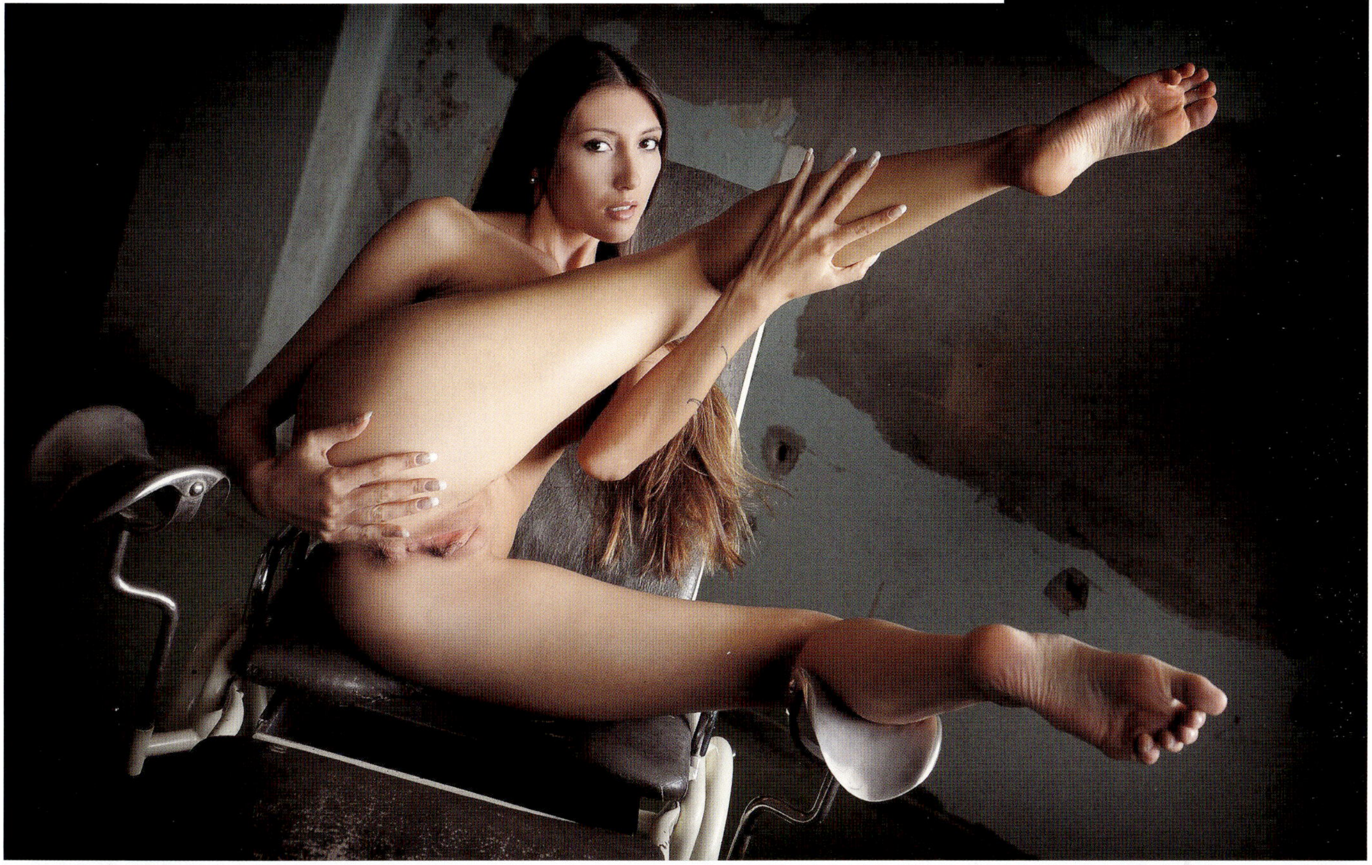

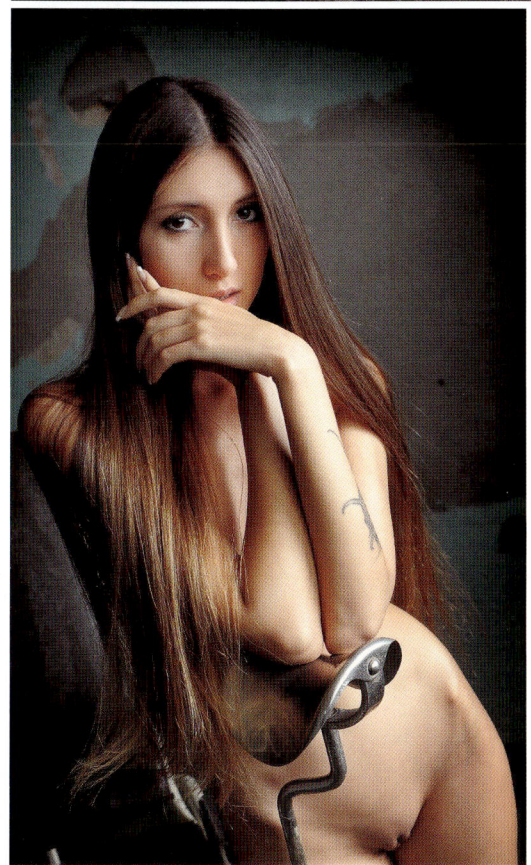

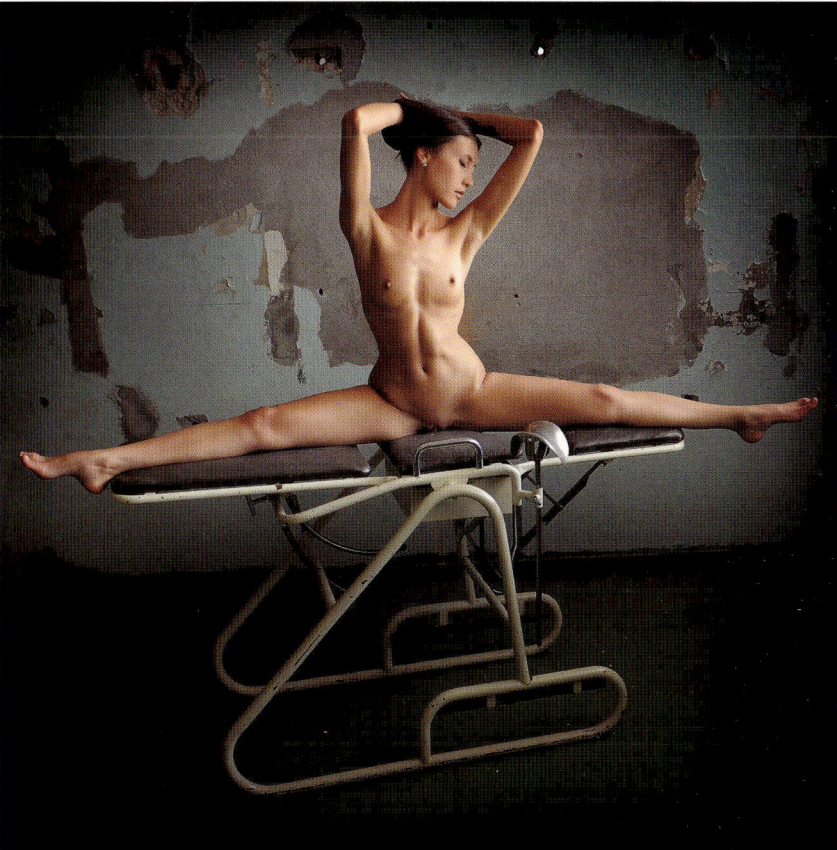

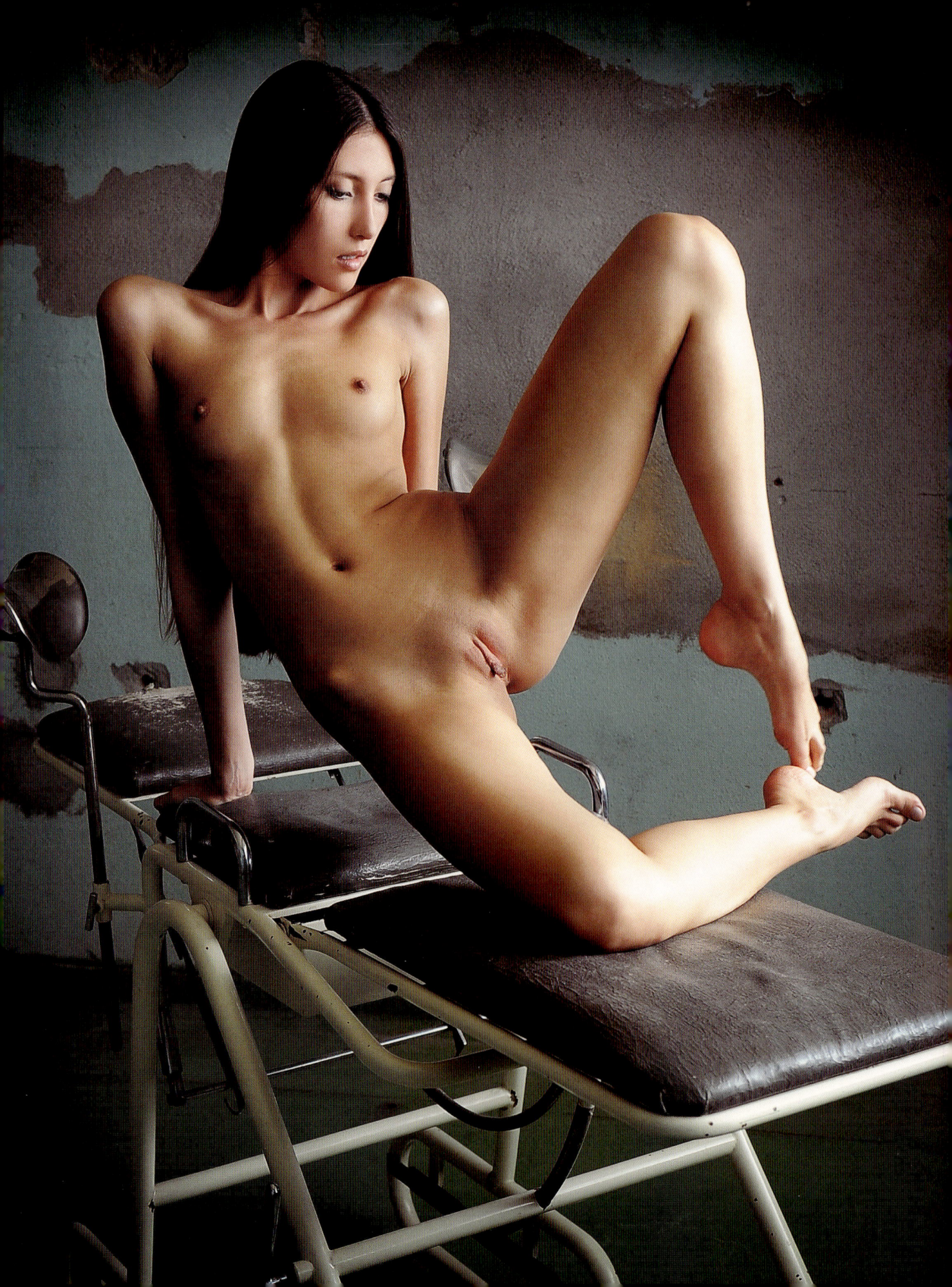

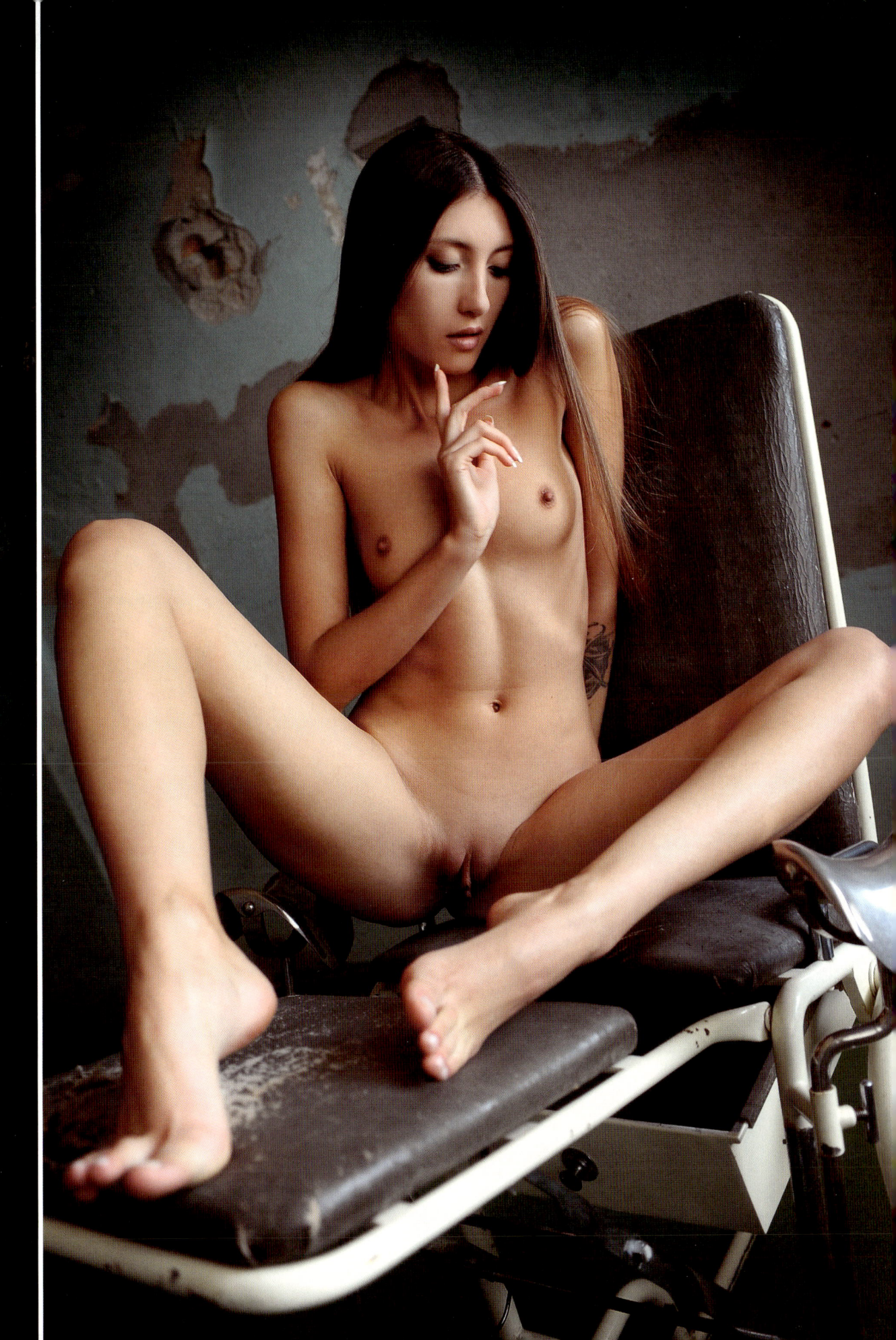

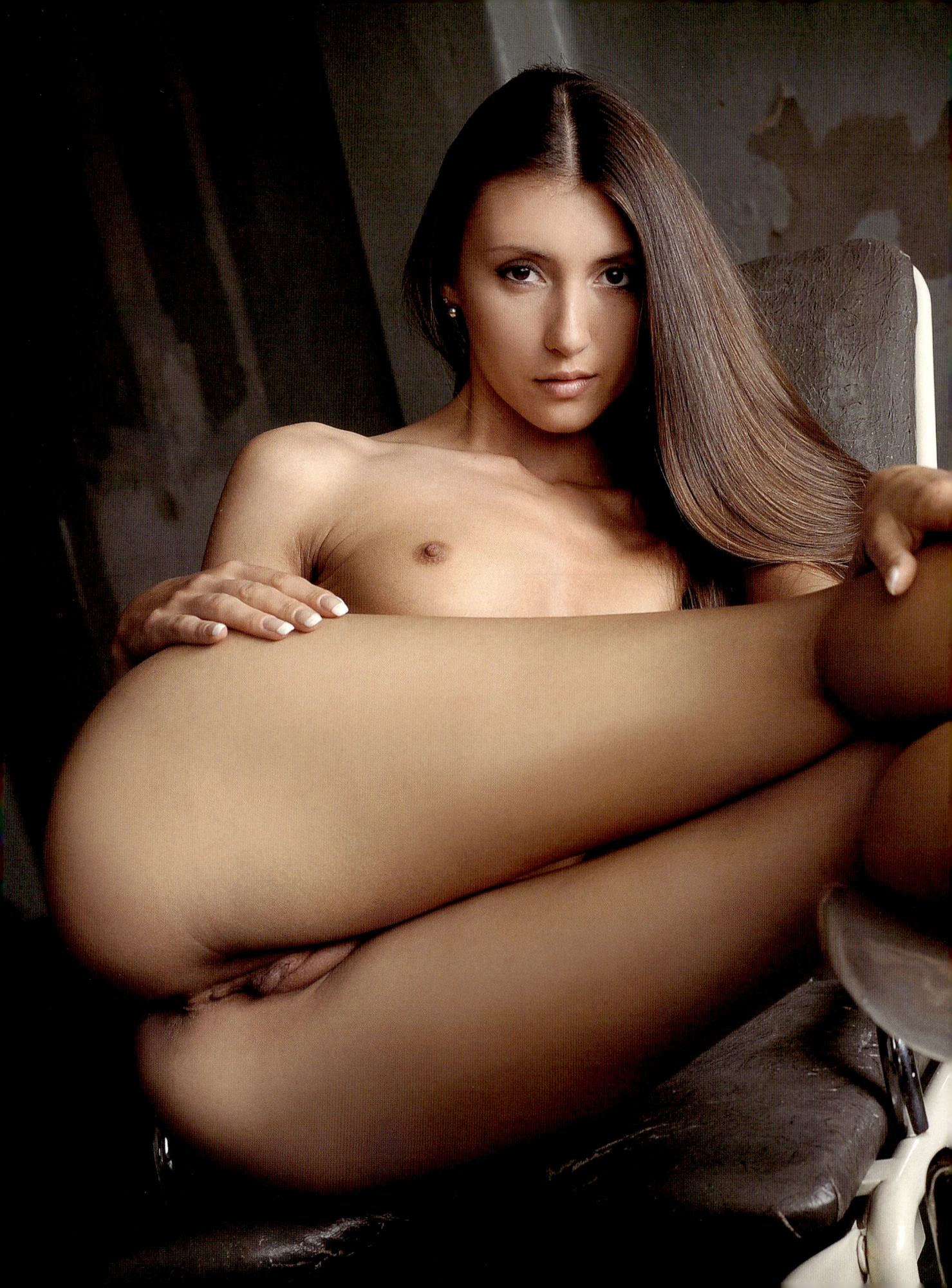

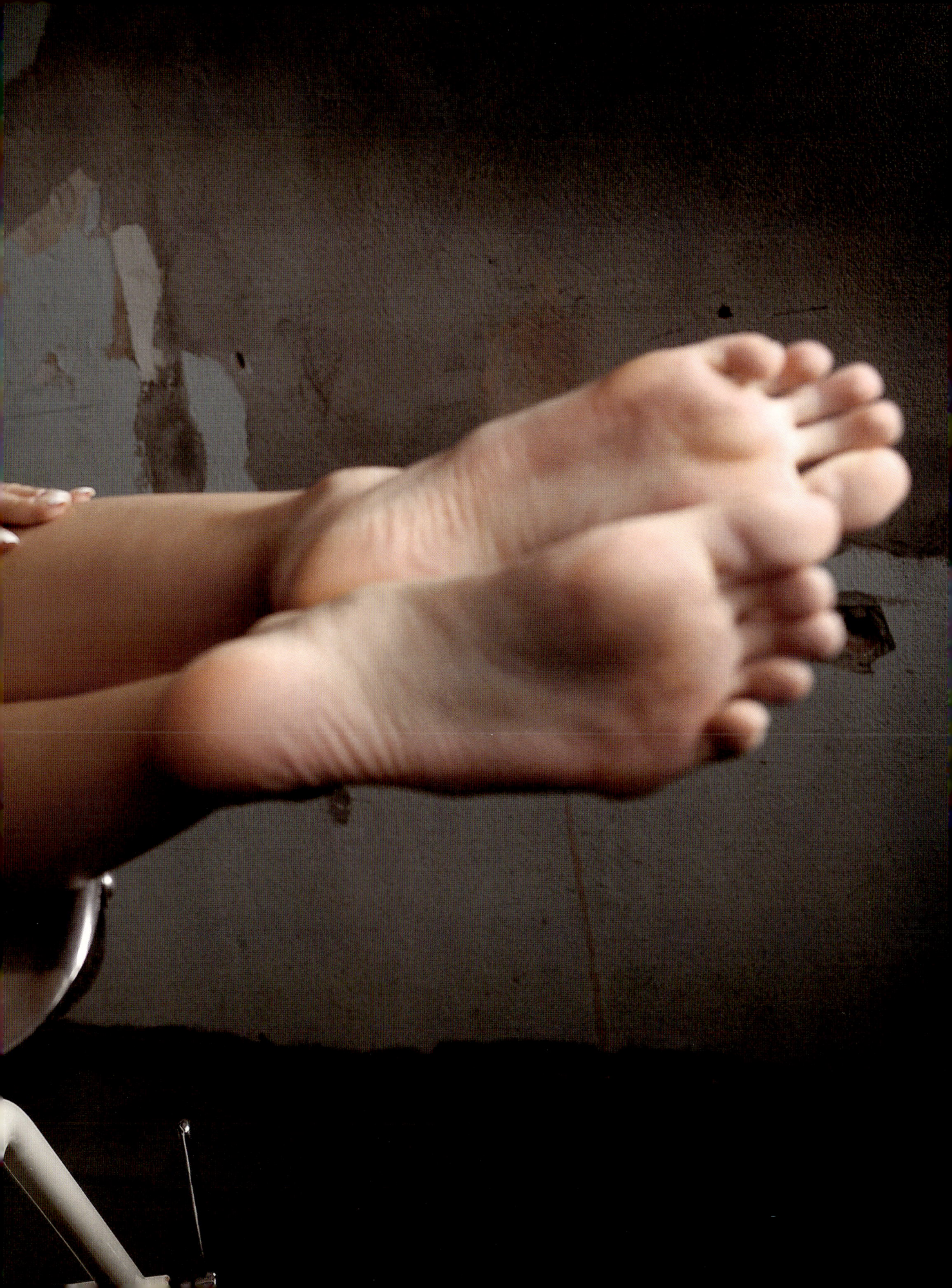

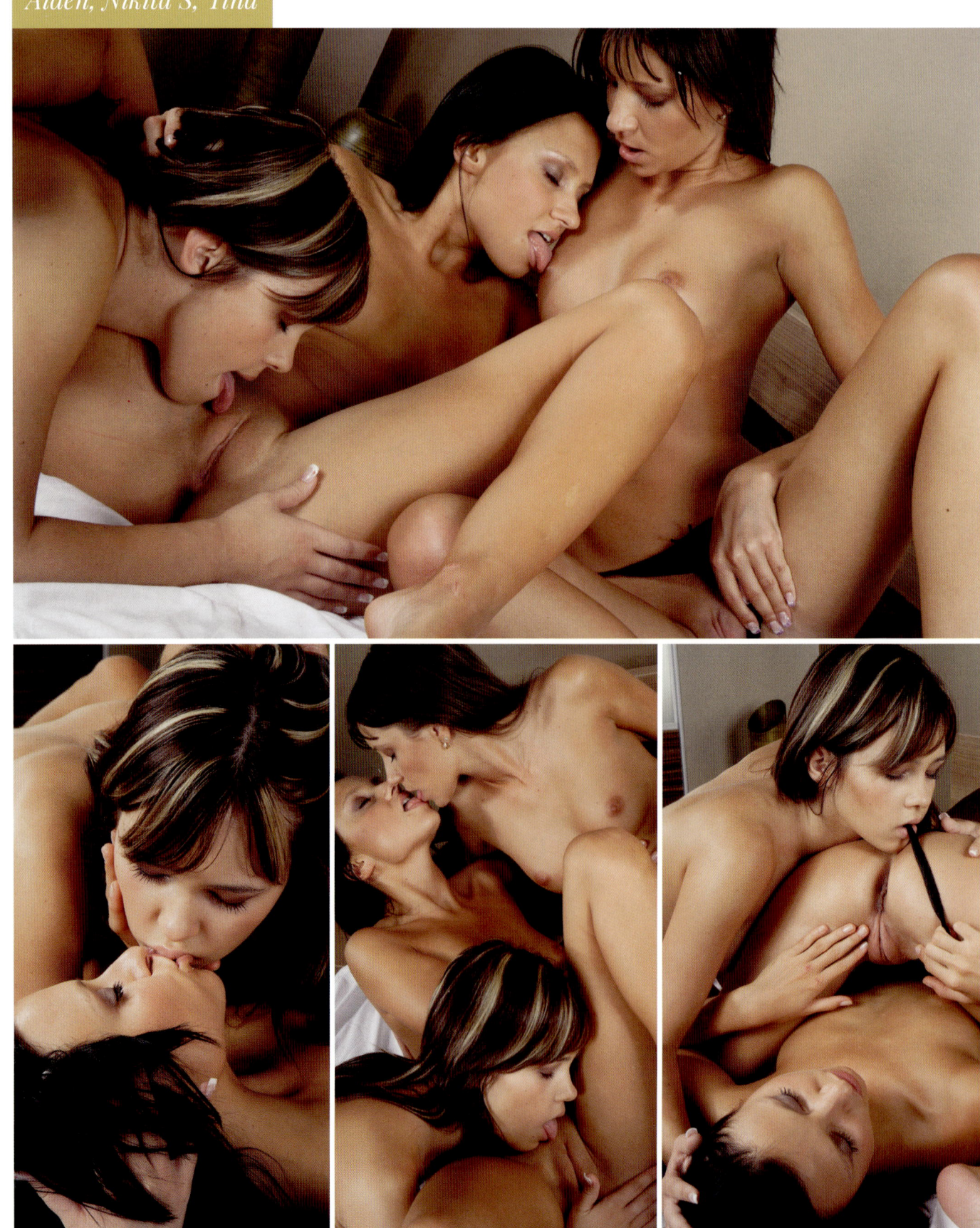

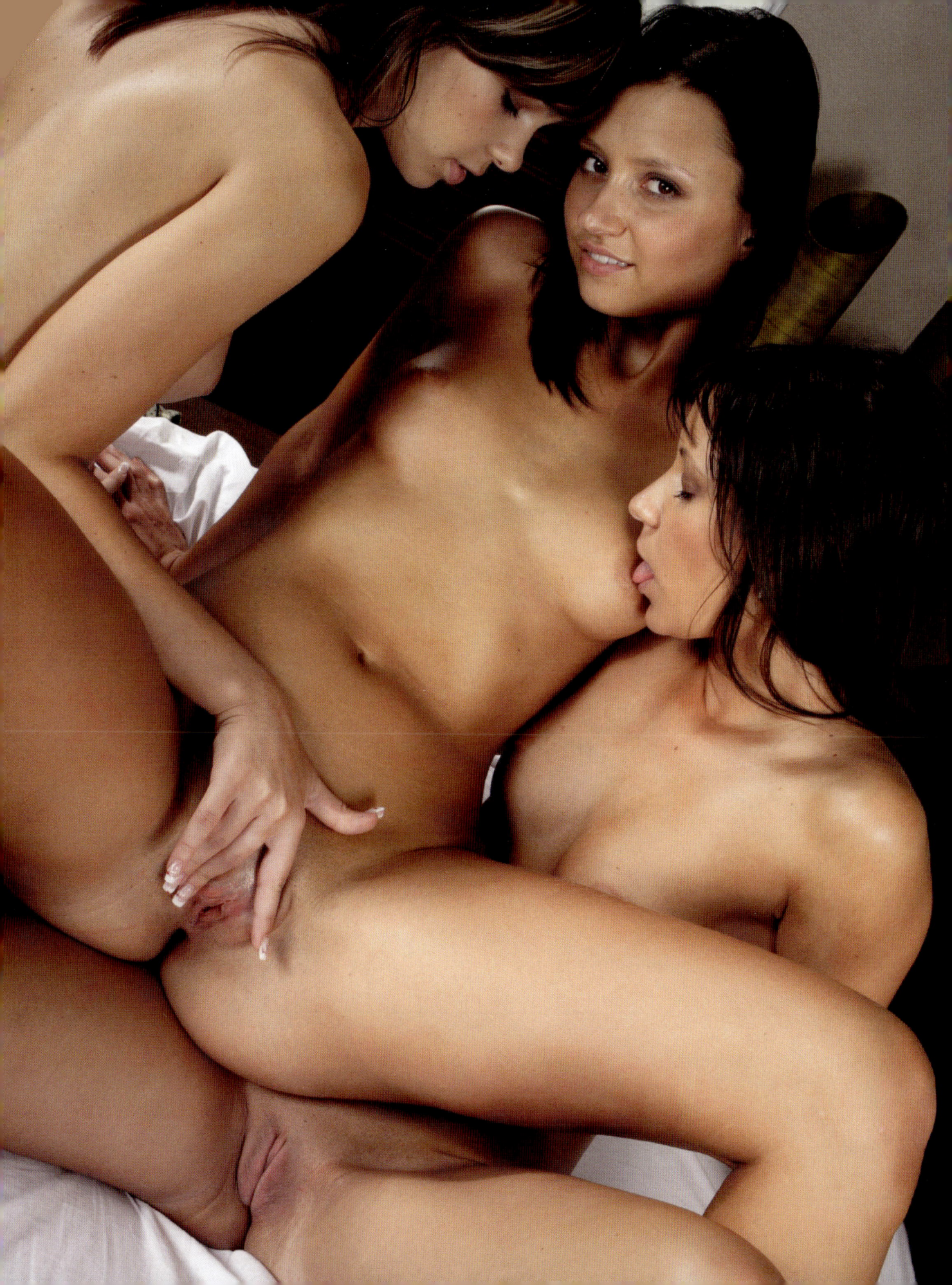

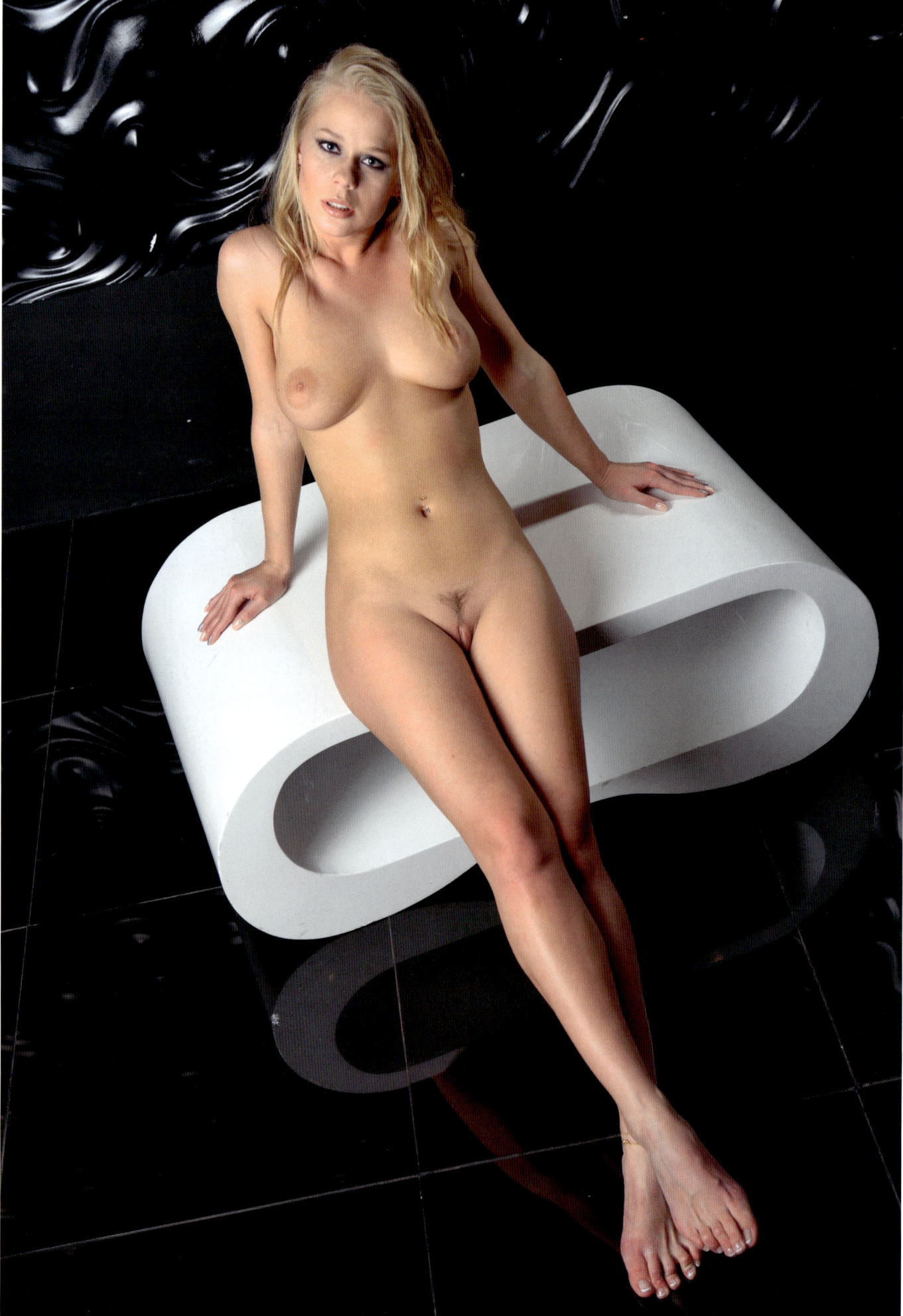

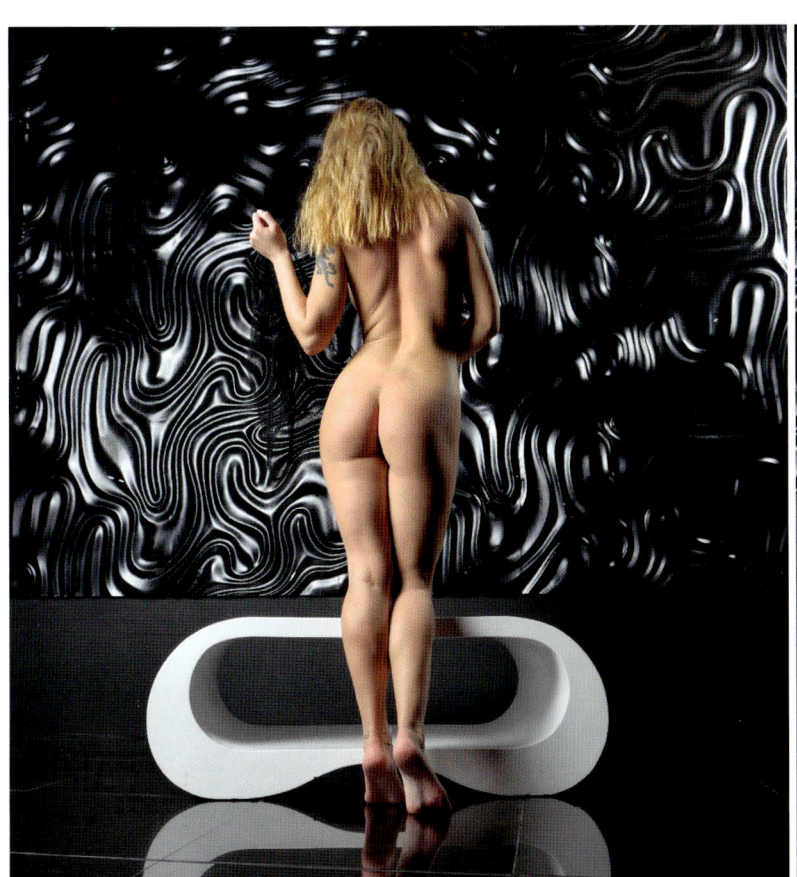
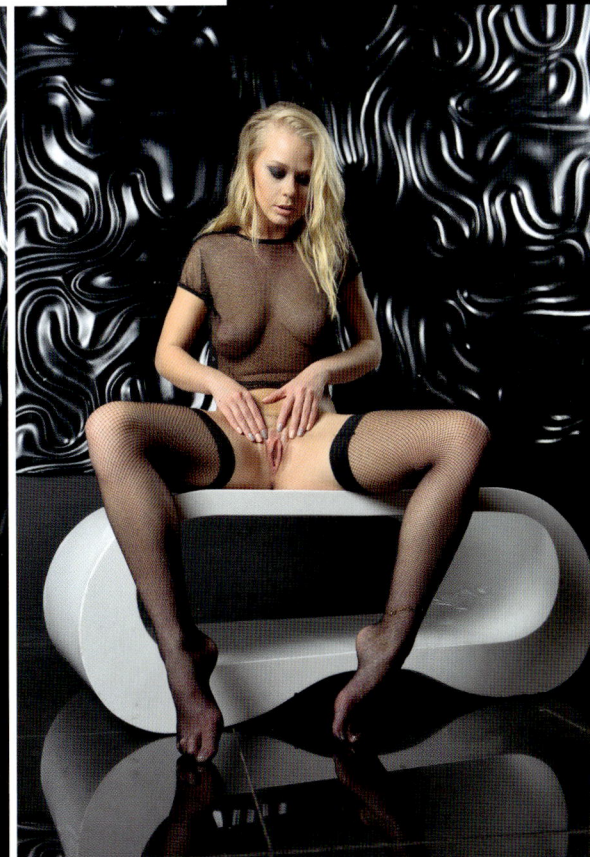
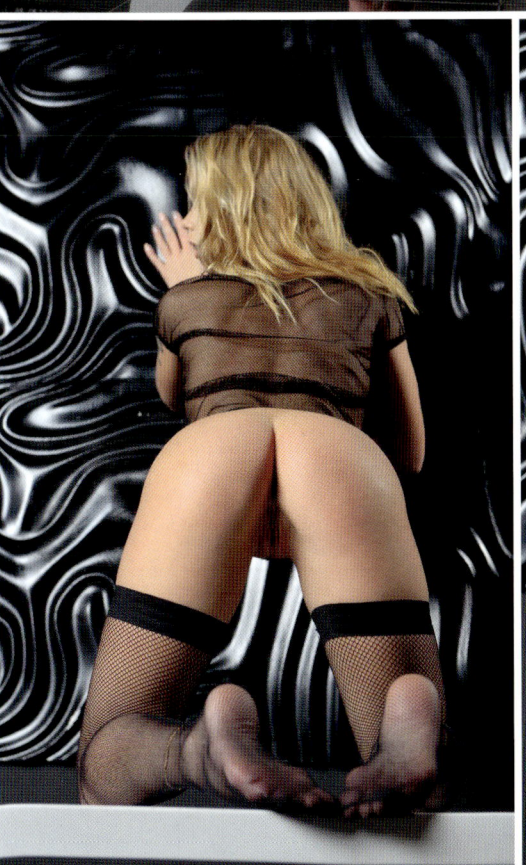
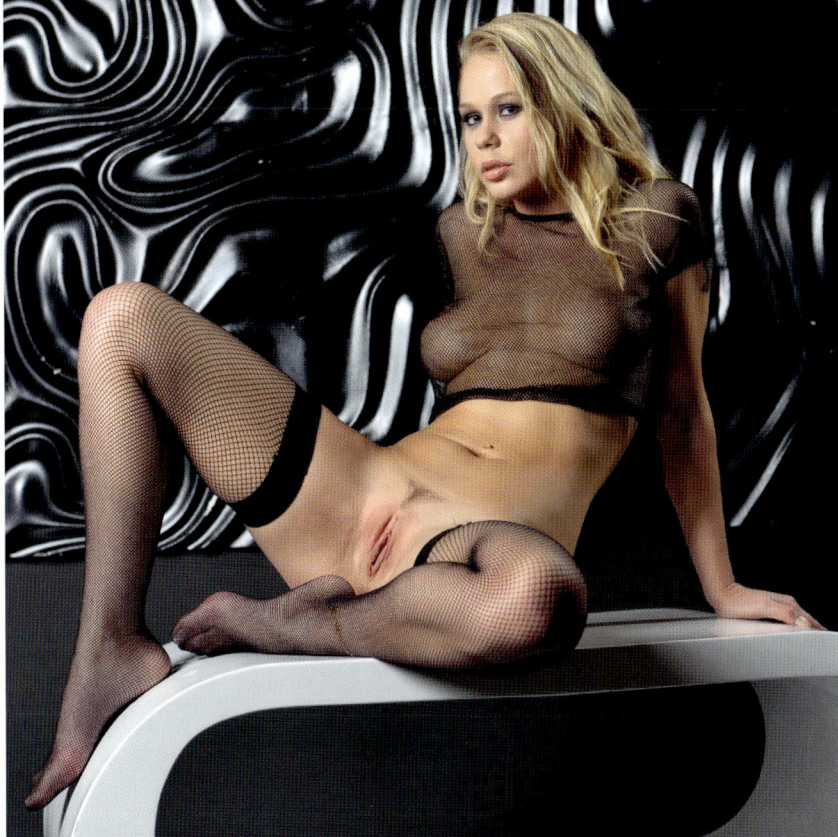

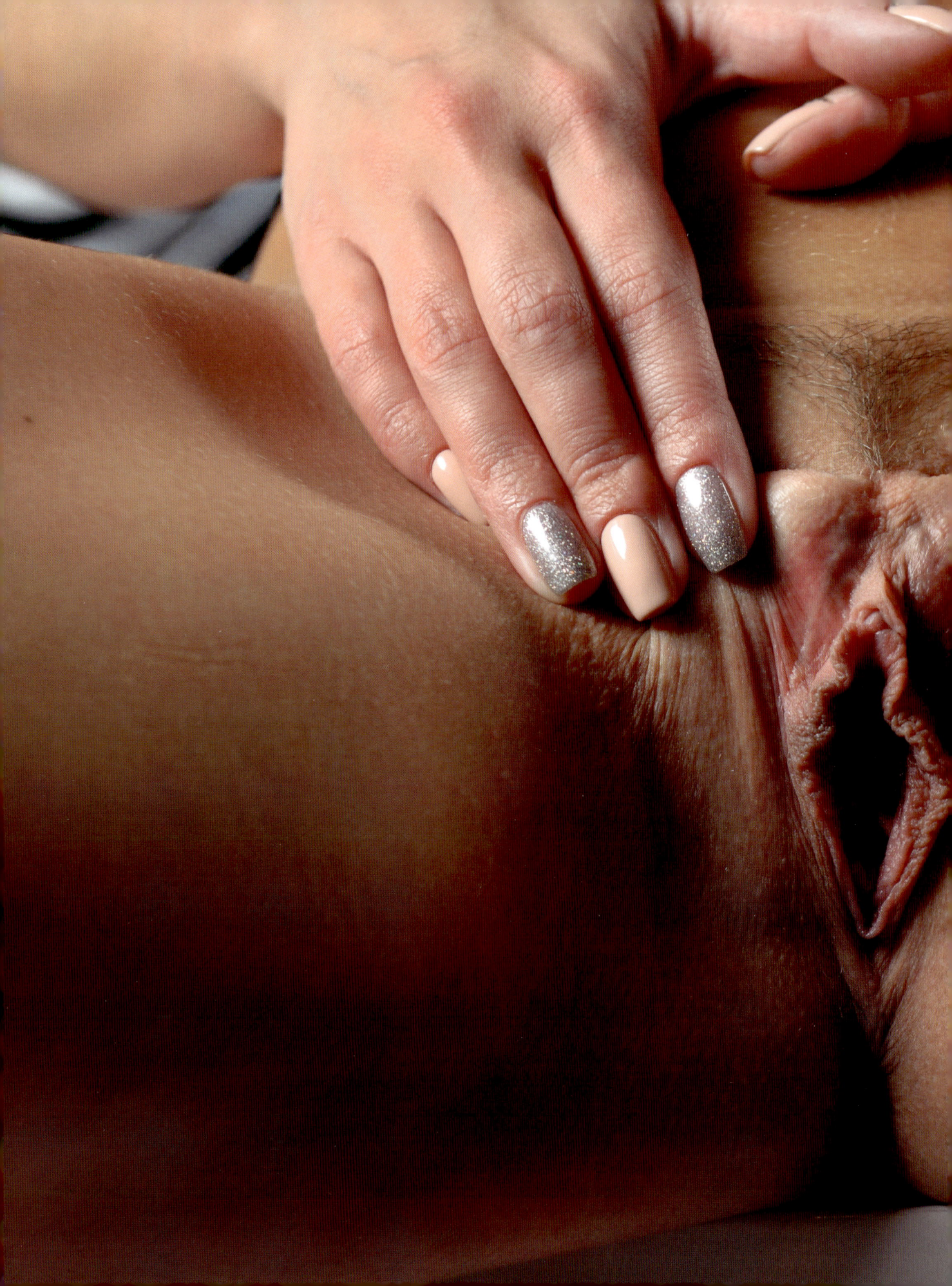

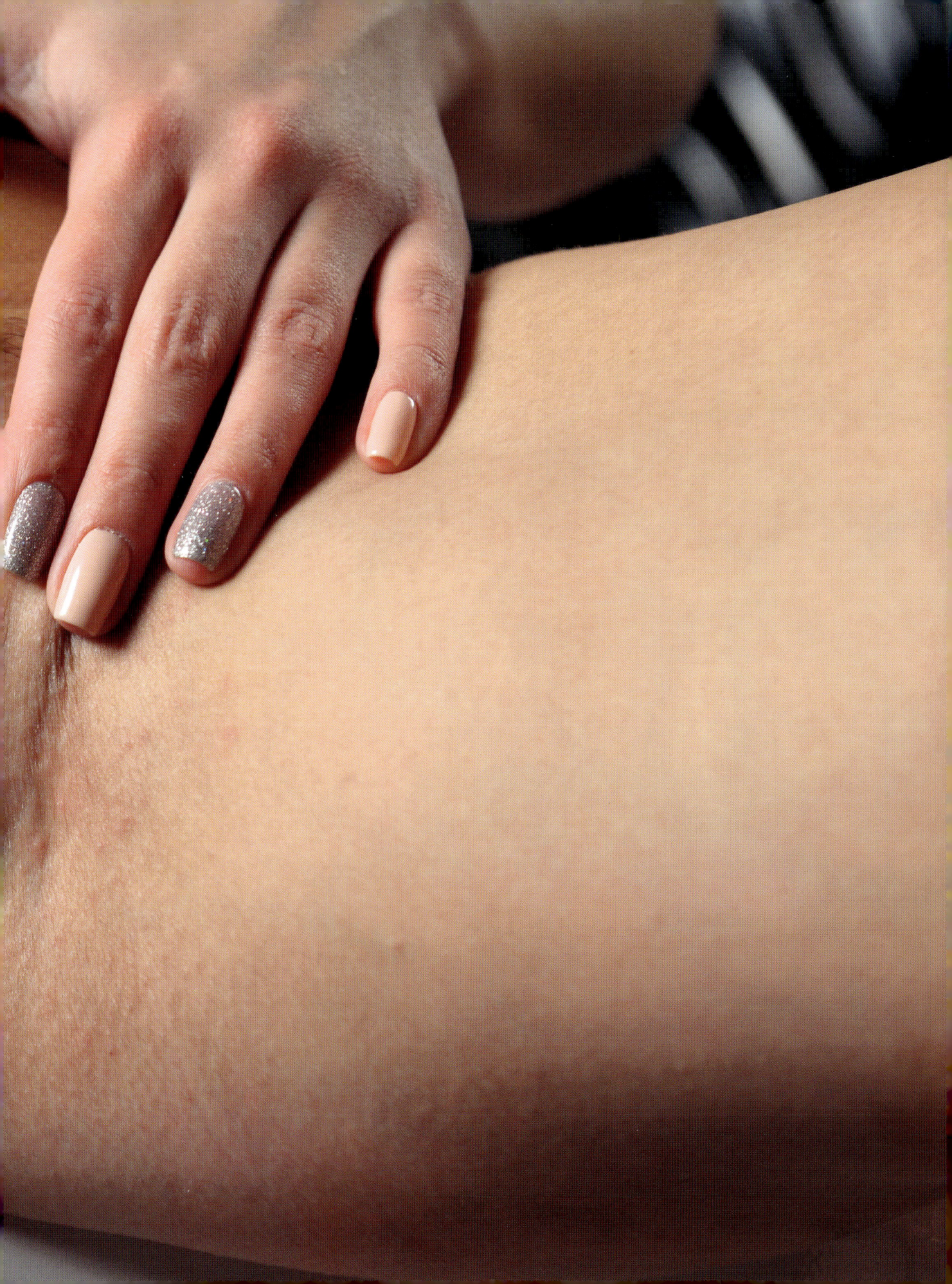

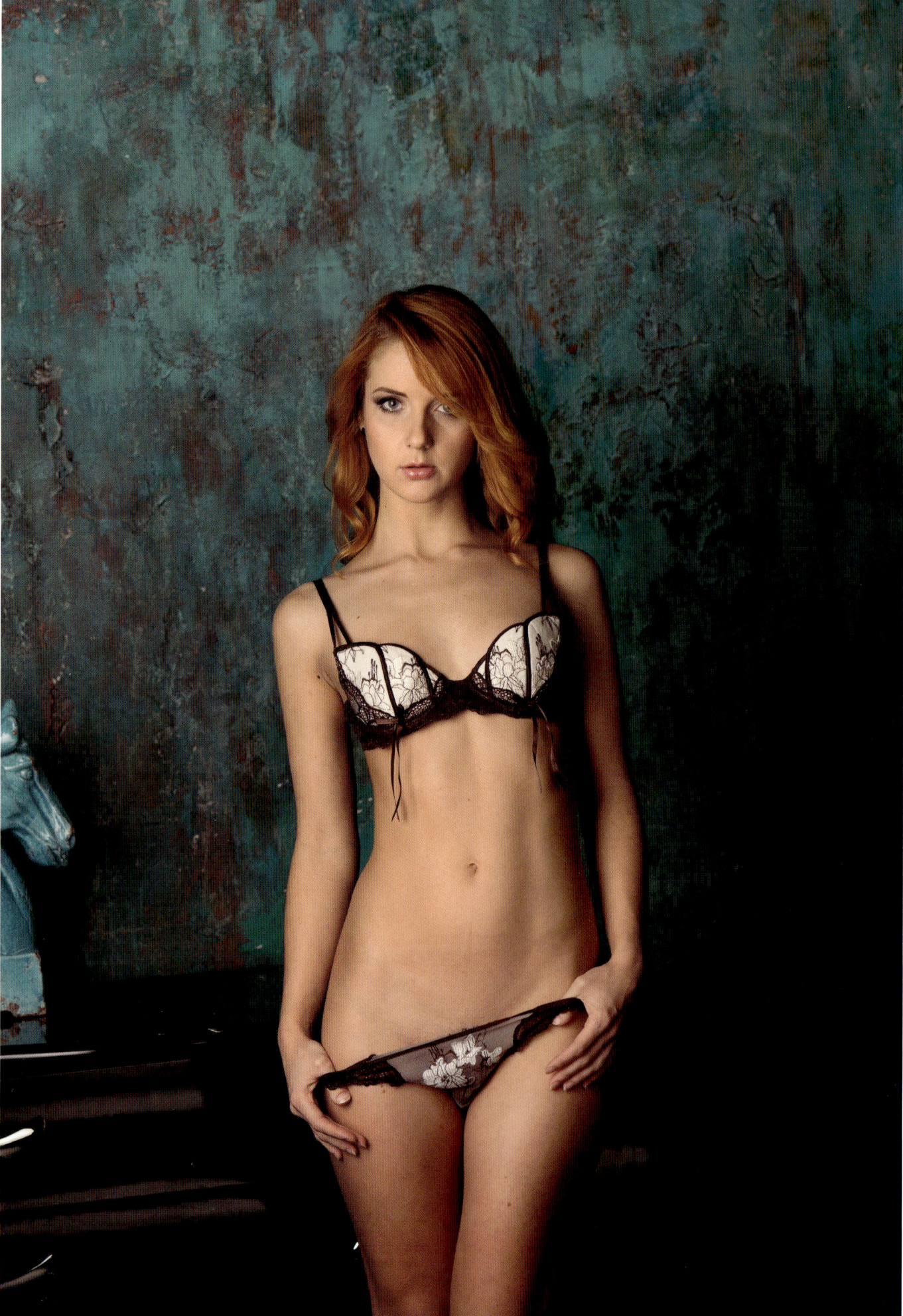

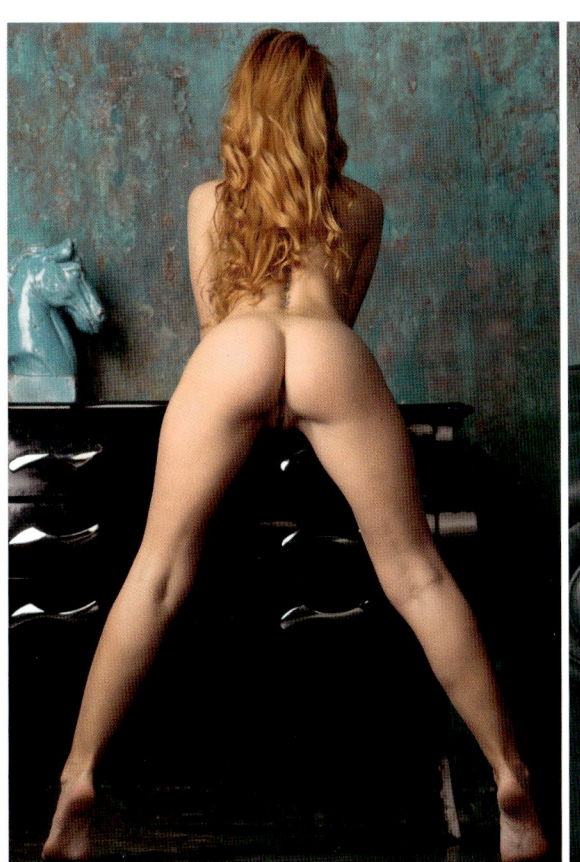

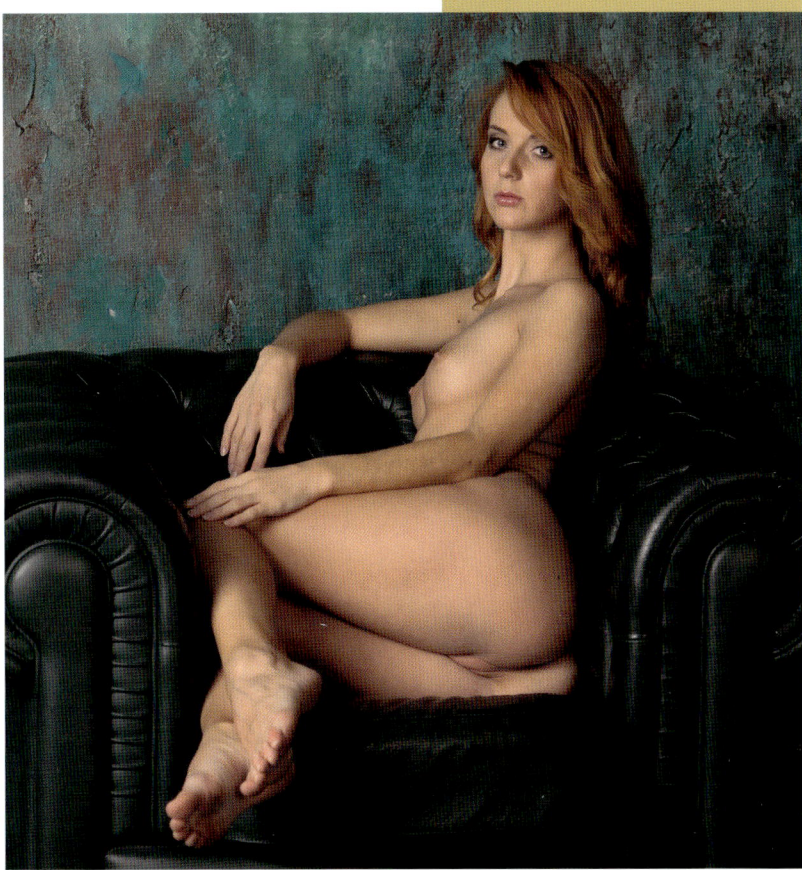

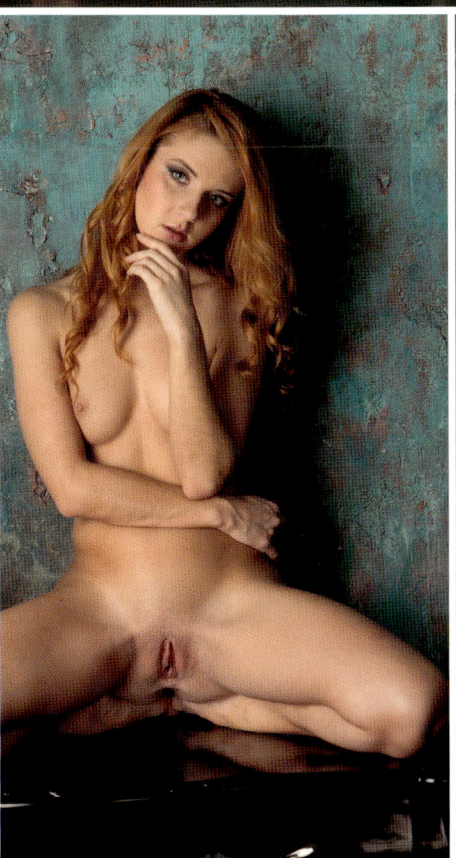

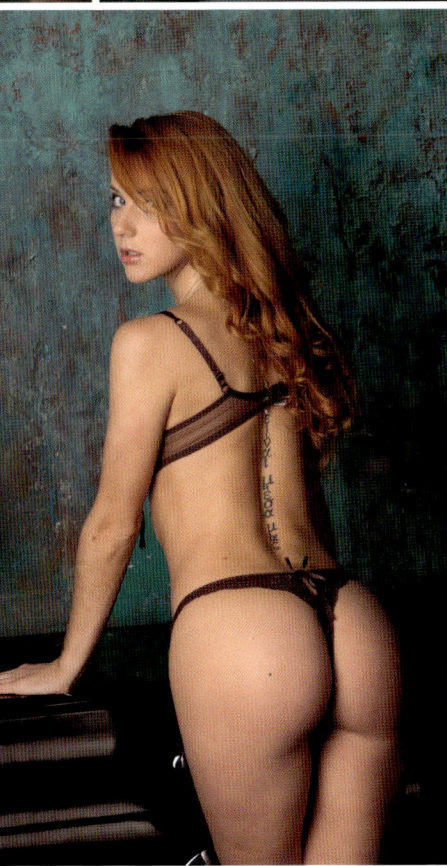

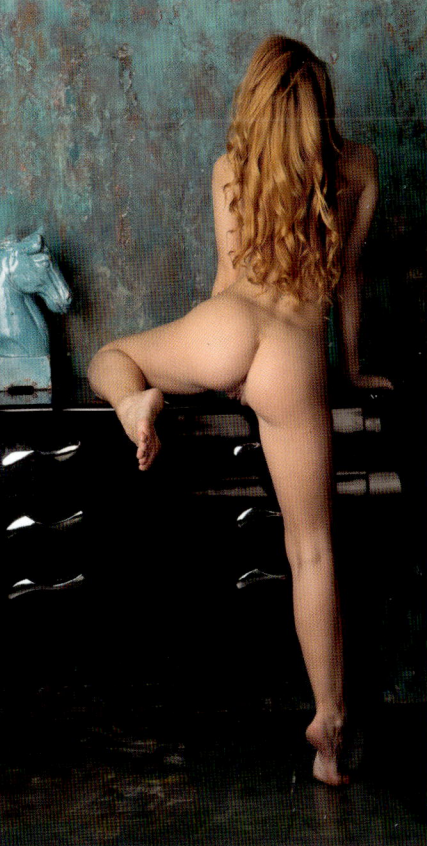

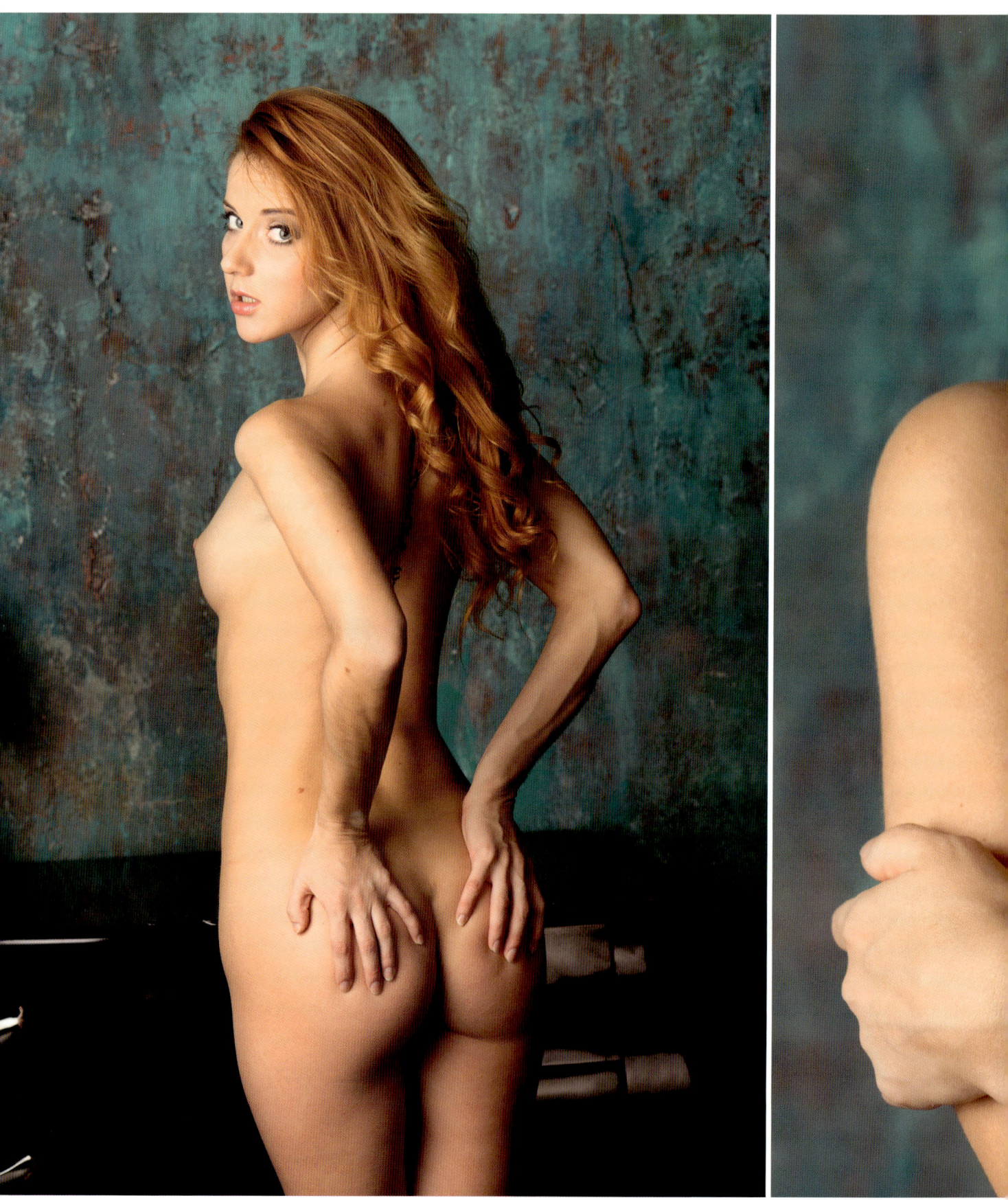

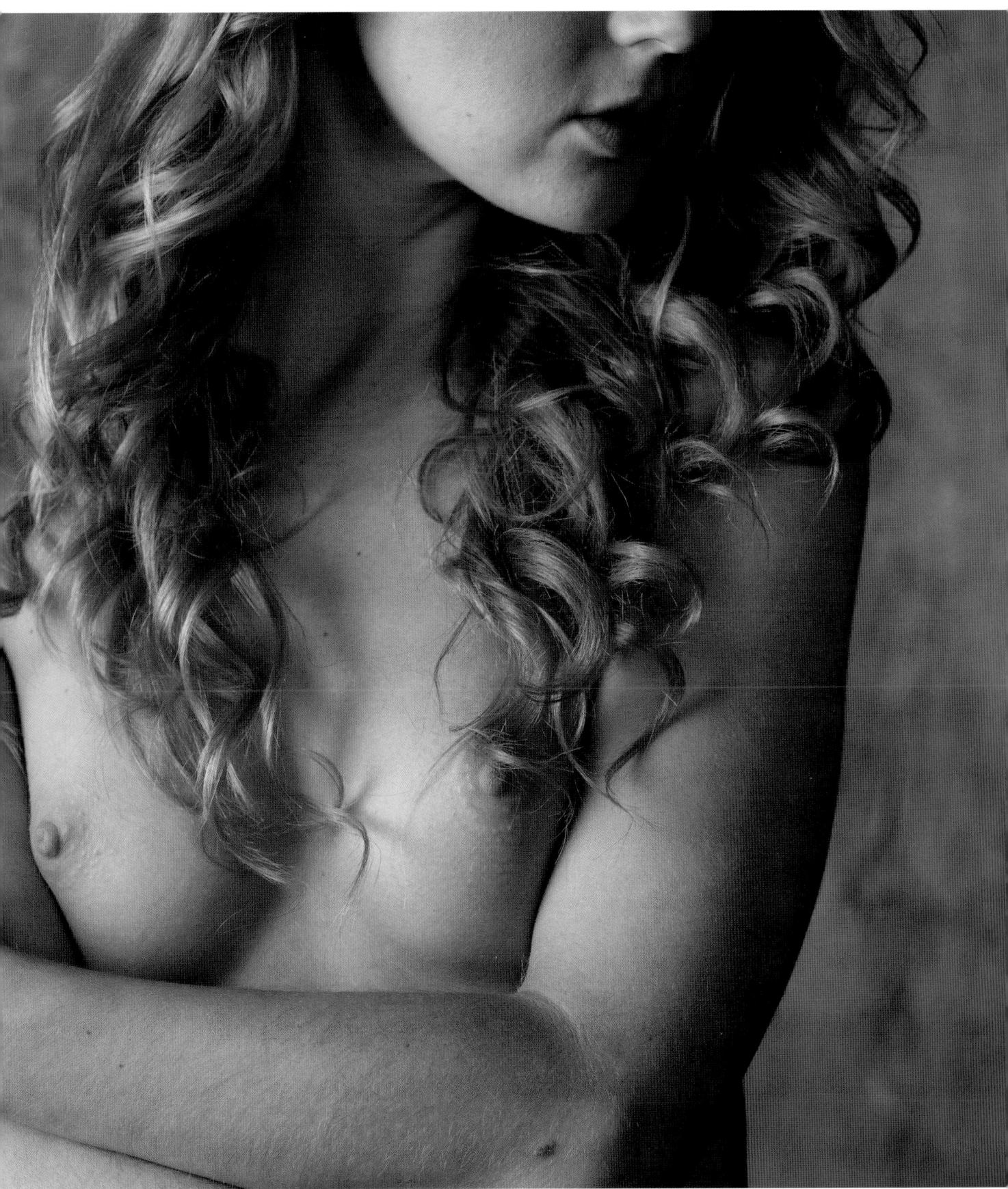

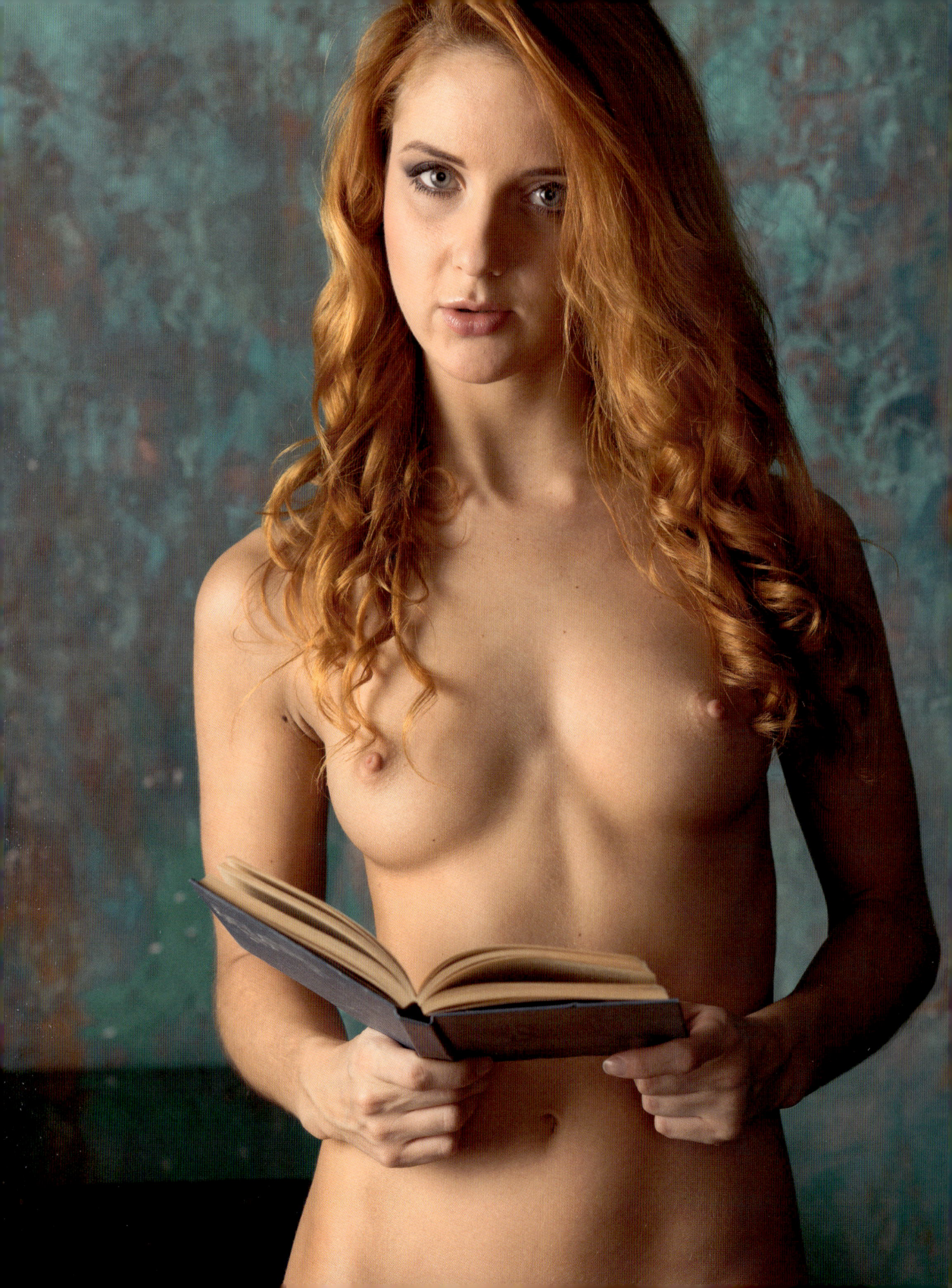

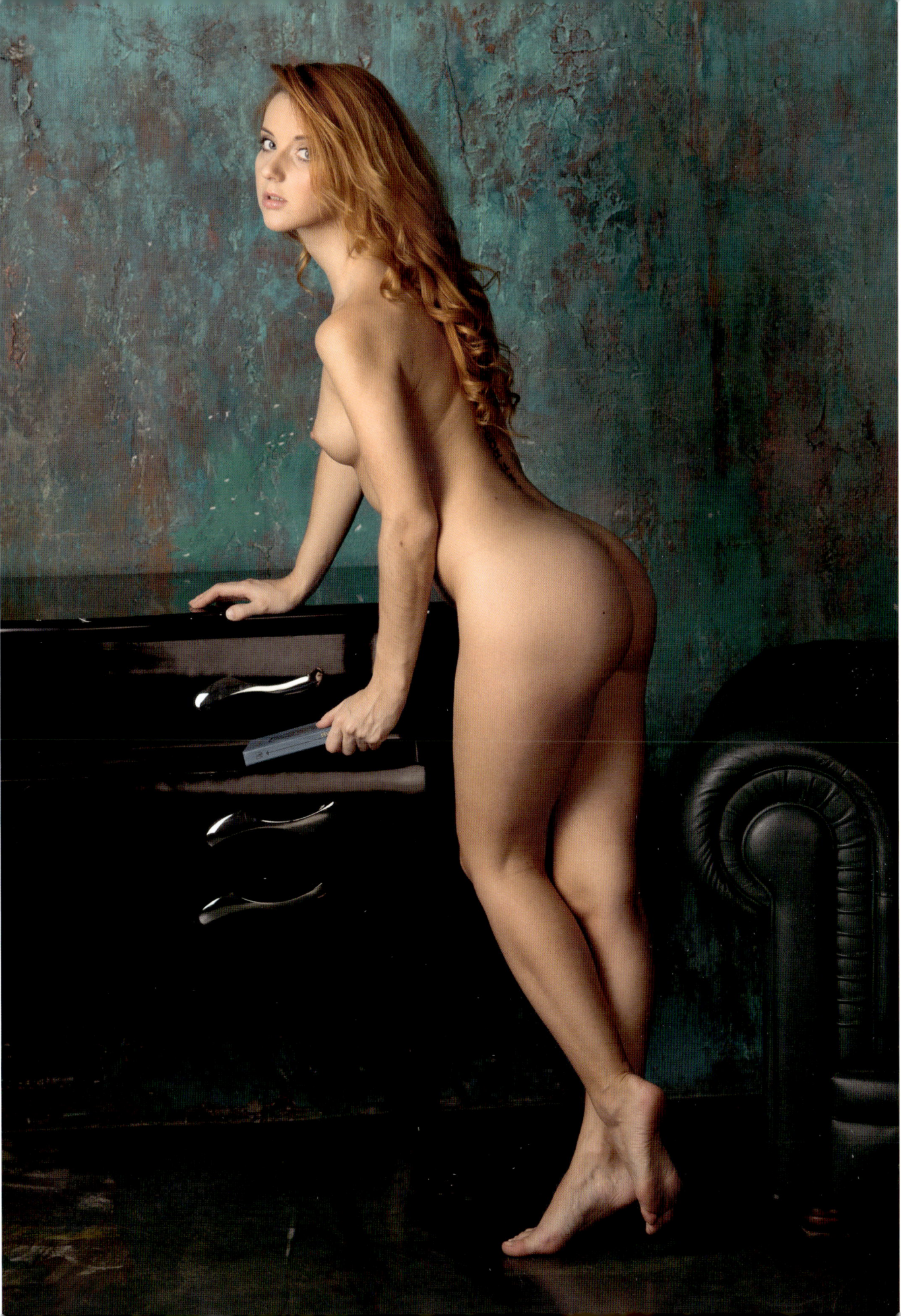

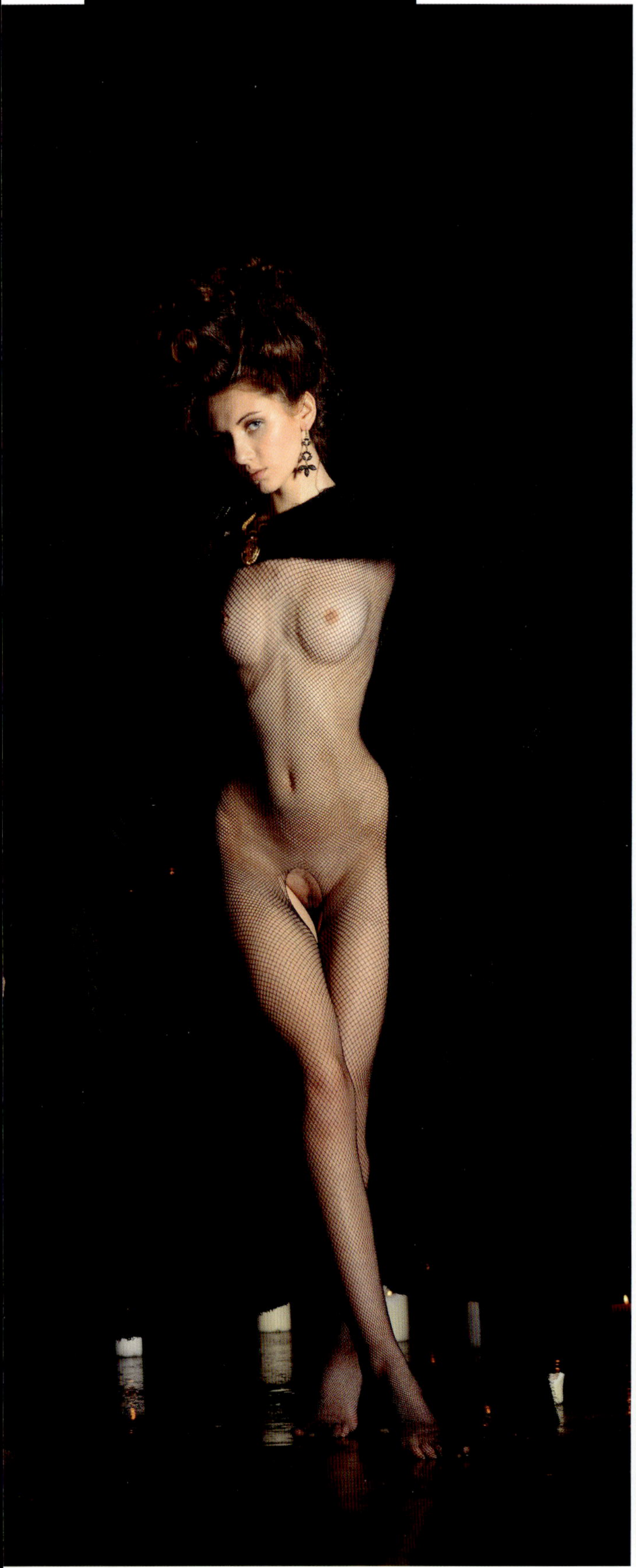

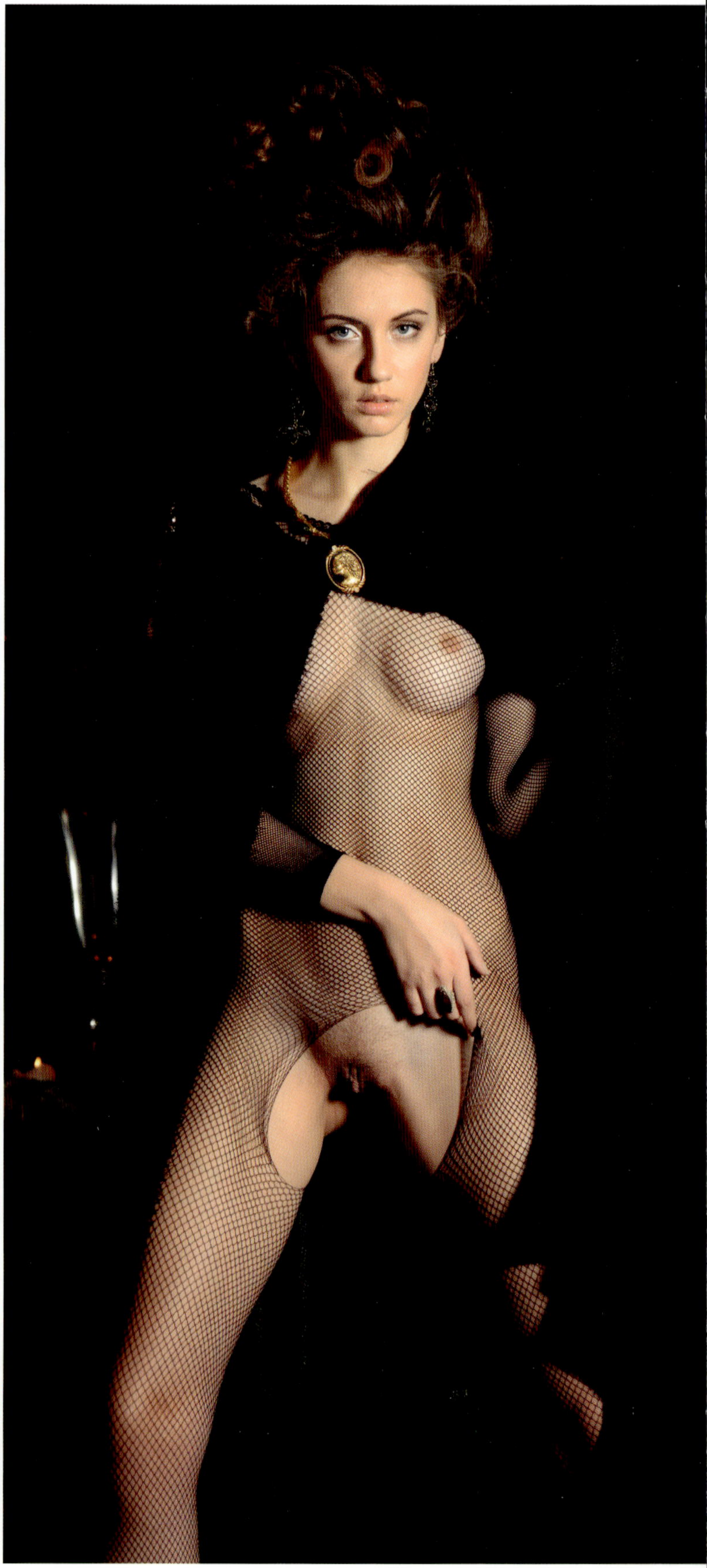

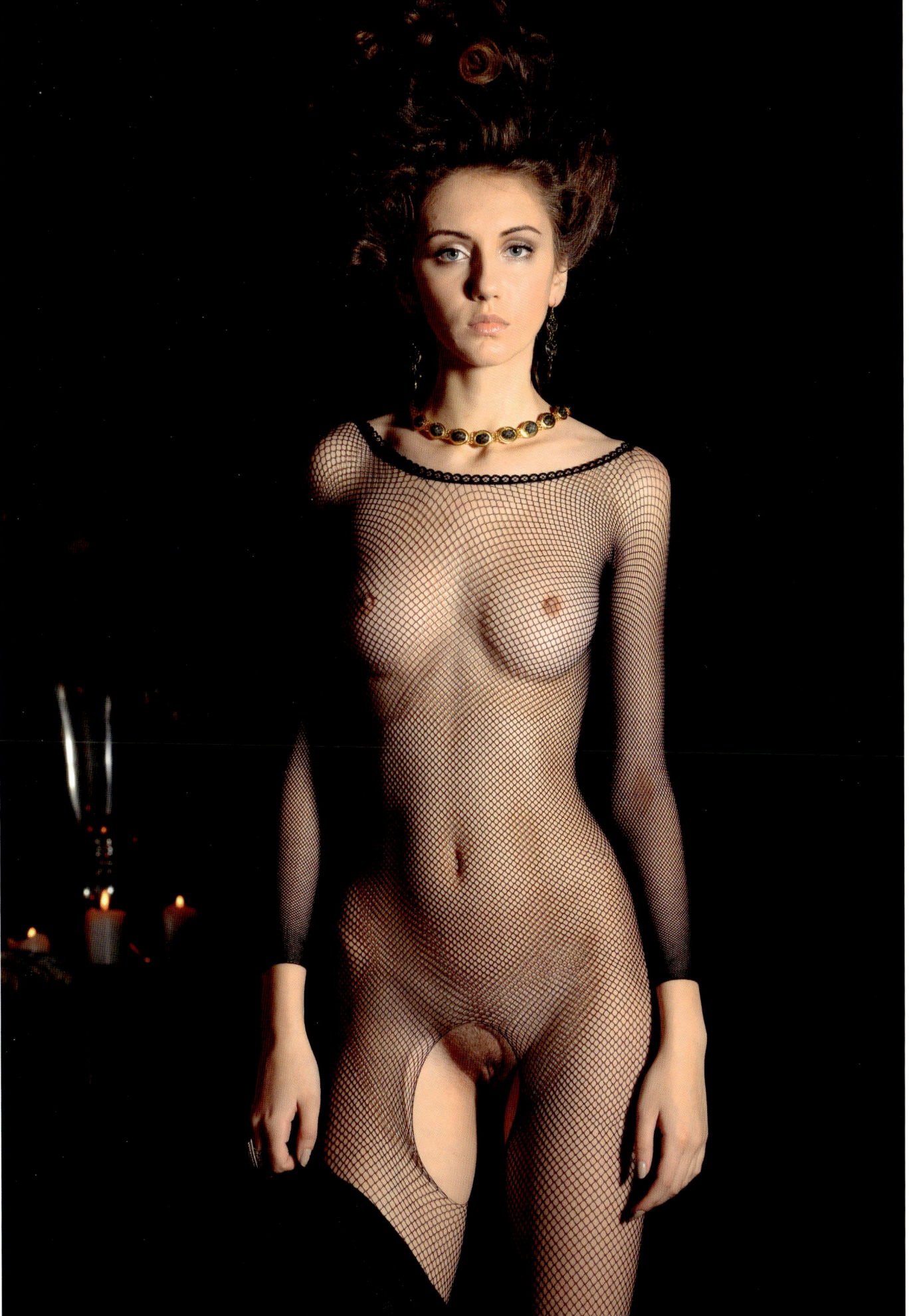

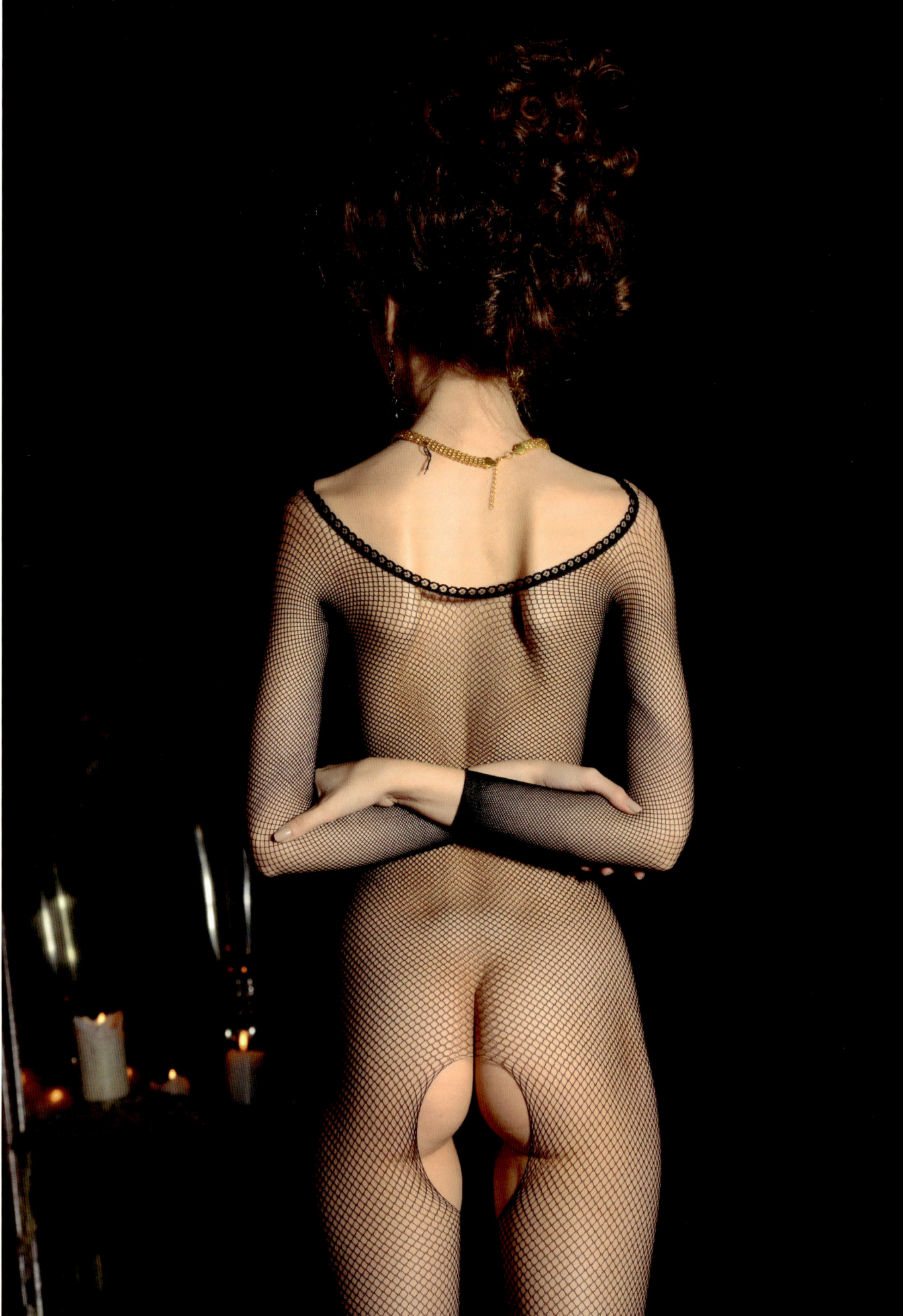

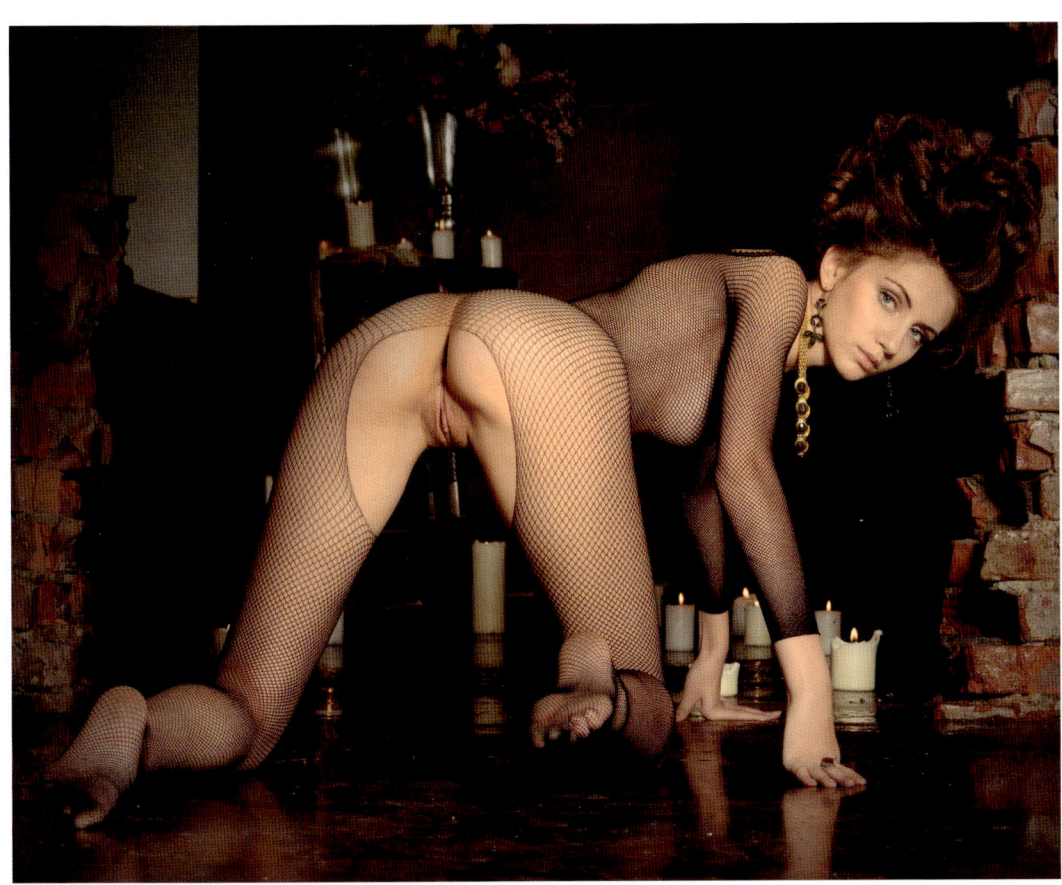
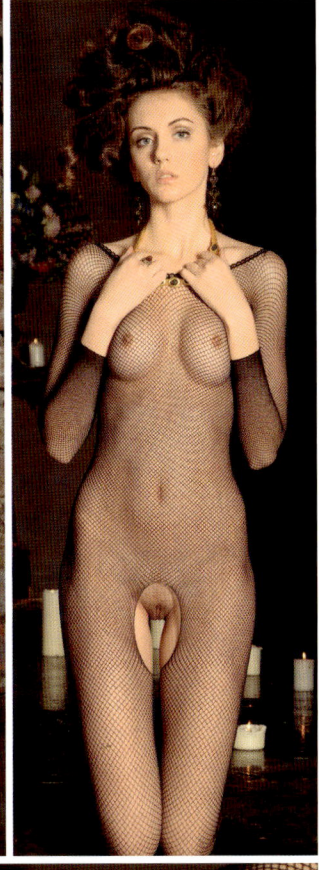
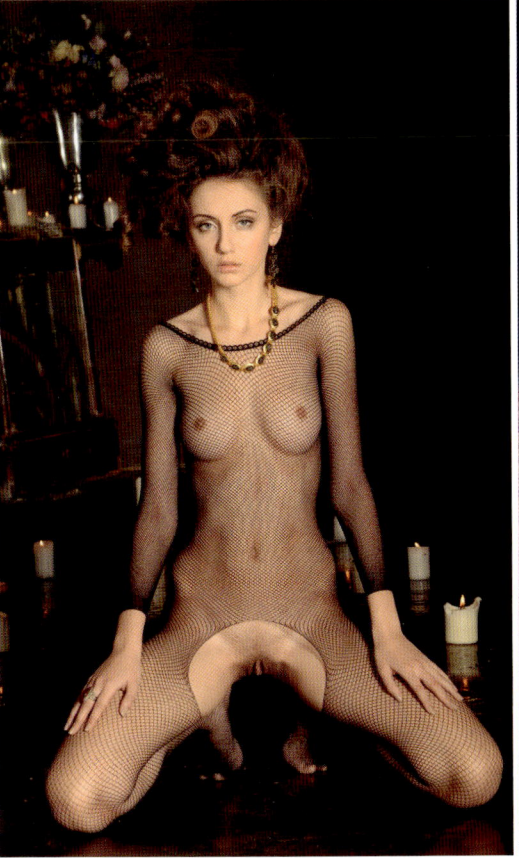
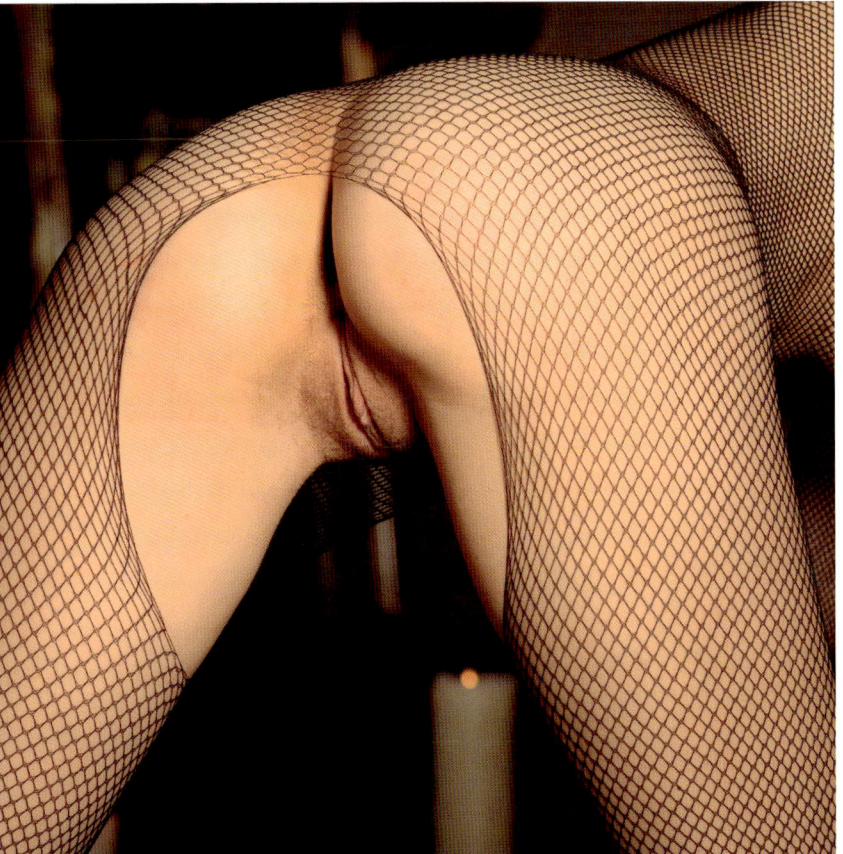

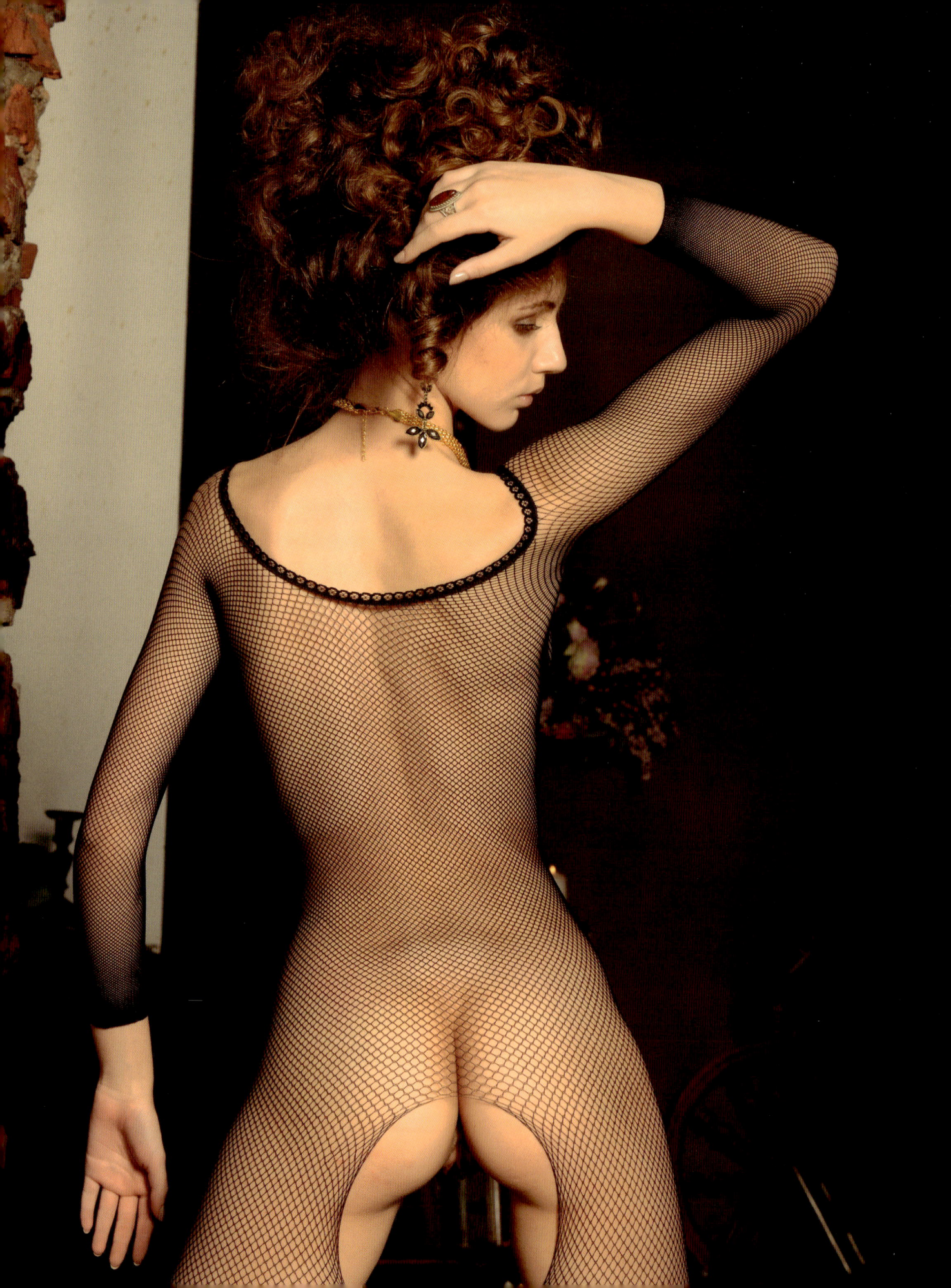

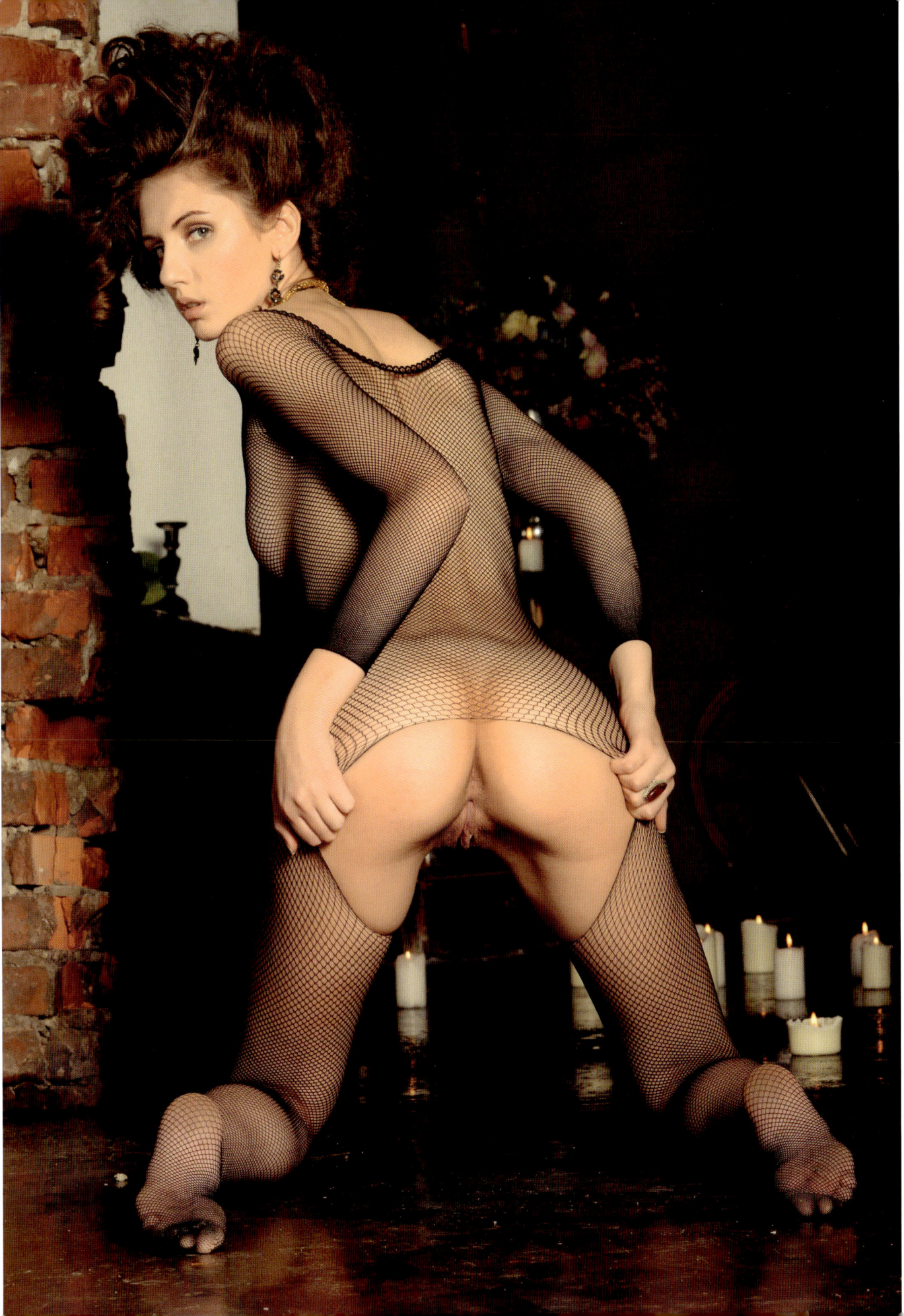

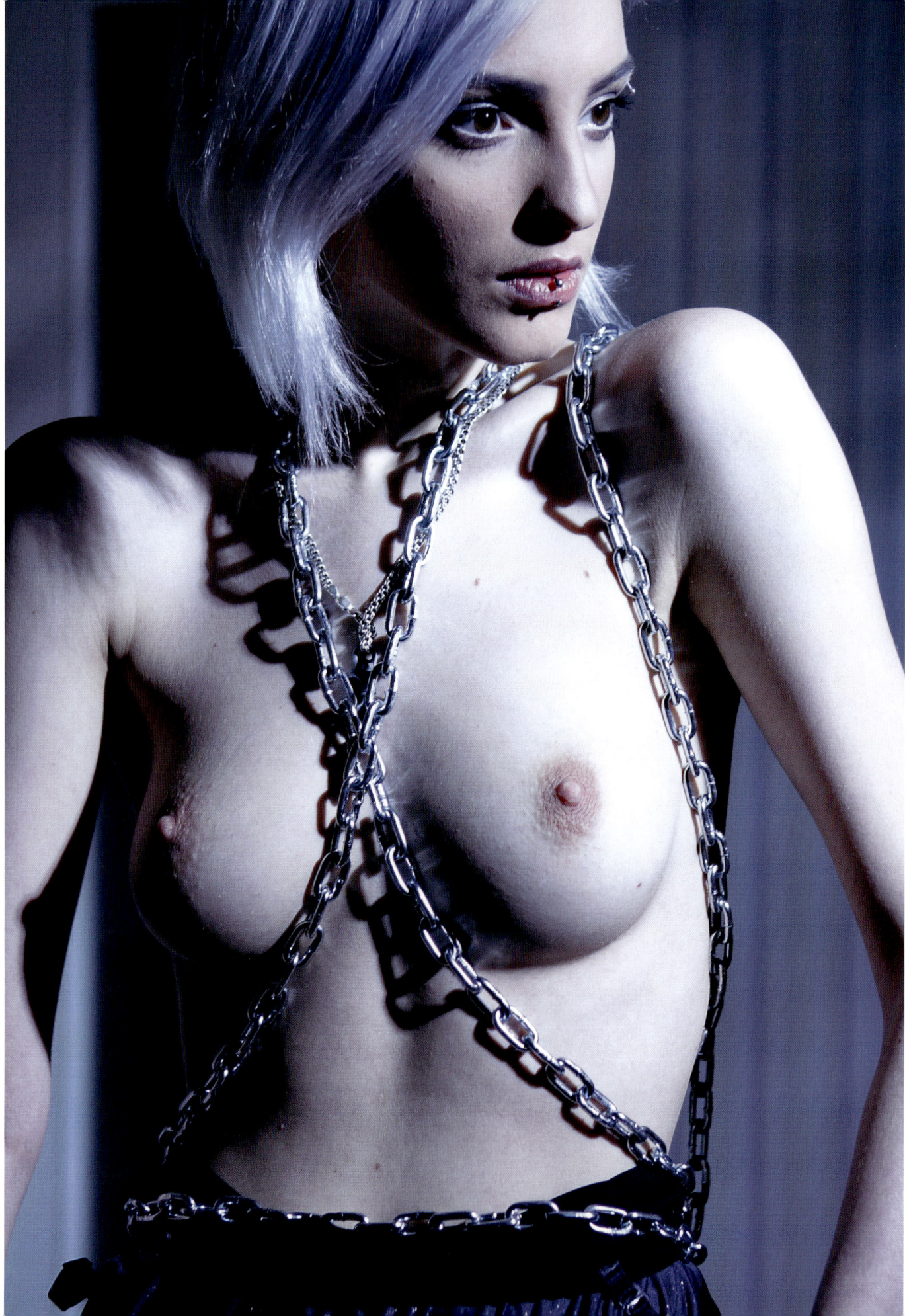

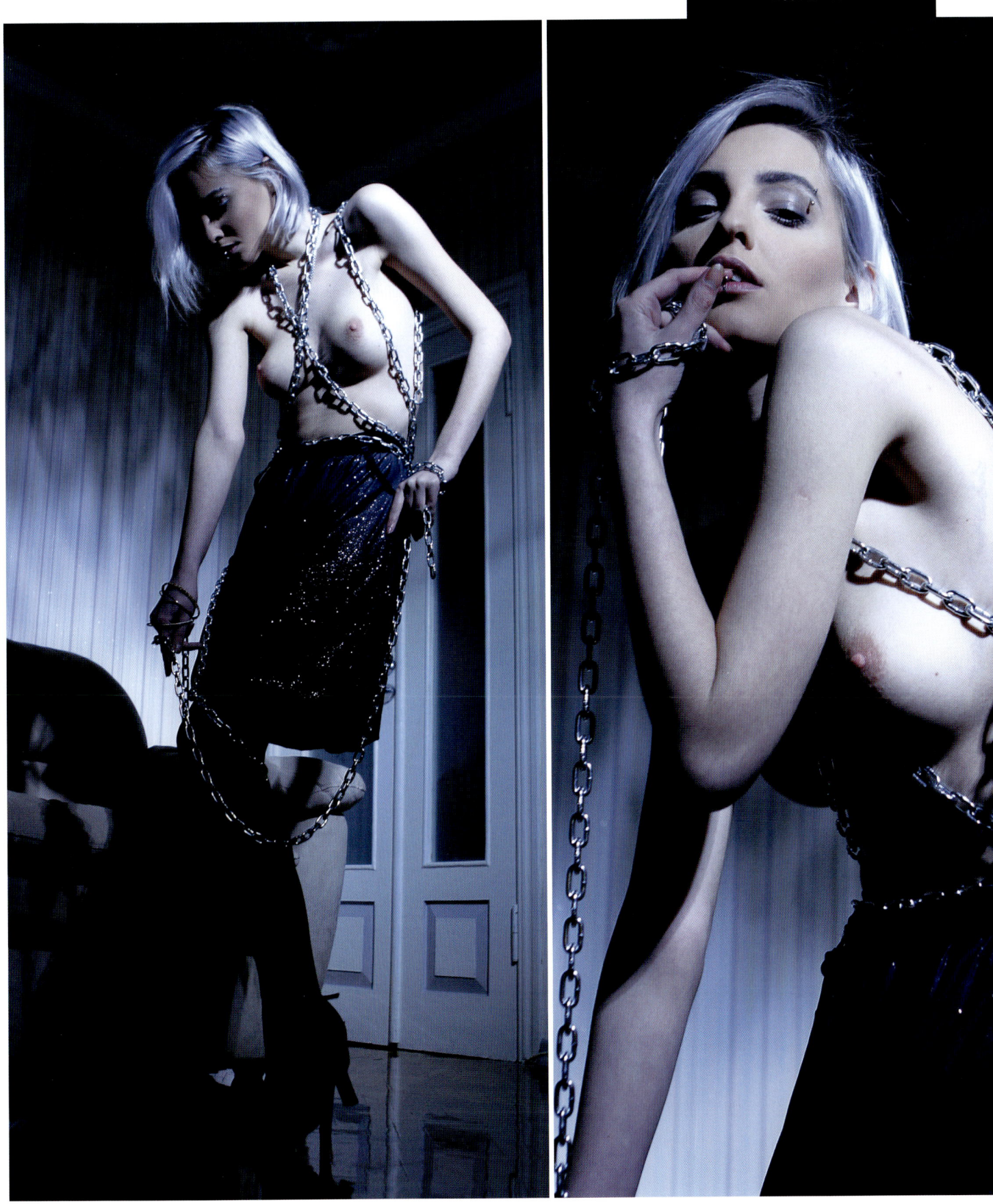

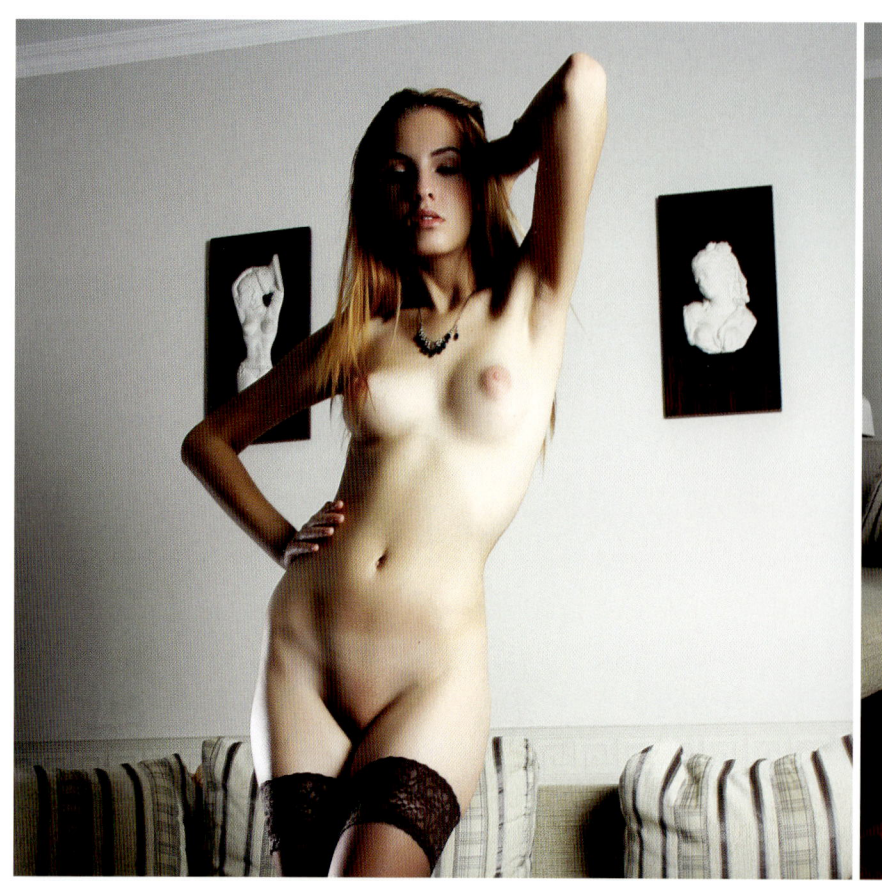
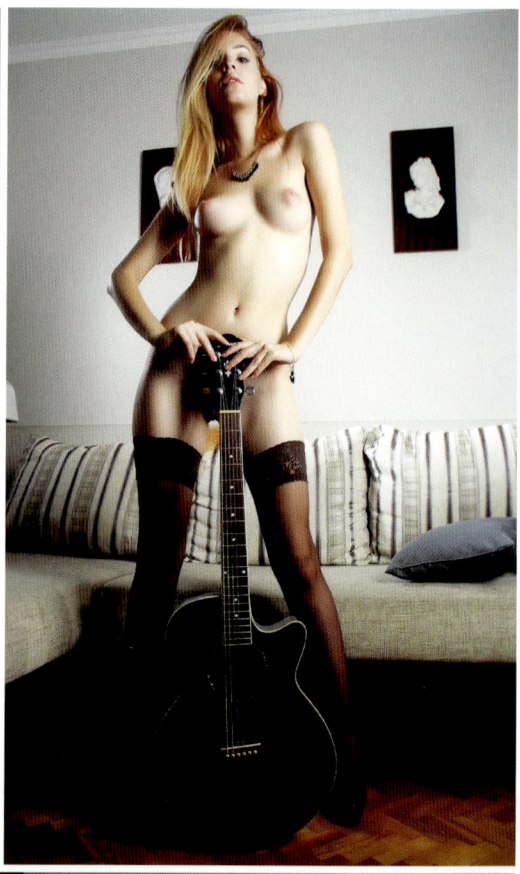
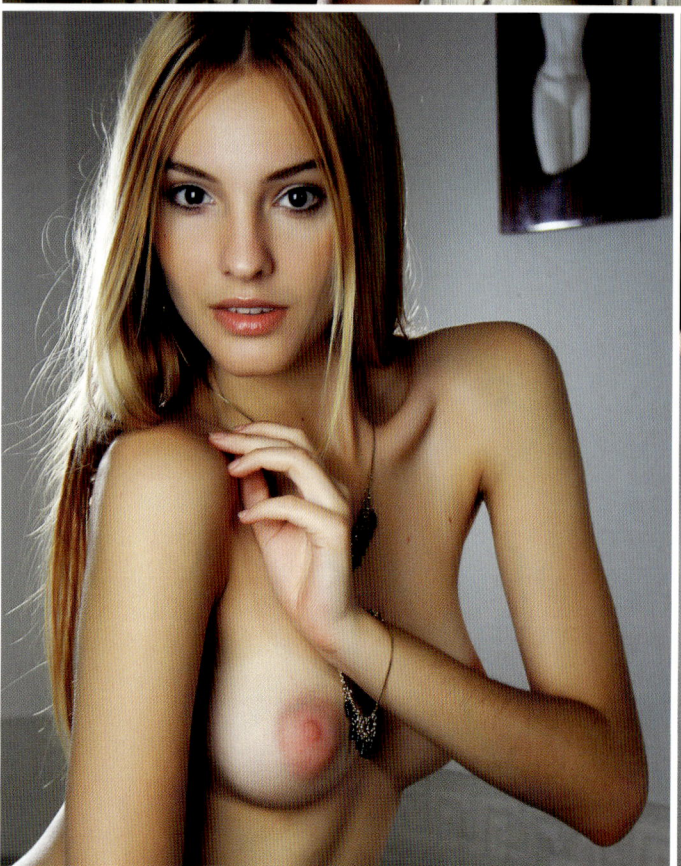
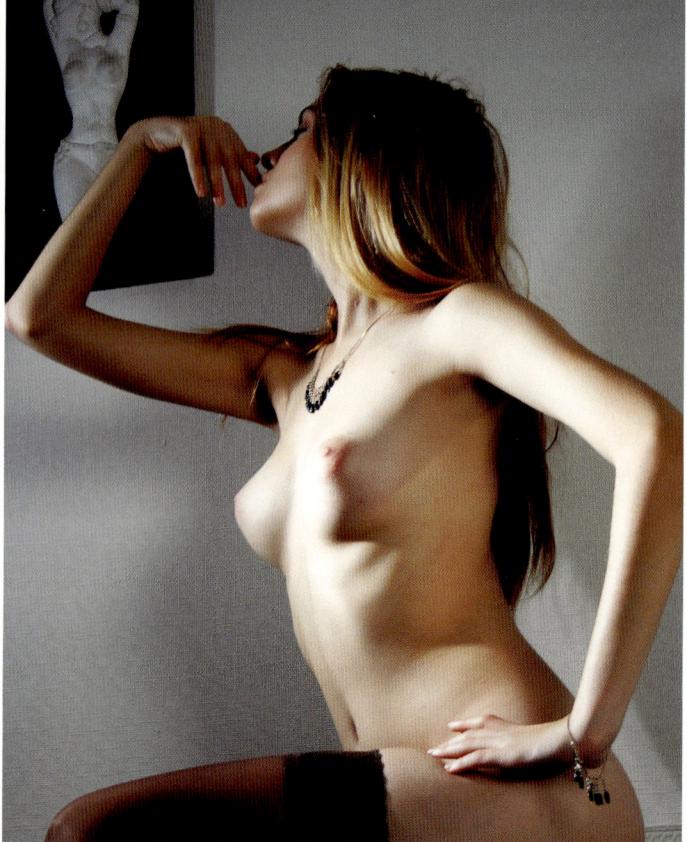

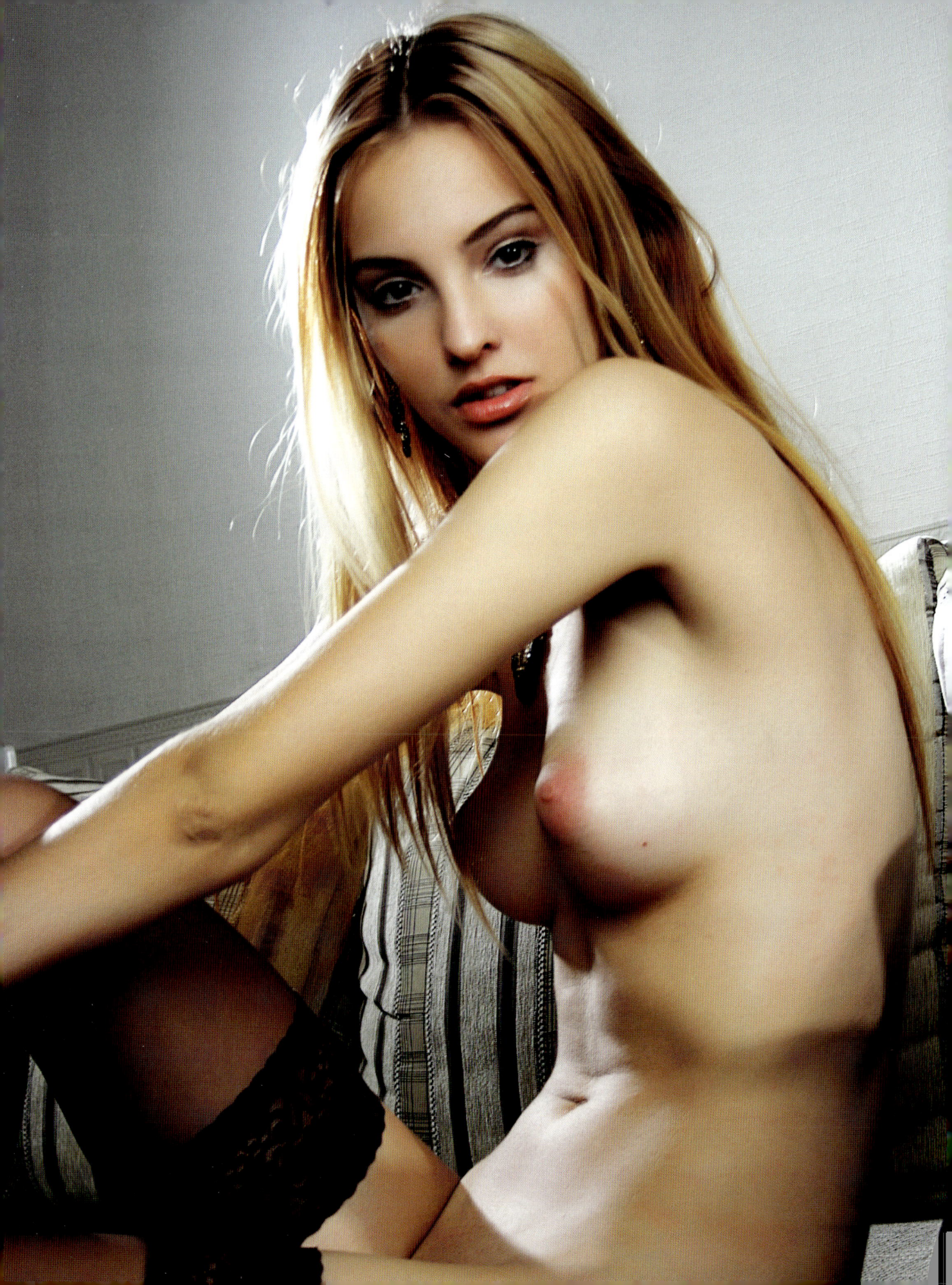

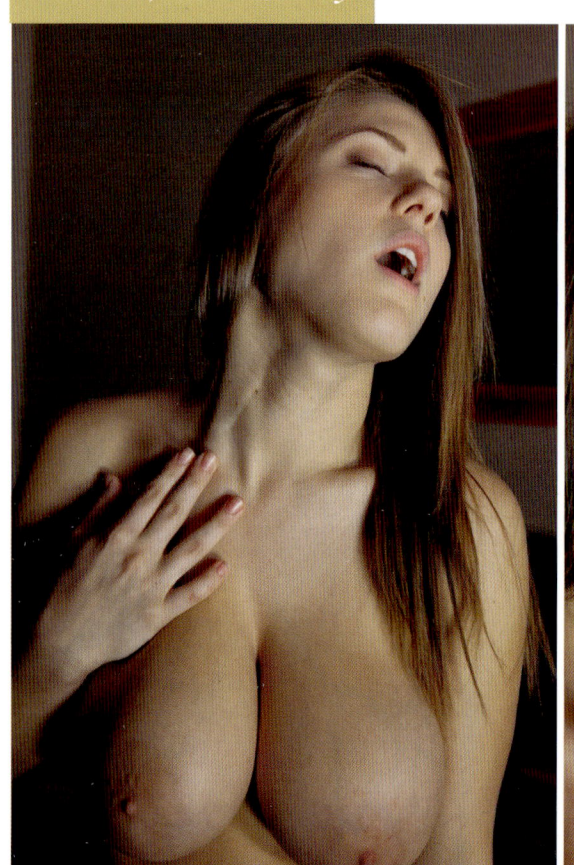
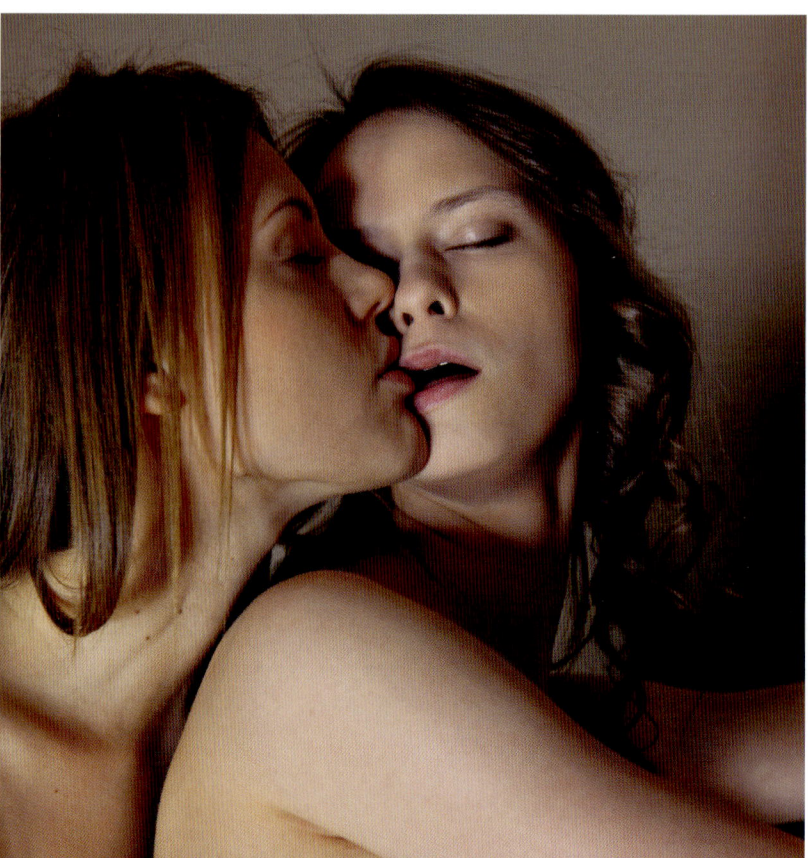

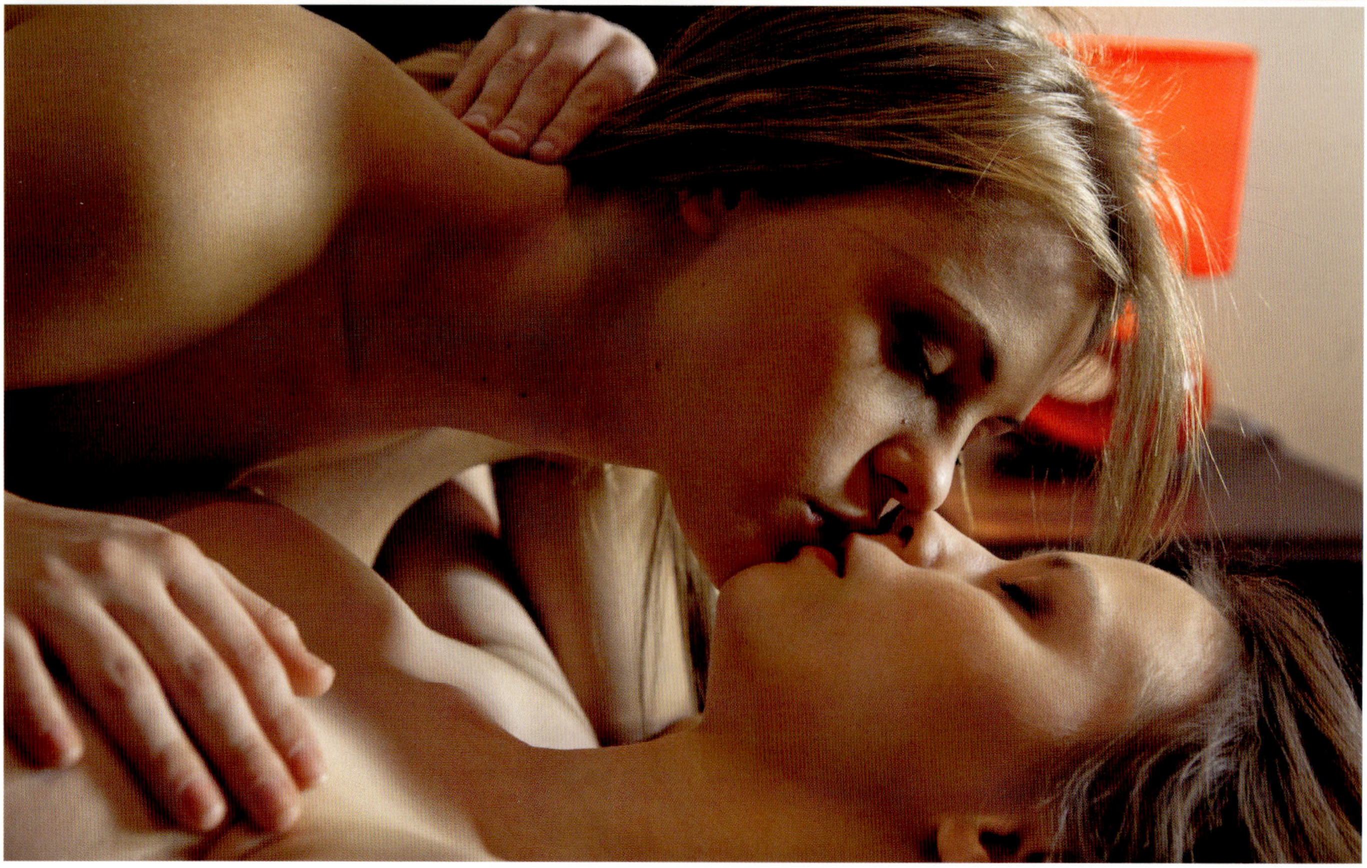

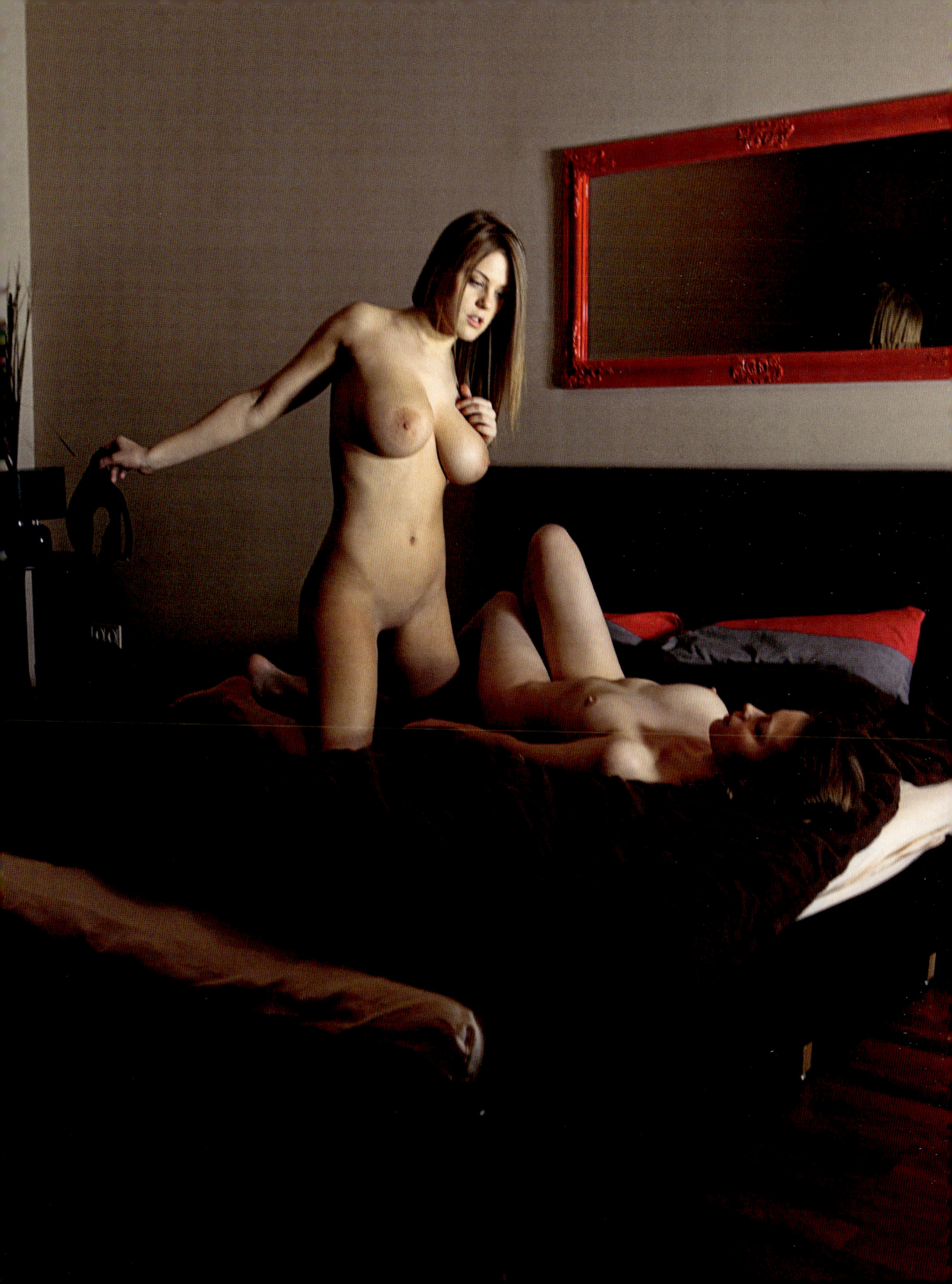

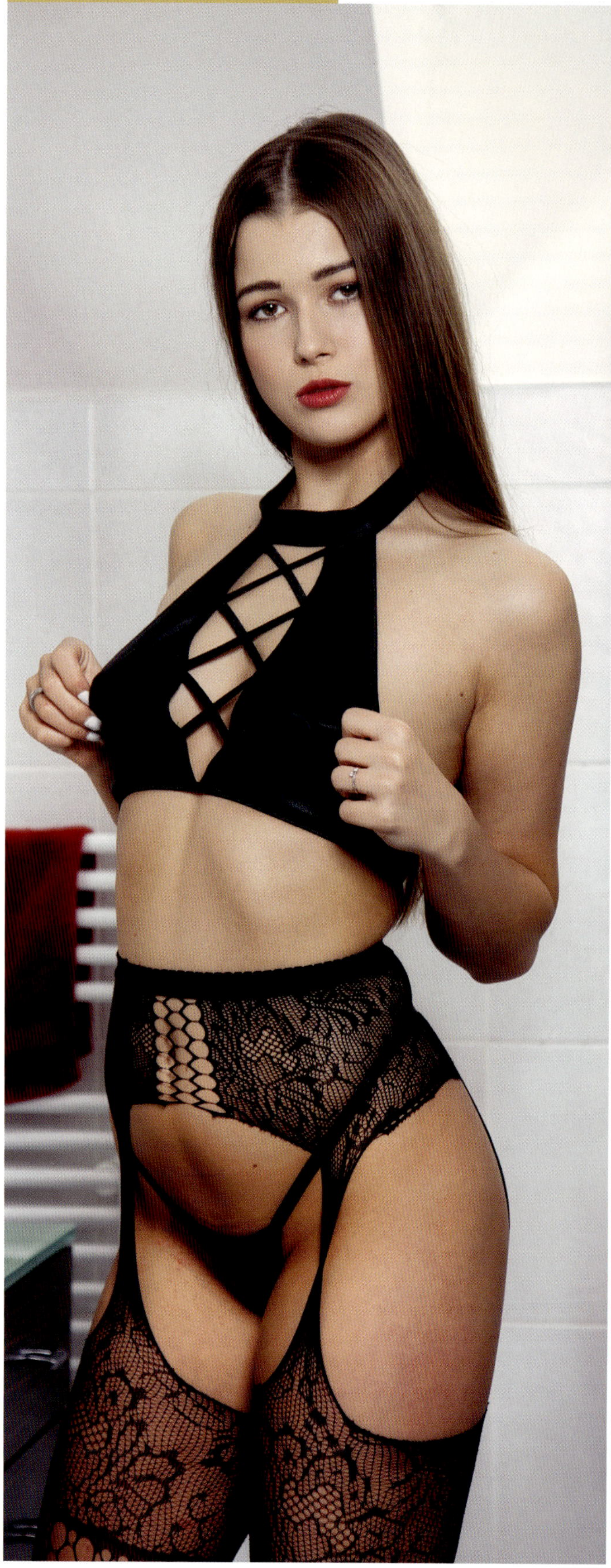

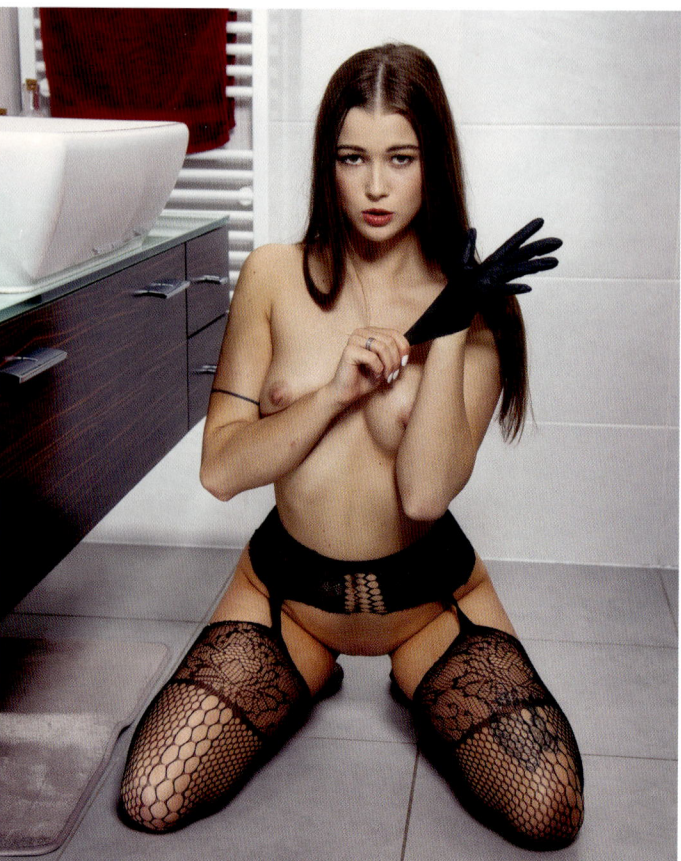

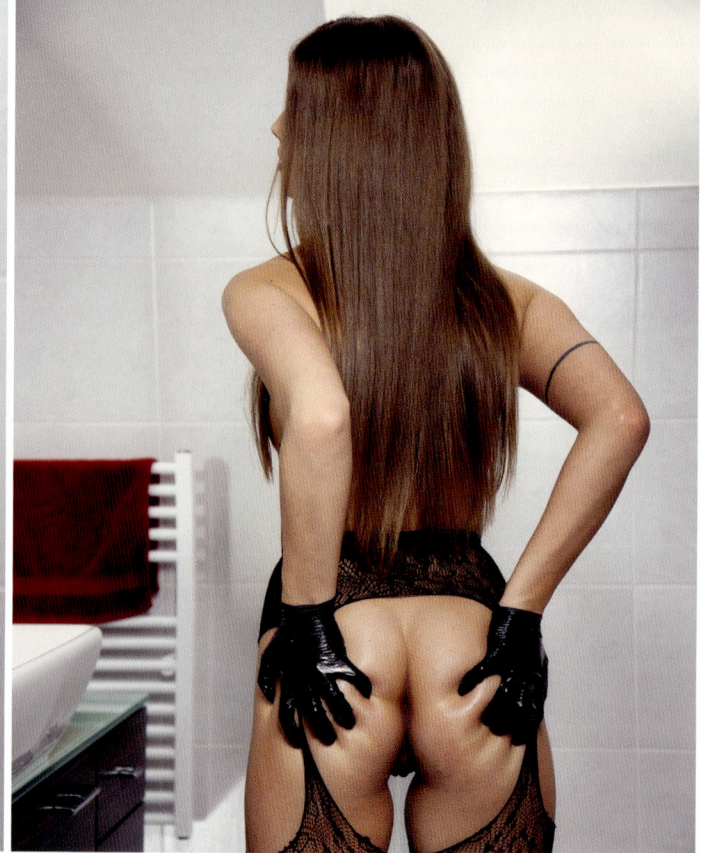

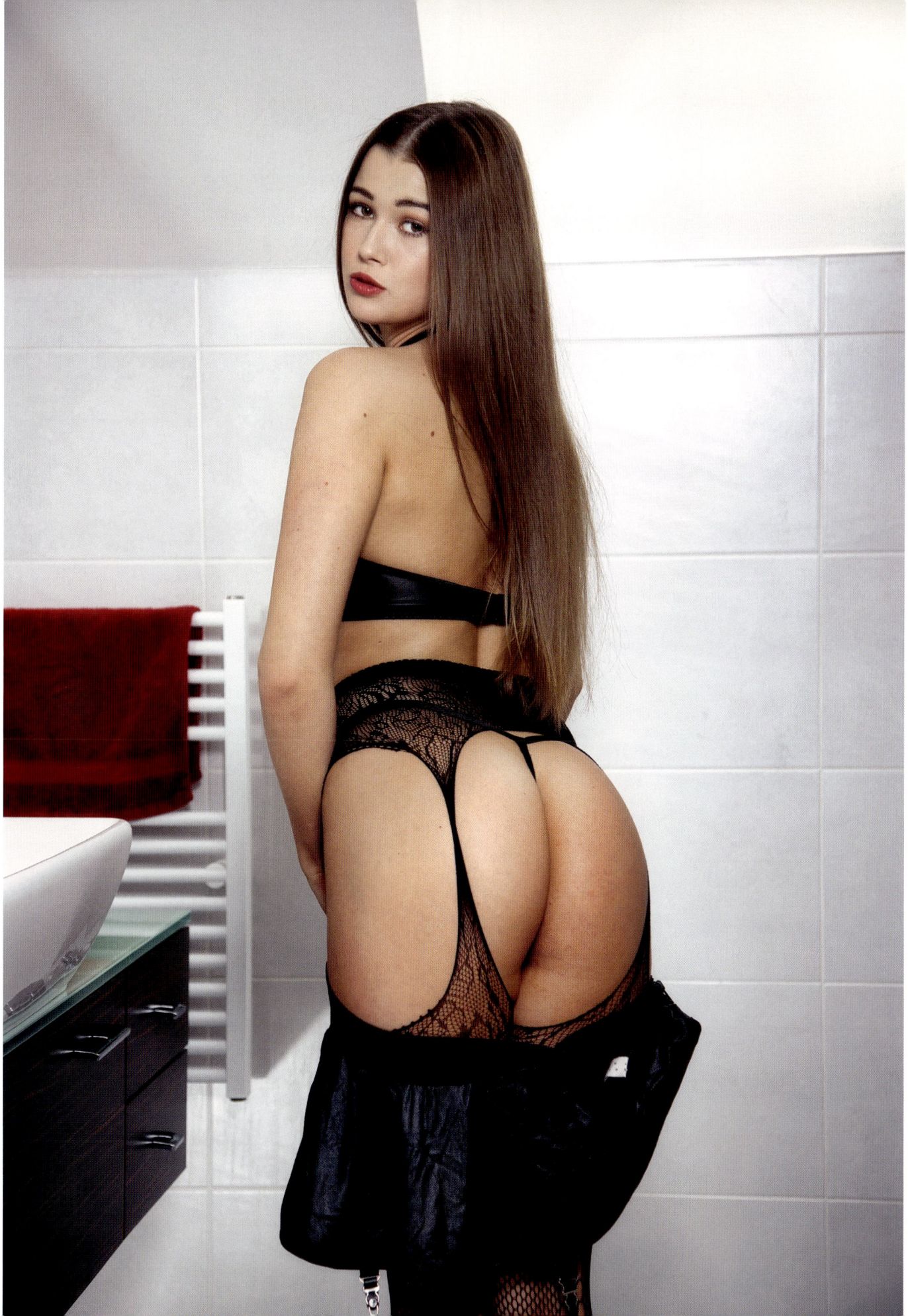

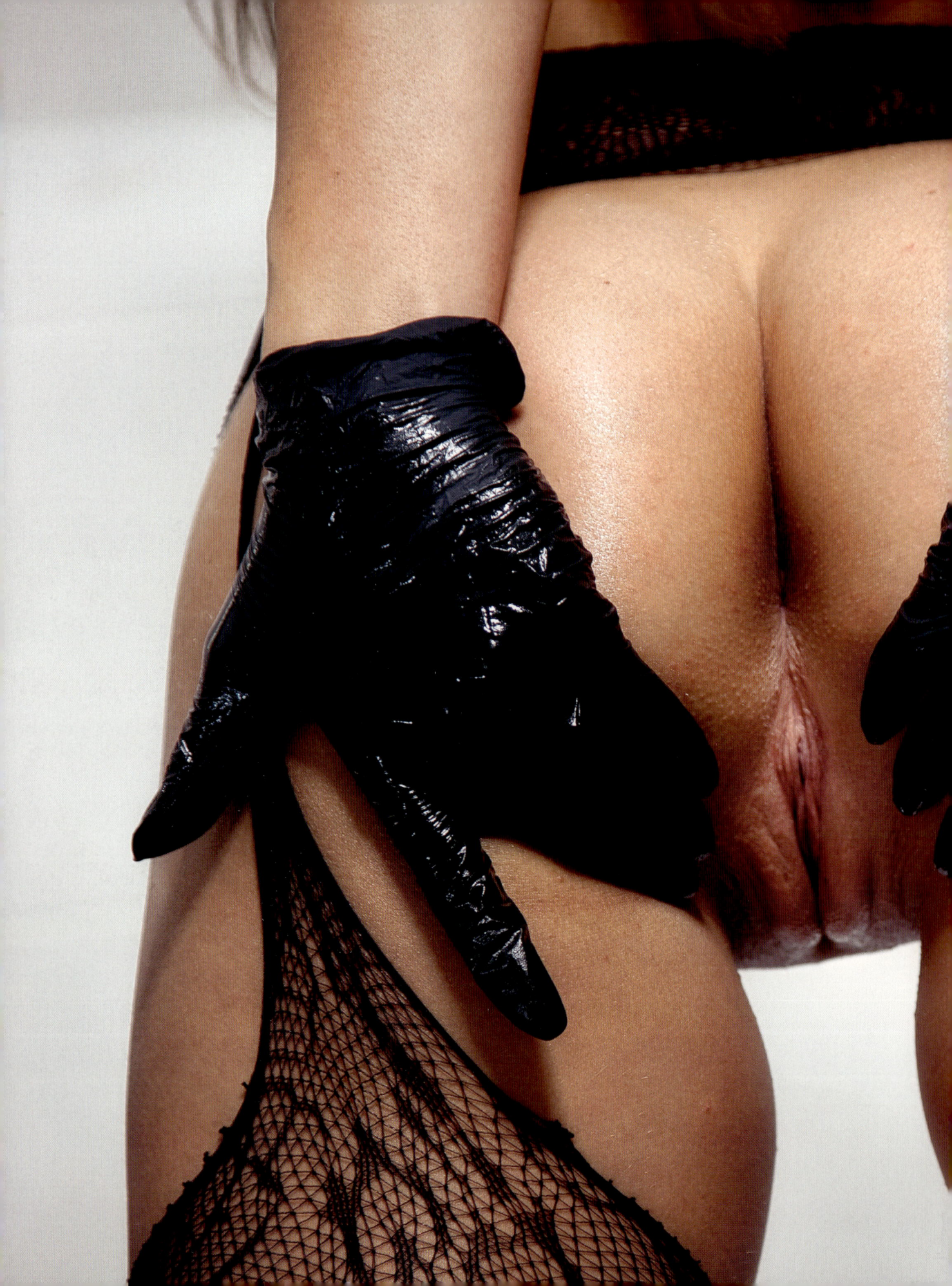

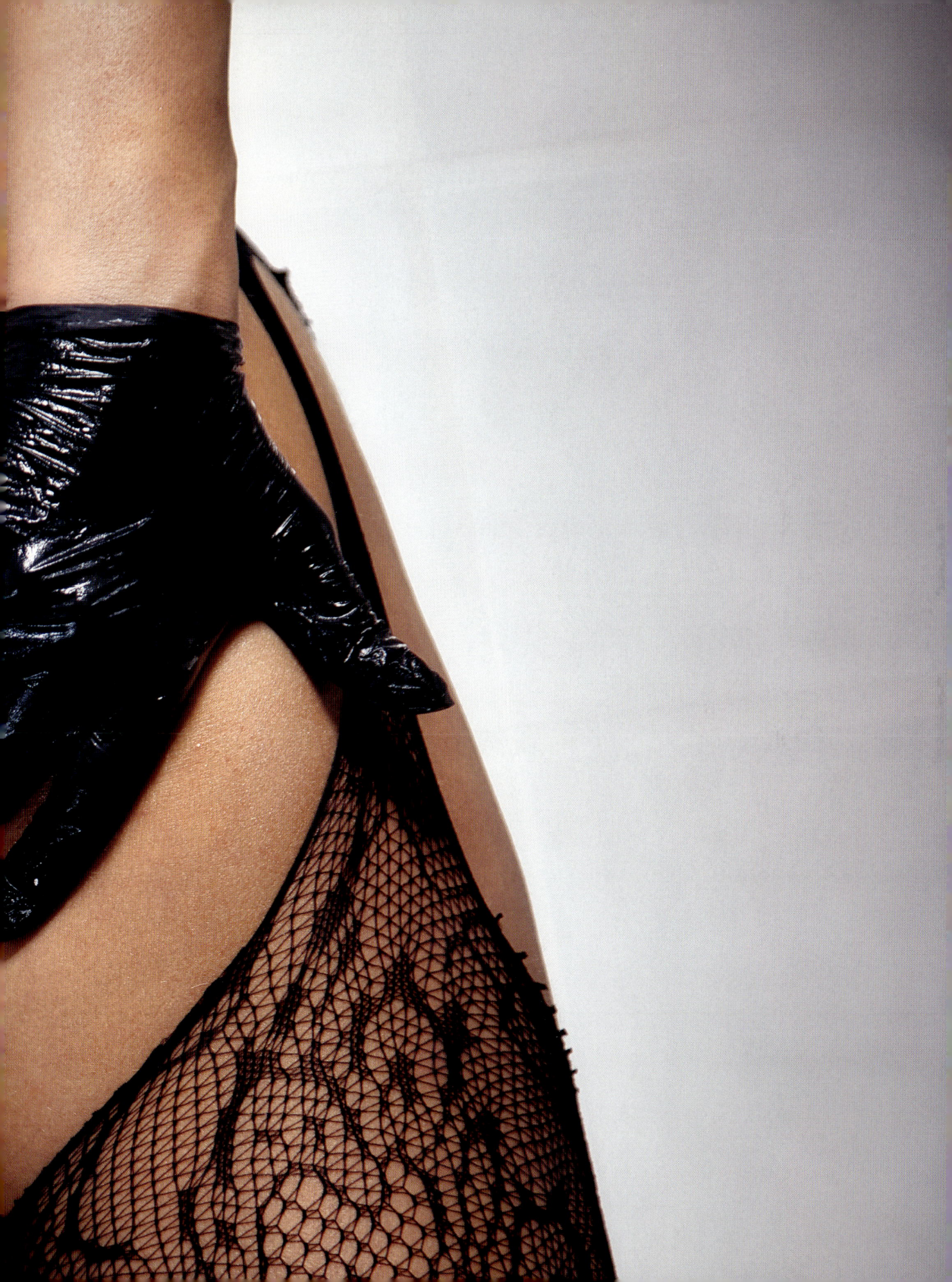

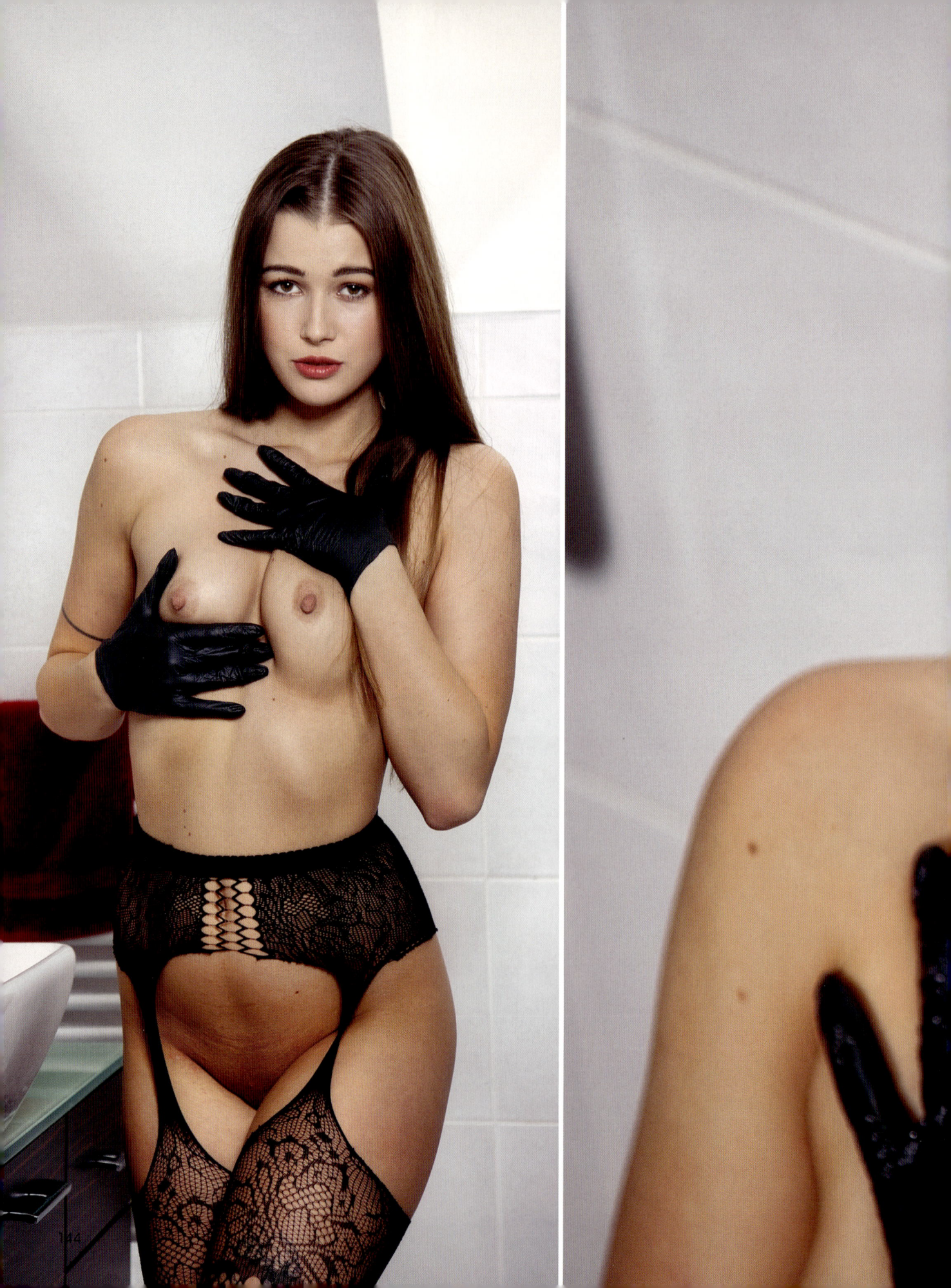

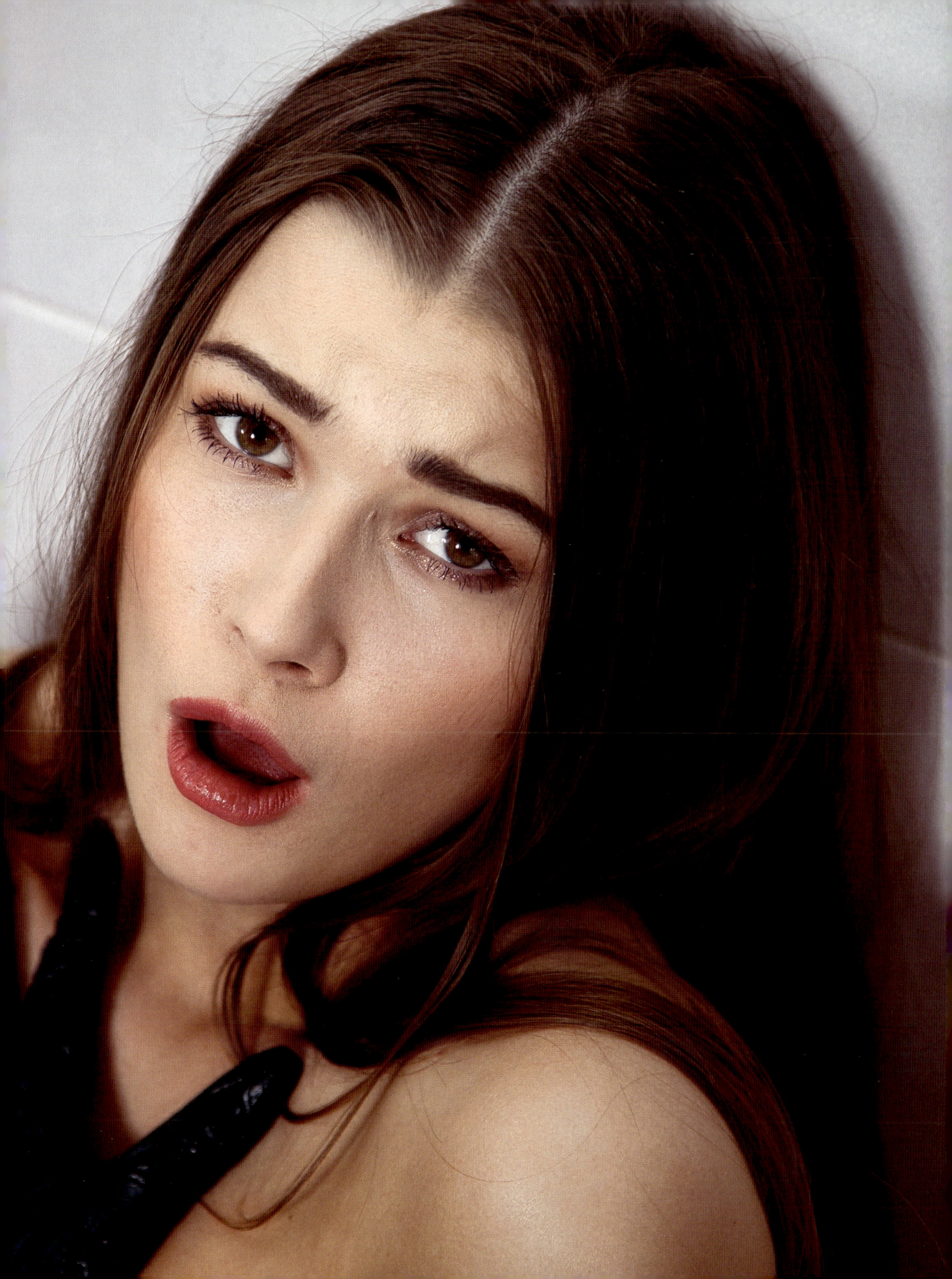

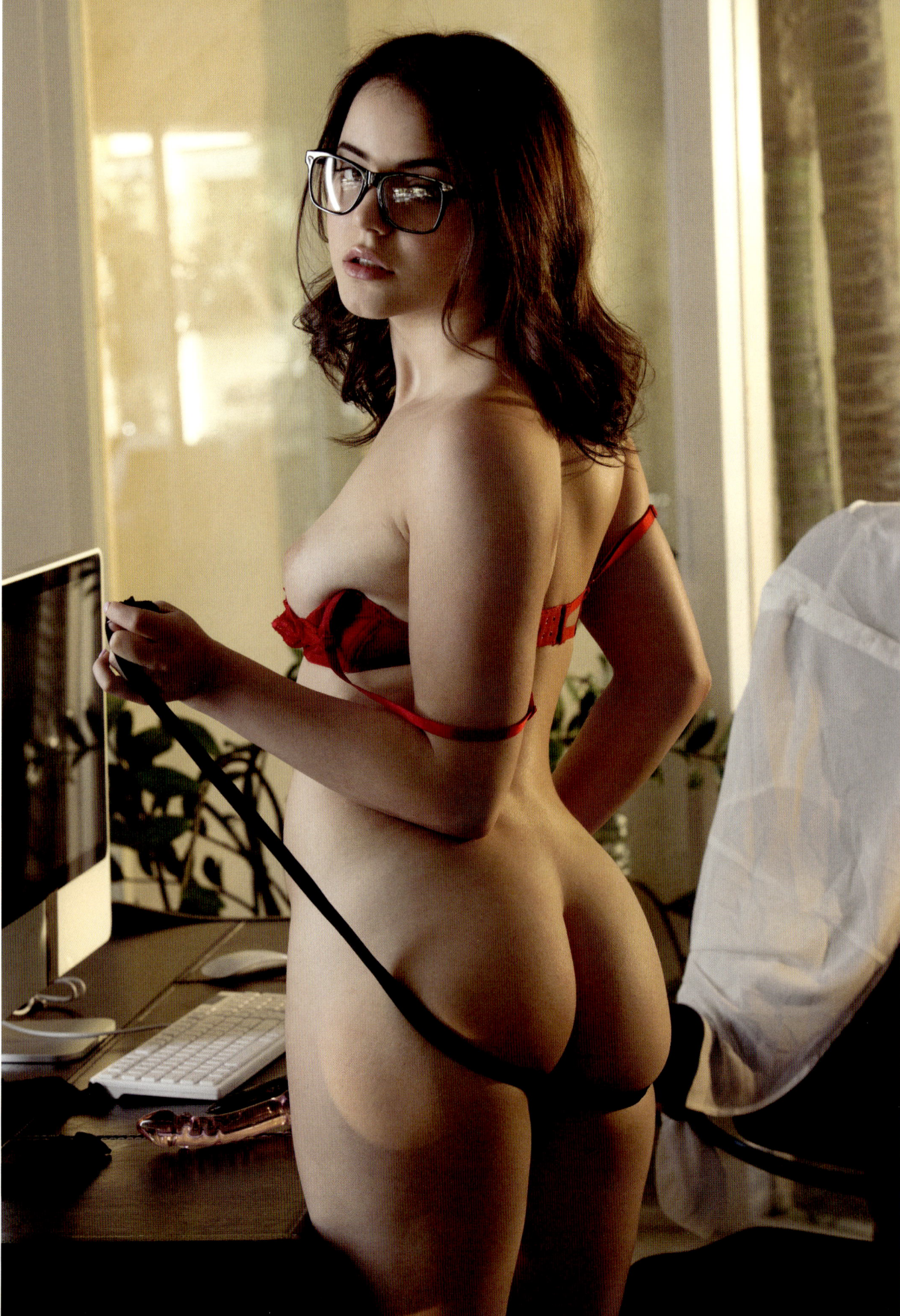

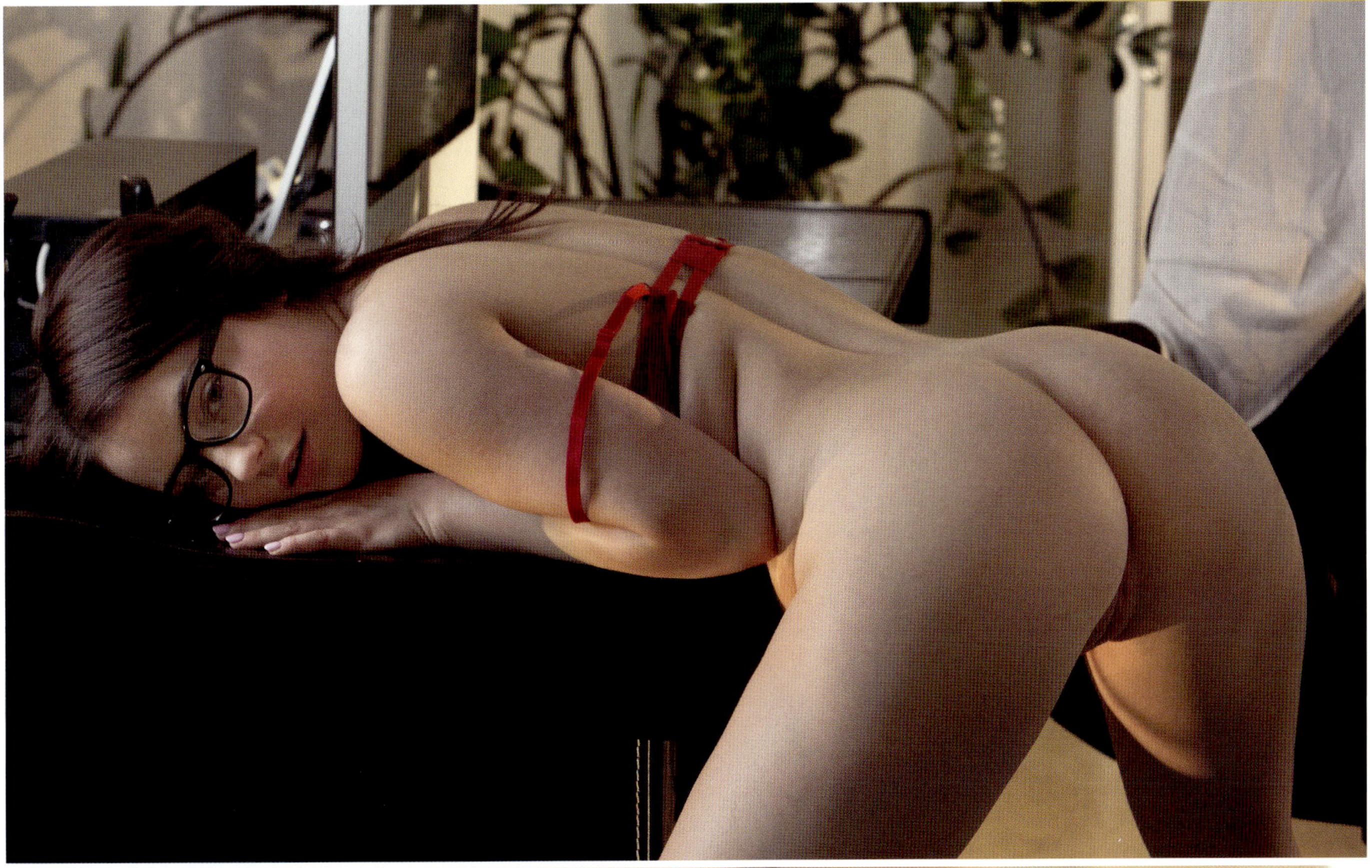

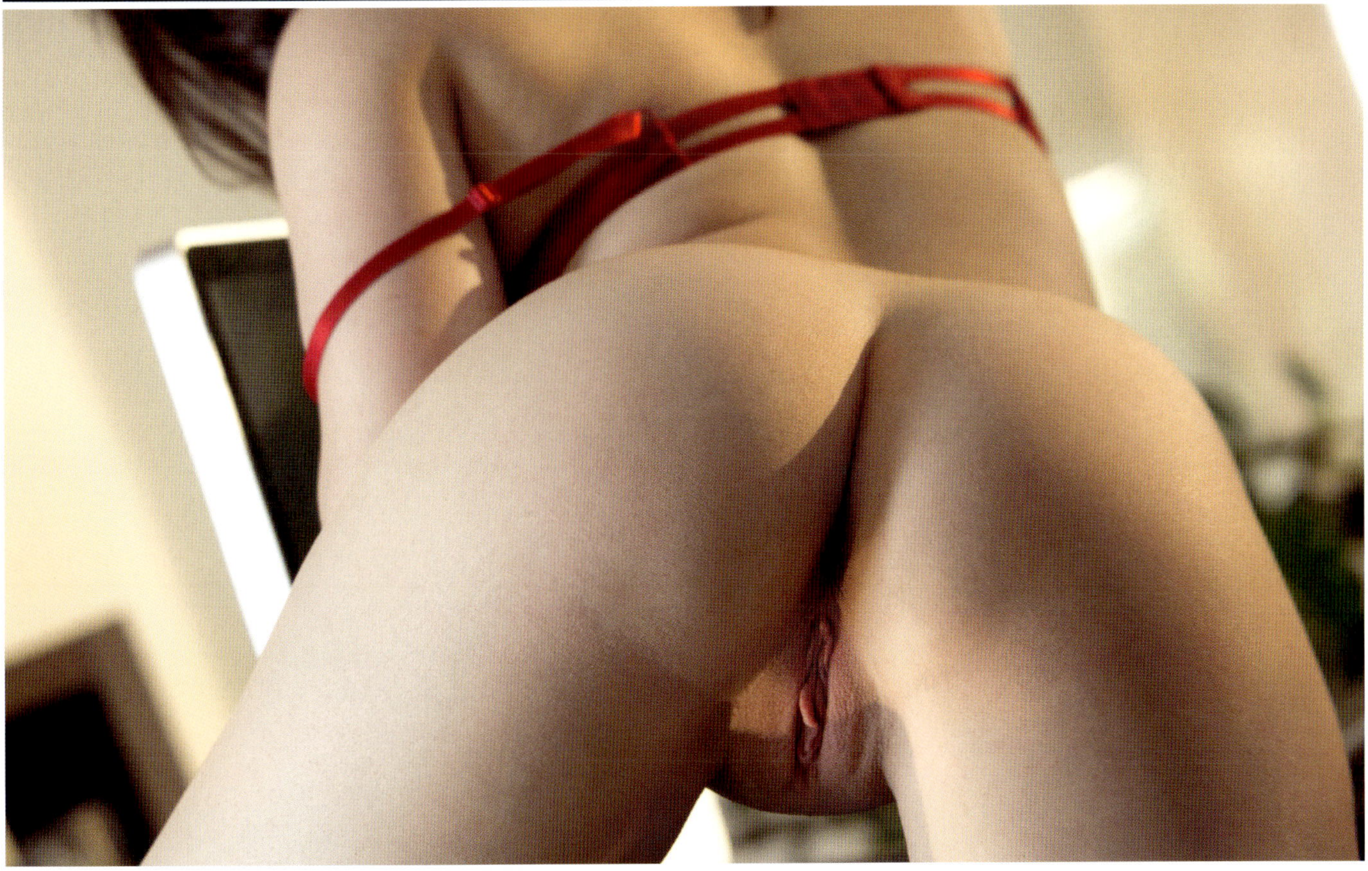

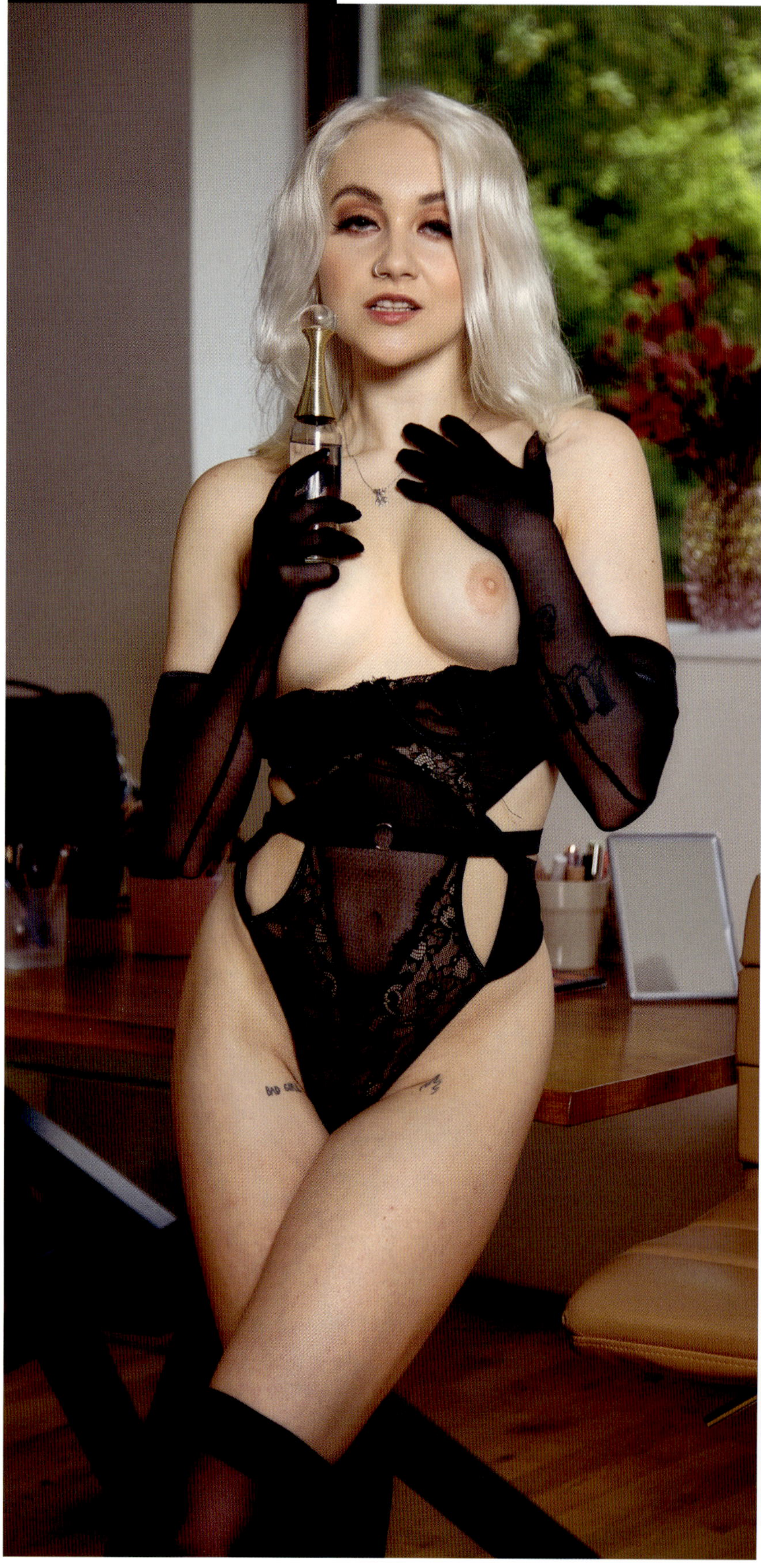

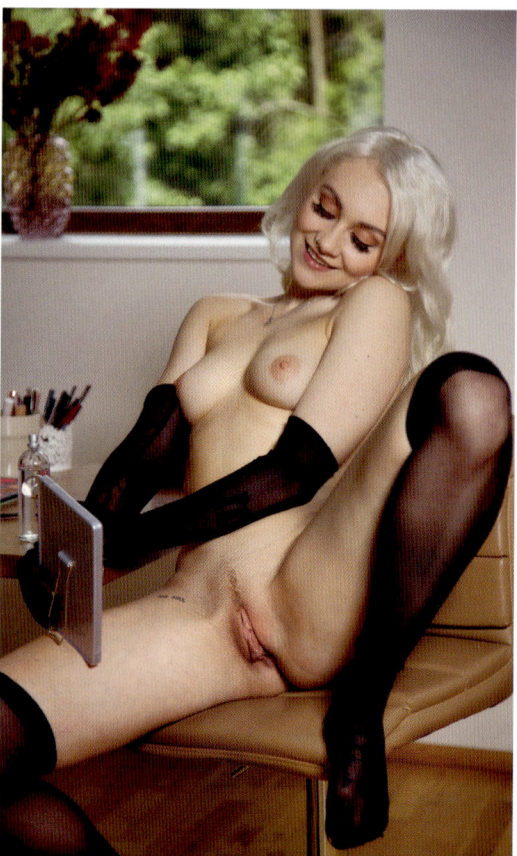

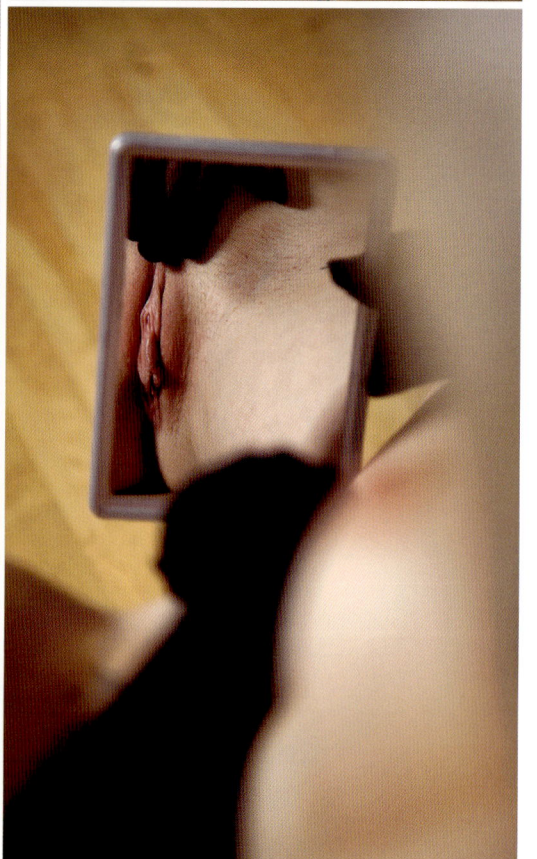

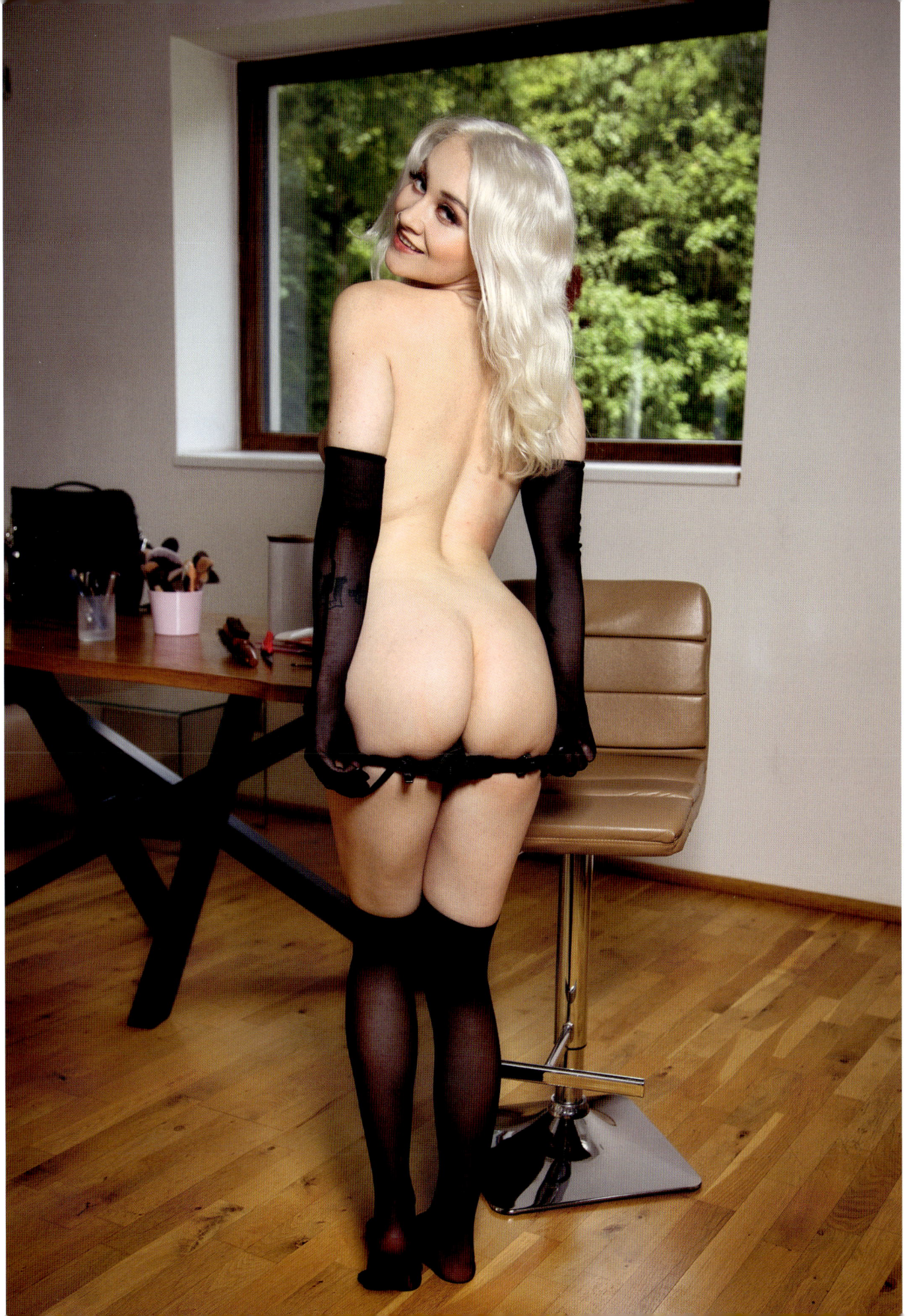

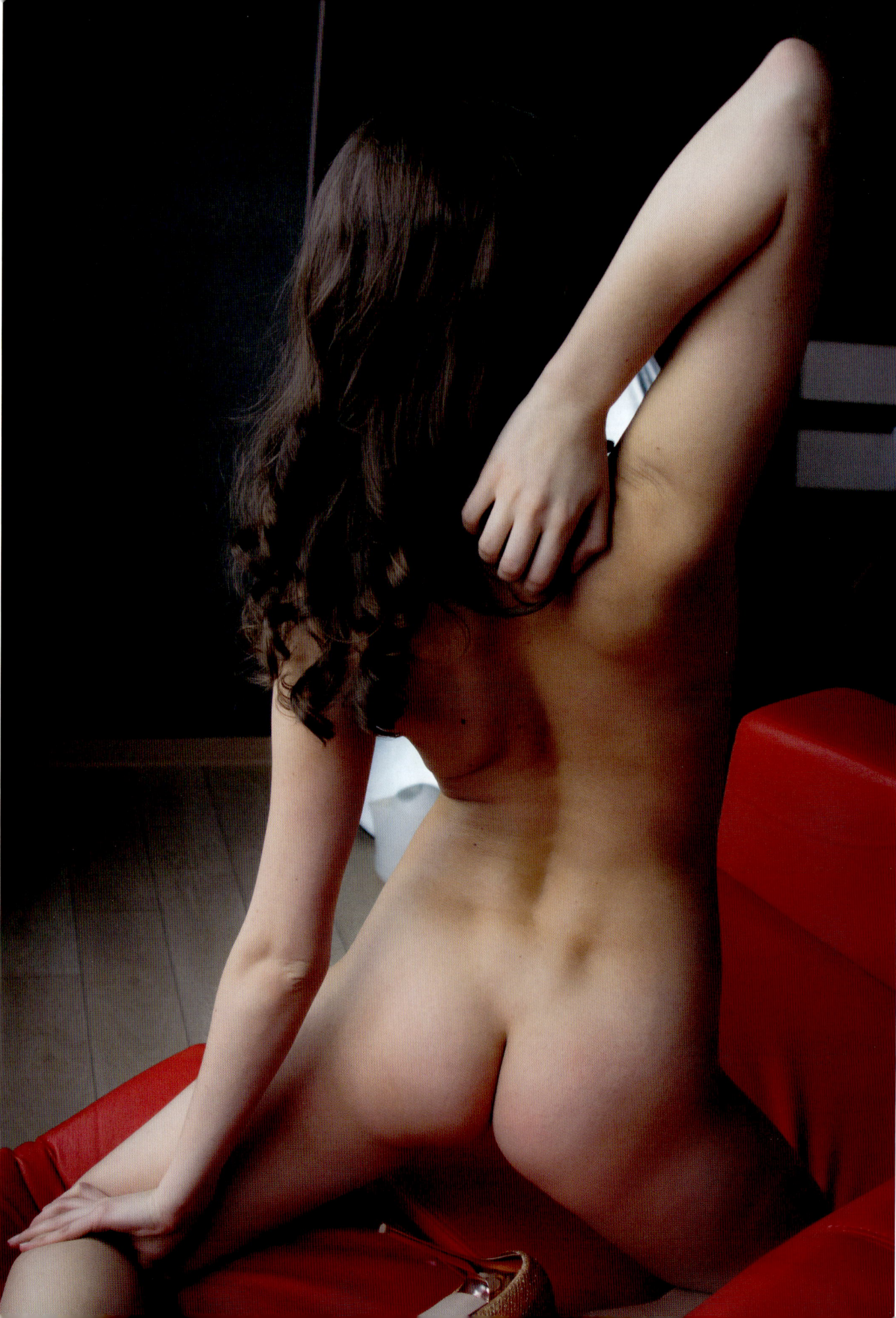

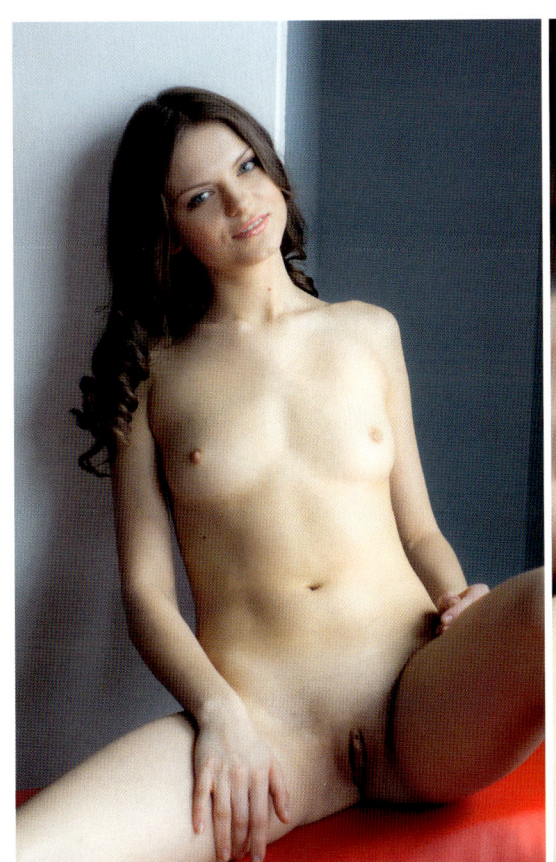

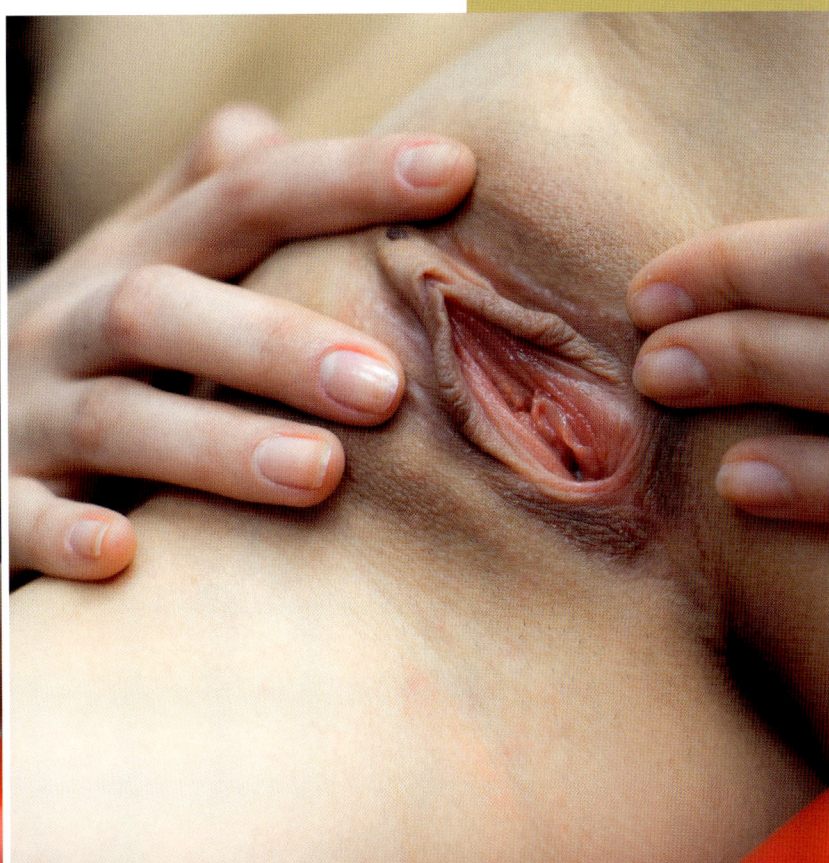

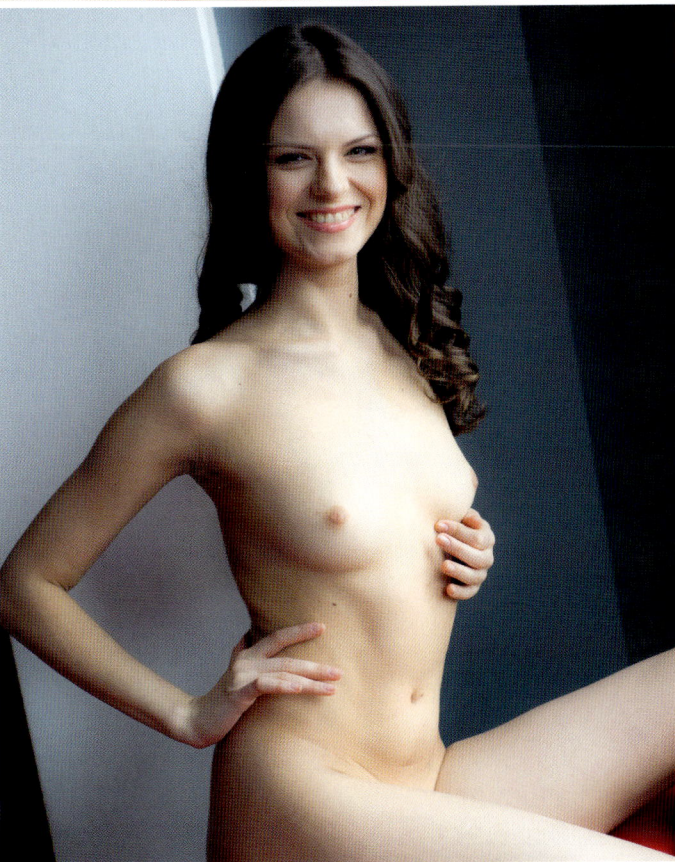

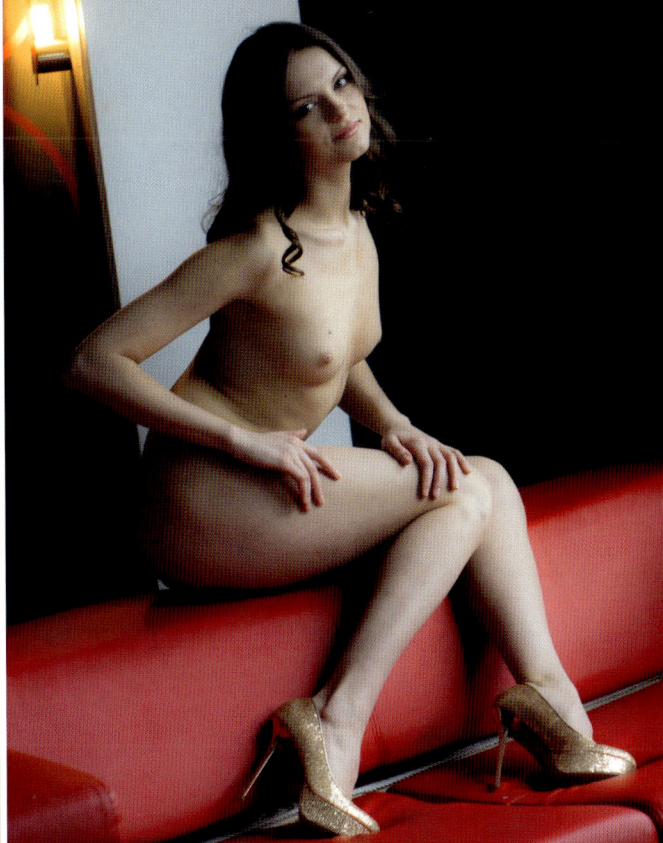

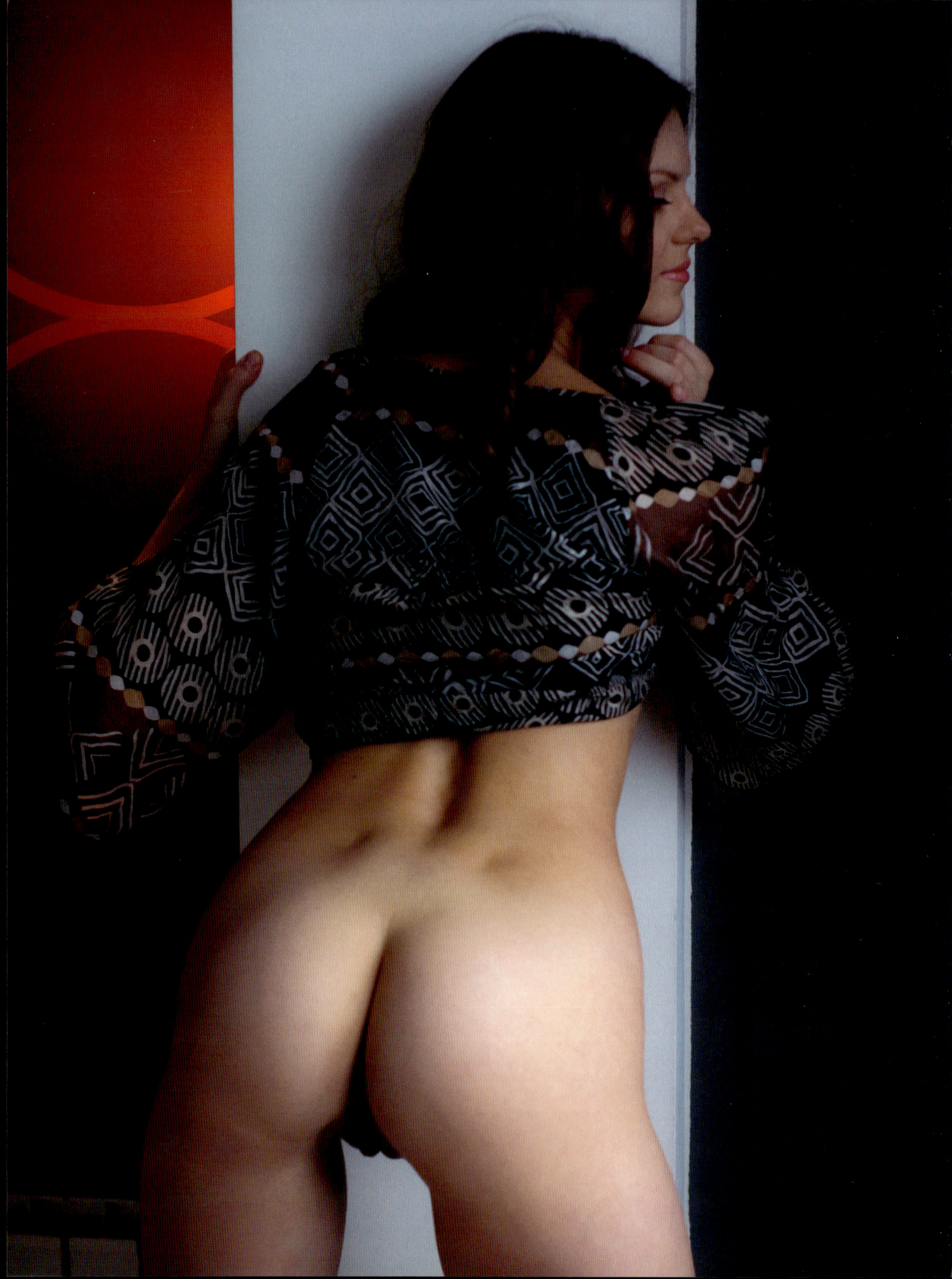

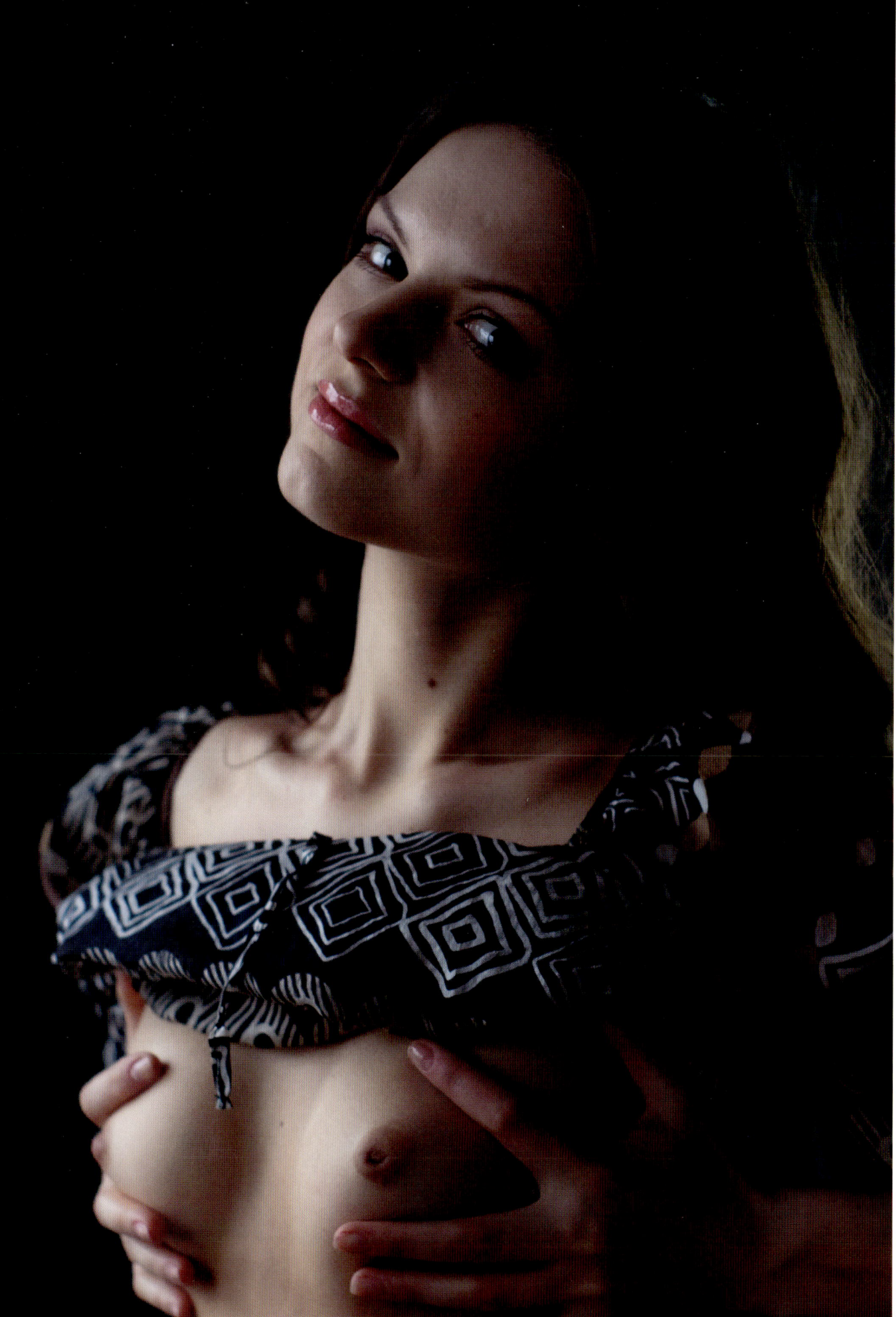

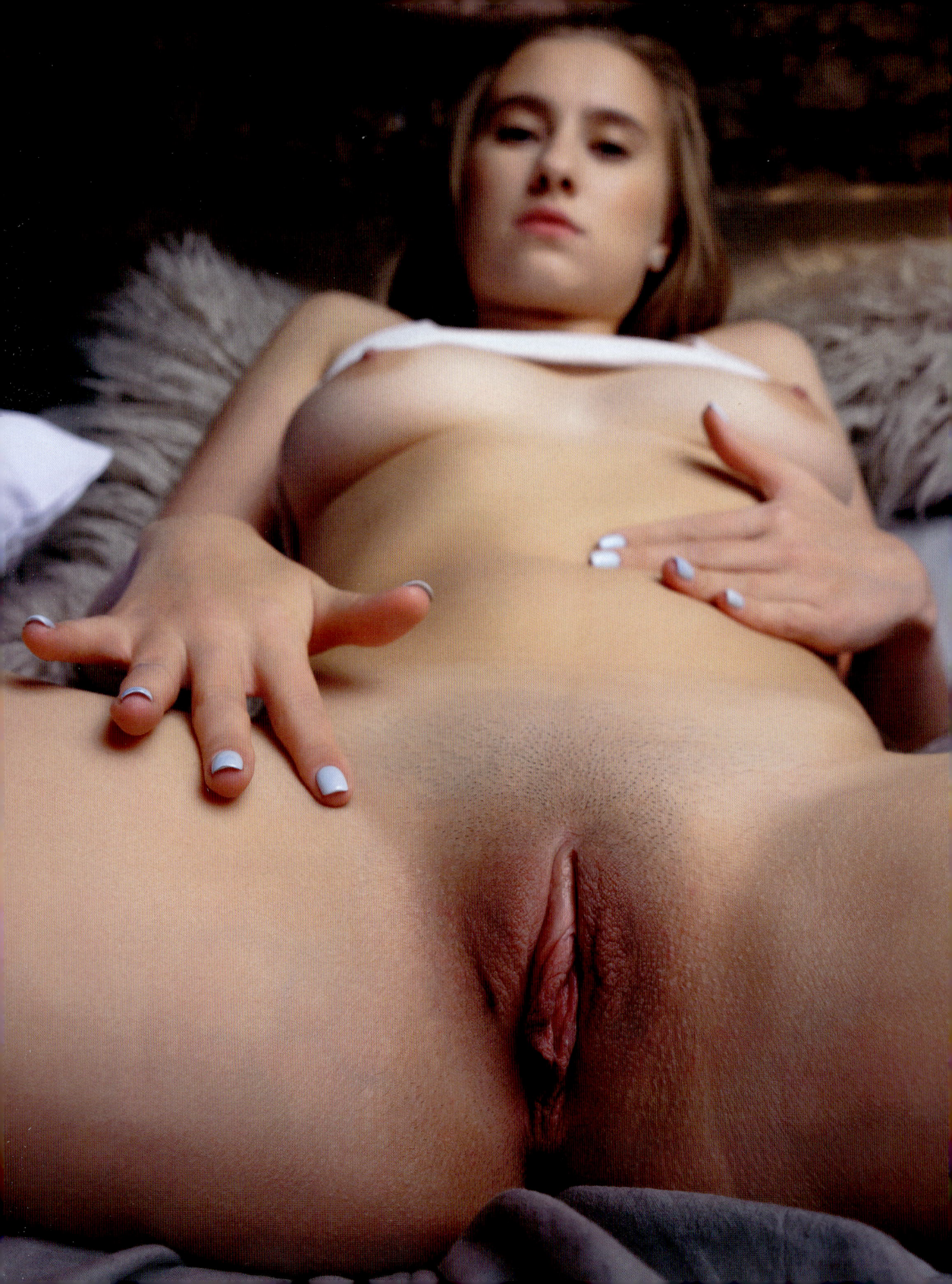

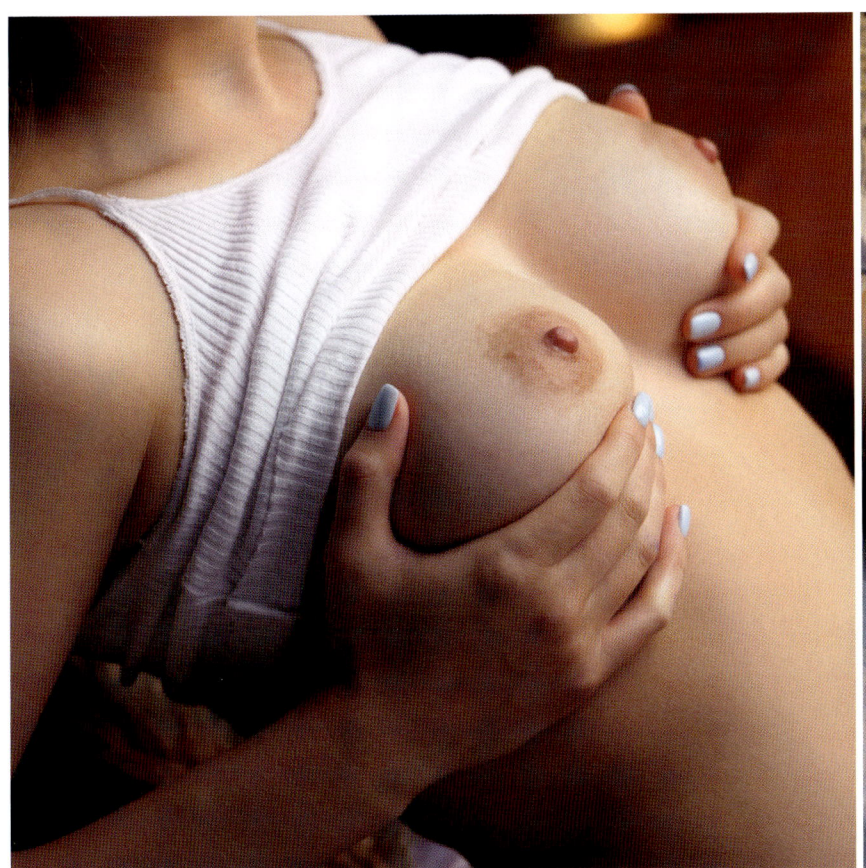

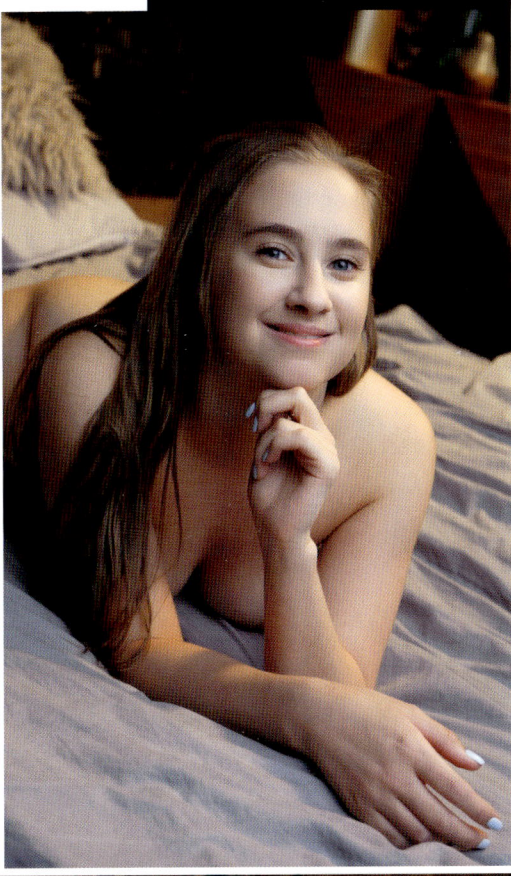

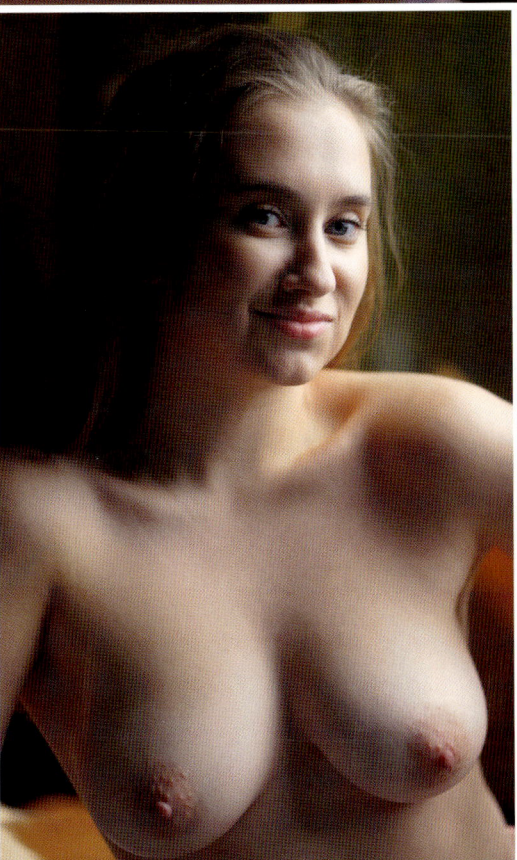

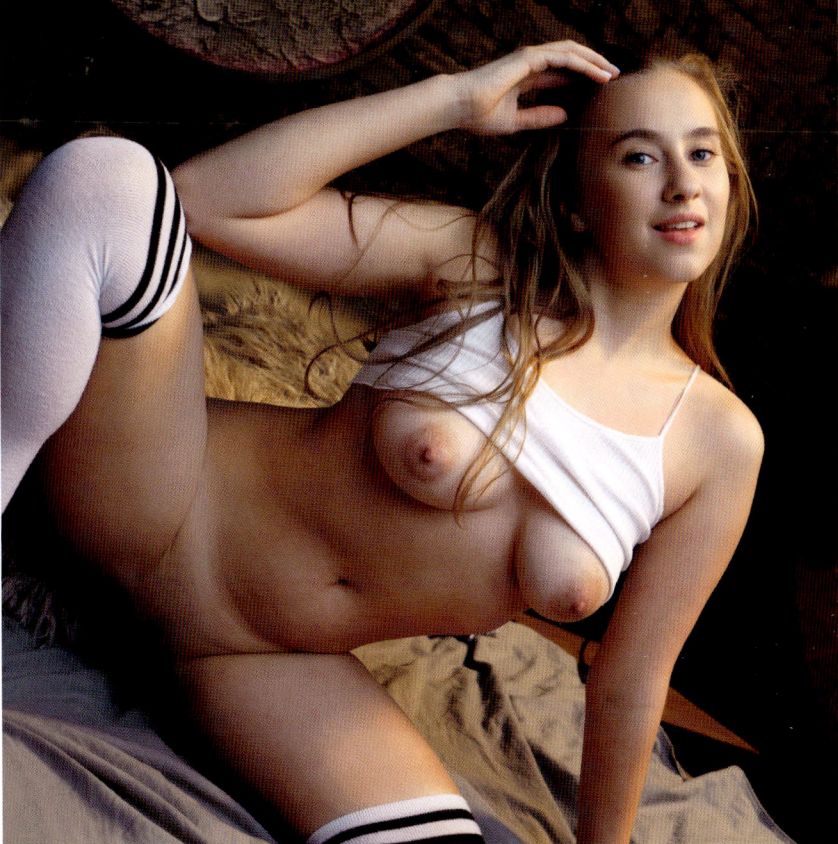

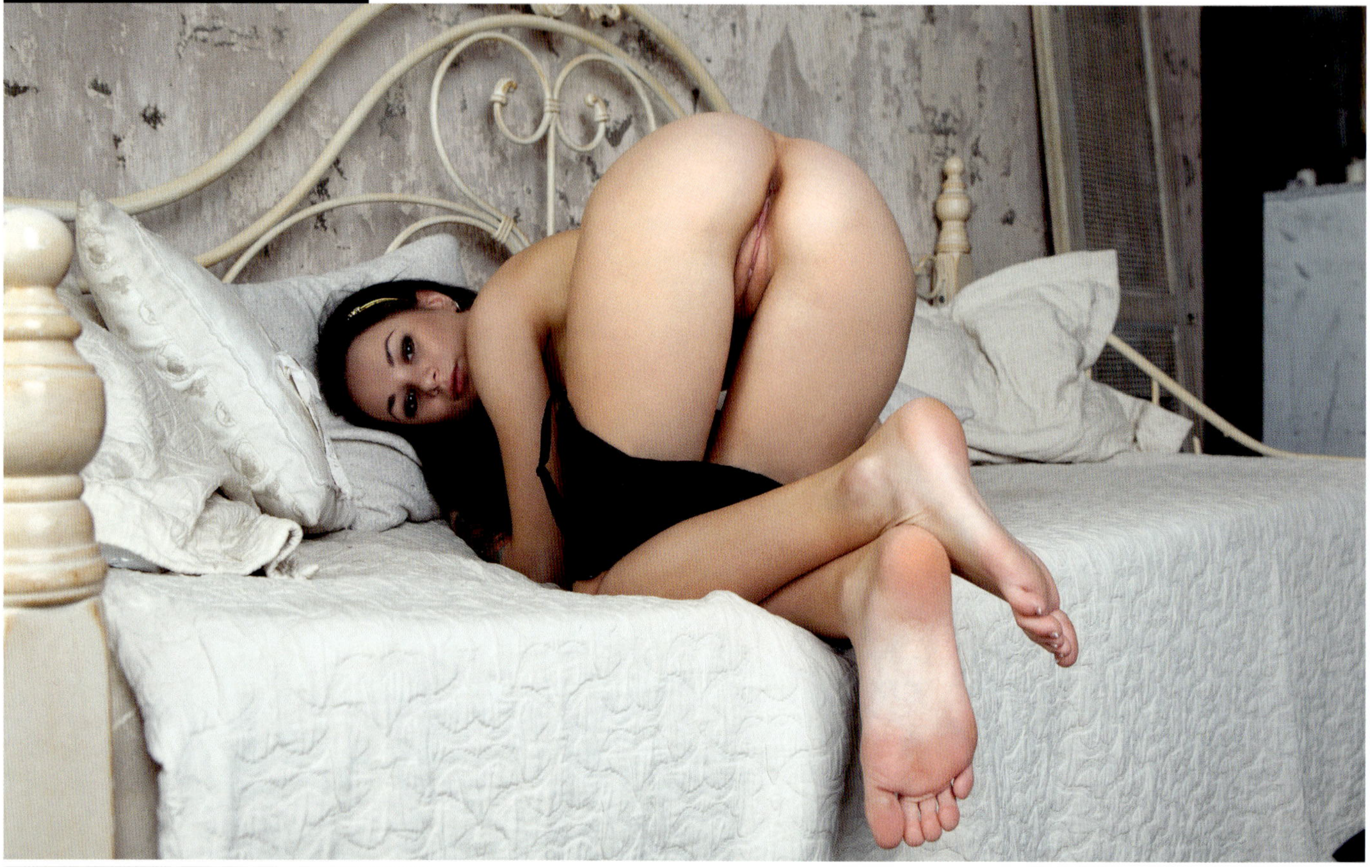

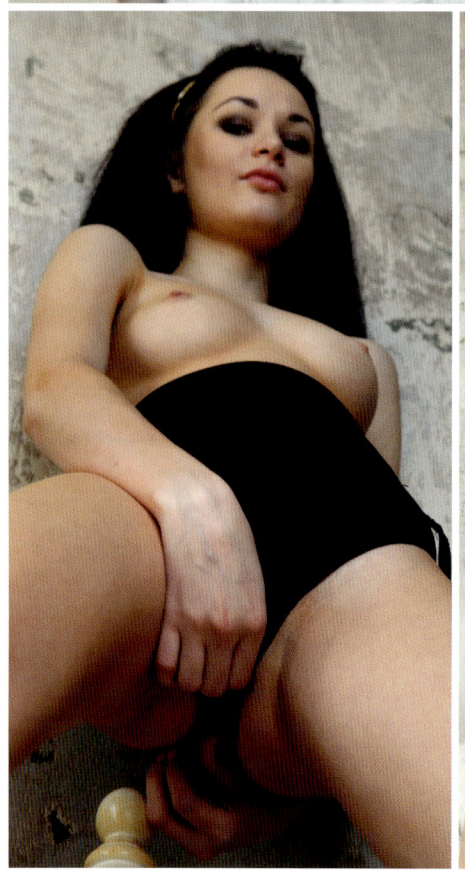
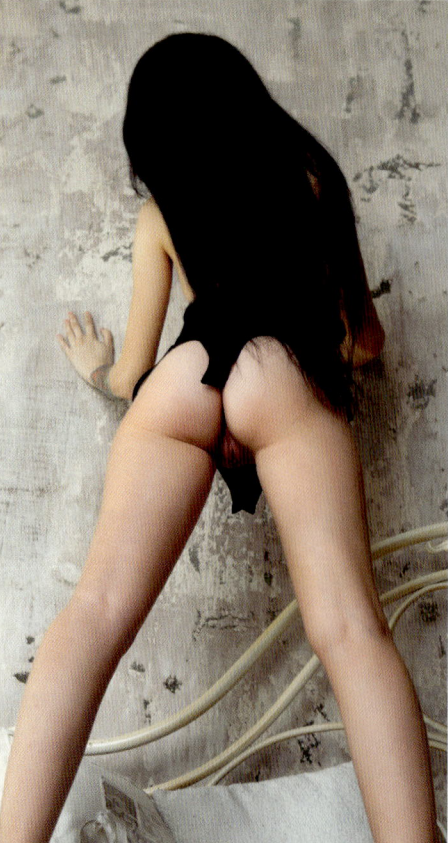
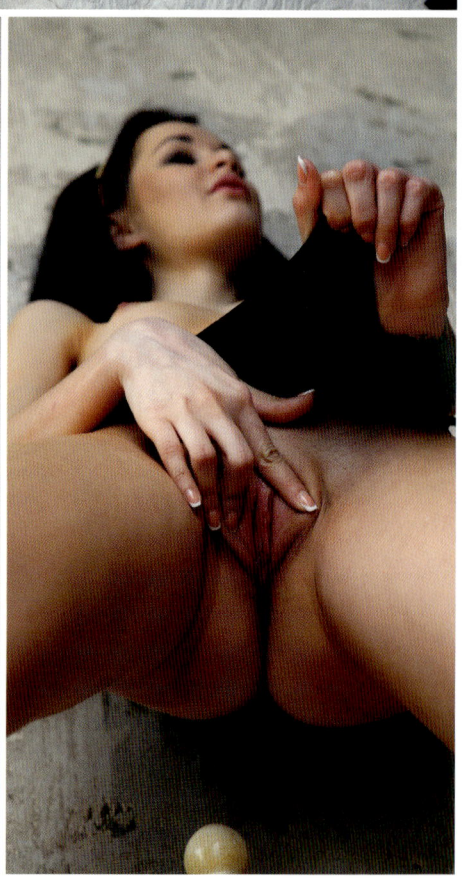

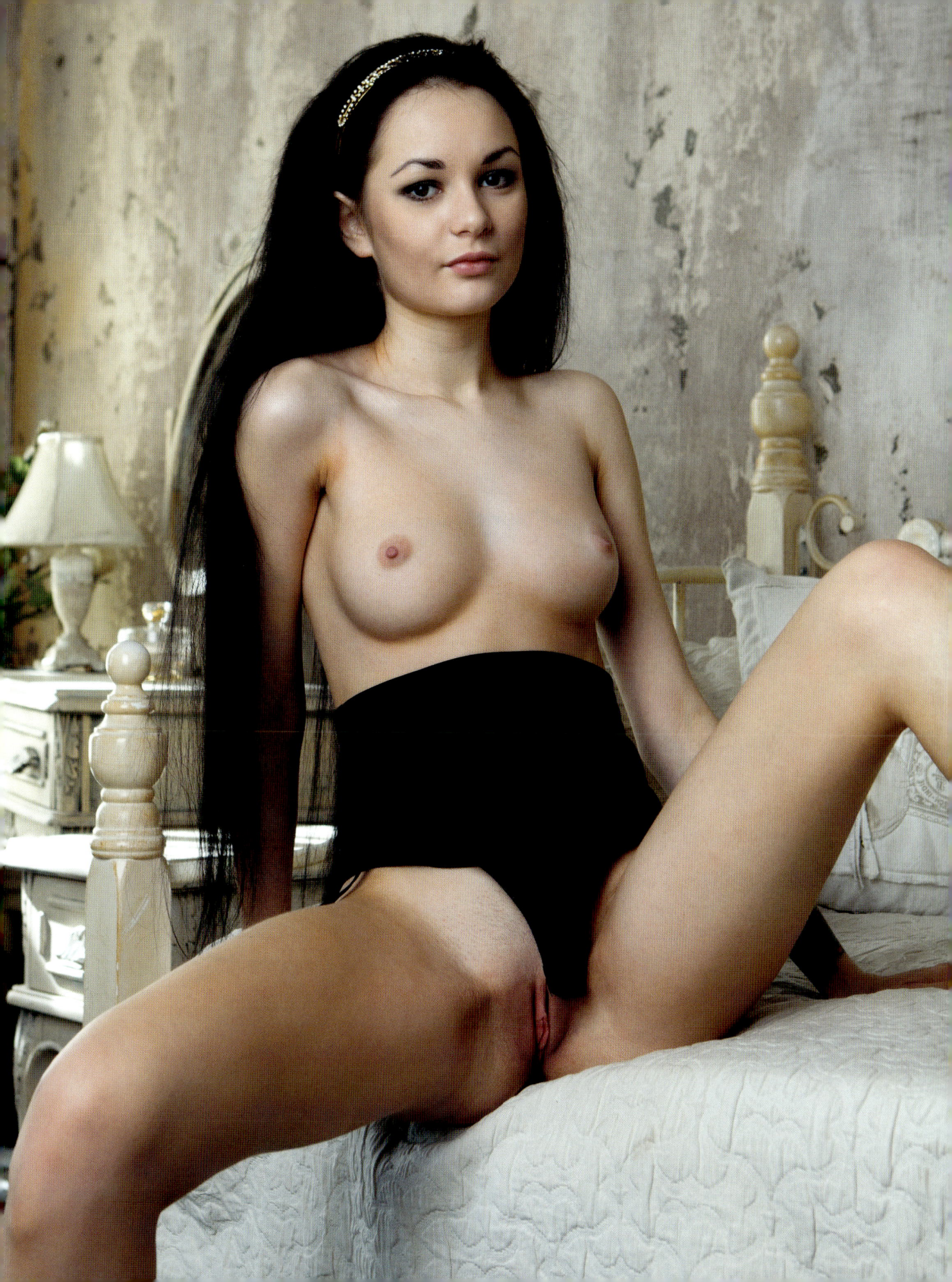

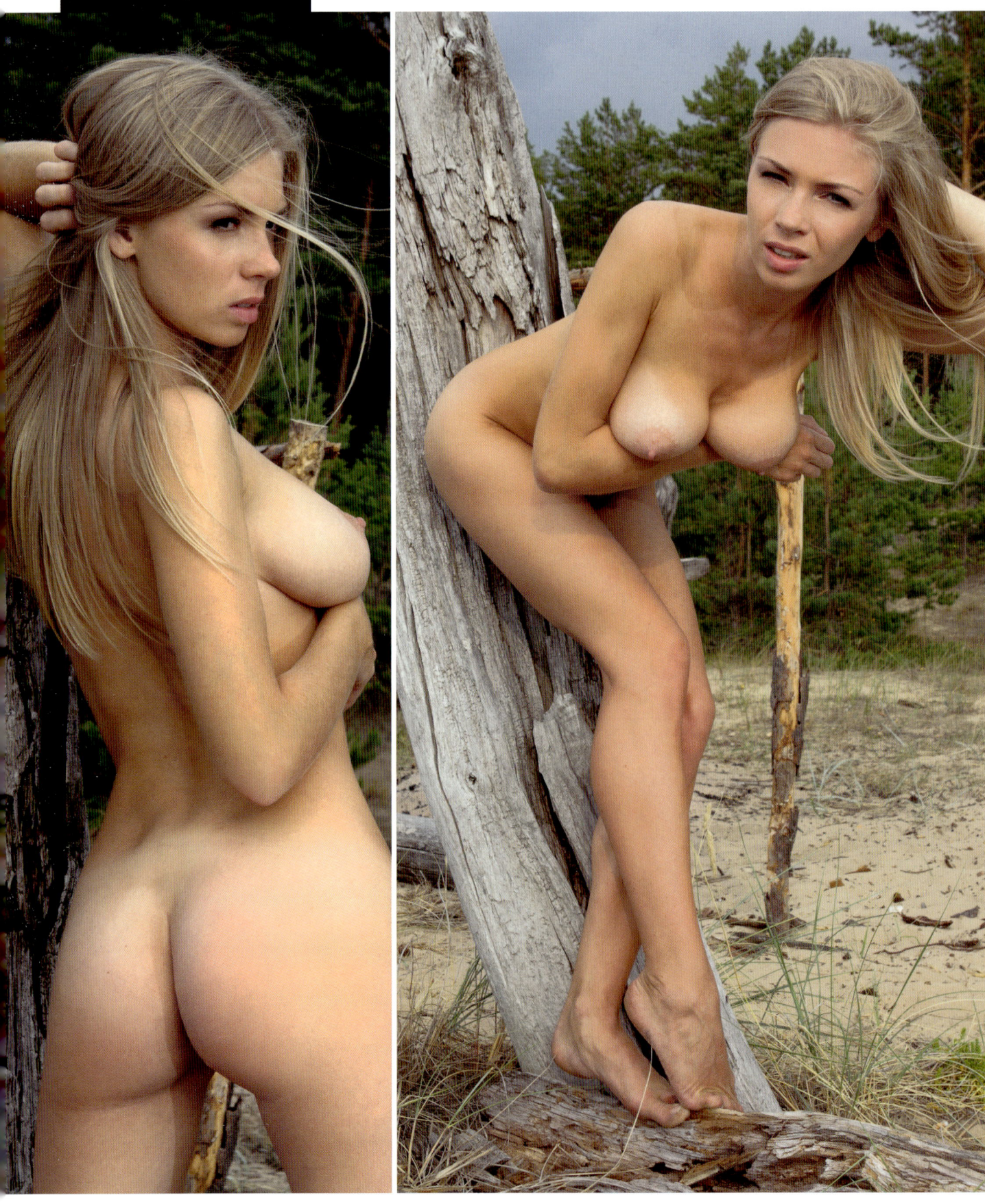

Lolly O

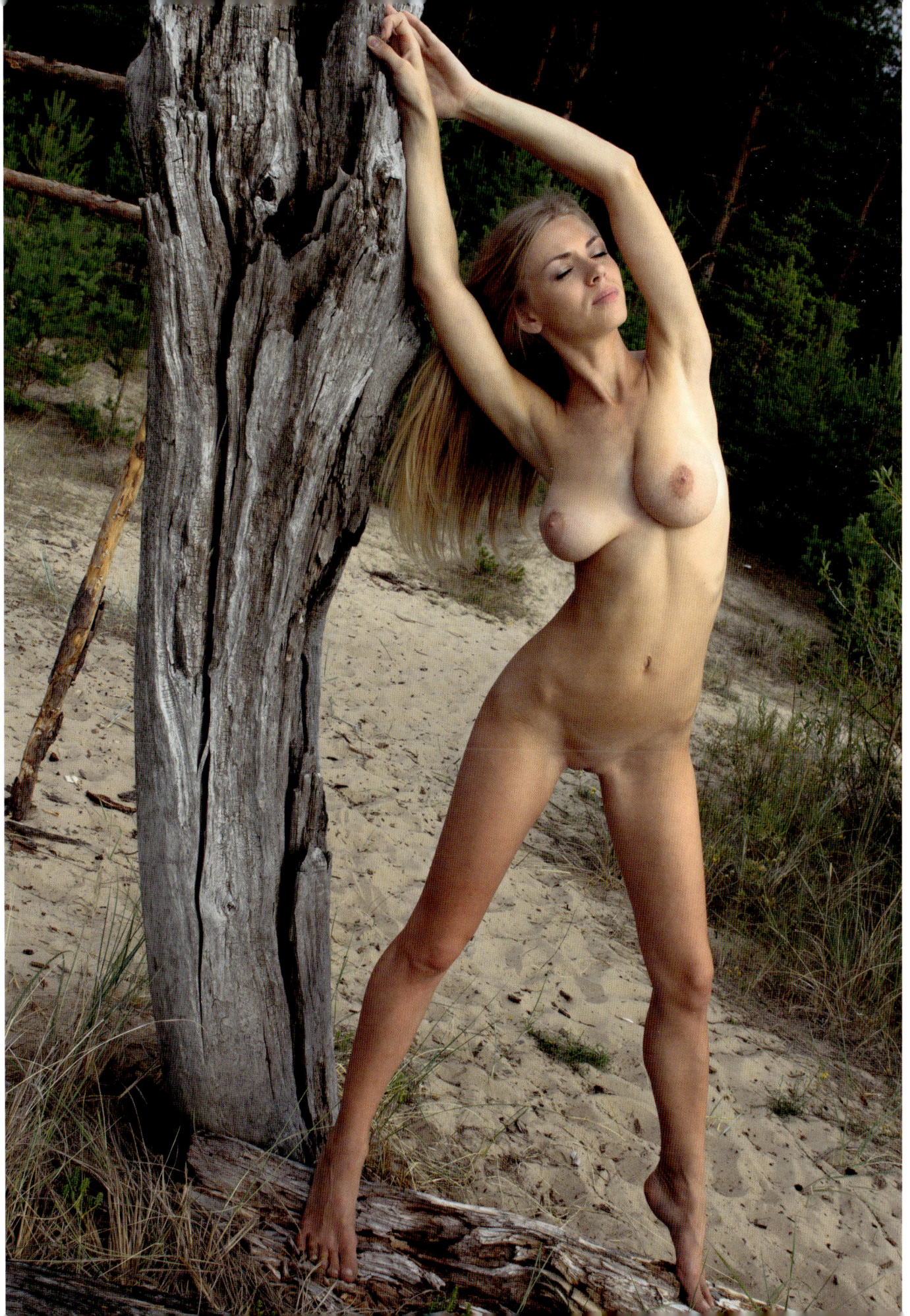

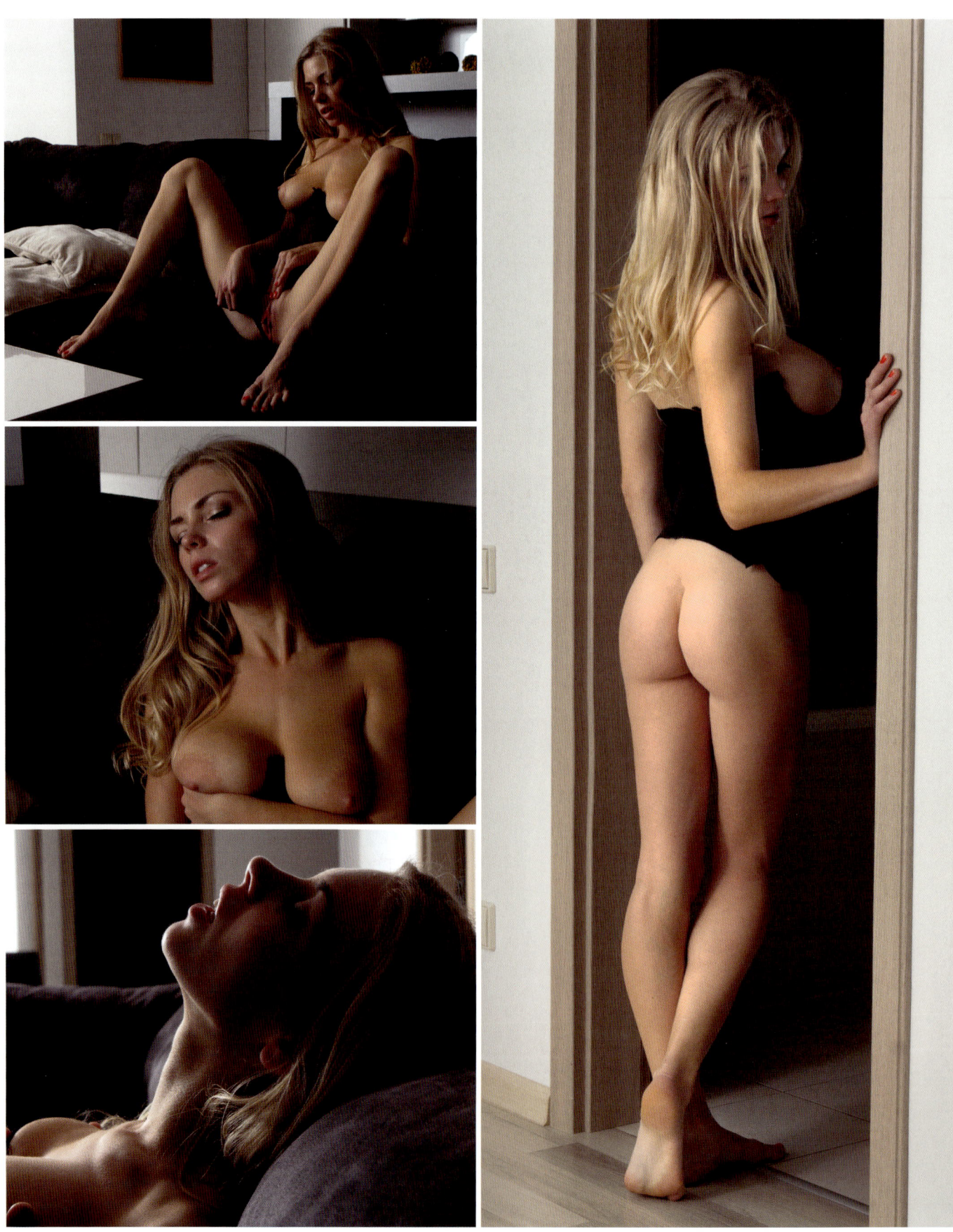

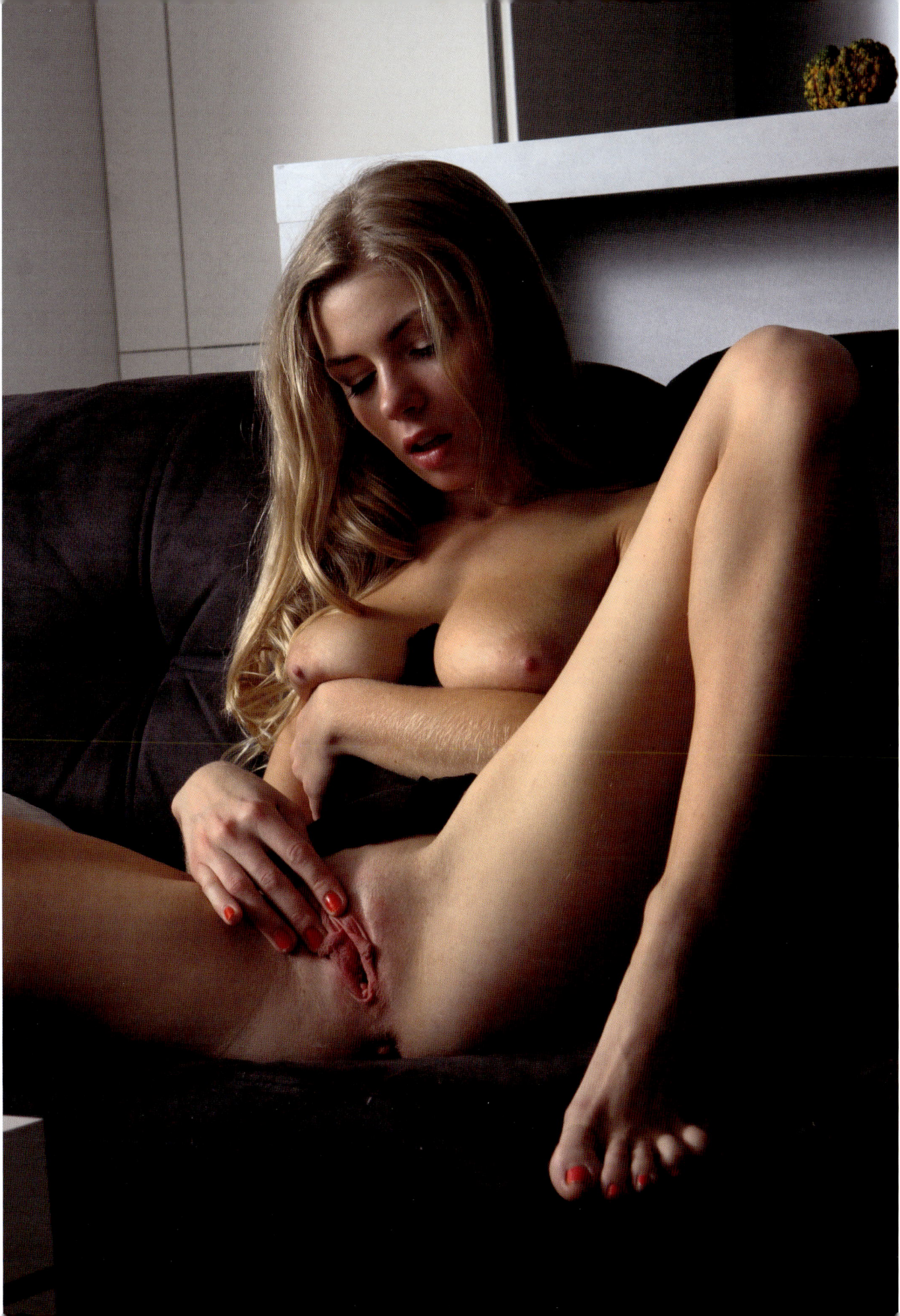

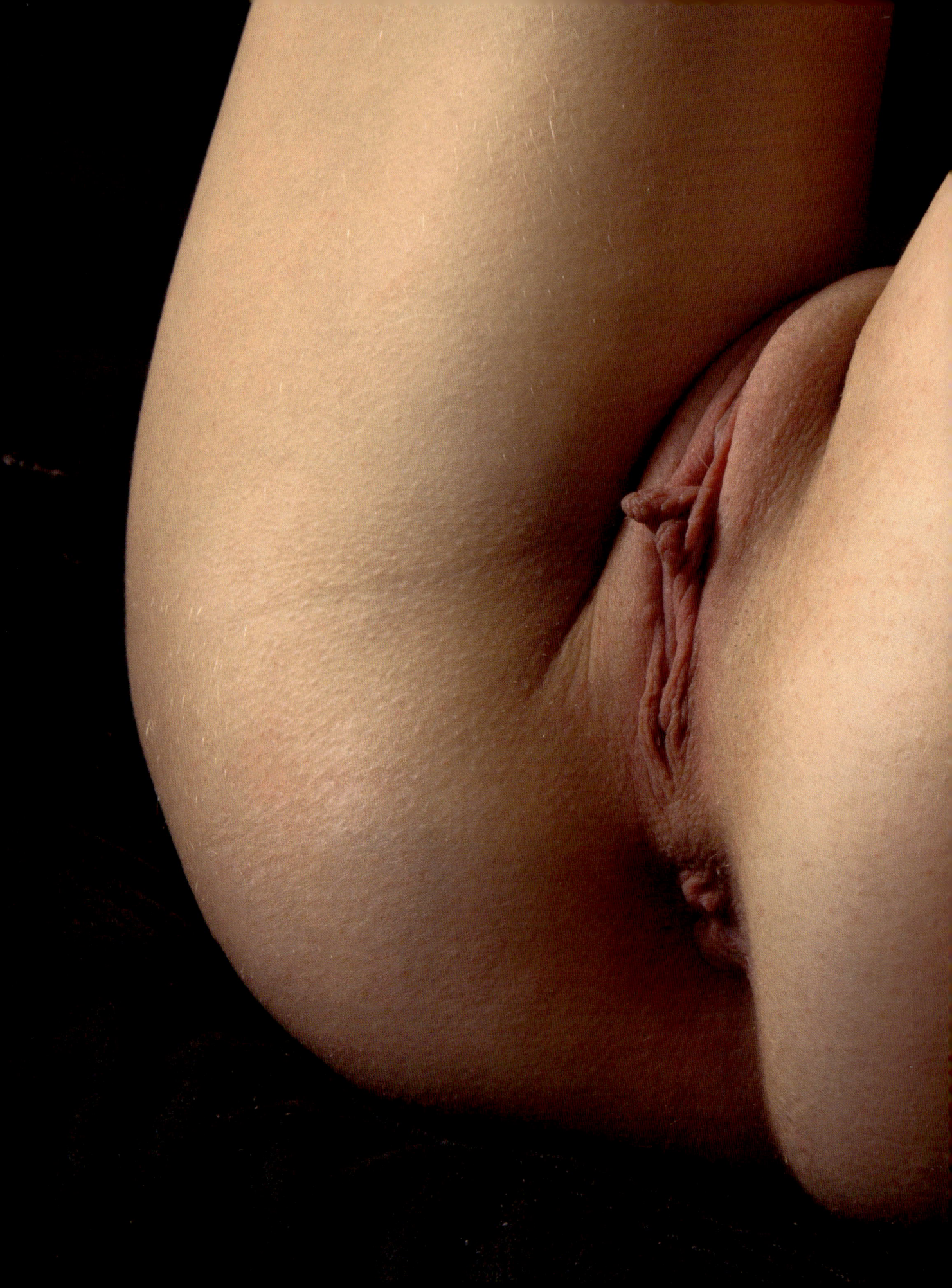

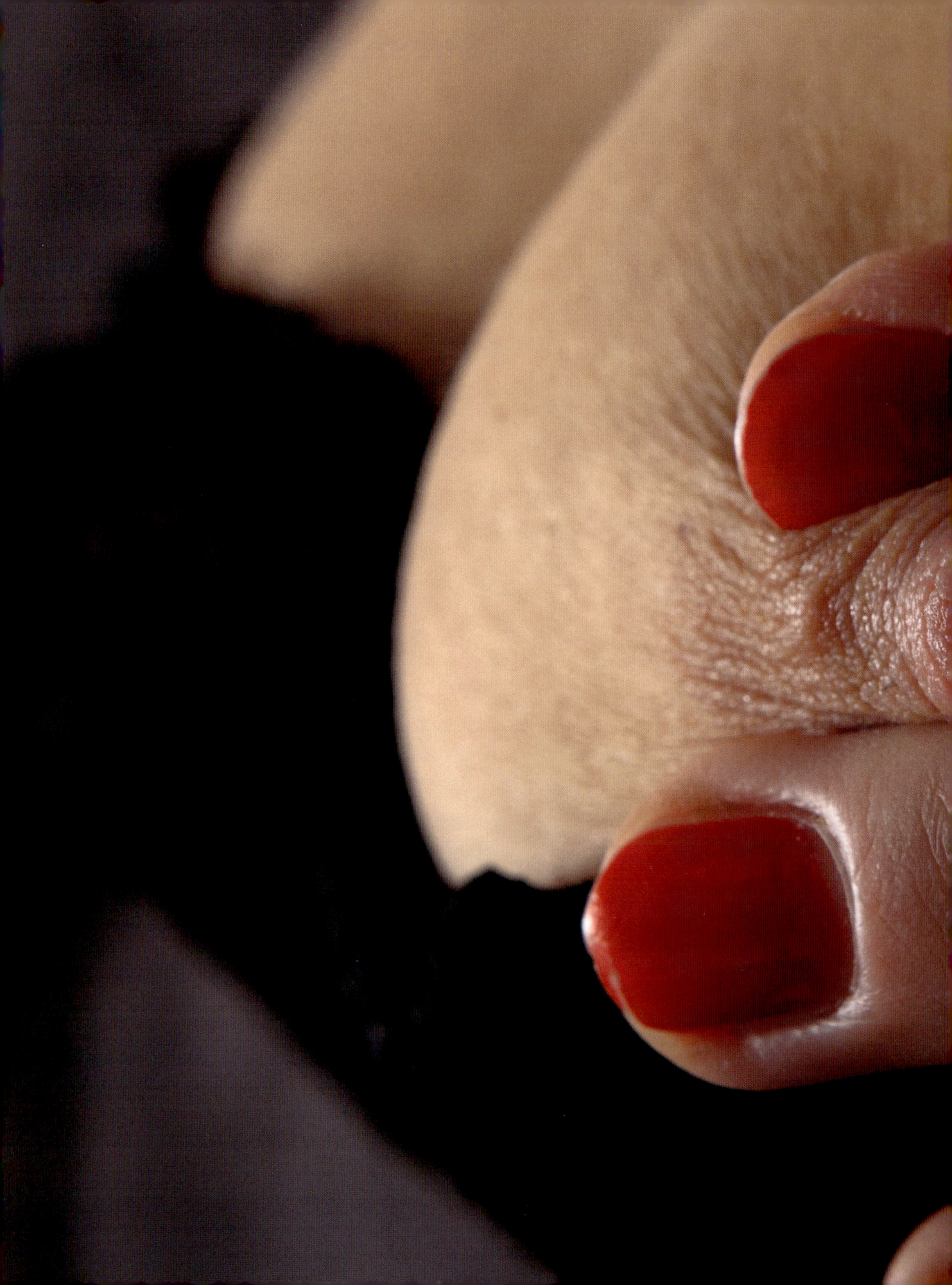

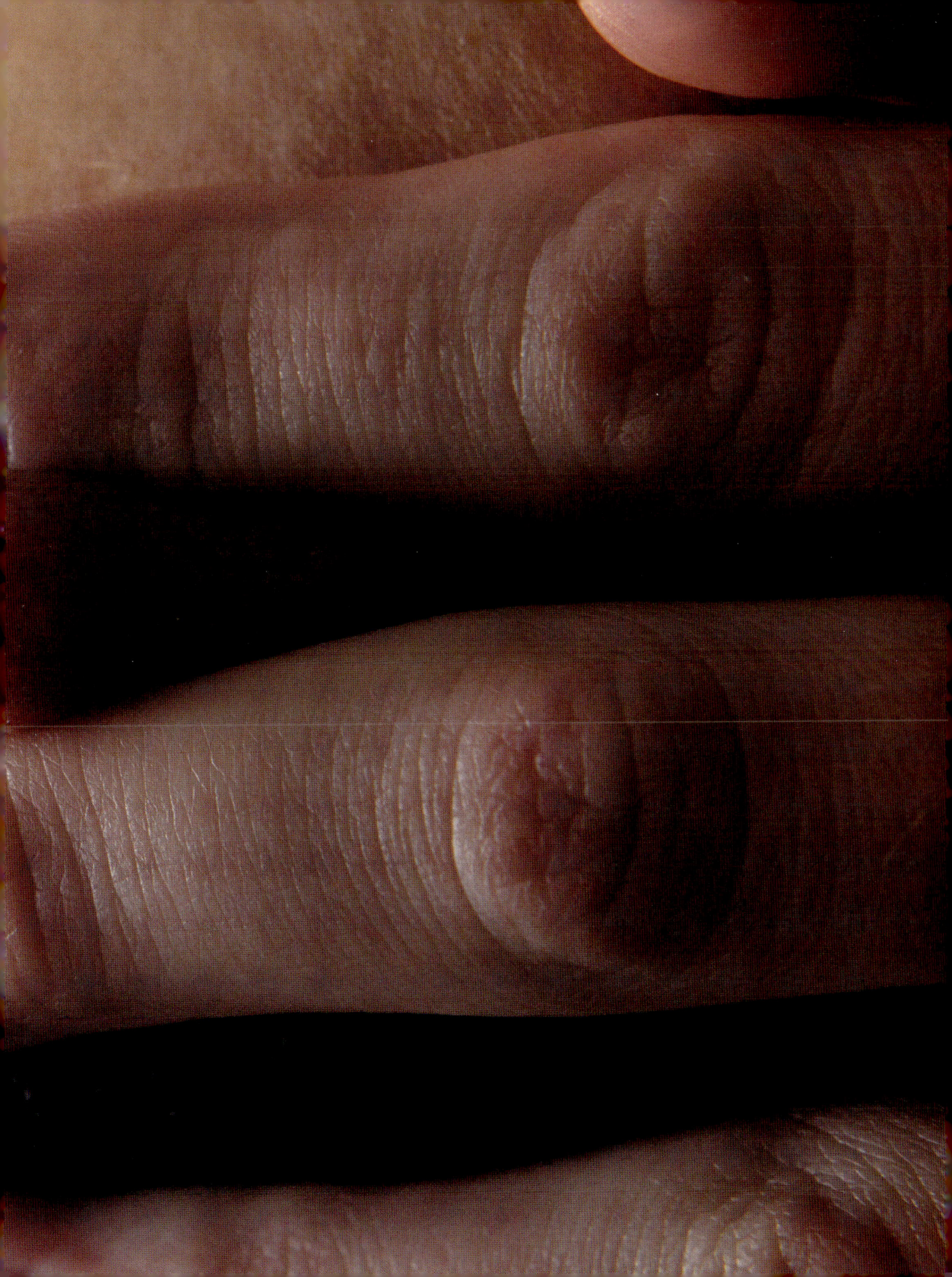

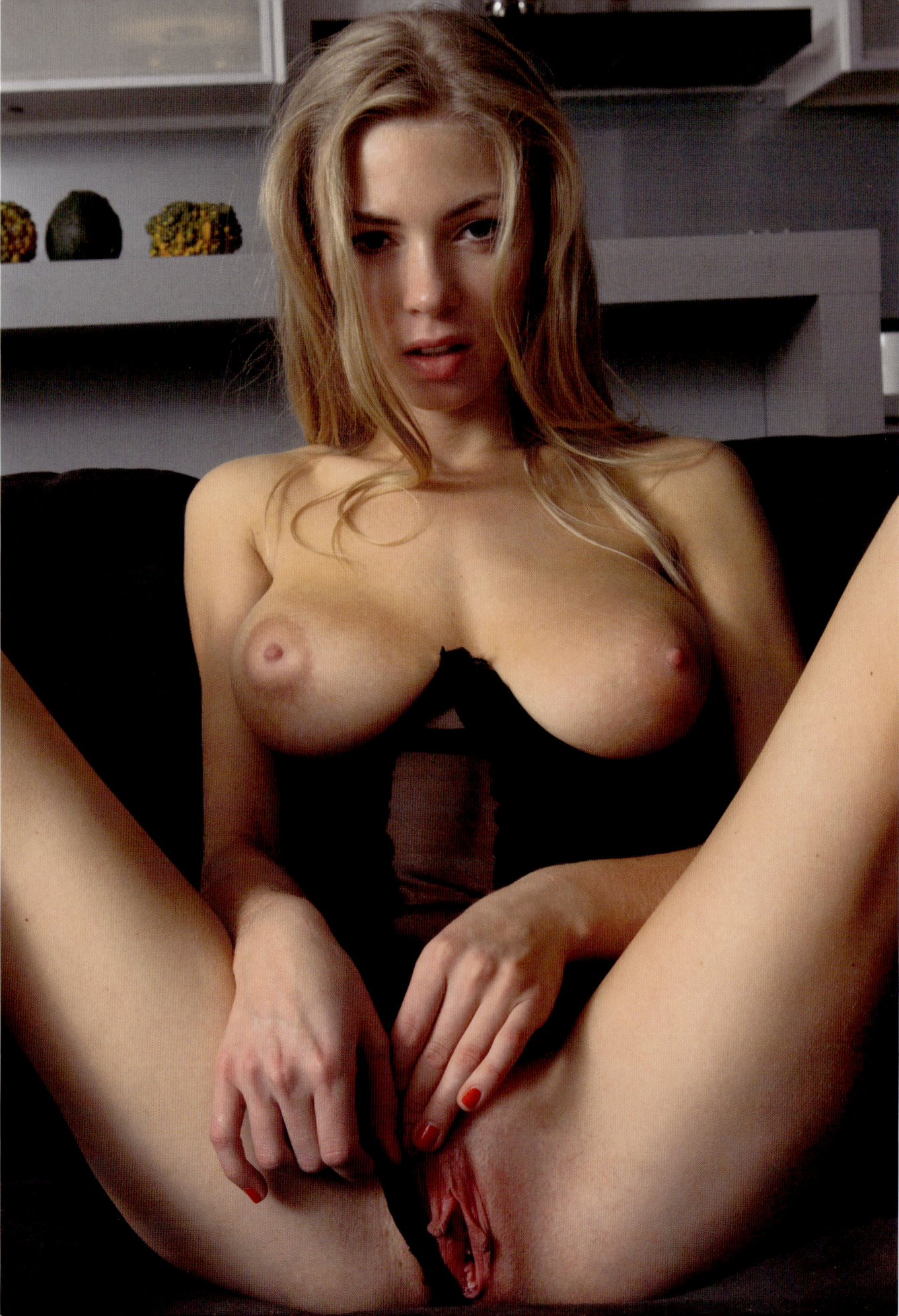

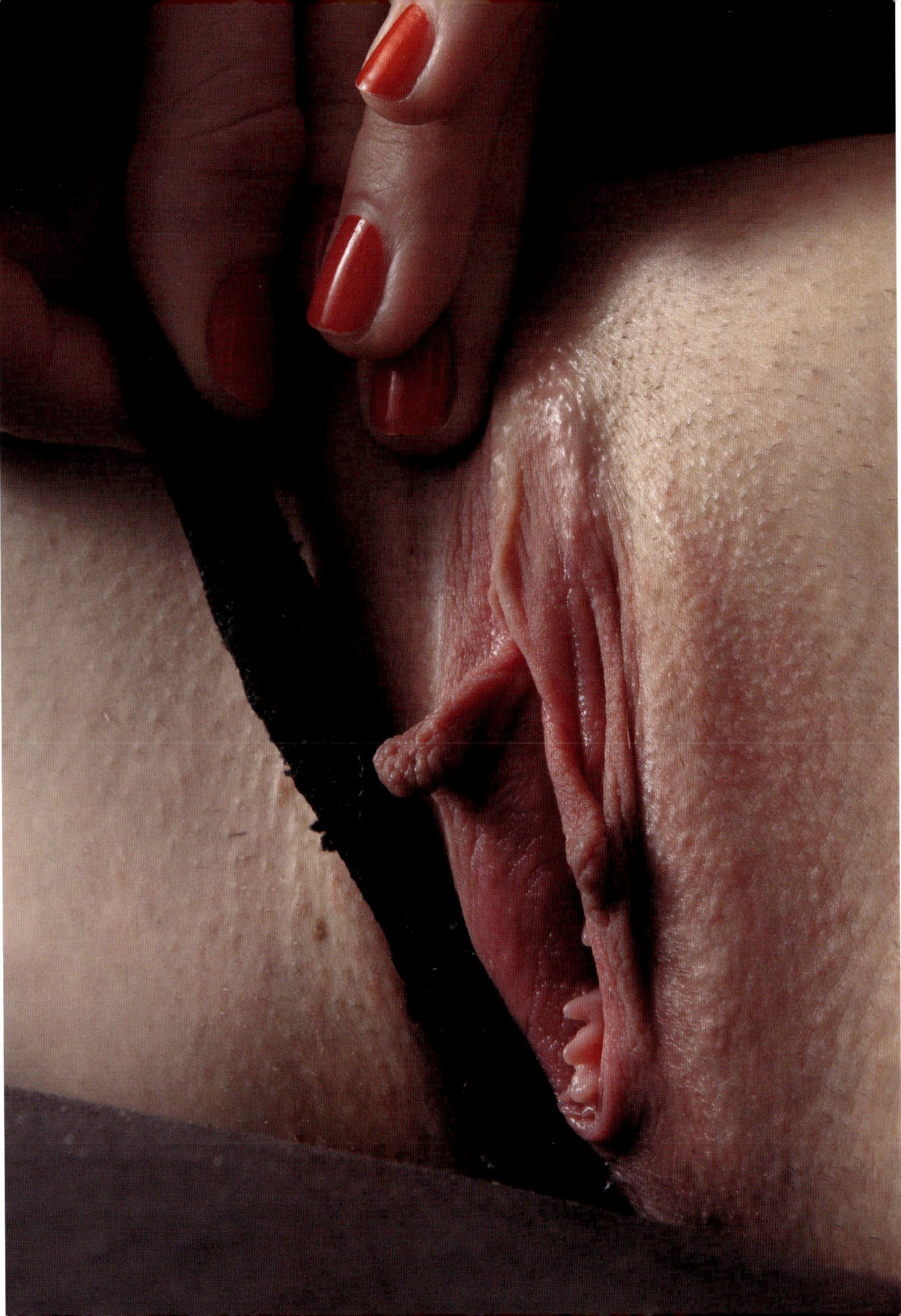

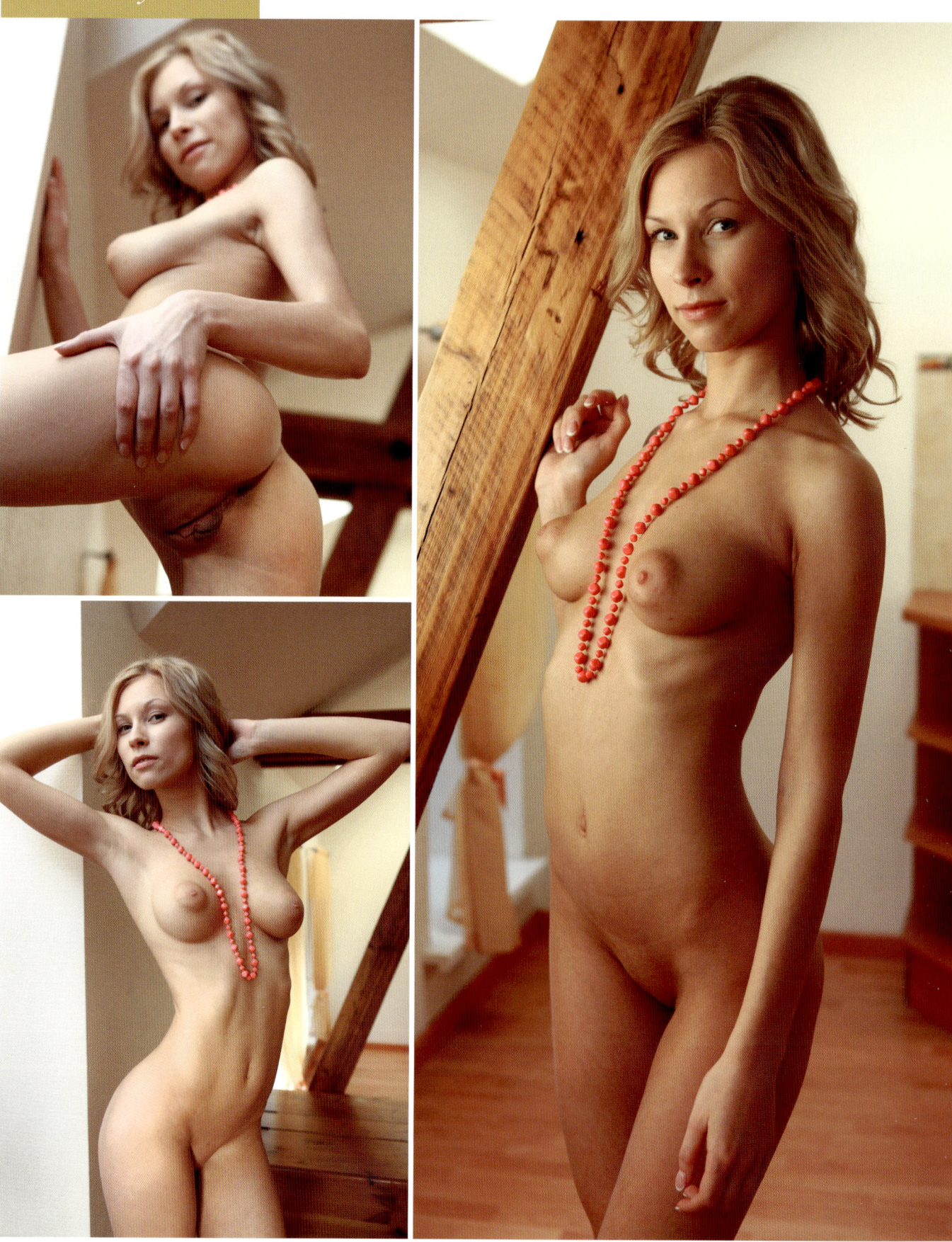

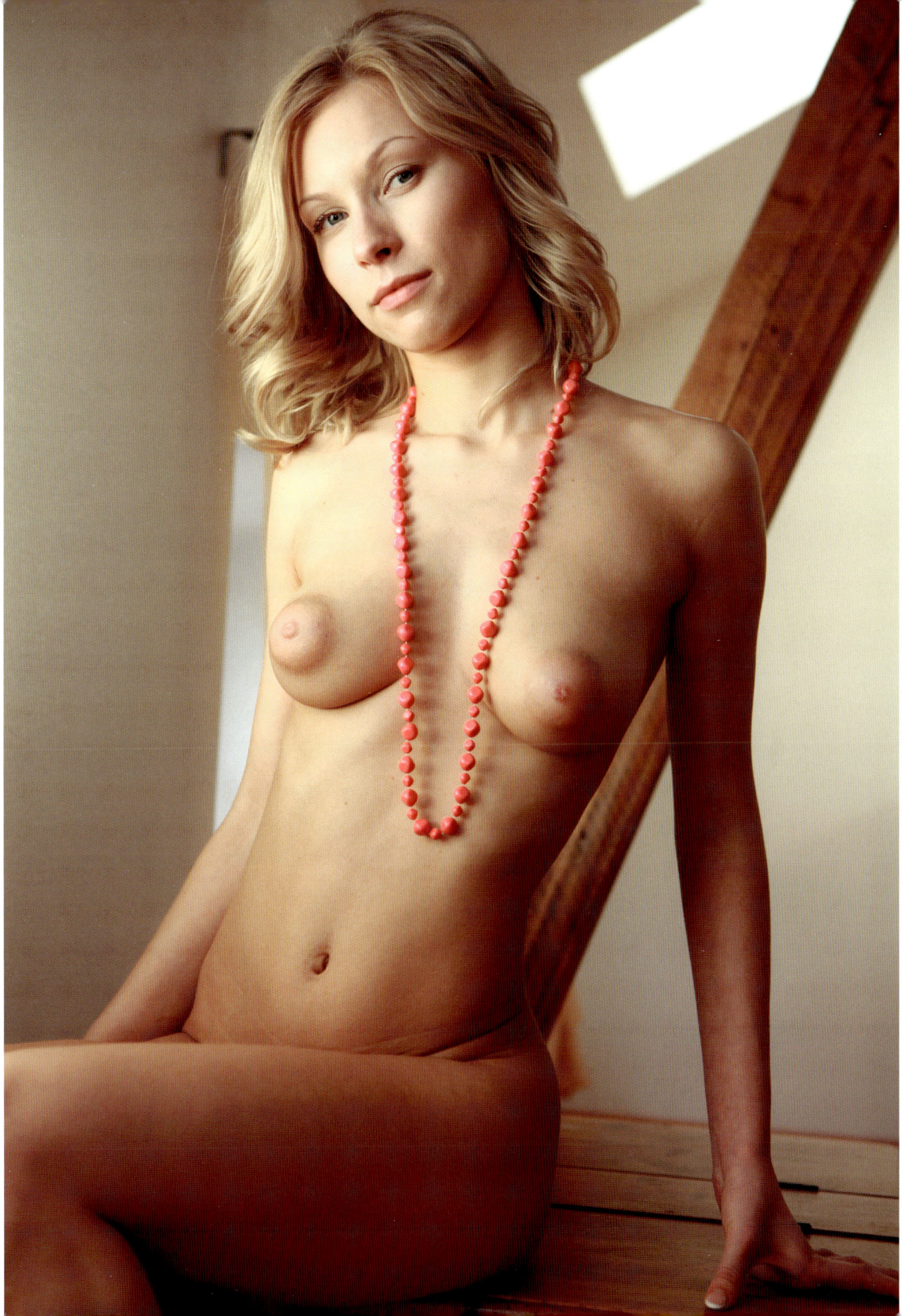

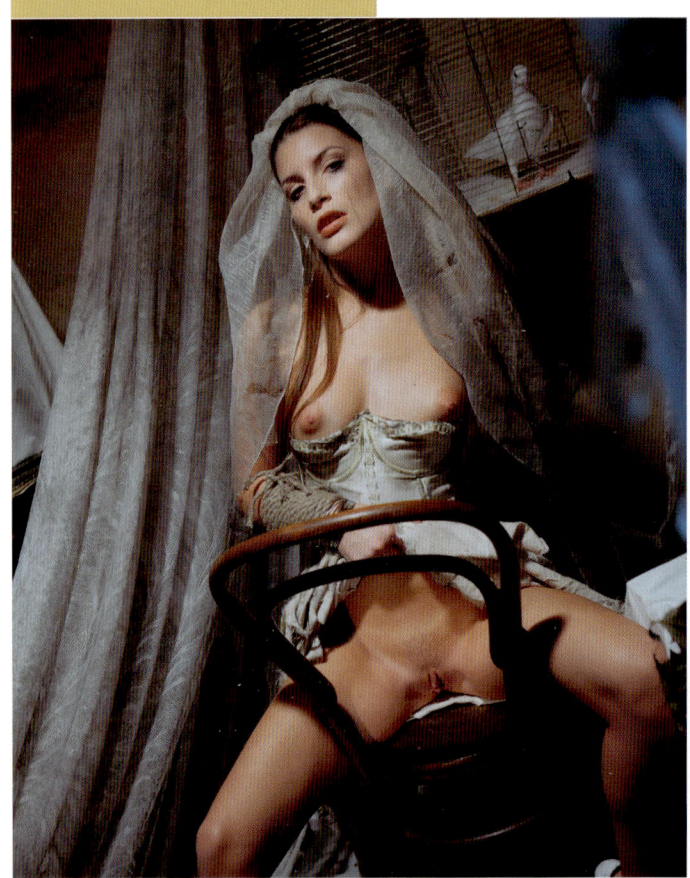
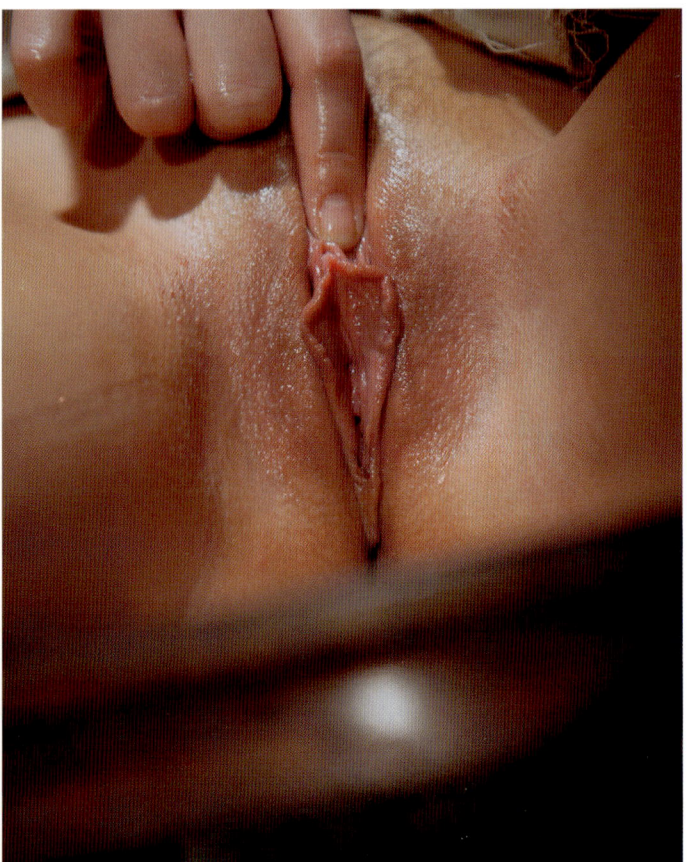

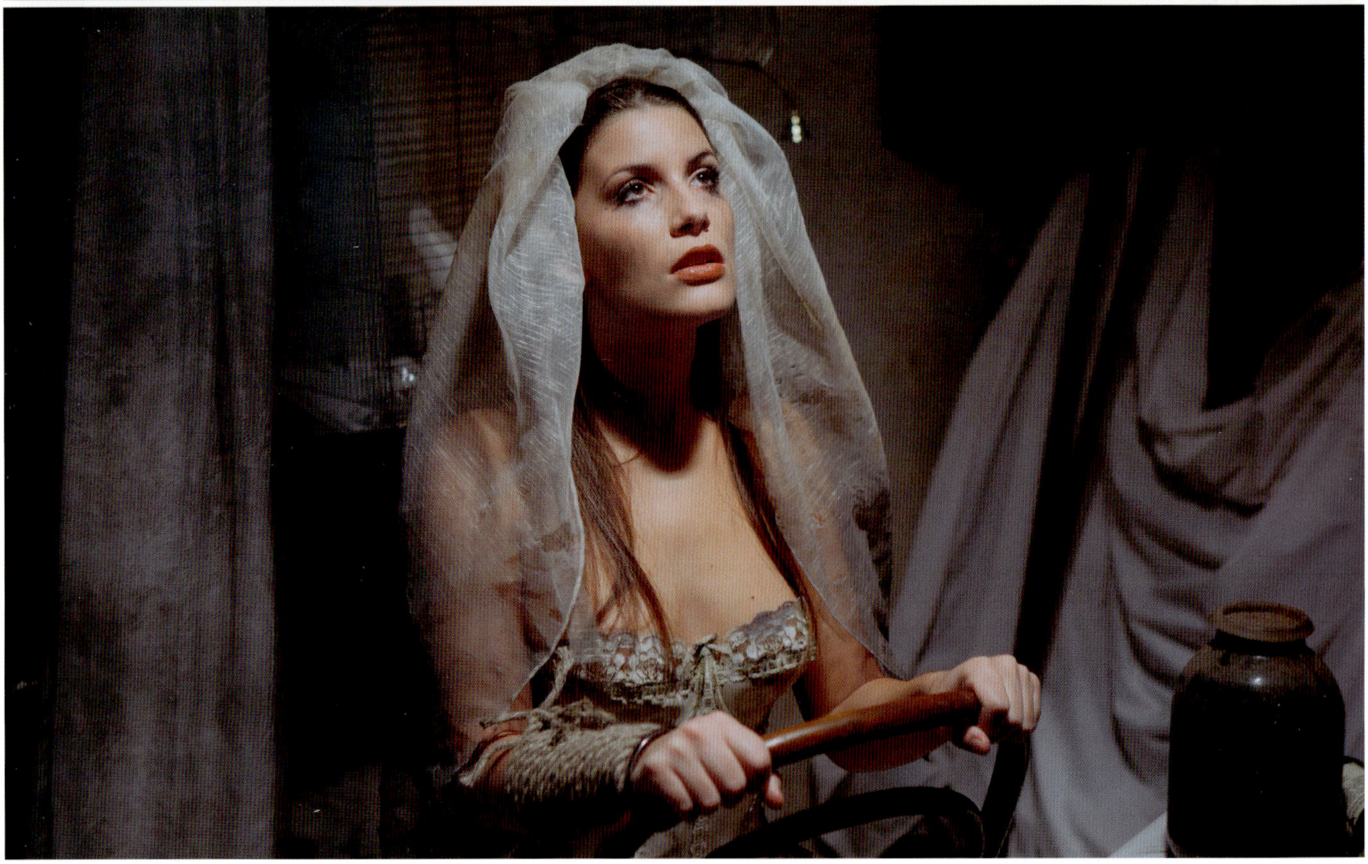

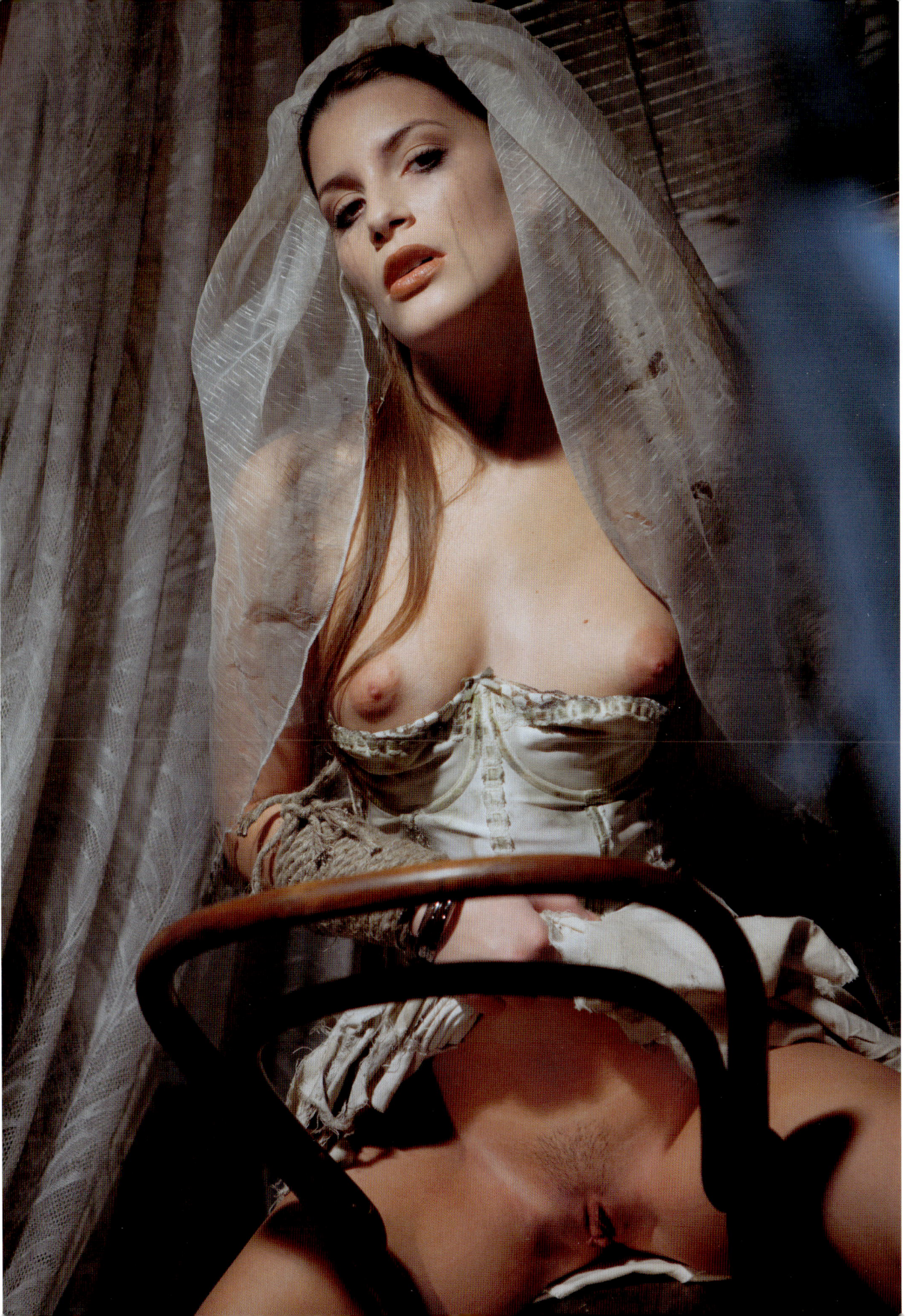

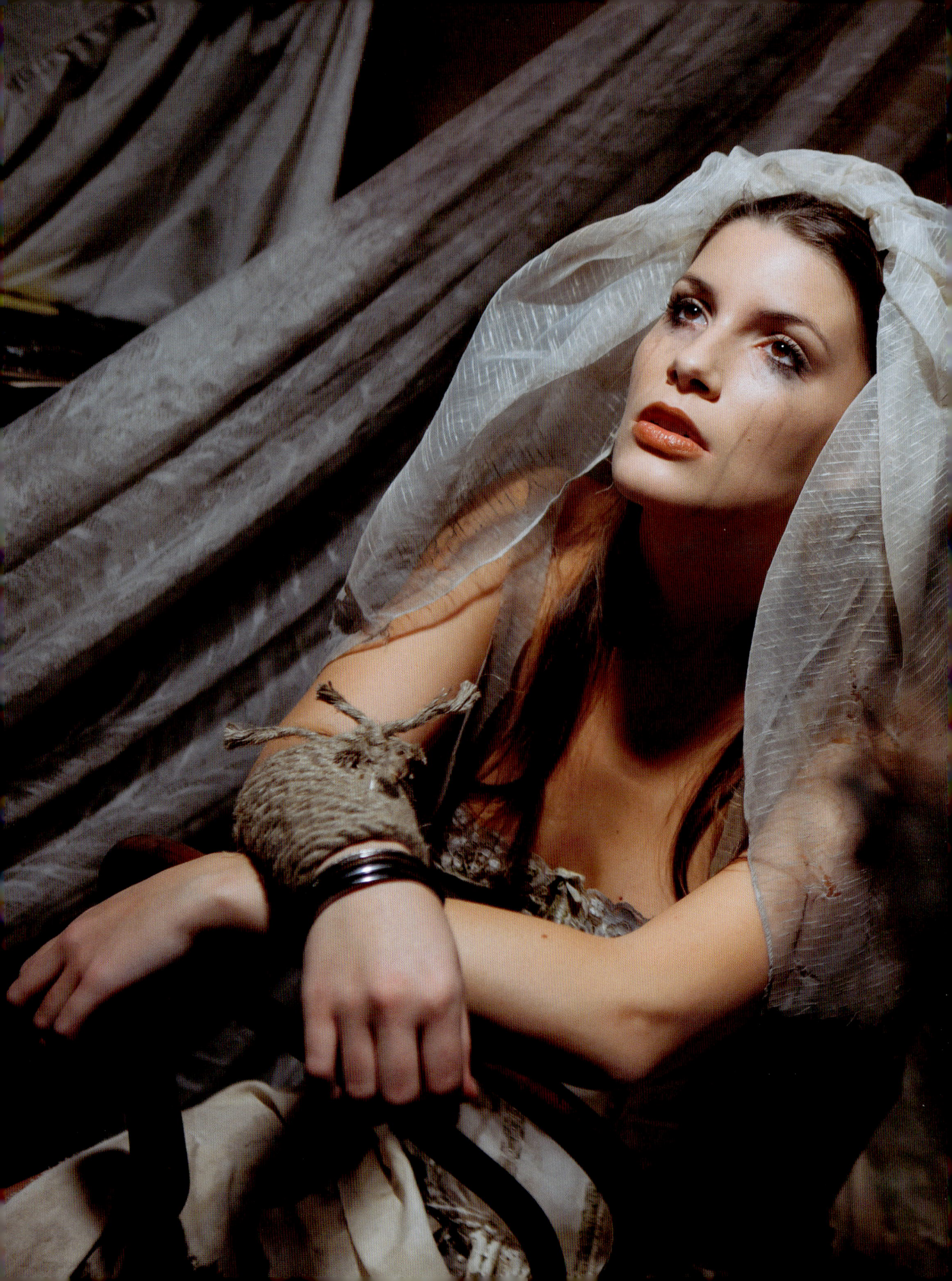

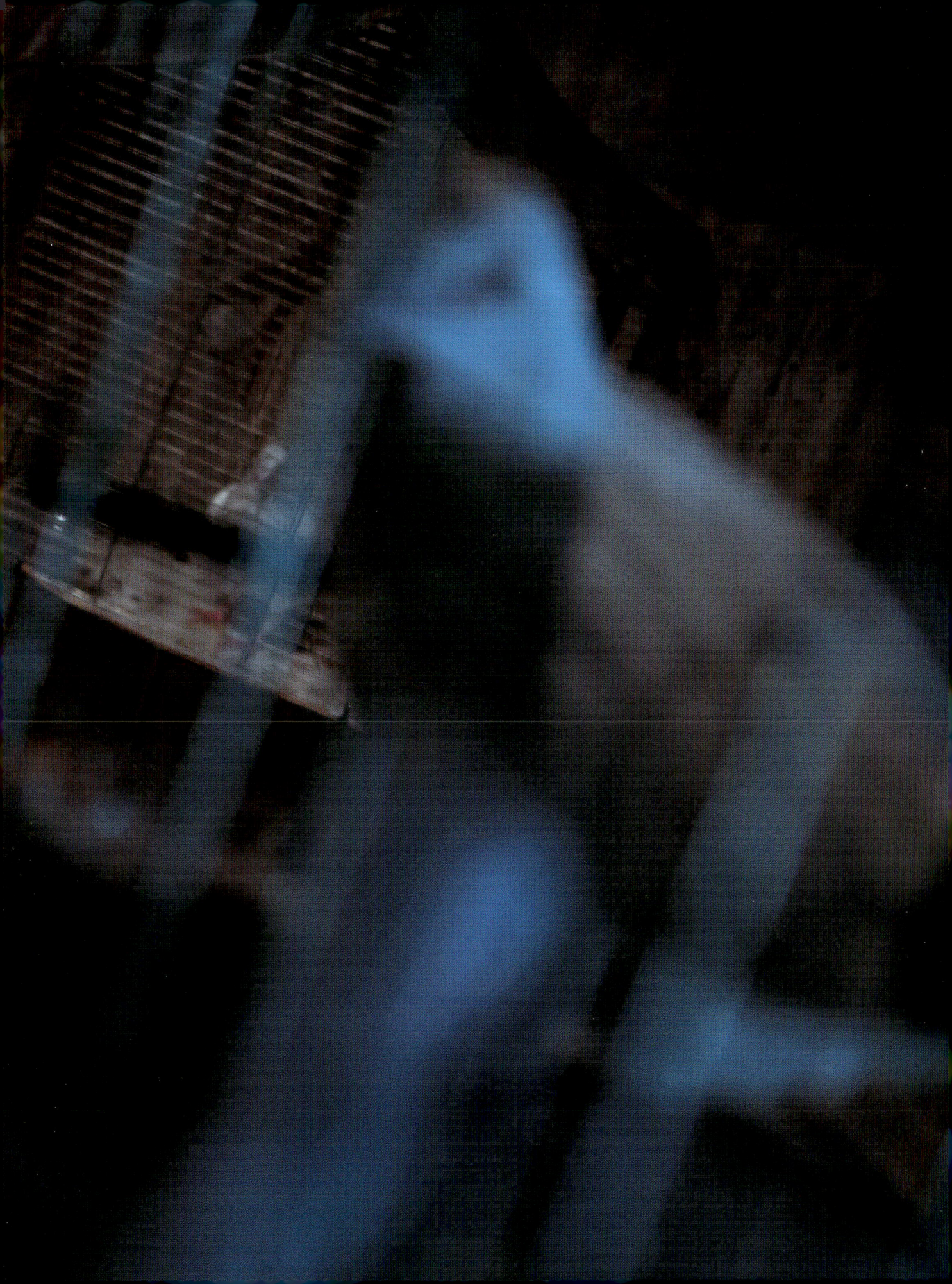

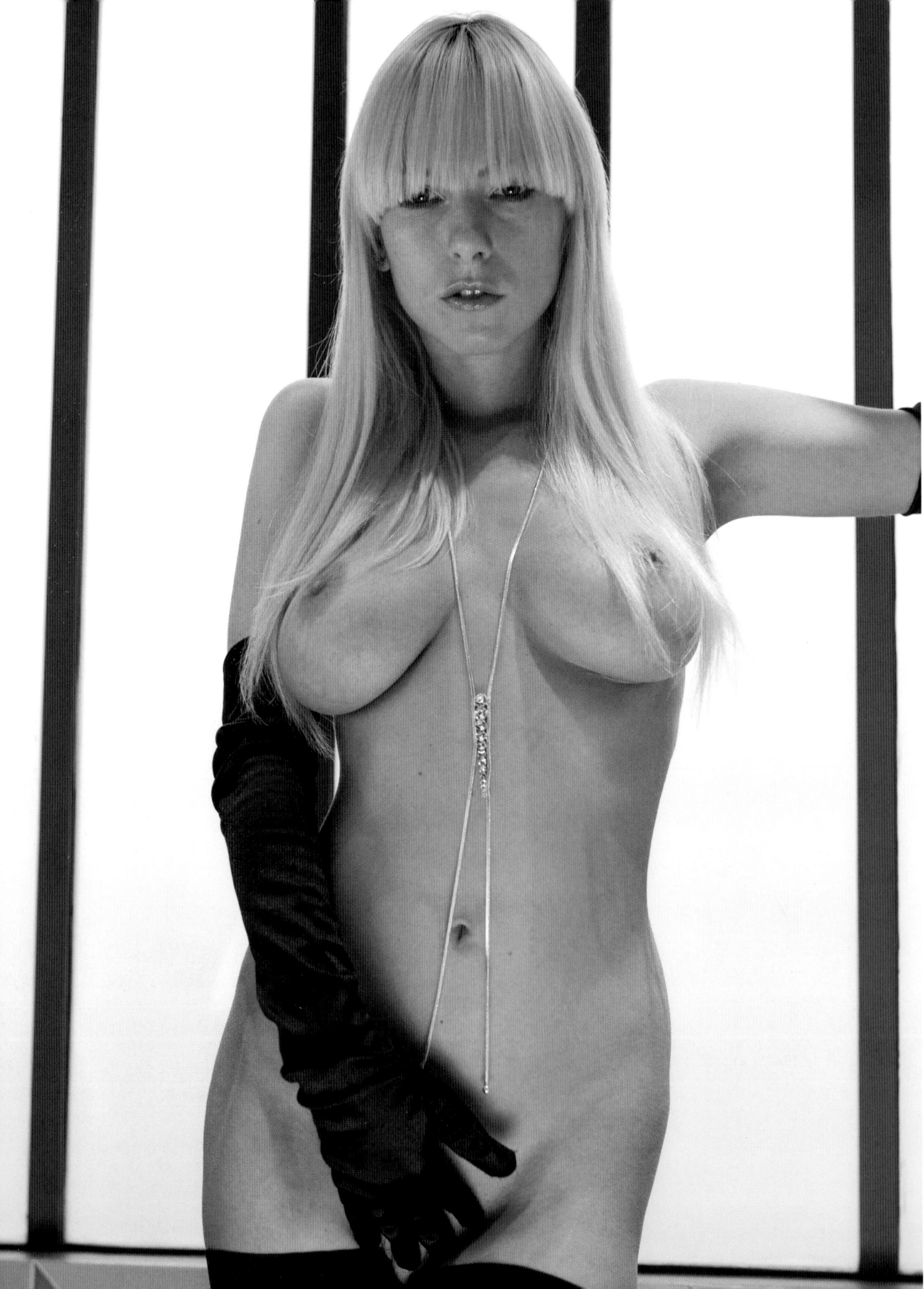

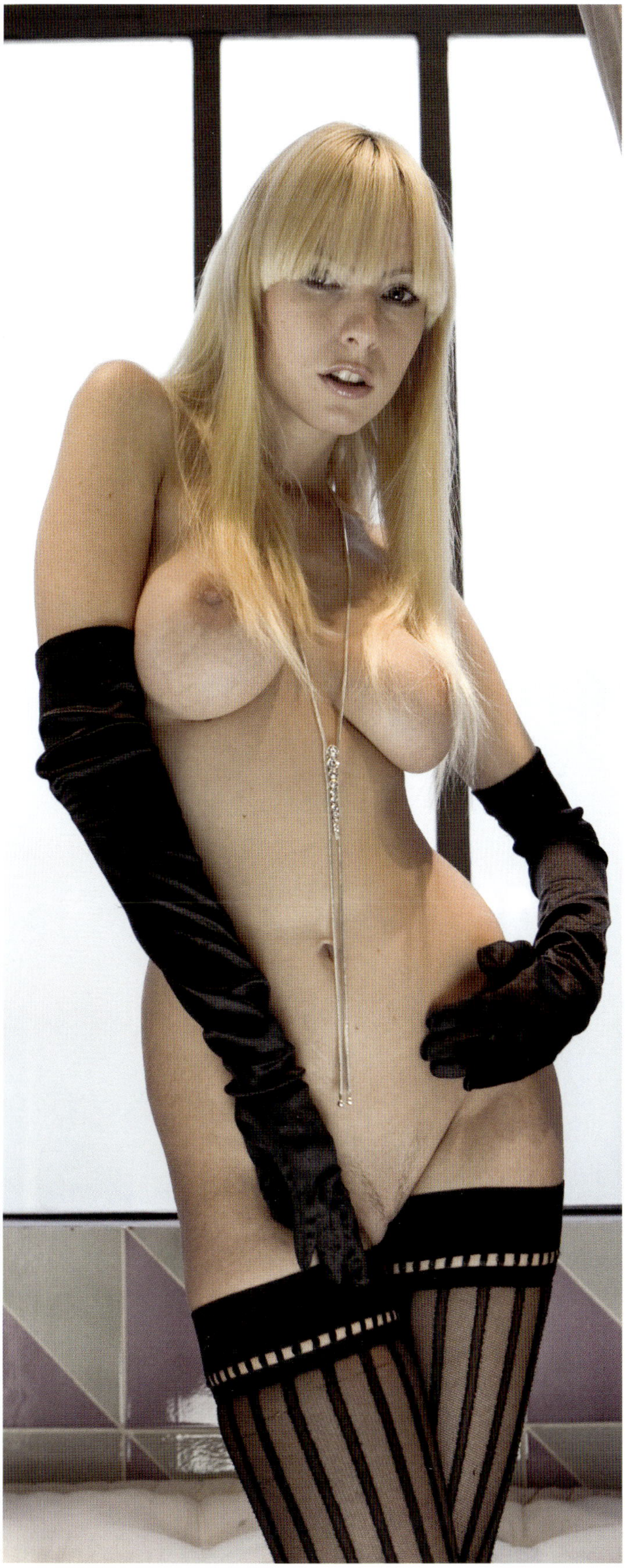

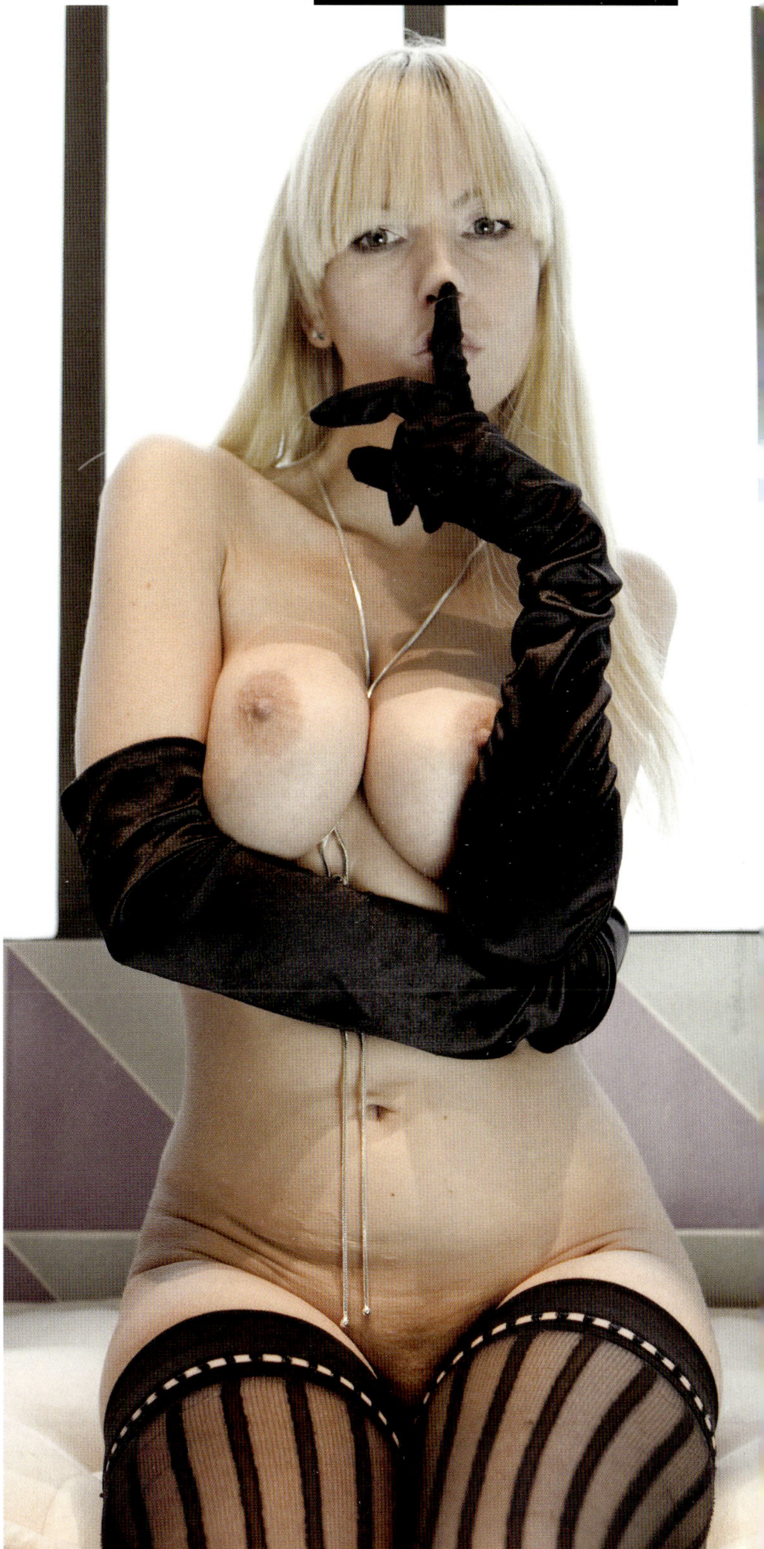

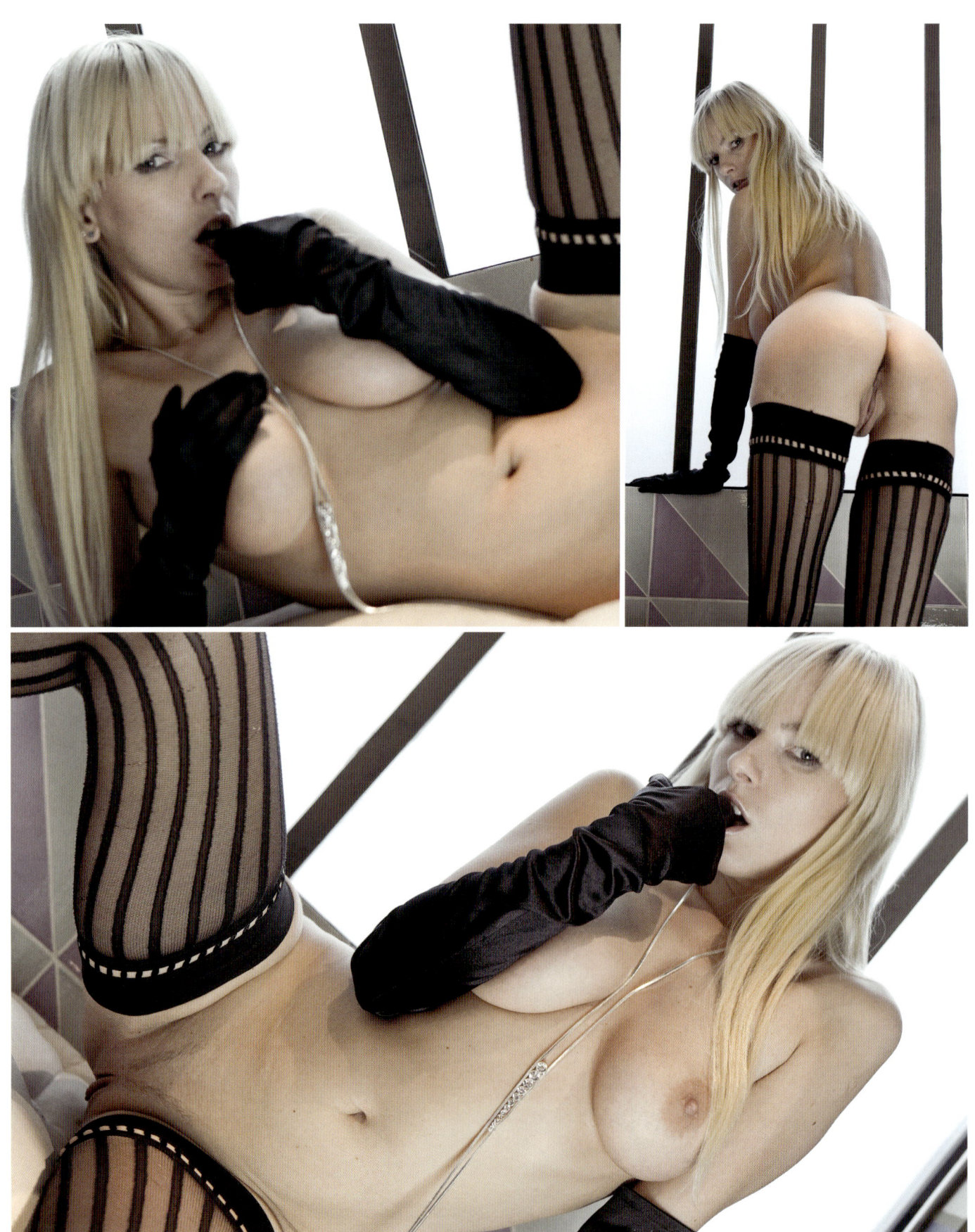

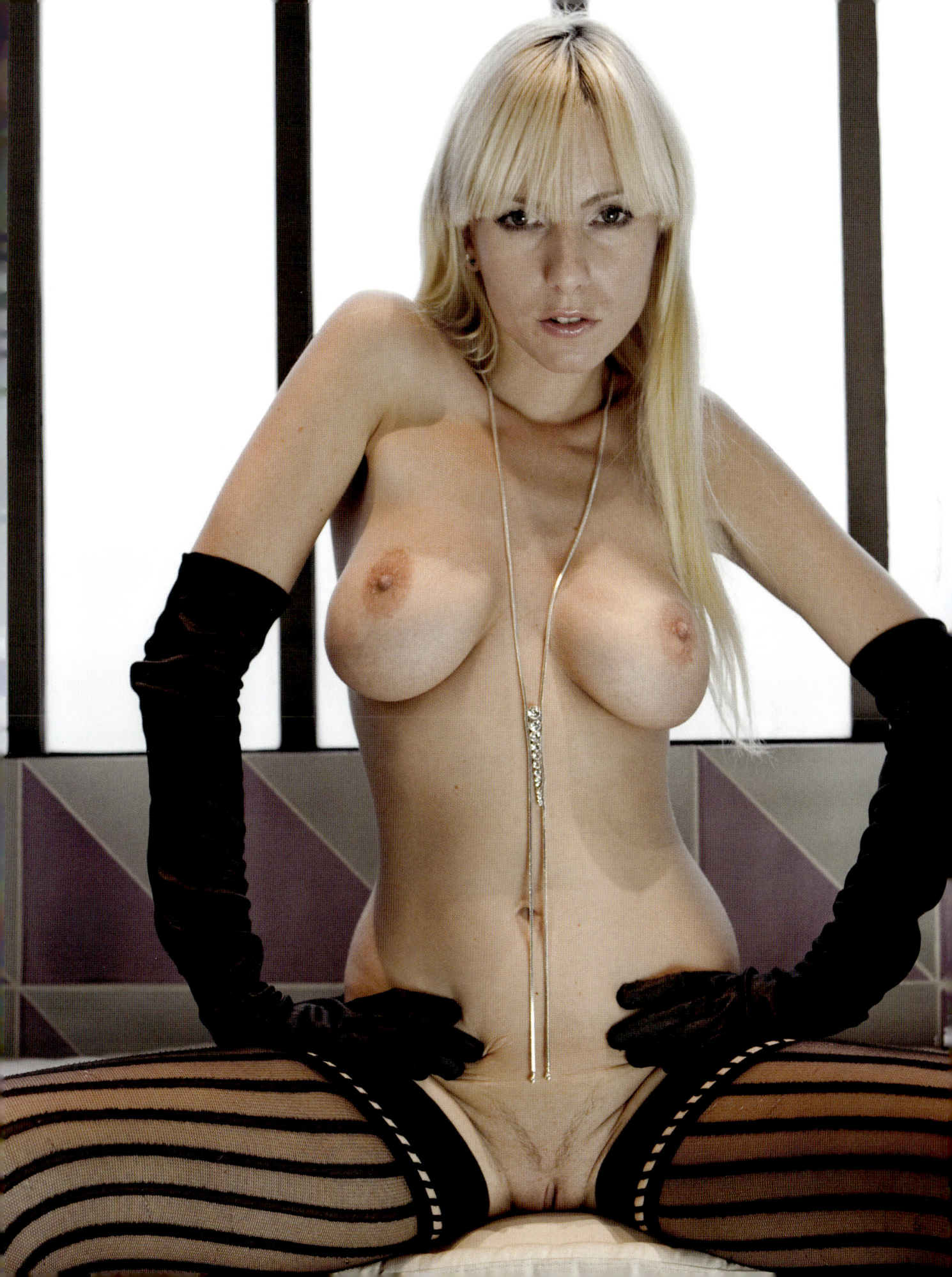

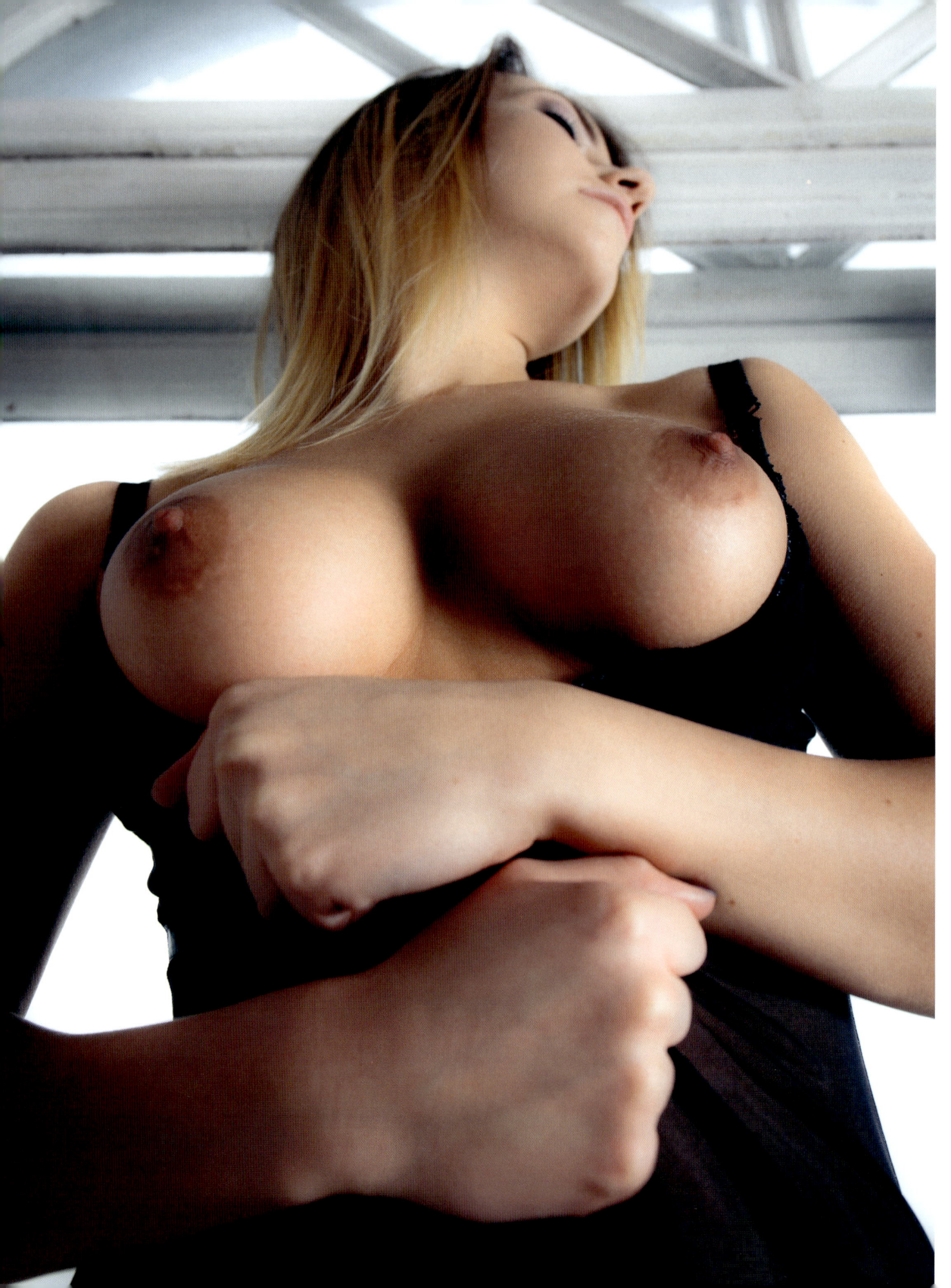

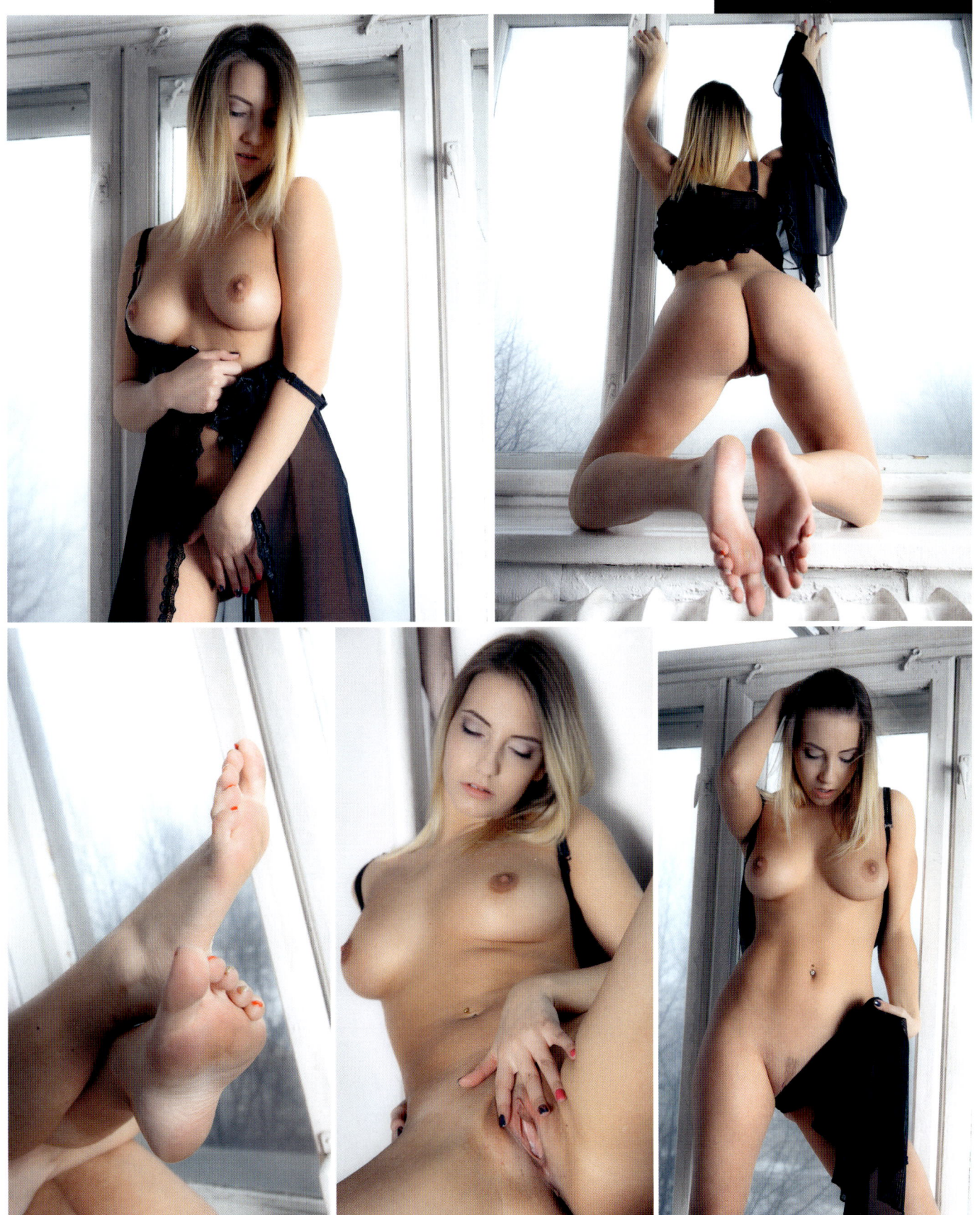

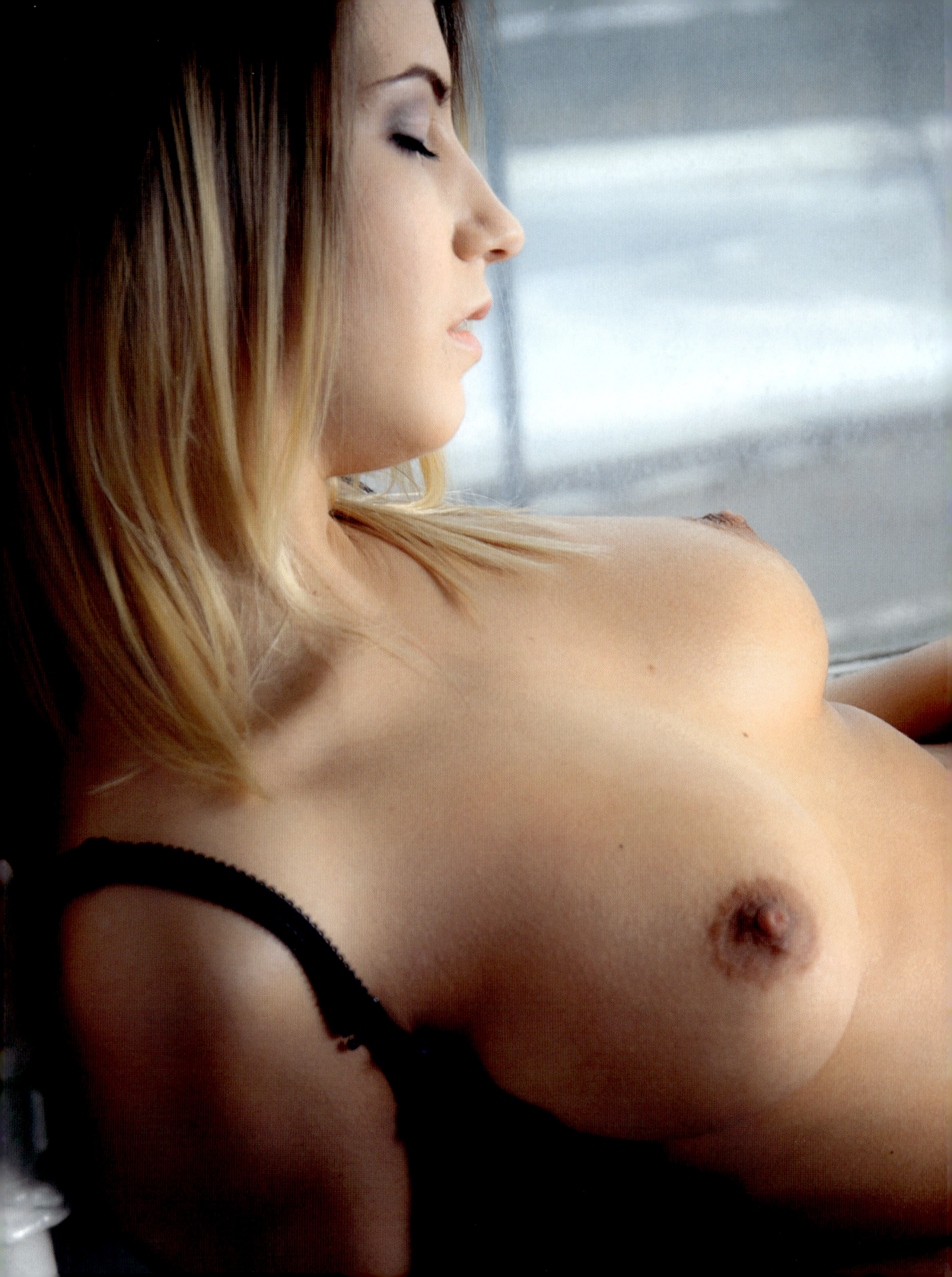

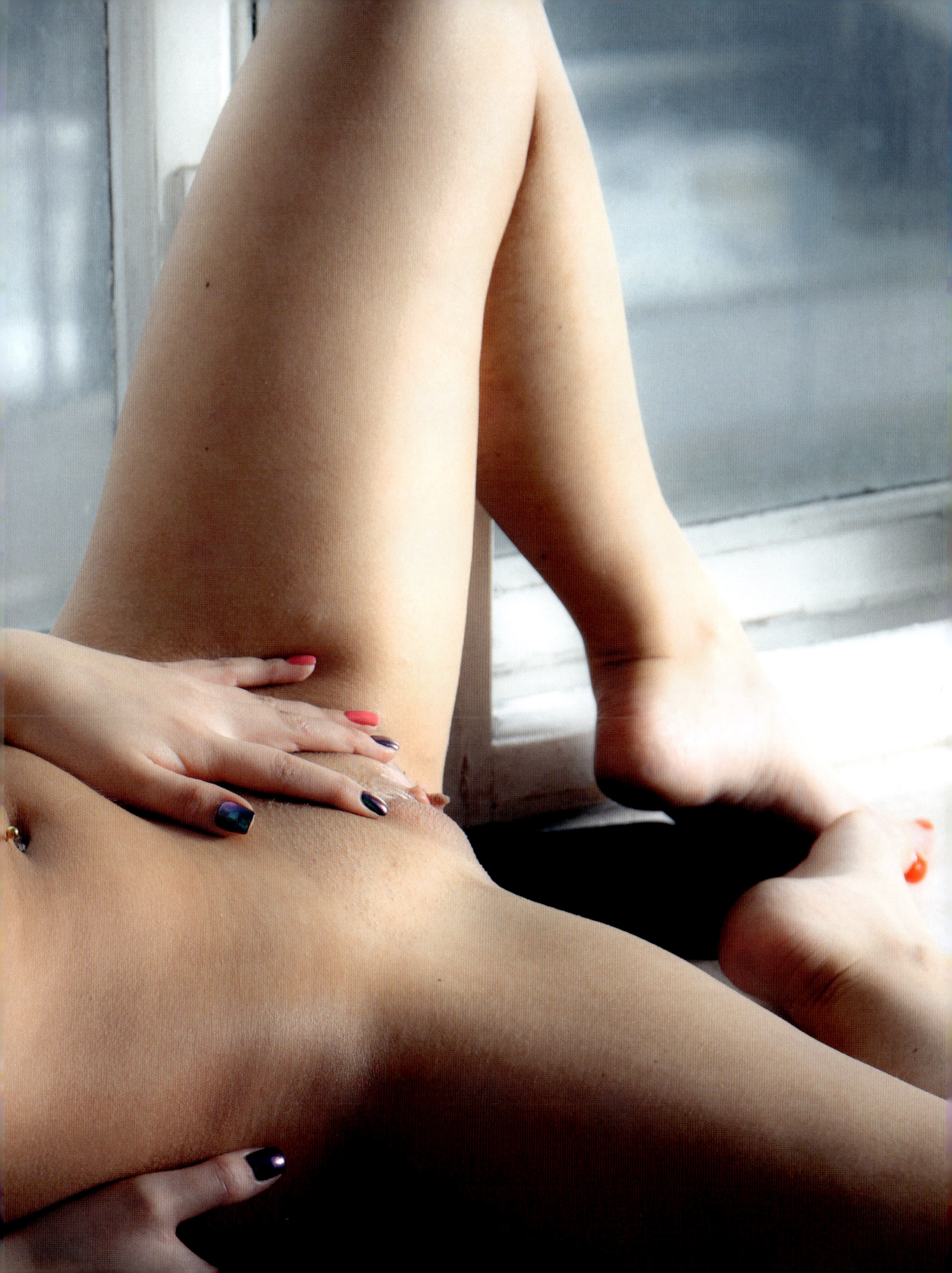

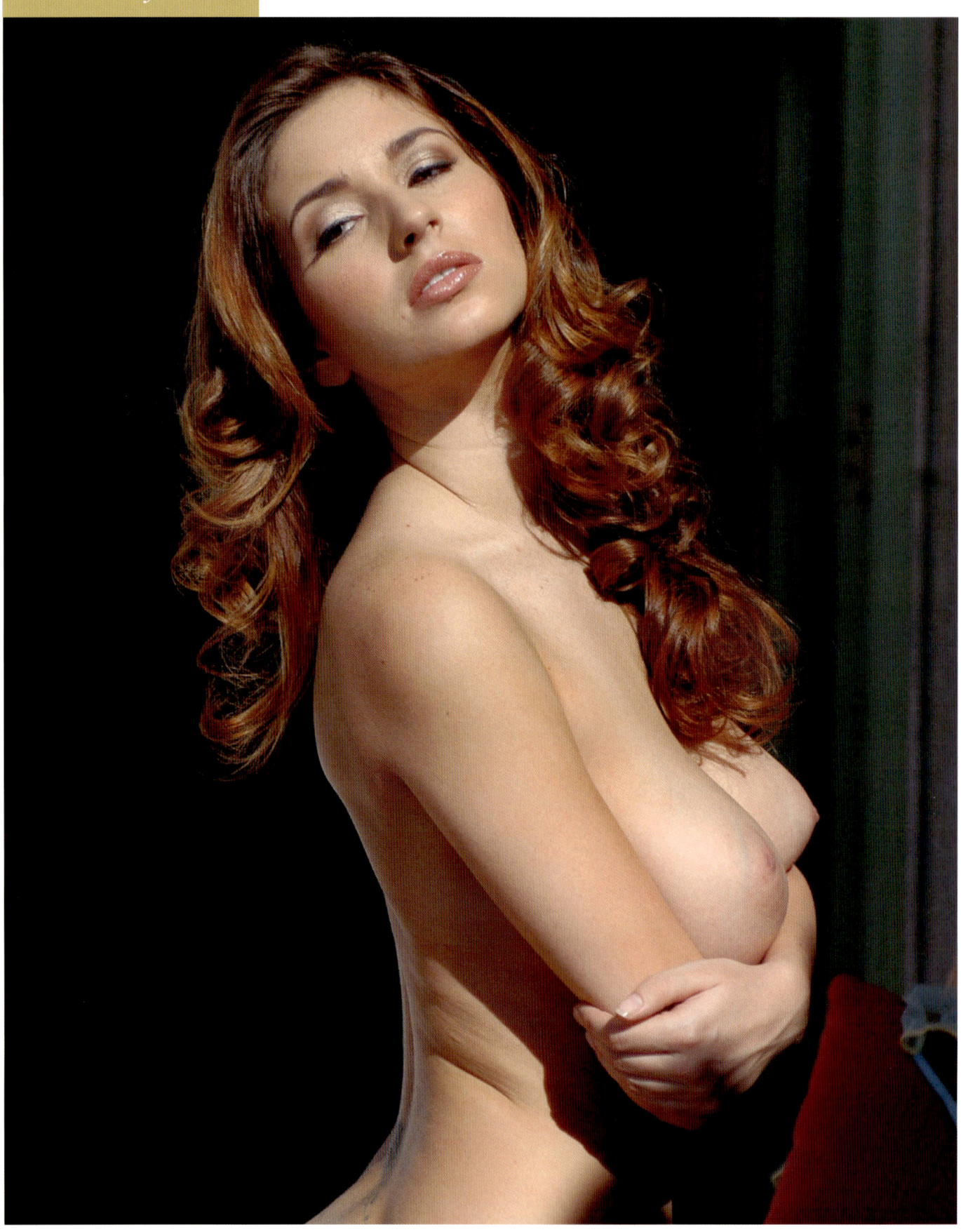

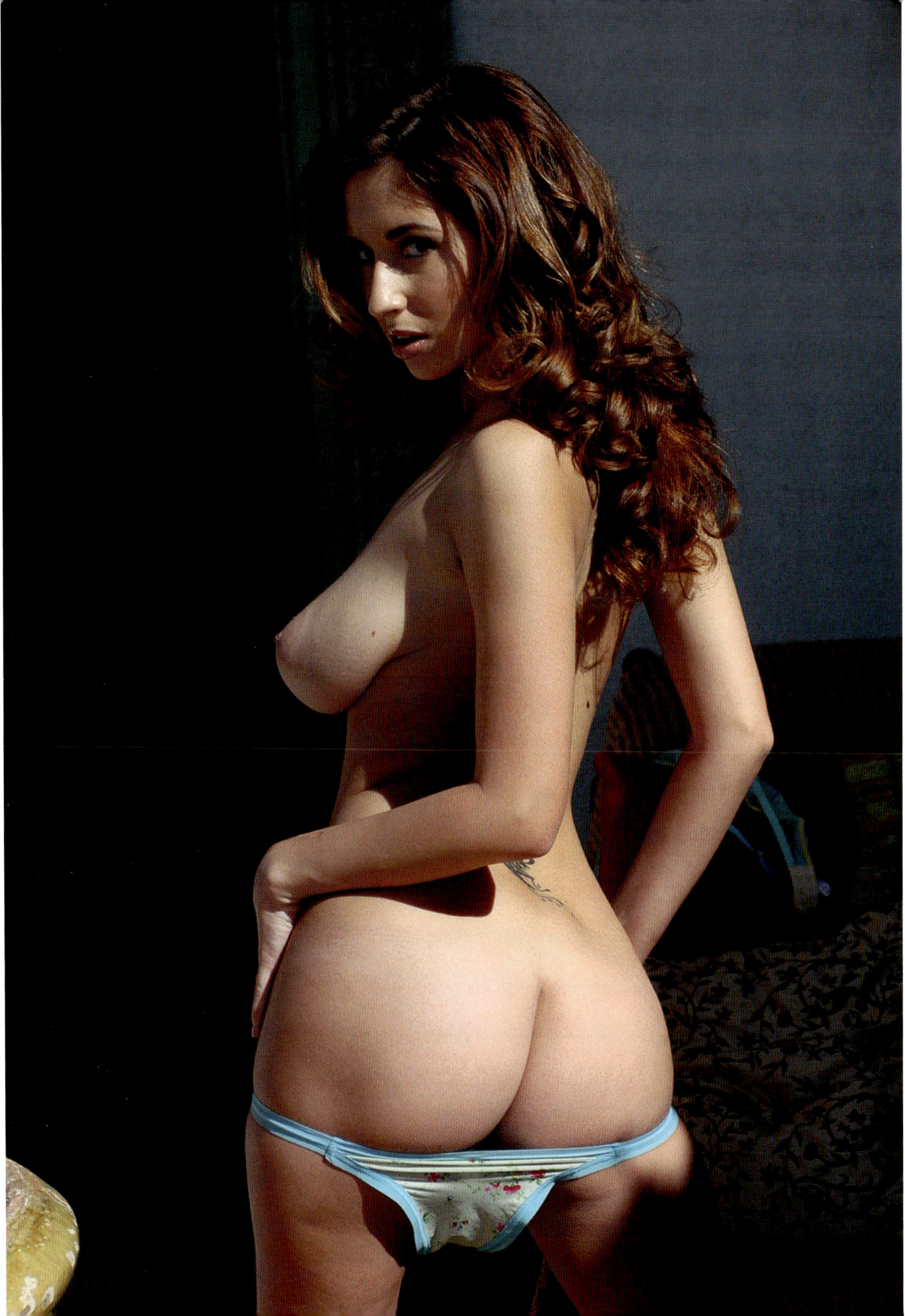

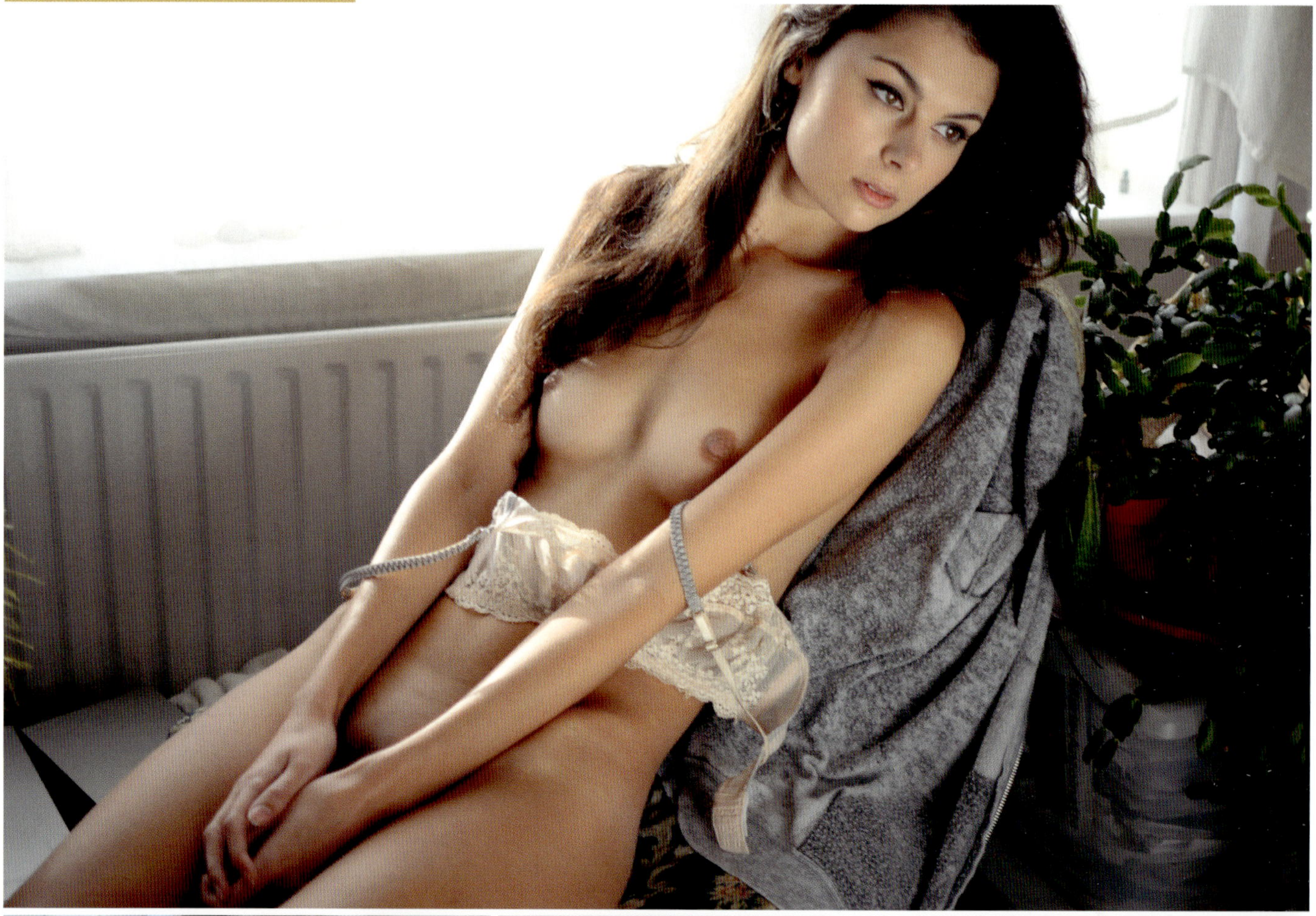

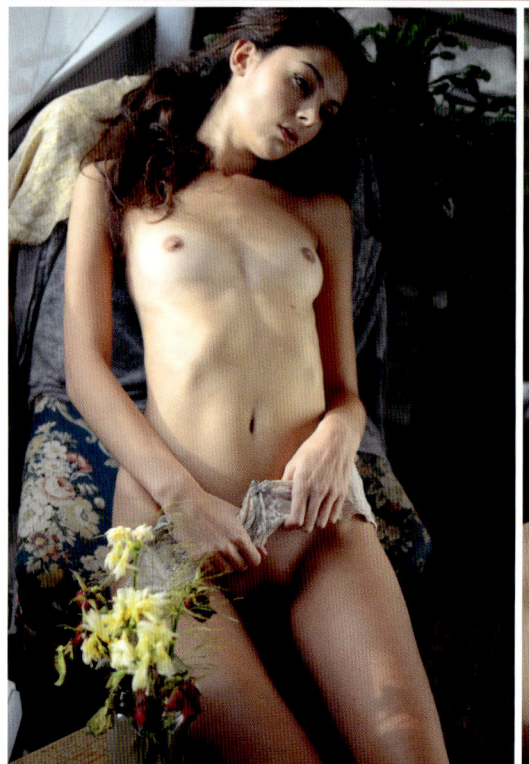

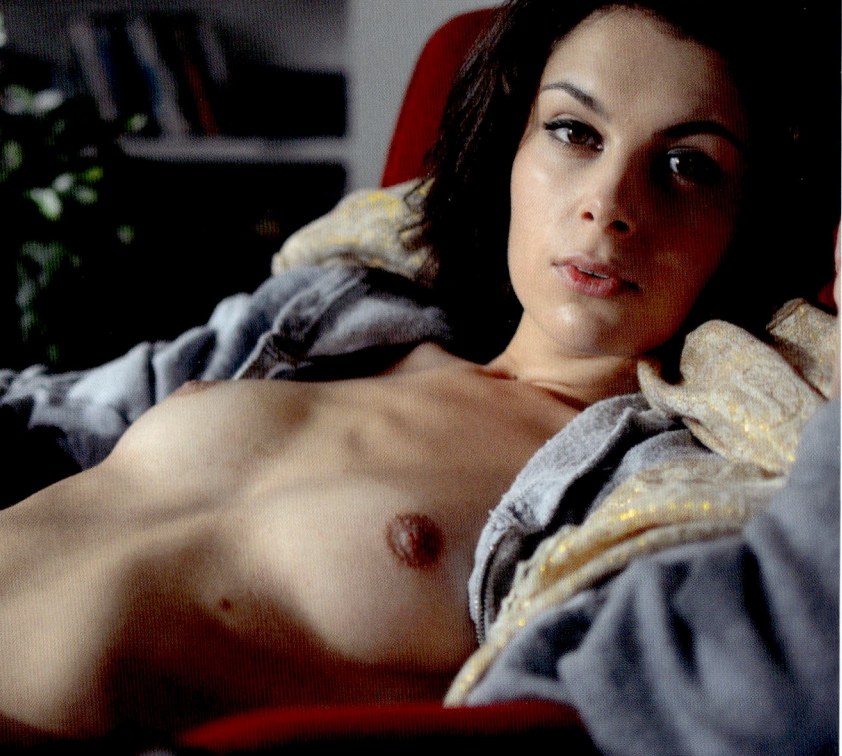

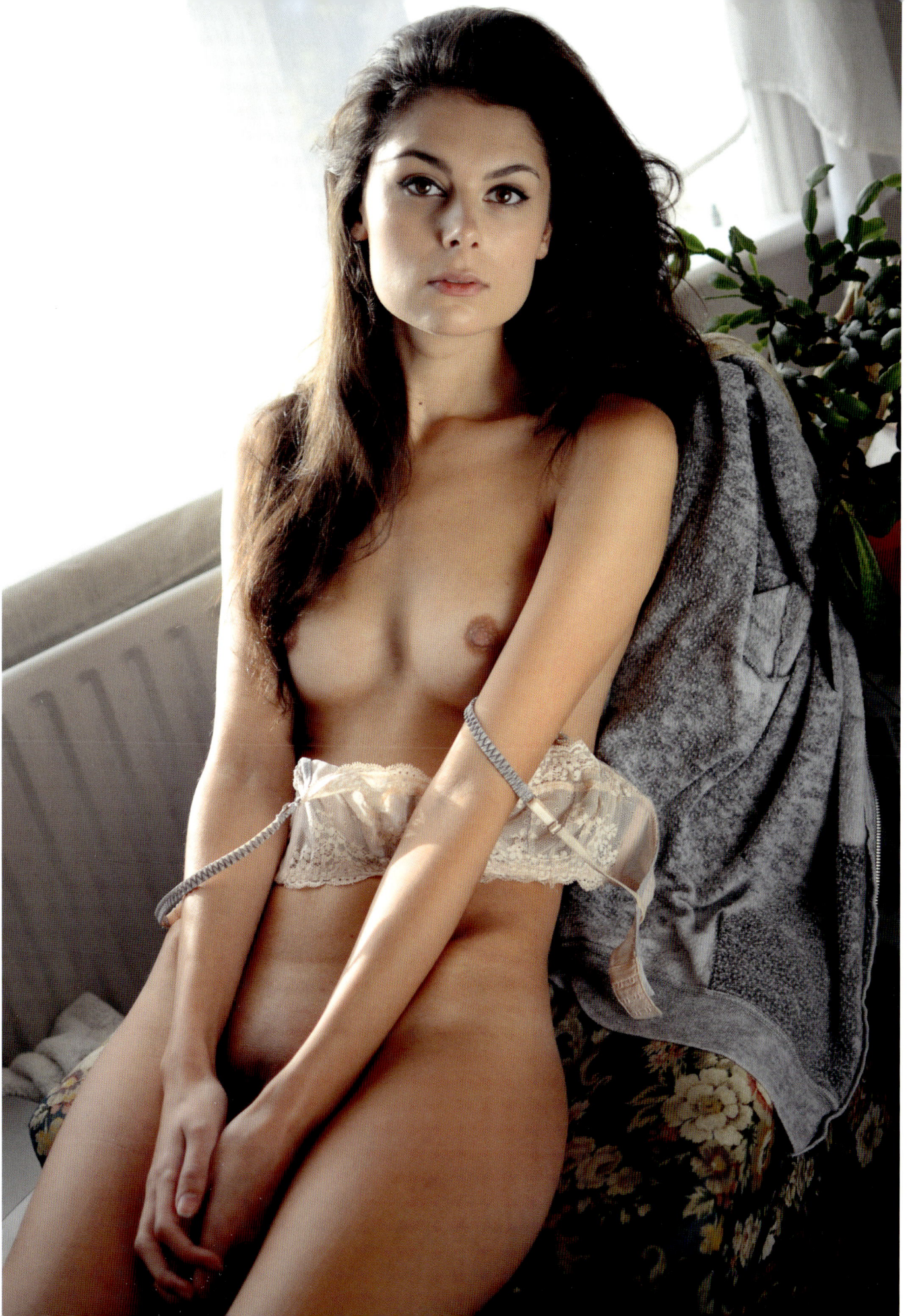

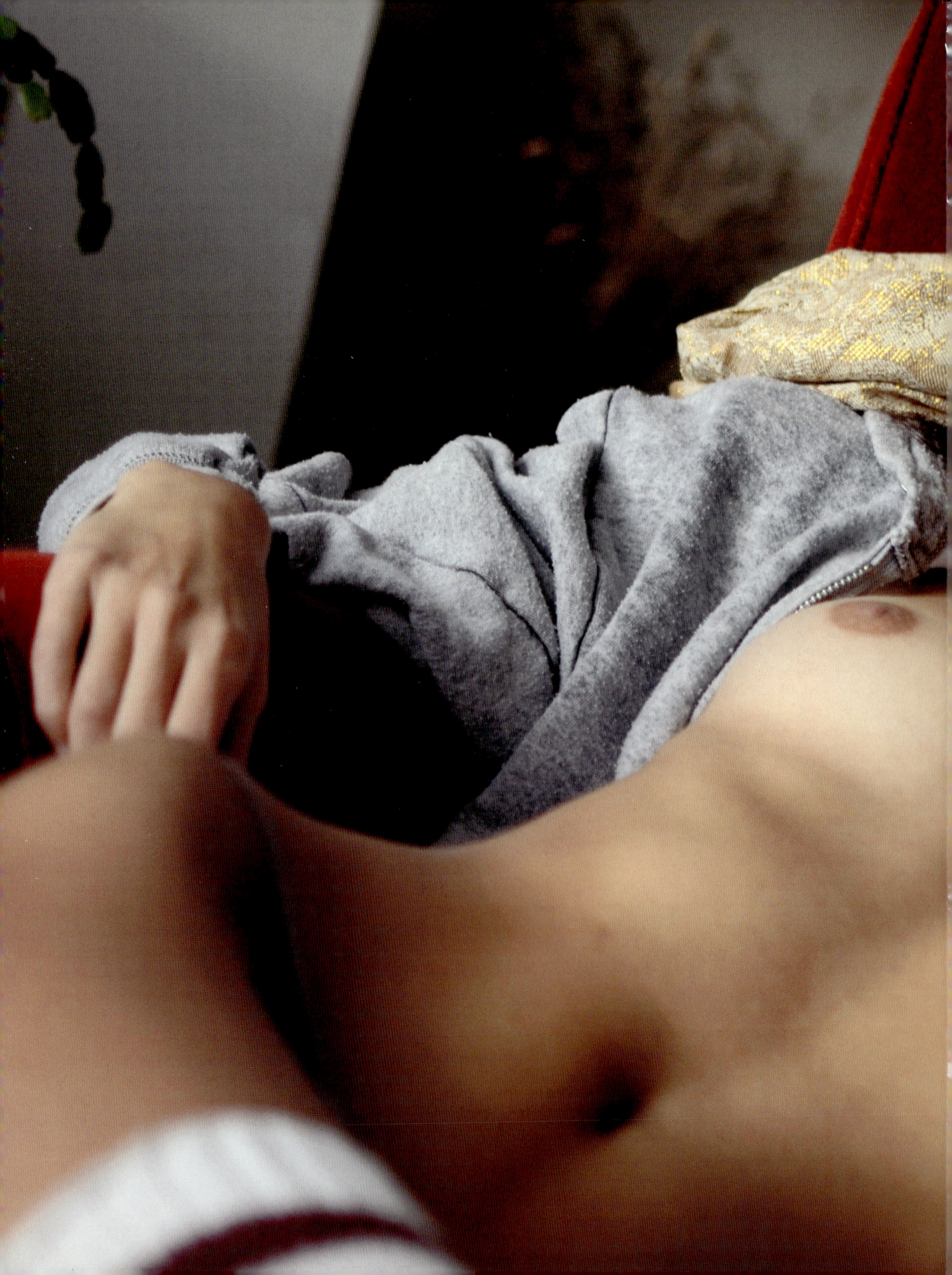

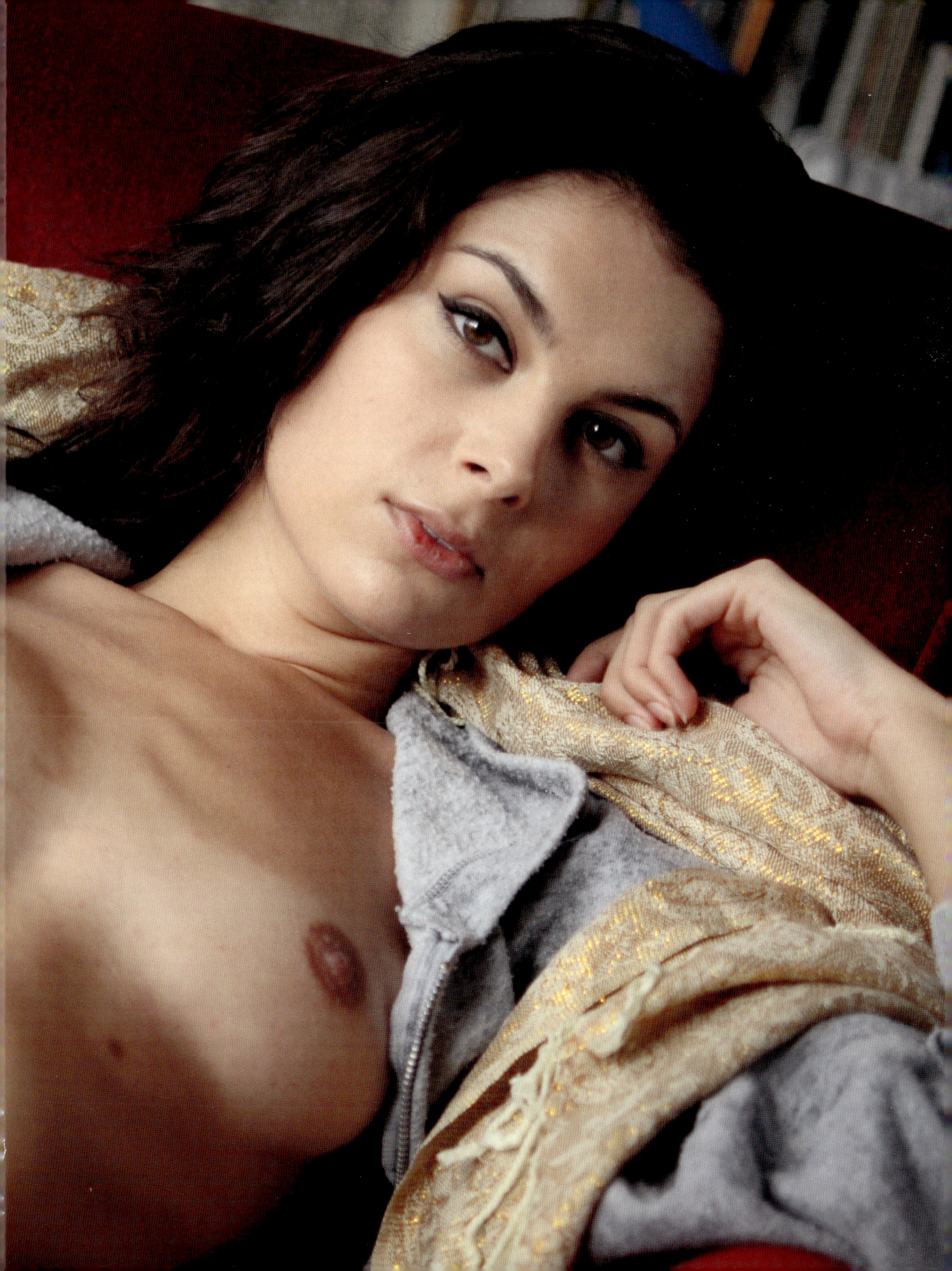

MODEL	PAGE	EYE COLOR	HEIGHT	WEIGHT	MEASUREMENTS
Aiden	116	brown	160cm	47kg	81/61/86
Anney	184	brown	173cm	50kg	86/64/86
Amelie Belain	28	brown	168cm	54kg	86/61/89
Angelica	178	blue	168cm	57kg	84/74/79
Alexis A	175	green	170cm	50kg	89/56/89
Alex Tifony	82	green	173cm	50kg	89/61/86
Alisa G	104	blue	178cm	55kg	91/61/91
Areana Fox	92	blue	168cm	52kg	84/61/84
Beata B	138	brown	170cm	57kg	91/61/91
Bree Haze	22	blue	155cm	56kg	84/61/84
Daisy A	168	blue	165cm	50kg	81/66/86
Guna	50	brown	168cm	49kg	89/61/91
Helen-H	94	brown	165cm	47kg	86/58/87
Joselina Joker	66	brown	163cm	53kg	81/61/89
Josephine	156	hazel	160cm	45kg	86/58/84
Juana	46	brown	157cm	49kg	86/71/84
Kalisy	62	brown	165cm	48kg	84/64/86
Kira W	136	brown	173cm	48kg	89/58/86
Kylie Quinn	146	brown	165cm	54kg	84/74/79
Lara	46	green	160cm	52kg	86/71/84
Leda	102	brown	168cm	51kg	84/61/84
Lilian A	106	brown	168cm	49kg	86/58/91
Lolly O	158	blue	175cm	50kg	94/61/94
Lo Lynn	6	blue	170cm	57kg	91/74/86
Maribel	100	hazel	160cm	52kg	86/74/86
Marie S	58	blue	170cm	50kg	89/64/89
Marilyn Sugar	148	green	165cm	52kg	84/61/84
Milla	154	green	168cm	47kg	88/58/89
Nedda	88	brown	160cm	42kg	84/56/84
Nikia	68	blue	168cm	50kg	86/58/89
Nikita S	116	hazel	160cm	50kg	86/74/86
Olia	76	blue	157cm	53kg	84/74/79
Olivia Sparkle	140	brown	177cm	58kg	86/61/86
Patricia-B	34	blue	160cm	53kg	71/74/81
Raeah	170	brown	168cm	53kg	86/66/84
Roberta Berti	122	blue	170cm	49kg	86/61/89
Sabrina-G	128	green	170cm	50kg	89/61/89
Saju A	110	brown	173cm	48kg	79/61/89
Sarika A	118	blue	165cm	48kg	89/61/89
Serena Wood	38	blue	165cm	45kg	89/58/79
Shay	182	hazel	163cm	49kg	86/74/86
Siya	52	blue	165cm	52kg	89/61/89
Sonya H	150	blue	137cm	49kg	76/58/76
Subil Arch	44	blue	165cm	51kg	86/61/94
Sunshine	64	brown	168cm	53kg	91/61/89
Sybil A	72	hazel	173cm	52kg	91/61/89
Tina	116	brown	168cm	52kg	86/74/91
Viola Bailey	84, 138	blue	175cm	55kg	94/66/89
Vita	21	brown	163cm	55kg	76/84/76
Yassa	14	brown	165cm	52kg	89/64/94
Zahyra	26	brown	163cm	49kg	86/74/91
Zoey-Taylor	12	green	163cm	52kg	86/66/84

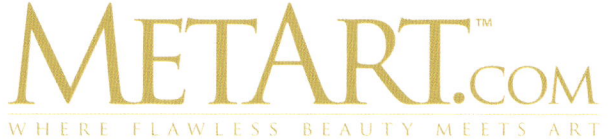

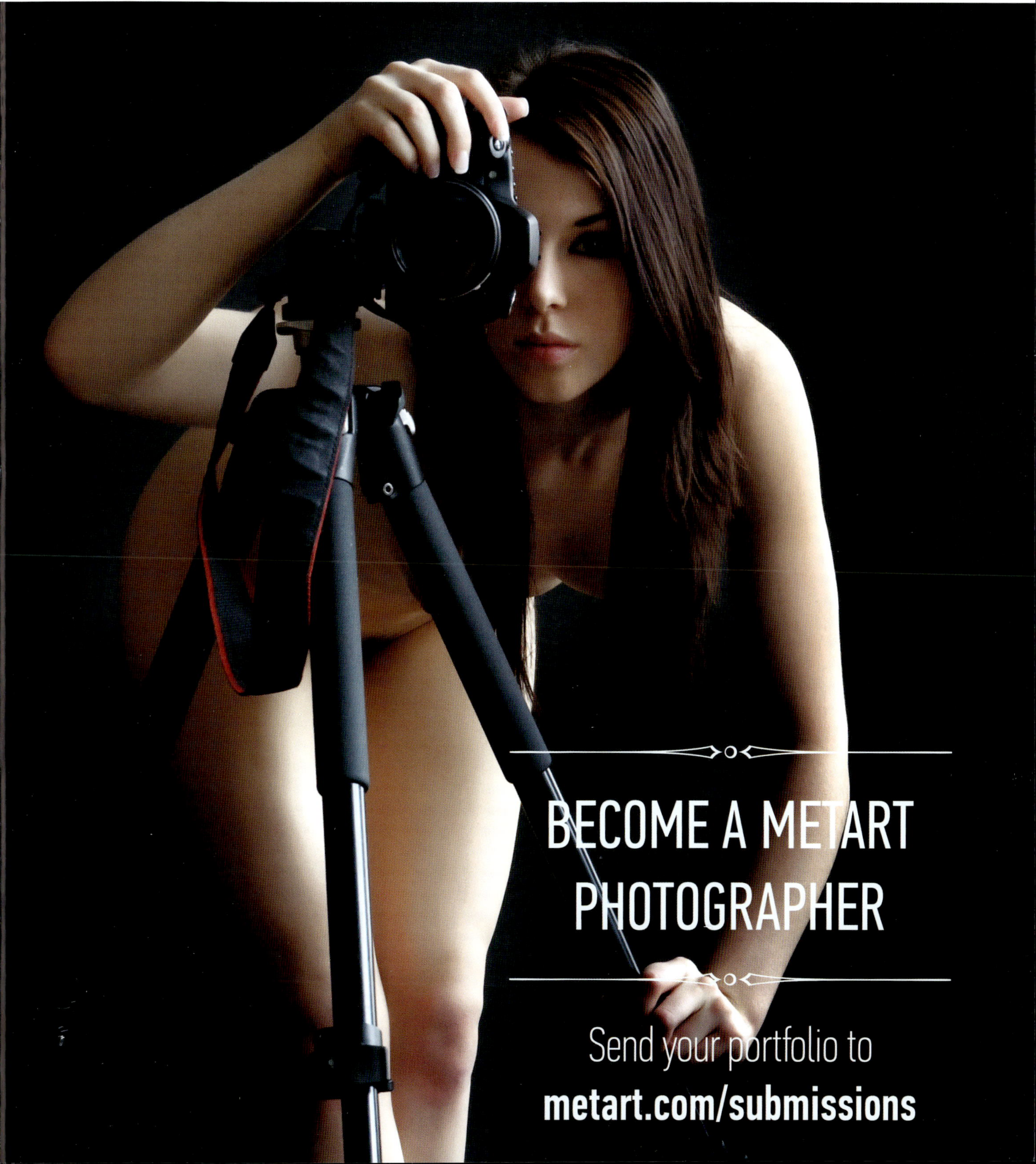

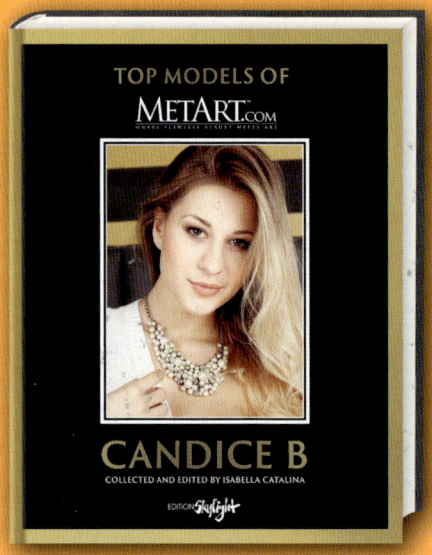
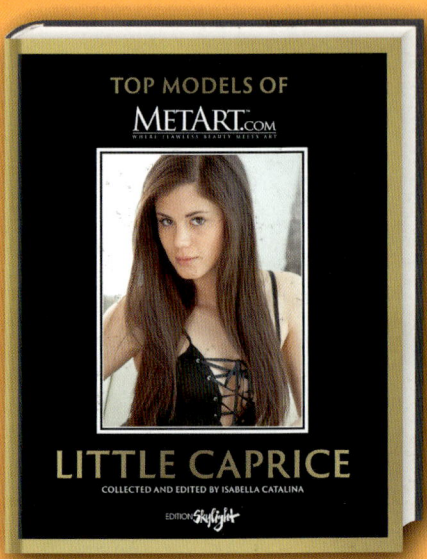
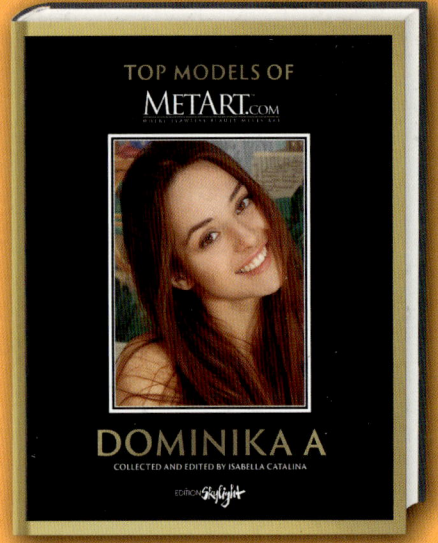
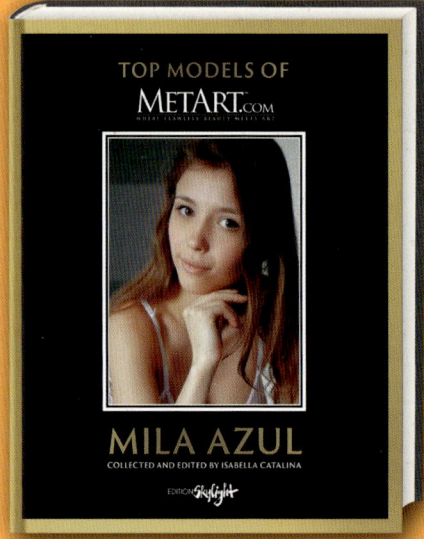
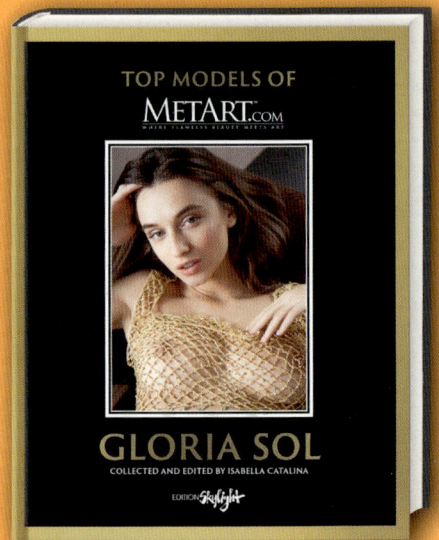